Music in American Life

A list of books in the series appears
at the end of this book.

DOOWOP

THE CHICAGO SCENE

Robert Pruter

University of Illinois Press
Urbana and Chicago

This publication was partially funded by a grant from
the National Academy of Recording Arts and Sciences, Inc.

This book is printed on acid-free paper.

Library of Congress Cataloging-in-Publication Data

Pruter, Robert, 1944–
    Doowop : the Chicago scene / Robert Pruter.
        p.   cm. — (Music in American life)
    Includes bibliographical references, discography, and index.
    ISBN 0-252-02208-4 (cloth : alk. paper).
    1. Doo-wop (Music)—Illinois—Chicago—History and criticism.
I. Title. II. Series.
ML3527.P78   1996
782.42164—dc20   95-19593
                                                              CIP
                                                              MN

To Margaret and Robin

Contents

Illustrations follow pages 70, 162, and 208

Preface

Folk music was all the rage in the early 1960s. A television show called "Hootenanny" beamed the music to millions of people in homes across America each week, and in most major markets, radio shows regularly programmed both traditional and popular forms of folk. Such trendy urban folk groups as the Kingston Trio, the Chad Mitchell Trio, and the Brothers Four got their starts on college campuses and regularly crisscrossed the nation on tour. I recall a show at my college in the spring of 1963 that featured a young and earnest handsome black folk singer named Willie Wright. At that time some black folk singers affected a quasi–West Indian appearance, with bandanna, rustic clothes, and no shoes, and Willie Wright shaped himself thoroughly in that image. He proceeded to entertain his audience with such traditional songs as "Cotton Eyed Joe" and "Wayfaring Stranger," but I was still steeped in rock 'n' roll and was unmoved. There was something artificial about the performance; like many folk musicians of those days, Wright came across as too self-satisfied over being a disseminator of true folk traditions, too self-congratulatory that he was not a purveyor of commercial pap.

Willie Wright was in fact a true folk performer, but his folk background had nothing to do with the Scots-Irish ballads that made up his repertoire. I didn't know it in 1963, but his folk roots were in doowop, an urban rock 'n' roll form that arose in the 1950s but which grew out of a decades-old tradition of a cappella vocal harmony. The onomatopoeic term "doowop" came from the nonsense syllables that ensemble singers used both in the lead and in the background, harmonizing and riffing to fill spaces in the absence of instruments. My appreciation for Wright might have soared had he chosen to go up on stage with a bunch of doowoppers and sing a type of music that was true to his own experience.

Doowop as a distinct vernacular form was familiar to the African American community in 1963, but it was not even known to the mainstream white culture. The term "doowop" apparently emerged in the early 1960s when a retrospective consciousness brought various 1950s styles, such as R&B vocal harmony, to the forefront. Doowop was mentioned as early as 1961 in the *Chicago Defender,* in reference to the Marcels' "Blue Moon."[1] But standard dictionaries reflecting mainstream knowledge of the form give 1969 as the year when the term first appeared in print.[2]

Vocal harmony groups have always constituted one of black music's richest traditions, an art form as deeply embedded as jazz, blues, or gospel. On recordings, black vocal harmony predates all other forms of black music. Evidence unearthed during the 1970s indicates that Columbia put a few groups on wax as early as 1894, and there have been African American vocal harmony groups on the popular music front since 1921, when the Norfolk Jazz Quartet made its seminal sides.[3]

Doowop drew on this long and rich tradition but it arose as part of the rhythm and blues revolution only after World War II. In the mid-1940s the Ink Spots, who used a natural high tenor and a contrasting bass to front their harmonies, were the most popular vocal ensemble in the United States, and they proved to be a tremendous musical influence in the African American community. Other groups soon came to the fore, notably the Ravens and the Orioles, who both hit the charts in 1948. The Ravens were close to the Ink Spots in their pop stylings, but in most of their recordings they remained well within a rhythm and blues style, especially as exhibited in the vocal textures of contrasting leads by bass Jimmy Ricks and natural high tenor Maithe Marshall. It was the Orioles who emerged as the crucial breakthrough vocal group, however, with their first hit record, "It's Too Soon to Know." The group, which is generally credited as being the first rhythm and blues vocal harmony ensemble, became wildly popular with black teenagers, youngsters who not only bought every Orioles record that came out but who were inspired to form vocal groups themselves.

The sounds of the earliest doowop groups were deep and mournful, rough and jumpy, smooth and mellow, and strange and somewhat exotic to the contemporary ear. In basses that burbled low, tenors that soared, leads that wailed, and choruses that chanted breathlessly in harmony, these groups made music that richly captures the atmosphere of the era, a long-ago sound that deeply touches the emotions. As rock 'n' roll emerged in the second half of the 1950s, the vocal groups tended to force more exaggerations in their presentations, so that some of them sounded not only baroque and exotic but downright bizarre. All that wailing, those soaring harmonies, and the wild vocal riffing—which many listeners scorned—represented the original creativity of youth and a real love of vocal harmony and rock 'n' roll.

The vocal groups of the 1950s were unsophisticated kids in matters of music, but what emerged from their use of vocal harmonies on America's urban street corners was a profound and genuine folk music that resonated in all later eras of black music and sometimes in popular music. They took, perhaps unconsciously, a music that most observers consider nothing more than a commercial rock 'n' roll entertainment and created an art form. In blending their voices they understood that, in harmony, timbre plays as strong a role as tuning. They composed songs that evoked the feelings and attitudes of kids growing to adulthood in the fifties. And for these reasons the vocal harmony groups formed one of the crucial strands of vernacular popular music that made up rock 'n' roll.

During the postwar years, rhythm and blues in the United States was recorded primarily in three cities—New York, Chicago, and Los Angeles. *Doowop: The Chicago Scene,* as a regional history of one of the principal recording centers, provides a basis for a fuller understanding of the emergence of rhythm and blues—and, by extension, of rock 'n' roll—by examining doowop, one of the preeminent substyles of both modes. The vocal groups were forces that made the city thrive as a music center during the 1950s. Using developments in Chicago as the model, I will show how these groups contributed to the emergence of rhythm and blues and that they were on the cutting edge of the rock 'n' roll revolution. The doowop groups, working in a symbiotic relationship with the city's record companies and radio deejays, arose out of a teen culture on the streets to create a new type of music, rock 'n' roll, which largely supplanted the old forms of rhythm and blues and pop music in Chicago. Doowop may have developed on the streets but it came to fruition in the recording studio.

Doowop: The Chicago Scene is intended to serve as a "prequel" to my book *Chicago Soul* (University of Illinois Press, 1991), in which I delineated the history of rhythm and blues recording in the city during the 1960s and 1970s. It is also a companion to Mike Rowe's *Chicago Blues* (originally published as *Chicago Breakdown,* Eddison Press, 1973), which gives a history of the city's postwar blues recording scene.

Doowop: The Chicago Scene provides histories of most of the labels and vocal groups in Chicago during the 1950s and early 1960s. The majority of the profiles are based on interviews with various members of the groups. I have also relied on many articles published in group "fanzines," and I have consulted every issue of the *Chicago Defender* from 1945 to 1965 to gather information about the different groups. The sources for each profile are given in notes at the end of each chapter. An invaluable resource for the years 1951 to 1957 has been a series of books called *First Pressings: The History of Rhythm and Blues,* edited and published by Galen Gart. This series, which compiles news, stories, ads, and reviews from trade publications of the era, has proved essential as I fleshed out my profiles on labels and groups.

I am gratefully indebted to all the persons who consented to be interviewed and who so ably offered comments, insights, and histories. Among the deejays, some of the most helpful interviews came from Herb Kent, Richard Stamz, and Lucky Cordell. Special thanks are due to people in the record industry, including Carl Davis, Tommy "Madman" Jones, Cornelius Toole, Bob Catron, Bill Erman, Lenny LaCour, Art Sheridan, and Charles Walton. Interviews with group members that have proved essential were those with Chuck Barksdale, Mickey McGill, and Marvin Junior (of the Dells); Cicero Blake and Dee Clark (Kool Gents); Joe Brackenridge (Von Gayles); Herbert Butler (Players); Gene Chandler and Earl Edwards (Dukays); Charles Davis (Trinidads); Bernard Dixon (Danderliers); Reggie Jackson and Robert Tharp (Ideals); Ralph Johnson and Homer Talbert (Debonairs); Sollie McElroy (Flamingos); Tony Gideon (Daylighters); Donald Jenkins (Delighters); Hilliard Jones and Reggie Smith (Five Chances); Earl Lewis (Five Echoes); H. Sam McGrier (Hambone Kids); Norman Palm and Charles McKnight (Pastels); O. C. Perkins and Millard Edwards (Sheppards); Kathleen Robinson and Vera Wallace (Versalettes); Howard and Robert Scott (Masquerades); Charles Perry and Carlton Black (Duvals); and Eddie Sullivan (Four Gents). I also extend appreciation to all those whom I may have neglected to mention here; your contributions have not been forgotten.

Heartfelt thanks go to my fellow record collectors and vocal group enthusiasts who provided contacts, interviews, and tapes of recordings from their collections. They include John Cordell, Wayne Jancik, Edward Keyes, Richard Murray, Bob Sladek, Bob Stallworth, and Steve Towne. I am also indebted to my copy editor, Carol Bolton Betts, whose fine editing improved the book in many ways. Finally, I thank my wife, Margaret, and my daughter, Robin, who gave me much-needed moral support.

Notes

1. Davis Jr., "Platters" [column].

2. *Merriam-Webster's Collegiate Dictionary: Tenth Edition* (Springfield, Massachusetts: Merriam-Webster, Inc., 1993): 345; *Oxford English Dictionary,* 2d ed. (Oxford: Clarendon Press, 1989), p. 959.

3. Seroff, "Polk Miller," pp. 27–41. Seroff discusses a variety of turn-of-the-century vocal groups in the context of black vocal harmony traditions. Also of interest: Seroff, "Pre-History of Black Vocal Harmony Groups."

DOOWOP

Introduction

In the early days of the record business, Chicago ranked second only to New York as a recording center. With its ideal midwestern location, Chicago became a center where the major labels—first Victor and Columbia and later Decca and Mercury—maintained studios and offices and recorded big band, Tin Pan Alley, country and western, classical, ethnic, and a variety of African American musical styles. The city developed a reputation as a jazz and blues recording center especially in the 1920s, when such companies as Paramount, Brunswick, and OKeh, as well as Decca and Victor, recorded many African American artists and maintained studios there. With its large South Side black entertainment district, from Thirty-first to Thirty-fifth streets along State Street, the city proved to be a particularly rich source of recording talent.

It was not surprising, then, that during the 1930s and 1940s, Chicago-based artists—notably Jelly Roll Morton, Louis Armstrong, and King Oliver—dominated the blues recording field and were most influential in pioneering jazz. Lester Melrose, a Chicago A&R (artists and repertoire) man who entered the music industry in the 1920s, claimed he recorded 90 percent of all blues talent for RCA Victor and Columbia while working out of the city from 1934 to 1951.[1]

During the late forties and fifties, the independent record companies seized control of the black-oriented recording market from the majors, and Chicago emerged as one of the principal centers for rhythm and blues music. In the mid-fifties, this music, along with country and western, fed the emerging form of popular music called rock 'n' roll. A large body of this new rock 'n' roll music was doowop, a vocal ensemble style from the urban centers, and record companies made it a practice to be on the lookout for vocal groups that they could sign.

The record labels, record distributors, and nightclubs all played roles in developing vocal group talent, but it was on the street where the doowop art form was created and nourished and where the doowop groups were sometimes discovered. So it is on the streets where one must first look for the genesis and the early growth of doowop.

The Street

Harmonizing on the street is an old tradition. A New Orleans researcher, Lynn Abbott, has found many sources dating back to the 1880s and 1890s that refer to the pervasiveness of close-harmony recreational singing by African American quartets in "schoolyards, lodge halls, barrooms, shoe-shine stands, railroad stations, and street corners," as well as in barbershops (which gave the form its original name).[2] One of Abbott's sources said that "it was typical, almost, for any three or four Negroes to get together and, they say, 'Let's crack up a chord! Let's hit a note!'"[3] This storied tradition was illustrated in *Harmonizing,* a well-known painting by the African American artist Horace Pippin. In this 1944 work, four black youths stand under a streetlamp, working out the harmonies for the latest hit.

Johnny Keyes, a member of the Magnificents, wrote a book called *Du-Wop,* a study of the doowop era of the 1950s, in which he noted, "All of the doowop groups had one thing in common. We started singing on the street corners, in the hallways and vestibules, in the boys bathrooms at school, and at the far end of the elevated platforms. Making music was very basic. The one who knew the words to the song was the lead singer. The remaining three or four singers imitated the sounds that the horns made in the background, in harmony. The bass singer started the songs, setting the tempo and giving the pitch. We voiced the chords, created and perfected the arrangements."[4]

Members of the vocal groups remember other sounds that made up the rich melange of noise on the street. Keyes mentioned the particularly vivid calls from the watermelon wagon:

> Usually three boys rode on the horse-drawn wagon, sometimes four counting the driver. You could hear them singing as they made their way slowly up and down the neighborhood streets on the South Side of Chicago in the '40s. It was one of the sounds of summer. The wagons would be piled high with the dark green melons. It seemed the street songs of watermelon hucksters could be heard for blocks. After all, everyone had their windows up to keep cool. There weren't very many air conditioners in the apartments, nor many automobile horns to compete with either.[5]

Keyes told of an additional sound of summer:

> Another entertaining form of street music was the hambone, a syn-
> copated sound made by slapping the hands against the hands and
> chest. If you're good, the mouth was added to the rhythm pattern. A
> rhyme went along with the hambone beat. The rhyme was spoken in
> a sing-song cadence, not unlike the vocals of the rap records of the
> '80s, with the ex-watermelon sellers slapping their thighs on the steps
> of the school and the front steps of the neighborhood buildings. These
> hamboners were the forerunners of the vocal groups. They got off the
> steps and took their acts to the legendary corners, underneath the
> street lamps.[6]

Levi Jenkins, a member of the Five Thrills, spoke about the instrumen-
talists and others who performed on the street:

> I can remember some groups in the late 1940s, they were not sing-
> ing groups, they were musicians, like guitar, tubs, scrub-boards—you
> know that kind of thing, a tub for a bass with a string. Guys like
> Tampa Red. They were all down there; Thirty-first Street was rich
> with talent then. Then the vocal groups became more common, be-
> cause we had some real popular groups then, say like the Ravens,
> Orioles, and the Clovers. They were our idols. The Orioles did things
> you could sing, copy more. The Clovers were more modern. They had
> more tricky things in there. Like a lot of groups didn't jump on the
> Clovers too much, because they had their things so sewed up.[7]

Keyes also remembered the vocal groups, noting that they "slowly replaced the blind man with the bottleneck guitar, who sang either blues or
religious songs. He was usually accompanied by a small boy who passed
a hat [around]."[8]

The legendary Bo Diddley started out as a street musician on Forty-seventh Street in 1945. He formed a group called the Hipsters, which featured
Diddley on guitar, Roosevelt Jackson on bass washtub, and Samuel Daniel
as a singer and sand dancer (a specialty involving dancing on a tray of sand,
to get a swishing sound). Diddley's music, which had an eclecticism that
was much exhibited in his later recorded work, had street origins. The
famed Bo Diddley beat perhaps was something he picked up from the hamboners on the street, although he always objected to that claim. He also must
have heard street-corner doowops, because a large body of his recorded
work involved the use of doowop harmonies.[9]

The vocal groups tended to look upon the blues singers as old fashioned
and perhaps lower on the social scale. "You see, everybody hated the blues,"
Maurice Simpkins, a veteran member of doowop groups, said. "Nobody

liked the blues. We used to laugh at the blues. All the guys thought it was funny. Our English was bad too, but their English was worst than ours. They say things like 'I'm a mannn' [a reference to Diddley's blues hit 'I'm a Man']. They would not say, 'man,' but 'mann,' and that would be kind of funny. You see we were going to school every day and these blues singers hadn't even gone to grammar school. That type of stuff was like old music. I got to like it for what it was years later."[10] Indeed, Simpkins wrote some excellent blues songs for Mighty Joe Young in the mid-1960s.

The vocal groups were not of the highest social standing either. Herb Kent, a deejay, said, "Without exception they came from underprivileged backgrounds, from the projects, poor neighborhoods, and they never had enough of anything. And as a result almost to a group when they did hit big time, they didn't know how to handle success. They were not even prepared for that. I never heard of such a thing as a middle-class doowop group."[11] Their style and manner were aggressive and typical of working-class blacks as well, as Kent noted: "All those guys would have processes, big eyes, and 'egregious' looks. A lot of the groups bought their clothes at Smokey Joe's on Maxwell Street."[12] Smokey Joe's, a store that in the 1940s would have offered zoot suits, in the 1950s supplied baggy suits with loud colors and exaggerated cuts that were favored by many working-class youth.

One of the great traditions of street vocalizing was the song battles, in which groups tried to outdo one another. Eddie Sullivan, of the Four Gents, recalled, "The main group we used to battle was the Debonairs. I remember one time we had a real big battle in the washroom of our park's recreation center, which we called the 'Children's Building.' The place was packed. The winner was determined by the crowd, whoever got the biggest applause."[13] Ularsee Manor noted, "Everybody had good harmony. If a group didn't have a high tenor it just sang in a lower range. But the lead singer was always the key. If you had a good lead singer then you could knock over a group. If you didn't have a lead singer people would give you a big hand, but you wouldn't win."[14]

Simpkins said, "We used to have what they called song battles in a place on Thirty-fifth Street in a hallway we named 'Echo Hall.' It was one of those things. Like Donald Jenkins got out of our group and found himself a couple of guys. So he came back with his group, the Fortunes, to prove to us that he could outsing us. Not only that, but in those days we used to have song battles all over the city. We go into different neighborhoods and find different groups."[15] Cities are collections of neighborhoods, and the groups of the 1950s often thought of themselves as representing a street, block, or neighborhood. The groups competed on that basis. Manor, whose Five Buddies group was from the Ida B. Wells projects, illuminated this point:

We mainly rehearsed right under the streetlight on Thirty-eighth Street, between Vincennes and Langley. We just traveled up and down that street. That was our street and anybody who came into our territory, they couldn't pass through unless they sang. From one territory to the next there would be singouts. Instead of fighting to get through, you had to sing to get through. That's what happened in those years, when we were fifteen, sixteen, and seventeen. It was actually a square block that we ran. For us it was very large block—the blocks were large in the projects—from Vincennes to Langley, and from Thirty-eighth down to Thirty-ninth Street. Every time you crossed another street you were in somebody else's singing group territory. The Five Frenchmen were from Vincennes to Rhodes, Thirty-seventh to Thirty-ninth Street. That was their territory.[16]

It is too easy to forget that, among the vocal groups in the 1950s, not all notable groups were the ones who made records. Tony Banks and the Five Frenchmen—comprised of pianist Banks, lead Reggie Gordon, baritone Henry Currie, baritone/bass Norman Cummings, first tenor Harold Foster, and second tenor Glen Phillips—never made a record but they were legendary; their reputation was so strong that they are still vividly recalled, decades later. Ularsee Manor recalled, "They were fantastic. They were on the 'Polk Brothers Amateur Hour' and were the first black act to win anything on that show. If they had been a little bit better organized they probably could have gone to the moon. That's how good they were."[17] Simpkins added, "They were a group known all over the city, record or no. Everybody knew the Five Frenchmen. Those guys could copy just about anything. They just did it real well, you know."[18] Gordon, the superb lead of the Frenchmen, attributed the group's success to Glen Phillips: "He was our arranger and vocal coach. He gave us our parts; he was our glue. He had a phenomenal ear, and without him we would have been an ordinary group. He was in a gospel group as well and came out of a gospel family."[19] Gordon recalled performing at the Trianon Ballroom with the El Dorados, and singing at such clubs as the Crown Propeller Lounge.

Another Thirty-ninth Street group of note was the Five Bells, consisting of Jerome Browne, Wardell Staples, Lester Armstrong, Rufus Hunter, and Julius Hawkins (brother of Jimmy Hawkins, of the Five Buddies). The group auditioned endlessly for Vee Jay records but never got signed; fortunately, most members of the Five Bells were of such caliber that they went on to record and perform with other groups.[20]

Simpkins noted another remarkable unrecorded group: "There were a lot of groups who never did get on record, but who were great. The greatest unrecorded group I know was the Cordovans. The El Dorados hung around them—they were just that great. The Cordovans went down to Chess. They had written a song, 'Heaven on Earth.' Leonard wanted to buy it for the Flamingos, but the Cordovans wanted it for themselves, so they didn't record. The only thing about them, they didn't have a good lead singer, but they had a background that was, whew, it was just something. I'd never heard anything like it since or today."[21] Clifton Carter, of the Five Cliffs of Dover, another unrecorded group, recalled, "The Cordovans started out at Twenty-ninth Street. They never had an opportunity to record, they did a lot of gigs, worked a lot of places along with us. They were pretty good."[22]

When the Five Chances were first working the street corner at Forty-fourth and Prairie, in the early 1950s, they met several unheralded, unrecorded groups. Reggie Smith, one of the Chances, said, "We used to have what they called group battles. We battled with the Five Thrills, the Knights of Rhythm, and some other groups I can't think of but didn't get any recordings out. The Knights of Rhythm, they came from Forty-fourth and Princeton. They were one of the toughest groups that you ever want to hear in your life. For them not to have had a teacher, they were one of the best harmonizing groups that I've ever heard in my life. They never really got the breaks because they never really tried hard. They just liked to stand on the corner and sing."[23]

Another talented musician who came around Forty-fourth and Prairie was recalled by Smith: "Curtis Mayfield was living around there before his mother and him moved to Cabrini-Green [on the near North Side]. His mother had bought him a banjo, something of that sort. He used to come around beating on the banjo and we'd tell him to get away from us with all that noise, cause we're trying to sing . . . and he went on to beat us to death. There was a lot of talent who came through our area."[24] But as Eddie Sullivan noted, "If you notice, among all these groups in Chicago there weren't any girl groups."[25] The vocal-group street scene in Chicago in the 1950s appears to have been a largely male domain, and few female group members can be found in this chronicle.

The story of the Five Cliffs of Dover was typical of the many unrecorded groups who used to compete on the street corners in the early 1950s. The original members were Perry Carter (lead), Clifton Carter (lead tenor, and no relation to Perry). Joseph Lester Thomas (bass), (James) Larry Halliburton (first tenor), and Louis Perkins (baritone), and they came out of the same environment as the Five Thrills, a group that was recorded. "What really started our group, as well as the Five Thrills," Clifton Carter said, "we used to sit around and listen to a lot of records. I was real close to Obie Washington, one of the Thrills, and his brother Fred. The three of us, we used to sit around and harmonize and imagine ourselves to be like some of the groups we heard. That should have been in the earlier part of 1953."

Within a few months, Obie and Fred Washington would go on to become a part of the Five Thrills and to sign with the Parrot label, and Clifton Carter went on to form the Five Cliffs of Dover. "At this particular time," said Carter, "the Five Thrills were really good. Levi Jenkins, their bass, knew something about music and that's what helped a lot. He was in the same community, but he was not what we called one of the regular fellows. He was on one side of the street, we were on the other. The Five Cliffs were also supposed to get an audition with [Al] Benson, but I don't know what went wrong."

The Five Cliffs were together for some four years before they broke up in 1957. At one point Louis Perkins was replaced with Gene Jordan, and Joseph Lester Thomas was replaced with Joseph Mays. Then Jordan dropped out, and for most of the group's history there were four members— Perry Carter, Clifton Carter, Larry Halliburton, and Joseph Mays. Although the Five Cliffs never graduated to the recording studio, they did progress to the club scene. They played such clubs as the Crown Propeller Lounge, the New Cotton Club, the Trianon Ballroom, the Old Grand Paris, and Martin's Corner. "We did a little bit of everybody's stuff," Carter said. "We did some of the Moonglows, some of the Flamingos, some of Billy Ward and the Dominoes, the Five Royales, Hank Ballard and the Midnighters. Then of course we had a lot of stuff of our own."

The Five Cliffs had started on the street corner, and Carter remembered fondly those early days of group competition, despite the song stealing that went on:

At that particular time, groups were somewhat rivals. If you were in a practice session and you happened to be around another group, and you hummed an unknown tune or say something too much, this other group would pick it up and they would do something with it. So you had to be mighty careful. Sometimes we would make a mistake and do some of our original stuff, like once at a Bud Billiken rally in Washington Park where a lot of groups were singing. Sometime later we looked around and sure enough the guys that were recording would wind up with our tune. It would be almost the exact thing that we sang.

Would you believe we did a little session at United? The man said, "Let me hear what you sound like," and we would go in and do one of our originals, and he would record it on a little tape. He would say, "You guys come back here; I'm kind of busy now but I'll set you up for an appointment next week." That's the way it would happen, and when you look around, a lot of stuff that you used in a practice session would be given to some of the groups that were already recording for them.

The Five Frenchmen experienced something just like that, as Reggie Gordon recalled: "We went down to Vee Jay, and they said we got enough groups, but while we were there they took one of our songs. They had a tape going on our audition. We had done something called 'Sweet Mama,' and they changed the lyrics and gave it to the Spaniels, who a couple months later came out with a reworking called 'I Really Do.'"[26]

Distrust, intense rivalry, and song stealing were not the experiences of every group. Stanley Vanorsby of another unrecorded group, the Junior Kingsmen from the Altgeld Gardens housing project, recalled harmonious relations, where all the groups would practice in the "Children's Building": "Practices would happen every day, anytime we were together you know. You could find groups out there—shoot, you'd find guys trying to sing, you'd find guys who *could* sing. They would all be kind of mixed up. Because you might be on the way home and a guy would come up to you and say, 'Man, show me how to do this,' and you stop and show him how to do this and teach him something else. Show others what you got. That was the attitude then. It wasn't like people stealing from one another songs and whatnot."[27]

The subject of stealing songs is a touchy one among many vocal group members. Like the blues, vocal harmony music has a strong folk character, and there was a body of songs and song motifs that was shared among the groups. But this meant that authorship invariably was a source of contention. Johnny Keyes called these folk compositions "street songs." He said, "A street song is an original that everybody sings, and a hundred people take credit for writing it. The Five Chances' 'Sugar Lips' is an example of a street song. Also, the bass line of our hit 'Up on the Mountain' came from a street song called 'Newborn Square.'"[28] During a 1991 radio interview, Keyes was agitated by a caller from his old neighborhood who contested the authorship of "Up on the Mountain." Keyes retorted, "The only part of 'Newborn Square' that went into 'Up on the Mountain' was the bassline, and, like a blues thing, that is public domain. You can't copyright a bassline."[29]

Groups were not always developing their craft on the streets, literally, especially in the wintertime. The Five Buddies, who made the pavement underneath a streetlight on Thirty-eighth Street their practice place in the summer, would go over their routines during the winter at a nearby YWCA, where Ella Jenkins, a folk singer, ran the institution's music programs. Manor, a member of the group, said, "Inside, it was the basement, hallway, boys room, anyplace there was an echo chamber."[30] Throughout the city there were community centers, park district buildings, and, of course, the schools where groups could practice and generally get together. Altgeld Gardens had the Children's Building, and in the Cabrini-Green projects on the near North Side there was the Seward Park recreation building; groups on the South Side gathered at the Lincoln Center, and on the West Side there was the Marillac House.

Private homes were part of the entertainment culture of vocal groups of that day, and "house rehearsals" were common. During much of the 1950s, Vee Jay, Chess, United, and other Chicago labels would contract with Al Smith to prepare vocal groups for recording sessions, helping them to work up and polish their material. "At that time all the groups in the city would rehearse in Al Smith's basement at 5313 South Drexel," Maurice Simpkins recalled. "There was a bunch of groups I remember down there one day. There must have been six or seven groups, and everybody was sitting around listening to everybody else sing."[31] That get-together had to break up, however, in order for Smith to rehearse for recording a new group that Vee Jay had just signed. Simpkins said, "Then Al said we would all have to stop rehearsing because he had to rehearse the El Rays. Someone said, 'They're still around?' Smith said, 'Yeah, Vee Jay decided to give them a shot.' That's when they did 'Dreams of Contentment.' They did that and about four other tunes down there." The joke in this story is that the El Rays, as the Dells, were *still* around in the mid-1990s.

"While we were down there another day," Simpkins continued, "some guys came in, a group called the Five Arrows. They had a record out at the time called 'Pretty Little Thing.' They came from New York, and they had a red Coup de Ville. Everybody was marveling over the car. None of us had even thought that far about a Cadillac! The Flamingos didn't even have a car like that red Cadillac. And they were the biggest group we knew of."

Simpkins remembered that "another popular house was Ted Daniels's house at 5162 South Indiana. That was where the Sheppards started, also the Five Thrills, the Calvaes, and the Rip-Chords." Daniels acted as manager for many of these groups. Willie Dixon's house at 5216½ South Calumet also served as a practice place for groups that Dixon would use on sessions. Johnny Keyes recalled, "Whenever he needed group things done for Chess record sessions he would call me and I would get Julius and Jimmy Hawkins and we'd go over to Dixon's house."[32]

Besides Daniels and Dixon, the principal record men in the 1950s who sought out groups were Samuel "Smitty" Smith of United, Calvin Carter of Vee Jay, Al Benson of Parrot, Levi McKay, and Bill Sheppard. In the early fifties, as vocal groups were ascending, people from Chicago record companies and independent operators such as Daniels and Sheppard increasingly redirected their searches from the clubs to places where they thought they could find the street talent, such as teen talent shows in the schools and theaters, and even the street corners themselves. Smith, an A&R director at United Records, discovered the Danderliers on the street corner, simply because he was driving by with his windows down. But despite the romantic notion of discovering talent on the street, most doowop groups were probably discovered through simple auditions at the record label, either arranged ahead of time or as walk-ins. The groups would hit the various spots around Forty-seventh and Cottage Grove or, later in the decade, would traipse up and down Michigan Avenue knocking on doors.

The Nightclubs

Chicago's nightclubs were the traditional venues where record men found recording talent and where in the early 1950s a number of the pioneering vocal groups launched their careers. The Flamingos, for example, were discovered by an important manager at Martin's Corner, and the Five Chances were discovered at the Crown Propeller Lounge by the man who would become their manager.

Club exposure for the vocal groups involved being a part of the regular revue-type shows produced by the nighteries, but the singers also entered amateur talent contests, usually conducted for many of the teen groups. Jimmy Hawkins of the Five Buddies recalled, "We would go on talent shows at the Flame in Thirty-ninth Street. In fact there were a lot of talent shows like that at the time, but we did the Flame basically. We also did the Crown Propeller on Sixty-third. The amateur show was in conjunction with the regular show, and it was who could get the most applause. I guess you could call it a song battle."[33] Another member of the Five Buddies, Ularsee Manor, who kept records of those engagements, recalled that "on June 22, 1954, at the Flame talent show we won third prize. We got three dollars each; we thought we were in heaven. McKie Fitzhugh was the master of ceremonies. The Five Echoes won first prize. They always won; they were a polished group."[34]

The owners of labels likewise found their talent in the clubs. Leonard Chess got into the business when he decided to record some of the acts he saw in his club, the Macomba. Art Sheridan, the owner of Chance, who began as a distributor, recalled finding several of his acts in the clubs: "I ran into some talent and decided to start my own label. Chicago had a lot of great black and tan clubs and I used to go to them often. Because being in the record business you hung out in all the clubs in town that had that kind of thing, even as a distributor. In those days it was the Crown Propeller Lounge. We also used to use the Crown often to have rehearsals prior to doing a session."[35]

Before most of Chicago's nightclubs that offered live entertainment in the black community bit the dust in the 1960s and 1970s, casualties of urban decay, record deejays, and the increasing cost of name entertainment, the city had a rich club life. The prestige clubs of the African American community, popularly called "black and tans" because they attracted both black and white clienteles, were noted for their fabulous revues featuring floor shows with gorgeous chorines, comedians, tap dancers, exotic dancers, contortionists, and nationally known singers and bands, as well as vocal groups. The revues were usually centered around a theme that changed every month or so and were under the direction of a producer and a chore-ographer. The music was usually supplied by a full-size house orchestra, such as Earl Hines Orchestra at the Grand Terrace, the Red Saunders Orchestra at the Delisa, the Hilliard Brown Orchestra at Joe's Deluxe Club, and the Mari Young Orchestra at the Rhumboogie.

Saunders told a *Tribune* reporter, "You had not just one nightclub, but four or five big ones going, and so many small ones. It was very, very nice. In those days you had the big ball hanging from the ceiling, with the lights on, and the mirrored lights. We had some great show producers in those days. They used to put on fabulous shows, costume them beautifully. The whites used to come from all over to see them."[36]

Most black clubs provided more modest entertainment fare, usually jazz combos, and in Chicago during the 1940s and early 1950s there were scores and scores of these groups—the Prince Cooper Trio, George Dixon Trio, Duke Groner and His Band, Leon Abbey Trio, Eddie Keyes Band, Johnny Pate Trio, and Cool Breeze and the Coolbreezers—playing the clubs. Most of these combos were instrumental jazz outfits, usually a guitarist, bassist, and pianist, that featured an occasional lead vocal. Generally one could find the same combo playing the same place for years, such as the Jimmy Gordon Combo, which played the Club Blue Flame for more than a decade.[37]

Some combos were what came to be known as jive groups, which featured vocal harmonies with instrumental, mostly string, accompaniment (guitar, tipple, bass). There were virtually no standup vocal groups in the clubs in the 1940s, but one could hear loads of marvelous vocal harmony in such outfits as Bill Pinkard and his Shades of Rhythm (regularly at Jimmie's Palm Garden), the Sharps and Flats (at the Morocco Cocktail Lounge), the Dozier Boys (at Martin's Corner), the Five Blazes (Club Bagdad), and Cats and the Fiddle (at the Pioneer Lounge for nearly two decades). Best known to blues fans was Willie Dixon's vocal harmony/instrumental group, the Big Three Trio.[38]

When the vocal groups emerged in the early 1950s, the most prestigious black nightclub area extended along Sixty-third Street, in Woodlawn. The nightclub reporters of the day called it "the stroll," but it was not the original stroll. In the fifties there were still name clubs left over from earlier thriving nightclub districts (or strolls) further north, along State Street from Thirty-first to Thirty-fifth streets, lining Oakwood Boulevard (Thirty-ninth Street), and around Fifty-fifth Street.

The original black nightclub district, which emerged during World War I and flourished during the 1920s, stretched from Thirty-first to Thirty-fifth streets along State Street. Perhaps the most famous nightery in this district was the Grand Terrace, home of Earl Hines and His Orchestra from the club's opening in 1928 to 1941. Originally located at Thirty-ninth and South Parkway, the place closed with much hoopla in early 1937. However, a new Grand Terrace soon established itself in the former Sunset Cafe and operated off and on in the business at that locale until the late 1950s. In the old Grand Terrace location in the Ritz Hotel, the Ritz Show Lounge became a major club in the 1940s, usually with uptown blues acts such as Dinah Washington, Andrew Tibbs, and Jo Jo Adams. Besides the Grand Terrace, the only other venues in the original stroll to make their presence felt in the 1950s were the Harmonia Lounge (3000 South Indiana) and the New Club Plantation (328 East Thirty-first).[39]

The building of the Regal Theater and the Savoy Ballroom in the late 1920s signaled the end of the original stroll, and during the thirties and forties new black nightclub districts emerged further south, principally along three main thoroughfares—Thirty-ninth, Fifty-fifth, and Sixty-third streets.

The Oakwood Boulevard (Thirty-ninth Street) stroll developed in the early 1940s when the Oakland area east of Cottage Grove changed from white to black.[40] Gloria Coleman, in a Chicago *Reader* feature, recalled, "Most exciting of all was Drexel Square—'the Point'—where 39th Street, Oakwood Boulevard, Drexel, and Cottage Grove came together. We'd spend hours taking in the sights and sounds, the colorful characters."[41] The area went downhill rapidly during the late 1940s, and by the early 1950s the only venue of note was the Flame (809 Oakwood), a successor to the Morocco Cocktail Lounge in the Morocco Hotel. The club regularly conducted amateur contests in which the local groups used to compete. The Five Echoes, the Fasinoles, and the Five Buddies practically made the club their home.

Garfield Boulevard (Fifth-fifth Street) was another famous stroll and during the 1930s and 1940s could boast of some of the most famous black and tans in the history of black entertainment.[42] They included the Club Delisa (5521 South State), the Rhumboogie Club (343 East Garfield), and the Hurricane Show Lounge (349 East Garfield). By the early 1950s the street was down a bit and only the Club Delisa was making any kind of impact.

The Delisa was not a club that regularly booked name talent. Approximately six times a year it featured revues produced by Walter Dyer, who also choreographed the shows and chorine line. The Red Saunders Band provided the music. Featured were mainly no-names, who, upon playing the Delisa, became name talent—performers such as Lurleane Hunter, George Kirby, Joe Williams, and LaVern Baker. Each revue featured a variety of acts—an exotic dancer, a tap dancer, a singer, a comic, and usually a contortionist (namely Viola Kemp, Red Saunders's wife). The Delisa on occasion booked vocal groups, and in the early 1950s the Sheppards and the Flamingos both played there. The Flamingos shared the bill in November 1952 with China Doll (a shake dancer), Jo Ann Henderson (a vocalist), Allen Drew (a comic), Lonnie Simmons (an organist), eight chorines, and the Co-ops (a headlining dance act).

During the late 1940s, Sixty-third Street from South Parkway (now King Drive) east to Cottage Grove developed into the principal stroll.[43] The most prestigious of the clubs was Joe's Deluxe Club, opened in 1938 by Joe Hughes, which had both a large cabaret room and a spacious cocktail lounge. The club began with a conventional entertainment policy but by the mid-1940s was presenting a female impersonator revue produced by its star, Valda Gray. Joe's Deluxe Club became a center for "visiting show folk," according to the *Defender,* especially its Monday night celebrity parties.[44]

Right around the corner of South Parkway on Sixty-third were two of the more sophisticated small clubs in the area, the 411 Club and Harry's Show Lounge. Both were strictly upscale and attracted people who presumably were not interested in blues singers, rhythm and blues vocal groups, and discordant jazz combos. The 411 Club (411 East Sixty-third) was owned by Ily Kelly, one of the city's wealthiest operators of a policy wheel (lottery). The club had been around since the early 1940s. In 1950 it began booking jazz pianist Calvin Bostic, whose keyboard work was tasteful, expert, and not likely to unsettle anybody's dinner. For the next decade Bostic was the centerpiece for the club. Charles Walton, a drummer in many combos on the stroll, described the 411's clientele as "almost like Cafe Society, like in New York—the Cafe Society. It was a fast crowd."[45] Walton referred, of course, to Downtown Cafe Society, the hippest jazz club in the country and the place where Lester Young built his reputation.

Harry's Show Lounge (432 East Sixty-third) was opened in 1947 by Harry Fields and Harry Smith. Reflecting the tastes of their clientele, described by Walton as what would now be called young urban professionals, Harry's featured in the early 1950s such acts as the Leon Abbey Trio (in which Walton was a member) and Olivette Miller ("America's Foremost Swing Harpist"). Miller was the daughter of the famed entertainer Flournoy Miller, and she played a string harp, not the blues "harp."

Halfway between South Parkway and Cottage Grove on Sixty-third, several notable clubs were established. The Kitty Kat was opened in early 1953 at 611 East Sixty-third and became a favorite venue of Sonny Stitt and other more art-oriented jazz musicians. Walton noted, "The Kitty Kat was a gay bar; it was predominately gays there. But everyone went there. When it was prominent, some scenes from *Raisin in the Sun* were filmed there."[46] For a time, the disc jockey McKie Fitzhugh used to broadcast from the place.

The centerpiece of the black clubs around Sixty-third and Cottage Grove was the Pershing Hotel, at Sixty-fourth and Cottage Grove, which had three venues, a ballroom, a lounge, and a supper club. When the hotel was taken over for black residency in 1944, the supper club in the basement on the Cottage Grove side was leased by Charlie Cole and Harry Fields, who opened it as the El Grotto. The hotel's two other entertainment spots, called the Pershing Ballroom and the Pershing Lounge, opened up on the Sixty-fourth Street side. The El Grotto became one of the prestigious black and tans, with fully produced shows, chorus lines, and name entertainment. It later became the Beige Room, where Larry Steele produced the shows, and in 1955 was called the Birdland (a name quickly changed to Budland). Budland at first was a jazz club, but as the decade came to a close it regularly booked vocal groups such as the Spaniels and Moonglows.

The color line in Woodlawn broke across Cottage Grove in 1951 with an explosion of clubs catering to African Americans. Two of the most prestigious clubs of the district, Club Bagdad (840 East Sixty-third) and the Crown Propeller Lounge (868 East Sixty-third), opened on Sixty-third east of Cottage Grove. The *Chicago Defender* reported in August 1951 that "with the Crown Propeller Lounge as standard bearer, 63rd Street is today rated the new Broadway with no less than six places in the swing groove."[47] Upon its opening, the Crown Propeller Lounge featured three different bands and Little Miss Sharecropper (LaVern Baker in a gingham dress, in her imitative Little Miss Cornshucks phase). For the first few years the club featured a giant lighted fishtank containing five hundred gallons of water and a woman named Atlantis, who would swim around in a mermaid outfit. The Crown Propeller differed from the Delisa in that it regularly booked name entertainment.

When the Moonglows first emerged as hitmakers on Chess with "Sincerely," they played at the Crown Propeller Lounge in October 1954. But their rock 'n' roll stylings were not appealing to the clientele and the group was replaced by the Rhythm Aces, another vocal group that had a more sophisticated sound. The Flamingos in their early club days were among the few vocal groups to play there regularly, and the club was the venue for out-of-town biggies, such as the Orioles and the Clovers. The Crown Propeller was another of those clubs that regularly conducted amateur contests in which vocal groups would compete.

The West Side nightclubs were largely concentrated on Madison and

Lake, east-west arteries, and the most prestigious were the Club Paris (1652 West Madison), Ralph's (2159 West Madison), Joe's Rendezvous (2757 West Madison), and Martin's Corner (1900 West Lake). The Club Paris, booked by showbiz veteran Finis Henderson, provided a traditional black and tan variety bill, and the Flamingos were the only vocal group to play there.

Martin's Corner was one of the most venerable black and tans in the city, having been established in the 1930s. Charles Walton pointed out that "it was owned by a gangster, a real policy man; it was just a little club."[48] Martin's Corner, although small compared to the Delisa, featured the standard floor shows with a chorus line, dancers, novelty acts, comics, and singers. It would serve as a venue for many of the early 1950s vocal groups. Both the Flamingos and the Five Echoes played the club regularly, and other groups who played there were the Fasinoles and the Five Thrills. Chuck Johnson was the producer of the revues at Martin's Corner, and when the Five Echoes played there in December 1953 they headlined the bill with Lady Jewel (an exotic dancer), Chuck and Nedra (dancers), George Green (a balladeer), and Rose "Cyclone" Morann (a comedienne).

Electrically amplified southern-style blues made famous by such artists as Muddy Waters, Little Walter, and Eddie Boyd was sweeping Chicago in the late 1940s and early 1950s, and several clubs were established that catered to this trade, mostly on the South Side. The famed 708 Club (708 East Forty-seventh) in the early 1940s was booking combos, but in 1948 it began booking such blues artists as Memphis Minnie and Roosevelt Sykes and rapidly became the premier blues club in the city. Silvio's (2254 West Lake) was the best known of the West Side blues clubs. It was rare for vocal groups to play in these clubs, but the Ideals once sang at Silvio's.[49]

The city's nightclubs were thus the venues where rhythm and blues vocal groups made their professional entrance into the world of show business. But the adult world of glittering night spots and the stroll was soon to be overshadowed by a new entertainment involving the earnest and youthful activities of the teenage vocal groups that were rapidly springing up in every neighborhood of the African American community, imitating the new rock 'n' roll sound of doowop.

The Recording Industry

In New York, Los Angeles, Chicago, and a few other cities, there were usually key areas where the record business was concentrated. In Chicago that area was called "Record Row," and in the early 1950s, as far as the rhythm and blues recording industry was concerned, it was located on the South Side in the vicinity of Cottage Grove Avenue and Forty-seventh

Street.[50] Independent record companies such as King, Vee Jay, Chess, United, Chance, and Parrot, as well as United, Bronzeville, and other distributors made their headquarters there. In 1954, after Vee Jay moved from Gary, Indiana, all the major independents were in the district. Chess Records and Aristocrat Distributing Company, both owned by Phil and Leonard Chess, was at 4750 South Cottage Grove, and across the street at 4747 was Vee Jay, owned by the husband-and-wife team of Vivian Carter and James Bracken. A block south were George and Ernie Leaner's United Record Distributors, at 4806, and Parrot, owned by kingpin deejay Al Benson, at 4848. Parrot was also the headquarters of Benson's Bronzeville Distributing Company, which was headed by Cy House. Further south at 5052 South Cottage Grove was the headquarters of United Records, which was owned and operated by a tailor, Leonard Allen.

Several blocks east of Cottage Grove on Forty-seventh street were several more firms. King Records was at 1232 East Forty-seventh, and the offices served as both a distribution branch and a company branch office for the Cincinnati-based outfit. Sheridan Record Distributors at 1163 East Forty-seventh and Chance Records at 1225 East Forty-seventh were two operations owned by Art Sheridan.

Just south of Chicago's downtown section, another Record Row was developing on South Michigan Avenue. By 1954, M.S. Distributing Company, which was founded by Milt Salstone in 1946, was located at 2009 South Michigan. Other distributors on the stretch in 1954 were James H. Martin, Inc., at 1343; Capitol Records Distributing Corporation, at 1449; and Midwest Mercury Record Distributors, at 2021. The following year they would be joined by Garmisa Distributing Company, at 2011, and by All State Record Distributing Company, at 2023. During the remainder of the decade most record companies and distributors from Forty-seventh and Cottage Grove gravitated toward South Michigan Avenue, and by the early 1960s the street had fully blossomed as a new Record Row.

The preeminent studio in Chicago during the 1950s was Universal Recording Corporation (usually called Universal Recording), founded in 1946 by World War II vets Bill Putnam, Bernie Clapper, and Bob Weber, on top of the Civic Opera House at 20 North Wacker Drive. The studio is famous as the site of the first echo chamber. Art Sheridan, who worked in the studio, recalled:

> Bill Putnam and Bernie Clapper were sergeants in the army during the Second World War and were stationed in the Civic Opera building in the communications division. They knew all the wiring and electrical connections in the building, and after the war [they] opened a studio there. They rented a penthouse for the recording studios

adjacent to the ladies washroom. So they produced sessions up there. And then they developed the first echo chamber by putting a microphone and a receiver in the ladies washroom, which was that old-type tile thing—it had great resonance—and while we were doing a session we put a guard outside the door so that nobody would come in and flush the toilet.[51]

The introduction of the echo chamber into the recording process was a significant development in the emergence of rock 'n' roll, particularly in vocal groups. These groups, with their untrained voices, had always worked on their harmony in tiled bathrooms, hallways, and subways, anywhere an echo could give resonance to their music. The use of echo in the recording process not only helped the groups obtain more presence on the records but also created the sound that the groups were trying to achieve.

Universal Recording moved around the near North Side during the 1950s. In 1954 it was located at 111 East Ontario, and by late 1956 it was at 46 East Walton. Nearly everything recorded by the independent labels was done at Universal. Sheridan remembered that all his Chicago-produced records were done at that studio and that Aristocrat sessions were carried out at the studio in 1947. Another important studio was that of RCA at 445 North Lake Shore Drive, also on the near North Side. Other studios included Columbia Records at 410 North Michigan, Modern Recording Studio at 55 West Wacker, and Boulevard Recording Studio in the downtown at 25 East Jackson (at 632 North Dearborn in 1958). Boulevard was owned by Eleanor and Hal Kaitchuck and briefly, during 1955–56, had a rhythm and blues label, Ronel.

Notes

1. Rowe, p. 17.
2. Abbott, "'Play That Barber Shop Chord,'" p. 290.
3. Ibid.
4. Keyes, *Du-Wop,* preface (unnumbered pages).
5. Ibid., p. 1.
6. Ibid.
7. Jenkins interview.
8. Keyes, *Du-Wop,* p. 3.
9. Bo Diddley, liner notes, "Bo Diddley"; Palmer, liner notes, "Bo Diddley."
10. Simpkins interview, January 16, 1979.
11. Kent interview, March 31, 1993.
12. Ibid.
13. Sullivan interview, July 2, 1993.
14. Manor interview.

15. Simpkins interview, August 7, 1977.

16. Manor interview.

17. Ibid.

18. Simpkins interview, August 7, 1977.

19. Gordon interview.

20. Keyes and Hunter interviews.

21. Simpkins interview, August 7, 1977.

22. This and subsequent remarks by Clifton Carter quoted in this introduction come from the interview with him.

23. R. Smith interview.

24. Ibid.

25. Sullivan interview.

26. Gordon interview.

27. Vanorsby interview.

28. Keyes interview.

29. Ibid.

30. Manor interview.

31. This and subsequent remarks by Simpkins quoted in this introduction come from the January 16, 1979, interview with him.

32. Keyes interview.

33. Hawkins interview.

34. Manor interview.

35. Sheridan interview.

36. "Music Personalities."

37. See Dance, *The World of Earl Hines.* In this book there is a discussion of many of these combos, whose leaders and members included an amazing number of alumni from the Hines band of the 1930s.

38. There has been much research on these groups, most of it by two rhythm and blues researchers, Rick Whitesell and Peter Grendysa. The following sources are most pertinent: Grendysa, "Blues and Jazz Collide in Chicago"; Grendysa, "The Four Jumps of Jive and The Big Three Trio"; Grendysa, Moonoogian, Whitesell, "The Cats and the Fiddle"; Whitesell, "The Lewis Bronzeville Five"; Whitesell, "The Three Bits of Rhythm"; Whitesell, "The Three Sharps and a Flat"; Whitesell, Grendysa, and Moonoogian, "The Four Vagabonds."

39. Information on the original stroll comes from the following sources. Dance, *The World of Earl Hines,* pp. 33–56, provides Hines's discussion of the original stroll, an account that is unparalleled for its evocative first-person look. Kenney, *Chicago Jazz,* an academic study, provides the best historical overview of the original stroll from its origins to its height in the 1920s. See also Pruter, "The Emergence of the Black Music Recording Industry"; Travis, "On the Trail of Chicago's Black Belt Ballrooms and Saloons," *An Autobiography of Black Jazz,* pp. 25–37; and Wang, "Jazz in Chicago," pp. 8–11.

40. See Coleman, "The Black Gold Coast." This evocative survey of Thirty-ninth Street dwells too much on the vice and not enough on the entertainment offered there.

41. Ibid., p. 1.

42. A solid survey of the street by a researcher who lived it is found in Travis, "Jazz Joints along East Garfield Boulevard," *An Autobiography of Black Jazz,* pp. 111–21.

43. I know of no published essay on Sixty-third Street.

44. Roy, "Joe Hughes' Club."

45. Walton interview.

46. Ibid.

47. "Sixty-third Street Goes Broadway."

48. Walton interview.

49. Spraggins interview.

50. Locations of the various firms were found in the *Red Book* 1954, 1955.

51. Sheridan interview.

1

Chance Records

Chance Records, along with Parrot, Chess, and United, was one of the pioneering labels in Chicago to record the new African American sounds that swept the city in the post–World War II years, the music of doowop harmony groups and Mississippi blues adapted to the urban scene with electrically amplified instruments. The company was in operation for only four years in the early 1950s, but during that time it recorded the Flamingos, Moonglows, Five Echoes, Five Chances, and Five Blue Notes, as well as a number of solo R&B and blues performers.[1]

Behind the label were two enterprising men, Arthur Sheridan and Ewart Abner Jr. Sheridan was born in Chicago on July 16, 1925, the son of the owner of an electronics factory. After World War II he caught the fever of the record business. His first experience was in developing pressing plants, having gone into partnership with an engineer who invented a new kind of press. Sheridan said, "He had the idea of manufacturing the presses and building pressing plants. In order to sell the pressing plants to other people, we built a pressing plant at Twenty-ninth and Wabash, behind my father's electronics factory. In any event, deciding that it was a demonstration plant, we thought we ought to take in some work to keep the plant going."[2] The plant was called Armour Plastics.

Sheridan noted, "There was a great desire in a lot of people right after the war to have pressing plants because of the great scarcity of phonograph records. Syd Nathan of King Records became a friend and was one of the first people we sold pressing plants to. We built a plant for him and we built a plant for somebody in Canada, and a couple around the States."

While Sheridan was being drawn into the business, Evelyn and Chuck Aron, a Chicago couple, were starting up a rhythm and blues label called Aristocrat. Evelyn was the principal force in the enterprise, and within a few months Leonard and Phillip Chess bought into it. In December 1949, the Chess brothers bought out the Arons and reorganized Aristocrat as Chess. Sheridan recalled,

> In taking in pressings from the various Chicago labels, I met the Arons. To make a long story short, Evelyn had gotten divorced from her husband, and I married Evelyn [on December 16, 1949]. Evelyn and I set up a record distribution company [called American Distributing Company]. So I spent a lot of time in the distributing business before I started the record business. I was a very quiet, bashful type of person, and when I went in the business with Evelyn I thought she was the sole person who knew everybody in the business from the distributing point of view. When our marriage broke up and I was left with the business, I was quite surprised that I could deal with it and come out of the woodwork and be able to deal with those record guys. It was a great learning place for me.

Then Sheridan was attracted to the recording end of the business. He said, "I spent a lot of time with Bill Putnam and Bernie Clapper, who had Universal Recording. For a while we became partners, and having sat in on a number of sessions and kibitzing with them and so on, I got accustomed to the art of being a producer." As a result of all the associations that he developed in the recording business, and also by hitting the city's black and tans, where he discovered unrecorded talent, Sheridan decided to start a label.

The Chance label was begun in September 1950 with headquarters at 2011 South Michigan Avenue. Ewart Abner Jr. joined the firm later. Abner was born, the son of a minister, in Chicago on May 11, 1923. In 1939 he graduated from Englewood High, where he had excelled both as an academic and as a leader, making the National Honor Society and being named to the graduating class "who's who," a list of students deemed the most outstanding. He went on to Howard University, where he majored in pharmacy, but he dropped out and joined the Civilian Conservation Corps. After a stint in the service, from 1943 to 1946, he continued his education at DePaul University, getting his accounting degree in 1949.[3]

Sheridan later recalled,

> At the time I met Abner he had graduated from college as an accountant. In those years a black man had a hell of a job trying to get a position as an accountant. He became our accountant in the distributing business and in the record plant, and ultimately for a while ran the pressing plant. After we closed the pressing plant, Abner became very much involved in Chance. In those years Leonard and Phil were

their own producers and A&R men, and I was my own producer and A&R man. Abner was basically the finance man, in the sense of being the accountant guy, bookkeeping and so forth.

Sheridan recorded both pop music and rhythm and blues, but the bulk of his output was in the R&B field. He explained why: "I was just in that particular area. The records we were distributing, for example. My great influence was Evelyn and to some degree Chuck." Sheridan came from an obviously upper-middle-class background, and it may seem strange that he developed a taste for R&B, but, he said, "I thought it sounded great, probably because I didn't know enough about music, per se, but I really liked the sound." His appreciation for rhythm and blues was such that he even substituted for an R&B deejay once, in 1952. As Sheridan recalled that experience, "Jessie Coopwood was a deejay at WWCA in Gary. I did a stint on his station when he went on vacation, because I wanted to learn what it was like to be a disc jockey. I did three months out there, and it was quite an experience. I learned a lot."

Chance started by recording a series of instrumentals by the tenor sax player Schoolboy Porter, a twenty-four-year-old native of Gary, Indiana, whose birth name was John A. Porter. He served in the navy in World War II and in 1948 joined the Cootie Williams Band, where he developed into a formidable honker. He was brought to the Chance label by Jessie Coopwood. His first release for the company, "I'll Never Smile Again," was something of a local hit in the early fall of 1950. He followed that in November with another local sensation, "Tennessee Waltz," which sold some ten thousand copies. Sheridan noted, "That was the era when the saxophone solos and the saxophone copies of popular tunes were very popular. Patti Page had a big hit with 'Tennessee Waltz,' and it was just a normal thing to put out an instrumental on a pop hit as soon as you heard one that seemed to be going somewhere."

Chance got into trouble in May 1951, when the American Federation of Musicians, at the behest of Chicago Local 208, revoked the recording license of the company for using nonunion musicians on the Schoolboy Porter session that produced "I'll Never Smile Again." Steve Chandler, a realtor who was associated with Chance, had reputedly supervised it. *Billboard* reported that his defense was that he "used boys who had union cards, but who, at the time of the sessions, were not paid up members. As a result, he held back the contracts and the union took action." *Billboard* said that the revocation of the license was the "first in a long time."[4] Sheridan had no recollection of Steve Chandler or of any AFM problems. As he said, "It could have happened, but I don't recall having a difficult time with the AFM."

In August 1952 Sheridan dissolved his distribution firm, American, and reorganized the company as Sheridan Record Distributors, with headquarters at 1151 East Forty-seventh Street. This brought both the distribution arm and the Chance label into closer proximity to the South Side's "record row." When the firm next door, at 1153 East Forty-seventh, moved out in August 1953, Sheridan's company was able to double its space.

Also in August 1953 the company added a subsidiary label, Sabre, with separate headquarters at 1225 East Forty-seventh Street. In September, Sheridan went into partnership with Dave Freed, Alan Freed's brother, in setting up another distribution outfit, Lance Distribution, Inc., working out of Cleveland.

After Schoolboy Porter, the rhythm and blues artists the company initially chose to record were mainly bluesmen, namely John Lee Hooker, Delta Joe, Homesick James, J. B. Hutto, Lazy Bill Lucas, and Big Boy Spires, on Chance; and Tampa Red (recording as the Jimmy Eager Trio) and Willie Nix, on Sabre. Many of these artists were actually recorded by Joe Brown, who had Sheridan distribute his imprints. As Sheridan said of Brown, "He recorded in some strange places. He would go out and record things, but didn't have the money to distribute them. So he'll sell the master or sell it with part of the royalty coming back." Sheridan himself always used Universal when recording in Chicago.

The blues artists recorded by Chance/Sabre were some of the top artists of the postwar Chicago bar-band era, but what the company produced was decidedly inferior to what Chess and other companies were putting out at the time. Mike Rowe has said that "there is little evidence that Art or his general manager Ewart Abner took anything like the pains that Len Chess did with his blues artists."[5] As it turned out, Chance became better known for its vocal group releases.

Under the direction of Abner, the company jumped on the vocal-group bandwagon by signing a host of groups in 1953, including the Flamingos and the Moonglows. The music recorded by the groups at Chance reflected the type of material that vocal groups were recording all over the country at the time. They did not typecast themselves as just balladeers or jump specialists; they tackled the whole gamut of rhythm and blues, recording blues, ballads, jumps, and Tin Pan Alley standards. The vocal groups became the focal point of the company, which even lent its name to one of them.

The Five Chances

The story of the Five Chances is the story in microcosm of the birth of the rhythm and blues vocal group sound, one of the essential strands that made up rock 'n' roll. The Five Chances were one of the pioneer groups who, under the streetlamps of the mean urban streets of Chicago's South Side, created and shaped some of the first sounds of R&B harmony.[6]

The Five Chances started during the very dawn of the vocal group era, in 1950, when the members of the group got together as eighth-graders in Felsenthal Grade School, at Forty-first and Calumet. The young men were Darnell Austell (lead), his brother John Austell (bass), Howard Pitman (baritone), Harold Jones (baritone and second tenor), and Reggie Smith (first and second tenor). (The Austell brothers were nephews of the long-time record entrepreneur Leo Austell.) Looking back, Smith asserted, "These are the originals, these are the ones who really started singing on the street corners."[7] They took the name El Travadors.

Things came together for the El Travadors when they won a talent show in 1954. "It was a big-time club on the South Side," Smith recalled, "the Crown Propeller Lounge. They had talent shows all the time. We won the talent show, and a musician there, Levi McKay, told us he could tutor us along, try to teach us our notes and really get us to singing. He took us under his wing and really started to teach us. The various Elks clubs let us use their halls and pianos for rehearsals. Levi taught us the old standard songs and this led us to auditioning for recording for the Chance label."

Abner liked what he heard and signed the group, but he renamed it the Five Chances. The group got its recording contract the day the members graduated from DuSable High. At the time of the signing, the group was made up of the Austell brothers, Reggie Smith, Howard Pitman, Harold Jones, and a fellow recalled as "Snooky." But McKay was experimenting with various lineups, drawing new members from other groups he managed. He brought in Eddie Stillwell from the Fasinoles and Clyde Williams from the Daffodils. (Stillwell would appear on records, but not Williams.)

The Five Chances recorded four sides for Chance—"I May Be Small," "Nagasaki," "California," and "Make Love to Me," but only the first two songs were released. Darnell Austell led on all the songs except "Nagasaki," which was led by Stillwell. (Stillwell was part of the group only for that session and also sang alternate lead on "Make Love to Me.") "I May Be Small," written by McKay, was the strongest of the four songs. It is a bluesy ballad but retains its attractiveness as a vocal harmony vehicle. The song was paired with the old Mort Dixon and Harry Warren song, "Nagasaki," which had been introduced onto the charts in 1928. The Five Chances—or Levi McKay—probably became familiar with the song from Doris Day's rendition in the 1949 film *My Dream Is Yours*. The group capably turned the fast fox-trot number into a fine R&B jump with slick complicated harmony, so one would never have guessed its pop origins. The record was released in August 1954 and got good regional sales.

"California" was an original jump written by McKay that was as strong as the released songs. The other unreleased number was "Make Love to Me," which was then a popular number on the charts by Jo Stafford. The music for the number, however, dates back to the 1920s. The two unreleased sides surfaced in 1964 on a Constellation album called *Groups Three*. When Chance closed shop at the end of 1954, the Five Chances found a new home with Al Benson's Parrot label.

The Five Echoes

The work of the Five Echoes on Sheridan's Sabre label ranks among the bluesiest ever recorded in the city. The group originally consisted of four kids from the South Side, in the vicinity of Thirty-fifth to Thirty-ninth Streets. They were Constant "Count" Sims, Herbert Lewis, Jimmy Marshall, and Tommy Hunt (who years later scored with "Human"). The group's hangout was the Morocco Hotel, at Thirty-ninth and Cottage Grove, home of a famous nightspot, the Flame. From it the group first took the name Flames.[8]

Around 1952 the Flamingos expelled their original lead singer, Earl Lewis. The banished singer loved to sing so he started looking for a new group, and the Flames gladly incorporated him into the group. Another, less-official, member was Freddie Matthews, who served as chauffeur and who also occasionally sang with the group. Not long afterward, the group changed its name to the Five Echoes after they discovered a previous claim to the "Flames" name. Earl Lewis told how the group got the opportunity to record:

> We ran into Walter Spriggs. He had heard about the Echoes. So he had come down to Thirty-ninth Street, where we hung out, and we would be like sitting around the street corner singing all the time. So he came by and said how would you guys like to go out on the road. "What we are going to do first is work a club for a time," said Spriggs, "so I can groom you guys like I want." There's a place up in Kenosha, Wisconsin, called the Right Spot owned by two Italian guys. Spriggs took us up there one weekend, and when we did this job there that night they had a nice crowd, which was the way Spriggs figured it. We did a good show for them that night and the crowd liked us. These two Italian guys told us to stay, and we stayed there 'bout a year.
>
> We did Orioles songs, Dominoes songs, everything. Then we started getting our material together. Walter Spriggs was knocking it around, writing songs. He wrote a couple, which was "Lonely Mood"

and "Baby Come Back to Me." So when Ewart Abner (we called him Little Abner) of Chance Records came out there, by that time we were swinging. We had the house packed every weekend. Abner asked us to record and that's how we started recording records.[9]

The first record, "Lonely Mood" backed with "Baby Come Back to Me," was released on Sabre in September 1953. Spriggs sang lead on both sides but was considered a member of the group only for the session; Sims sang baritone; Herbert Lewis, baritone; Tommy Hunt, second tenor; Earl Lewis, first tenor; and Jimmy Marshall, bass. According to Earl Lewis, both sides got radio play in various cities across the nation, but the record could not be called a big seller since it did not get on the charts nationally. It did, however, make the group known, so that when they were billed they had some name recognition.

After the record, Hunt was lost to the group. He had been drafted, leaving the Five Echoes short a member. The remaining singers in the group—Sims, the two Lewises, and Marshall—recruited Johnnie Taylor, a Kansas City native who was bumming around Chicago singing in a local gospel group, the Highway QC's. This was the same Taylor who became a hit-making phenomenon of the 1960s and 1970s. Given the fact that he had forsaken gospel for a blues group and sang R-rated songs years later, some might question whether Taylor was the right type to be in gospel in the first place. But according to Earl Lewis, Taylor was far from an apostate: "Johnnie was the type of guy who was stone religious," Lewis said firmly. "He was a gospel singer, he was *really* a gospel singer," he repeated for emphasis. "He just moseyed off into rhythm and blues."

With Taylor as a member, the Five Echoes' next record was "So Lonesome" backed with "Broke," released on Sabre in February 1954. "So Lonesome" featured Sims on lead but had Taylor coming in as second lead. "Broke" featured Sims as the sole lead.

By early 1954 the Five Echoes were becoming regulars in the clubs, playing such venues as the New Heat Wave, in January, and Martin's Corner, in March. April saw the group traveling to the Kansas City Municipal Auditorium to launch a tour of the Midwest. The group's most spectacular date was in September 1954, when they appeared on McKie's Variety Show at the Corpus Christi auditorium. On the bill were some twenty-two acts, among them the El Dorados, Five Chances, and Fasinoles.

The Five Echoes had one more session with Sabre. The company seemingly was trying to get the Echoes away from blues so it had them record a ballad, "Why Oh Why," and a jump, "That's My Baby." Hunt, while AWOL from the service, joined the group on this session, singing second lead on "Why Oh Why." Hunt was soon lost to the group again after the

FBI caught up with him and sent him to the stockade. Chance was apparently winding down at the time, because it closed its doors before the year 1954 was out. This may account for the fact that the songs from this session went unreleased but appeared in 1964 on the *Groups Three* Constellation LP.

The Five Blue Notes

The Five Blue Notes were thought for a long time to have come from Chicago, but the group was actually from the Washington, D.C., area. The members got together in 1950 while still students at Francis Junior High School in Georgetown, Maryland, where they took the name Bluejays. Original members were Andy Magruder (lead), Waymond Mooney (first tenor), Robert Stroud (second tenor), and Moise Vaughn (baritone/bass). The group practiced to music of such contemporary groups as the Orioles, the Five Keys, and the Ravens.[10]

In late 1952, the Bluejays won a citywide amateur contest, and other shows soon followed. A Korean War veteran, a Lieutenant Slaughter, heard them and began rehearsing them. He got the Bluejays on a Red Cross tour, playing before wounded veterans at military hospitals in the Baltimore and Washington area.

In late 1953, the group was taken over by manager William "Bosco" Boyd, who was managing several other local groups, notably the Clefs, of "We Three" fame. First tenor Waymond Mooney left to join the marines and was replaced by Jackie Shedrick. At the same time, lead tenor Fleming Briscoe joined the group and the group's name was changed to the Five Blue Notes.

On Boyd's suggestion, the Five Blue Notes went to Chicago to try to get a recording contract. After a month there they lucked out and signed with Chance Records. They recorded four songs, and all were released on the label's subsidiary Sabre label. The first release paired "My Gal Is Gone," a typical 1954 deep, brooding ballad featuring Magruder as the lead, with "Ooh Baby," a routine jump led by Briscoe. The second release paired "The Beat of Our Hearts," a more poplike and accessible ballad featuring Briscoe as lead, with a tuneful jump, "You Gotta Go Baby," with Vaughn on lead. What is interesting about these songs is that the Blue Notes used all their members, especially Shedrick, as an echoing falsetto and Vaughn as an interjecting bass.

The Five Blues Notes returned home and waited, but when it looked as though nothing was going to happen with the recordings, Magruder joined the marines. However, in early 1954 "My Gal Is Gone" went to number one in the D.C. area, and the group started playing local bills without him.

While on leave, Magruder had the bittersweet experience of seeing the Five Blue Notes perform "My Gal Is Gone" at the city's famed Howard Theater with new lead, "Ricky."

By the time Magruder was discharged from the service in 1958, the Five Blue Notes were history. But Magruder wanted his taste of fame and formed a new Five Blue Notes group, consisting of himself as lead, Stroud on second tenor, Vaughn on baritone\bass, Shedrick on first tenor, and Louis Smalls as a new lead tenor. The group recorded on the local Onda label, but the two sides, "My Special Prayer" (led by Stroud) and "Something Awful" (led by Smalls), were hardly special and perhaps a bit awful. A follow-up in 1959, which paired "My Special Prayer" with "The Thunderbird," also did nothing. This new group stayed together until 1960, when they broke up.

Magruder then joined a later Spaniels group, and recorded on their last hit, "I Know," in 1961. He stayed with the Spaniels until 1963, when he tried to go it alone as a solo act. Magruder managed to get one record out by himself, under the name of Andy Mack, for the Chess label. The titles were "Do You Wanta Go" and "Later Than You Think," and he was backed by a young D.C. group, the Carltons. Aside from a few plays in the D.C. area, the record bombed.

The Flamingos

The Flamingos, with their smooth, delicate harmonies, featured an elegant sound never successfully imitated by any other group. It was a true ensemble sound with four- and five-part harmonies that were often intricate and always technically polished and pristine. Unlike many of the vocal groups' members, the Flamingos were adults, and they sang with a serious approach to their art that made them one of the most respected and famed groups in rhythm and blues history

Many collectors believe that the Flamingos' Chicago years, when they appeared on Chance (1953–54), Parrot (1954–55), and Checker (1955–56), were their golden years. This is a purist view that contends that the group essentially forsook rhythm and blues after they left the Chicago labels. It is a view I do not wholly share, for I am a great fan of their Decca (1957) and End (1958–63) material; nevertheless, I find their years in Chicago the most intriguing part of their story.[11]

The unique sound of the Flamingos stems from the members' unusual heritage. Except for the lead singers, Sollie McElroy and, later, Nate Nelson, the group's other members—cousins Ezekial (Zeke) Carey and Jacob (Jake) Carey, and cousins Johnny Carter and Paul Wilson—were all related and were all Black Jews. Earl Lewis, a neighborhood pal who started with the group, noted that "the Flamingos were all part of a choir in their church. They sang hymns, Jewish hymns I think. Kind of solemn, like in a Catholic cathedral." Nate Nelson, when interviewed by Wayne Jones, said, "This is where all our harmonies came from. Our harmonies were different because we dealt with a lot of minor chords which is how Jewish music is written."[12]

An explanation is in order concerning the Flamingos' religion. They have been called Black Jews, and indeed members of their particular denomination—the Church of God and Saints of Christ—are commonly called by that name. Its believers hold it as a matter of faith that they are the chosen people, descendants of the Jews of the Holy Land. This church, however, unlike other, more orthodox, Black Jewish groups, has a partial Christian content, evidenced by the fact that its service uses a choir instead of a cantor, as would an Orthodox Jewish congregation. One source says that the Church of God and Saints of Christ combines elements of Pentecostalism and black nationalism with the holy days and rites of Judaism.[13] If the church is indeed influenced by Pentecostalism, its music is surprisingly devoid of any gospel content, as Lewis and Nelson made clear.

Music in a minor key has overtones of sadness and darkness, and this feeling is present in the songs of the Flamingos, particularly their later Checker ballads, "Dream of a Lifetime," "Whispering Stars," and "Would I Be Crying." Like all R&B groups of the fifties, the Flamingos did an equal number of jump tunes ("Jump Children" and "Carried Away," on Chance), but these are less successful than their ballad material—they're too controlled. Peppy, up-tempo numbers seem to require a little more spirited anarchy. Yet throughout the Flamingos' career they were as much a jump-tune group as they were balladeers, despite the overemphasis collectors over the years have placed on their ballad material.

The Careys usually tell interviewers that the Flamingos were formed in the fall of 1952, when the group was discovered by its first manager, Fletcher Weatherspoon.[14] Before that time the Careys feel they were just an informal group of boys singing harmony. But that history of the group does not seem to allow for less than a year's time between their formation and their signing with Chance Records early in 1953. In fact, their genesis dates to at least two years earlier.

The Carey cousins grew up in Baltimore, down the street from Sonny Til of the Orioles. (Zeke Carey's older brother attended high school with Til.) In 1950, the Careys moved to the Douglas community on Chicago's South Side, and while singing in the choir of a Black Jewish congregation at Thirty-ninth and State they met Johnny Carter and Paul Wilson. The four young men were soon found around Thirty-fifth or Thirty-sixth and Lake Park, doowopping on the street corners. Eventually Carter and Wilson became related to the Carey cousins through marriage.

The group found a lead in Earl Lewis, the first of several "outsider" leads. Lewis, a friend in the neighborhood, dated the sister of one member of the group. Lewis recalled the group's early days: "We started together, oh, about 1949, 1950, and were all just neighborhood guys who started singing. We used to sing and, man, we would have a big crowd around us. Every night we would sit around, just sitting out on the front steps, and all the kids would come around and listen to us sing."

With Lewis in the lead, the group at first went under the name the Swallows. They kept that name for about six to eight months, until they discovered another group called the Swallows and changed their name to the Five Flamingos, a formulation typical in Chicago, where just about every group put a number before its name.

The Five Flamingos eventually were discovered by Weatherspoon, and the group graduated to house parties. Speaking about Weatherspoon, Zeke Carey mentioned that "he would take us to three or four house parties on the South Side in one night. We sang very close harmony, and that was unusual at the time. We sang the hits of the day, and people got off on that. The house party thing did a lot for us. We had never sung that type of music in front of audiences before. We had sung in churches Sundays, but this was a unique experience for us. The feedback we got gave us a second notion that maybe we should take singing more seriously."[15] Lewis also recalled that Weatherspoon, as a member of the Elks, took the group to entertain before a number of gatherings of that fraternal organization.

Probably sometime early in 1952 Lewis was ejected from the Five Flamingos; he readily gave the reason: "Girls," he laughed. "You know, not making rehearsals, just things like that. They were tired of my messing up." Although this was still before the group signed with Chance, Lewis recalled rehearsing two of their later Chance sides, "Someday, Someway" and "If I Can't Have You." He went on to become one of the members of the Five Echoes and was replaced in the Flamingos by a new "outsider" lead, Sollie McElroy, who was discovered by Weatherspoon in a talent show.

"There used to be a theater off Fifty-first, the Willard Theater," said McElroy. "I had gone there to perform in a talent show. I had been singing in church, but it wasn't a thing I felt. I never forgot the song I was singing, 'Cry' by Johnnie Ray. And I sang that, and I was so excited so that when I got to the high part I lost control of it. And this guy stuck the hook out and pulled me off the stage. The audience goes 'no no no, let him go on again.' The orchestra started up and I sang the complete song. I won second prize."[16]

Weatherspoon, impressed by what he heard, brought McElroy to the Five Flamingos and they accepted him as their new lead. Lewis, who was still hanging around the group, told of a bizarre early rehearsal: "'September

Song,' I remember at rehearsal Sollie showed up and sang the song. But he sang it so high and, you know, he put so much into it, he collapsed and just fell over and fainted. We all just stood there and stared because we never saw anything like it."

Weatherspoon had a friend who owned a nightclub, Martin's Corner, and had the Five Flamingos perform on an amateur night. In the audience was a representative of King Booking Agency, operated by Ralph Leon. The upshot was that Leon became the group's manager and Weatherspoon stepped aside. (Weatherspoon was getting drafted at the time, making it easier for him to bow out.)

Leon felt the group was ready to record, and probably sometime in early 1952 he took the Five Flamingos to audition at United Records, then the largest R&B label in the city. But the company rejected them. Zeke Carey recalled, "We sang a capella for them, we were told we sounded too good. So we came back a year later. There were other things we wanted to sing, and then we were told we didn't sound black enough. We weren't raw enough. The harmony was too close, too perfect."[17]

By late 1952 the Five Flamingos had left house parties far behind and were playing Chicago clubs with some regularity. In October they performed at the Indiana Theater (219 East Forty-third Street), and in November and December they were appearing at the famed Club Delisa.

Leon then took the group to Chance, which signed the act in January 1953 and shortened its name on record labels to simply the Flamingos. In the clubs, however, the group for the next two years used the number in its name. In March, the label put on the street "Someday, Someway" backed with "If I Can't Have You." Although the midtempo "Someday, Someway" was the superior side, by June the flip was doing well in several regional markets, especially Detroit and Philadelphia. The ballad flip exhibits two leads, McElroy the first and Carter the second. Zeke Carey said, "Sollie sang the lead to the song basically. I think if you listen to 'If I Can't Have You,' and if you remember the Orioles you'll probably recognize to a certain degree that we were influenced by the Orioles. You'll recognize how the second lead would come in. He would sing a little part and the main lead would then come back in."[18] Most early 1950s groups looked to the Orioles for inspiration, and the Flamingos were no exception. In 1955, when the Flamingos were on Checker, they redid "If I Can't Have You" infinitely better as "Nobody's Love."

In July, Chance released "That's My Desire" backed with "Hurry Home Baby." "That's My Desire" is a divine version of the Frankie Laine hit from 1947, but the flip side is an imitation Ravens number that made nobody forget about the Ravens. By August, "That's My Desire" was racking up strong regional sales.

September saw the release of the Flamingos' classic Chance recording of "Golden Teardrops." The beauty of this song is marvelously enhanced by the intricate harmonizing, especially the way the voices are dramatically split in the intro and the close. McElroy's impassioned vocalizing helps immeasurably in giving the legendary "Golden Teardrops" its reputation as a masterpiece. "Carried Away," the flip, is a pleasing jump, but nobody noticed, so strong was the A side.

Given the regional successes of their singles, the Flamingos were touring regularly by the latter part of 1953, playing Detroit, Cleveland, and other midwestern cities, as well as making a tour of East Coast cities. In November the group signed with Associated Booking Corporation and began a tour with Duke Ellington at the Regal Theater. In February 1954, the group appeared with Ellington at the Howard in D.C. and the Apollo in New York City.

Meanwhile, the Flamingos' recording career was not going as well. Late in 1953 Chance issued two less-than-stellar sides in "Plan for Love," a blues, and "You Ain't Ready," essentially a variation of "Someday, Someway." Neither side sold. March 1954 saw the release of "Cross over the Bridge" backed with "Listen to My Plea." Neither the cover of the Patti Page hit nor the bluesy "Listen to My Plea" was appealing enough to sustain the Flamingos' name with the public. "Cross over the Bridge" got some play in Chicago and other cities, however, and some collectors swear by its quality.

In October 1954, the group put out two more sides that hardly thrill vocal harmony fans today: "Blues in a Letter," a stone-solid blues, and "Jump Children" (alternately titled "Vooit Vooit"), a cover of a James Williamson record on Chance. The latter is a terrific number, but it didn't excite the public in 1954. "Jump Children," which is not what collectors usually look for in groups today, was most typical of the era, and the group used the song in its live performances for years afterward.

"Jump Children" was the last release by the Flamingos on Chance before the label folded, but that did not complete their output on that label. "September Song," a song left in the can, was eventually released on a 1964 Constellation album.

The Moonglows

The Moonglows were nominated to the Rock and Roll Hall of Fame in 1990 and again in 1993 but failed to get inducted both times. Presumably, if one were to go by the strict criteria of impact on the charts, the Moonglows are not deserving members, having produced just three top-forty singles on the pop charts. But if any vocal group signaled the birth of rock 'n' roll—by which rhythm and blues emerged out of its black subculture into mainstream teen culture—it is the Moonglows. This group's career paralleled that of its mentor, the legendary deejay Alan Freed, who played Moonglows records from his early days in Cleveland to his triumph in New York radio as the foremost rock 'n' roll deejay in America. The Moonglows performed in the very first rhythm and blues concerts sponsored by Freed in Cleveland and later made appearances in Freed's rock 'n' roll movies, during the height of his fame. Any hall of fame located in Cleveland would be remiss not to induct the Moonglows.

The Moonglows began their career as a rhythm and blues act, and their earliest records reflected the era when vocal groups sounded bluesy and mournful on the ballads and rough and jumpy on the upbeat material. By the mid-1950s, when they emerged as rock 'n' roll stars, they were singing smooth ballads and upbeat tunes with a feel of pop, and some of their songs came from old-line Tin Pan Alley tunesmiths. What made the group distinctive was the outstanding polish and perfectionism the members developed in their harmony techniques, one of which was "blow harmony," by which they built harmonies with notes that made a blown breath a part of the sound. The harmonies then sounded as though they came from deep within the chest.[19]

The story of the Moonglows is mainly the story of Harvey Fuqua and Bobby Lester, two remarkable natives of Louisville, Kentucky. Fuqua, born July 17, 1929, was a cousin of Charlie Fuqua, a longtime member of the famed Ink Spots. Harvey Fuqua's entry into music was almost ordained, as he commented to journalist Steve Propes. "I wanted to be famous like my uncle, but I didn't like guitar. I wanted to be a drummer, but I ended up playing piano."[20] While attending high school in the city, he met Robert L. Dallas, known later as Bobby Lester. Lester was born on January 13, 1930. Fuqua and Lester hooked up while still in high school, singing as a duet but also performing with Lester as a solo singer accompanied by Fuqua on piano. The pair's first professional gig was in a Louisville club, in 1949. Eventually Fuqua and Lester joined the Ed Wiley Band. Wiley, a tenor saxophonist, got a hit on the charts in 1950 with "Cry, Cry Baby" (vocal by Teddy Reynolds), so he was hot. Fuqua and Lester toured the South with Wiley. Around 1952, however, Fuqua moved up to Cleveland, Ohio, leaving Lester behind in Louisville.

In Cleveland, Fuqua soon found himself involved in the burgeoning vocal group scene. Because of the success of the Orioles, the Clovers, the Dominoes, and other groups of the day, singers were getting together, forming groups. Fuqua joined with bass Prentiss Barnes (born April 12, 1925, in Magnolia, Mississippi) and tenor lead Danny Coggins (born in Tennessee) to form the Crazy Sounds.

The Crazy Sounds sang a range of material—jazz, pop, and rhythm and blues—probably a reflection of Fuqua's experience in the Ed Wiley Band. "We were singing jazz," Fuqua recounted, "James Moody and Eddie Jefferson type of things. It was three part harmony in the beginning, doing bop, pop, and jazz things. We were called the Crazy Sounds because we were singing jazz. Then we started into other types of music; we loved the Dominoes and all those things."[21] It's interesting that Fuqua's reference to jazz was to artists associated with the "vocalese" style of jazz singing, in which the vocalist, such as Eddie Jefferson, would sing the exact notes from a saxophone rendition, such as one by James Moody. The Crazy Sounds were obviously working on vocalese jazz, which was becoming popular in the early 1950s.

Prentiss Barnes told the R&B historian Peter Grendysa that the group got its break in the business when it was discovered by a local blues singer, Al "Singin' Fats" Thomas. Prentiss said, "At the time we were hanging out at a club called the Loop. We auditioned there one Friday morning and Fats Thomas happened to be there. Right away he called Alan Freed. Even today, I still don't know what he heard in us that sounded so good to him. We were kind of rough but, whatever he heard, he liked it."[22]

Freed did not care for the group's name, the Crazy Sounds, however, and dubbed them the Moonglows, which derived from his deejay moniker, "Moondog." Freed formed a new label, Champagne, with promoter Lew Platt, and the group made its first recordings in February 1953. The release featured "I Just Can't Tell No Lie," led by Fuqua, and "I've Been Your Dog (Ever Since I've Been Your Man)," led by Barnes. Both titles were credited to Freed, but Barnes has claimed to have written both sides. Barnes asserted, "Alan Freed wrote no songs for us, that's for sure. He never wrote no damn songs. He just got credit for them because we didn't know any better."[23] The record featured a new member of the Moonglows, Bobby Lester, because just prior to the session the group drove back down to Louisville and recruited Fuqua's old partner.

The Champagne record did well in Cleveland, according to Fuqua, mainly because of Freed's unceasing plugs for the record on his show. Fuqua said, "It got us a shot on some of Freed's shows—in Akron, Warren, Youngstown, like those towns, about a fifty mile radius. Freed was booking people like B. B. King, Charles Brown, Little Jimmy Scott, anybody who had a decent record, so we could work once a month."[24]

The first big show for the Moonglows was in August 1953, when they appeared on Freed's Big Rhythm and Blues Show, held in the Cleveland Arena. Also on the bill were Fats Domino and Joe Turner. As John A. Jackson demonstrated in his remarkable biography of Alan Freed, *Big Beat Heat,* all of Freed's Ohio shows were rhythm and blues shows that attracted mostly blacks. They were not the first rock 'n' roll shows, as legend would have it. Elsewhere in the country the Champagne release was out of earshot and hence got no airplay.

One person who was apparently less than impressed was Danny Coggins, who decided that the entertainment business was not for him and left to pursue more stable employment in his gas station. Replacing Coggins was first tenor Alexander Walter (born April 17, 1936, in Alabama), who went by the name Pete Graves. He was a friend of Prentiss Barnes.

In October 1953, Freed brought the Moonglows to the Chicago-based Chance label. For the group's first release, the company put out "Baby Please" backed with "Whistle My Love." The top side, led by Fuqua, is a low-key bluesy ballad, and the flip, featuring a duet lead of Fuqua and Lester, is a steady rocking jump. Neither side did anything in the market, despite heavy promotion by Freed in Cleveland.

Because of the approaching holidays, the Moonglows' second release was "Just a Lonely Christmas" backed with "Hey, Santa Claus." "Lonely Christmas," led by Fuqua, is an Orioles type of droopy ballad that appeals to today's collector, and "Hey, Santa Claus," led by Barnes, is a routine jump heavily derived from the old rhythm and blues tune "Be Baba Leba," made famous by Helen Humes in 1945. Neither side is particularly Christmasy, and it was obvious that neither Gene Autry nor Charles Brown had anything to fear from the Moonglows. However, "Hey, Santa Claus" made a surprise appearance many years later in film, in *National Lampoon's Christmas Vacation.* In one scene, Chevy Chase looks across the street and there's a black band playing and singing "Hey, Santa Claus" (actually lip-synching to the Moonglows' original). Christmas 1953 saw the Moonglows playing at a Freed revue at the Akron Armory, in Akron, Ohio, along with the Dominoes and Little Walter.

At a recording session in Chicago in January 1954, the Moonglows waxed six more titles, presumably songs that were more saleable. One was a cover rendition of Doris Day's "Secret Love," which was popular at the time. The Day version had been featured in the film *Calamity Jane.* Although the Moonglows' version was recorded with a backing band that provided inappropriate doowop chord changes instead of what the song called for, it was particularly effective in their harmonized intro with falsetto top that segued into Lester's emoting lead. "Secret Love," as the Moonglows' third Chance release, was paired with a spectacular jump, "Real Gone Mama," featuring Fuqua as lead. The *Billboard* reviewer gave the latter four stars and "Secret Love" only three stars. The record, released in February 1954, made the most noise of all the Moonglows' Chance sides, and Sheridan said that in March it was the company's top seller. In April, the Moonglows appeared at Freed's Moondog Ball in the

Akron Armory, sharing the bill with Charles Brown, Paul Williams, and Margie Day.

June 1954 saw the release of "I Was Wrong" backed with "Ooh Rockin' Daddy." "I Was Wrong," featuring Fuqua as lead, has a nice switch-off approach, opening with Fuqua's sultry low-key lead and switching off to high-powered chorusing and seguing into Lester's screaming lead. Fuqua asserted, "That was the strongest song, I think, before 'Sincerely.' It made quite a bit of noise in Cleveland, Chicago, and I believe, the West Coast. We never got a count on sales, so it doesn't matter. Wherever we went, people would request 'I Was Wrong.' That's why I think it had a shot."[25] The record never made the national charts, but it picked up what were then called regional sales.

"Ooh Rockin' Daddy," with Lester on lead, is an R&B jump, but with the searing sax break and the aggressive approach to the "rock, rock, rock" refrain, one could call it a proto–rock 'n' roll number. The *Billboard* reviewer preferred the rocking side and gave it four stars.

The Moonglows' fifth and final Chance release, "219 Train" backed with "My Gal," came out in October 1954, as the company was fading and the group was hunting for a new label deal. The pairing was barely distributed and proved to be the group's rarest record, now fetching collector prices from five hundred to a thousand dollars. "My Gal," led by Fuqua, is an uninteresting jump partially saved by an excellent sax break by Red Holloway, but the bluesy "219 Train" is something else, with a great emotional melismatic lead by Bobby Lester.

Chance had left some fine Moonglows sides in the can, supposedly forever, but in 1964, after Ewart Abner and Art Sheridan founded Constellation Records in August 1963, the new company put out a series of reissue LPs, one of which was a twelve-side collection of the Moonglows' Chance material. Two unreleased sides in the bunch were an appealing jump, "Fine Fine Girl," and a pleasant ballad, "My Love." Neither song was hit material, to be sure, but both were certainly worth retrieving.

*   *   *

The closing of Chance in December 1954 has always been characterized as a business failure. But it appears that this interpretation is incorrect. Sheridan and Abner were getting deeply involved in the business dealings of James Bracken and Vivian Carter, two neophytes in the record business, who had recently launched Vee Jay and needed help in making their new label a success. Sheridan helped to secure national distribution for their initial releases, by leasing their first Jimmy Reed record and first Spaniels record for his Chance label. But, Sheridan later noted, "I just got tired of it, and I was spending a lot of time with Vivian, Jimmy, and Abner, and didn't want to be a producer." In all probability, Sheridan was losing his youthful enthusiasm for the business and had decided to pursue what became a highly successful career in real estate. After working briefly at United Distributors, Abner went over to Vee Jay to run the company.

What Chance produced during its four years of existence hardly ranks with the output of big labels in Chicago, either in quantity or quality, but there are a lot of collector items for both blues and vocal groups in their catalog, ensuring that Chance remains one of the legendary labels in the golden age of rhythm and blues. But Chance was not yet producing rhythm and blues records that could be characterized as rock 'n' roll. When the company closed, the rock 'n' roll revolution was just being launched. It was Chess that took Art Sheridan's principal acts, the Moonglows and the Flamingos, and turned them into rock 'n' roll stars.

Notes

1. Information about the Chance label comes from Rowe, *Chicago Breakdown,* pp. 106–13, and the Sheridan interview.

2. This and subsequent remarks by Sheridan that are quoted in this chapter come from the Sheridan interview.

3. Information on Ewart Abner comes from "Vee-Jay Boss Joins Urban League Board" and the Abner interview.

4. "Petrillo Nixes Art Sheridan's Disking License."

5. Rowe, *Chicago Breakdown,* p. 113.

6. Information about the Five Chances comes from Pruter, "Five Chances," and the Hilliard Jones, Howard Pitman, and Reggie Smith interviews.

7. This and subsequent remarks by Reggie Smith that are quoted in this chapter come from the September 28, 1989, interview with him.

8. Information about the Five Echoes comes from Pruter, "Five Echoes"; [Topping] and [Richardson], "Tommy Hunt Story"; Lewis interview.

9. This and subsequent remarks by Earl Lewis that are quoted in this chapter come from the Lewis interview.

10. Information about the Five Blue Notes comes from Goldberg and Redmond, "Five Blue Notes."

11. Information about the Flamingos' early years comes from: Fileti, liner notes for *I Only Have Eyes for You*; Hoekstra, "Flamingos Return"; Jones, "Nate Nelson"; McGarvey, "Flamingos Story"; Pruter, "Flamingos"; Sbarbori, "Sollie McElroy"; Tancredi, "Flamingos: Early Years"; and the McElroy, Lewis, and Zeke and Jake Carey interviews.

12. Jones, "Nate Nelson," p. 12.

13. O'Brien, "Church of God."

14. Zeke and Jake Carey interview.

15. Hoekstra, "Flamingos Return."

16. McElroy interview.

17. Hoekstra, "Flamingos Return."

18. Zeke and Jake Carey interview.

19. Information about the Moonglows comes from: Caldarulo, "Moonglows: Definitive Biography"; Given, "Moonglows"; Grendysa, *The Moonglows* liner notes; Hunt, "The Moonglows"; J. Jackson, *Big Beat Heat;* Marion, "Listening In"; Propes, "Commandments of Doo-Wop"; Pruter, "Moonglows' Sound" and "Prentiss Barnes"; White, "Harvey Fuqua"; and the Barnes interviews.

20. Propes, "Commandments of Doo-Wop," p. 11.

21. Ibid.

22. Grendysa, *The Moonglows* liner notes.

23. Barnes interview, September 26, 1992.

24. Propes, "Commandments of Doo-Wop," p. 11.

25. Ibid.

2

Parrot Records

Al Benson achieved fame on a truly legendary level as a Chicago deejay, concert promoter, and record company entrepreneur. He earned widespread popularity by feeding the appetites of the city's rapidly growing population of southern-born blacks, who were clamoring for the "real thing" in black popular music, which by the late 1940s was being called rhythm and blues. Born Arthur B. Leaner, Benson was an uncle of the record distributors Ernie and George Leaner, but there wasn't much family resemblance. While Ernie and George were well-spoken and cultivated, Benson was inarticulate and uncouth. His thick dialect made him at times sound like a mushmouth over the air, not the best attribute for a disc jockey. He walked with a limp, and one observer detected in Benson a bit of compensating arrogance. The deejay never hesitated in using his popularity to wield his power ruthlessly. No entertainer making records could cross him and still expect to be heard on black radio in Chicago.

For all his popularity as a radio personality, Benson was not that successful as a record company entrepreneur. His first enterprise was Old Swingmaster Records, started up with radio-station owner Egmont Sonderling in March 1949 at 154 East Erie Street. Sonderling was apparently president, Leonard Davis was general manager, and Benson was in charge of A&R. The company folded in the summer of the next year after only a few releases, none of them vocal group recordings.

Benson's second venture was Parrot Records, which lasted from summer 1953 to early 1956. A look at the way Parrot was run might explain Benson's failure as a record company owner. The Parrot label and its Blue Lake subsidiary, which began operating in 1954, were both under the umbrella of the Bronzeville Record Manufacturing Company. Located first at 4307 South Parkway (now King Drive), the company moved to the heart of the black record row at 750 East Forty-ninth in June 1954, and then relocated to 4858 South Cottage Grove the following January. The Bronzeville Distribution Company also operated out of those premises.

Much of the administrative operation of the company was conducted at Benson's South Side home, where he based his broadcasts in the early 1950s. Vocal group members who had dealt with him report that Benson seemed to run the company alone, almost as a hobby. He was president, administrator, A&R man, producer, and, in Chicago, distributor. Most of Parrot's sessions were recorded on the city's near North Side at Universal Recording. In recording his vocal groups, Benson made use of the city's many club performers, notably the saxophonists Paul Bascomb and Red Holloway, who provided so many of the great breaks heard on the vocal ensemble recordings.

Many of the Parrot and Blue Lake records are relatively rare today, in part because Benson apparently never established a secure distribution network for his company. In 1955, when two members of a group came back to him complaining that they could not hear their record in their home-town of Detroit, Benson thrust some copies of the record into their hands and gave them the name of a distributor they might entreaty to secure a distribution deal. Needless to say, a company operating on that level was not long for this world.[1]

Despite distribution problems, Parrot and Blue Lake were failures in only one sense: as commercial enterprises. Otherwise, the labels were a terrific success, because they handed down to us a legacy of the most splendid recordings by bluesmen, solo R&B performers, and vocal harmony groups of the early 1950s. The solo and blues acts have been discussed elsewhere, notably in Mike Rowe's groundbreaking historical survey of postwar Chicago blues, *Chicago Breakdown*. However, it is Benson's vocal groups, notably the Five Thrills, the Flamingos, the Five Chances, and the Orchids, that are of interest in the present study.

The Five Thrills

The Five Thrills flashed onto the R&B scene in Chicago for a year during 1953–54 and then disappeared forever. During that year, they were the most frequently recorded group on Parrot, but it's hard to understand why, when one listens to their records. Most of their "original" tunes were thinly disguised covers of records of the day, and their other material lacked any sort of distinction. Nonetheless, one can find some virtues in their songs. Although their "originals" may not have been that, their songs were competently and entertainingly done.[2]

The Five Thrills were basically an aggregation of young men who lived on Thirty-first Street and began singing together in 1950, while they were still students at Douglas Elementary School at Thirty-second and Calumet. The original members were Levi Jenkins (bass and piano), Gilbert Warren (lead tenor), Oscar Robinson (baritone), and brothers Fred Washington (baritone) and Obie Washington (second tenor). When the members went on to high school, they scattered to DuSable, Dunbar, and Phillips, all which served the South Side.

The group was discovered by happenstance on the proverbial street corner. "We were just singing everything that was out," Jenkins has said. "Yeah, you know, doowopping. We were on Thirty-first Street one day and a guy named Ted Daniels came by. He said he wanted a group and that we should come around to his house. He was around Fifty-second Street and Drexel. We had some material and we went around to several labels with it. First to United, then we went to a couple more. And then we ended up at Parrot. Al Benson liked us, so that's how we got started."[3]

The first release, "Feel So Good" (Fred Washington lead) backed with "My Baby's Gone" (Robinson lead), came out in December 1953 with less-than-grand success and less-than-original material. "Feel So Good" was actually the jump "Serve Another Round," made famous by the Five Keys, and "My Baby's Gone" was really the ballad "My Summer's Gone," originally recorded by the Four Buddies. The Thrills' songs got relatively good play in Chicago—via Benson, of course—and earned the group recognition locally. Elsewhere in the country the record did nothing, probably because of Benson's anemic distribution system.

By early 1954, Robinson had left the group and was replaced with Leon Pace, although maybe not right away. As members of the Sheppards (of United fame) remembered it, they took Robinson in as a member to improve their vocal harmony and gave Andre Williams to the Five Thrills in return. Williams, who would beef up the stage presentation of the group, was probably briefly a member before being replaced by Pace.

The Five Thrills, with Pace, came out in early 1954 with two new sides on Parrot—a ballad, "Gloria" (Warren lead), and a jump, "Wee Wee Baby" (Washington lead). "Gloria" as penned by Warren is a different song from the well-known Cadillacs' classic of the same name, and a few steps down, but it is the outstanding side of the Five Thrills. The high tenor wailing in the background and the blending of voices made the song the group's most modern and most entertaining number. "Wee Wee Baby," however, is an exceedingly weak remake of a Robins' song from 1949.

Jenkins recalled also recording, but not releasing, "My Saddest Hour" and "Rockin' at Midnight." A reissue label, Relic Records, in 1990 found "Rockin' at Midnight," a rousing jump, but they also found three other unissued titles—the very appealing "Ride Jimmy Ride" (a thinly disguised remake of Lloyd Price's "Mailman Blues"), "So Long Young Girl" (a bluesy jump), and an almost a cappella rendition of "All I Want," a song recorded by the Five Chances on the Blue Lake label in 1955. The Five Thrills' version of "All I Want" appears to have been recorded in 1953, yet the Five Chances have the composing credit on the 1955 release, so one wonders about the origin of this song.

Relic also found two unissued Parrot tunes by a group called the Earls. If the collectors Bob Stallworth and Dave Antrell are correct, the Earls were actually the Five Thrills. The two songs by the Earls—"Laverne" and "Darlene (Girl of My Dreams)"—appeared originally in the late 1970s on a bootleg LP called *Parrot Doowop,* and Antrell heard "Five Thrills" in the lead vocals. Stallworth brought the sides to the attention of Levi Jenkins, who said they were in fact by the Five Thrills. Subsequently, the two cuts were put out on a counterfeit Parrot single and credited to the Thrills.

Both "Laverne" and "Darlene (Girl of My Dreams)" are extraordinary. The former is a pleasantly bouncy jump with a subtle Latin rhythm. The tasty sax break by Paul Bascomb and the guitar break are outstanding. "Darlene" features a terrific blend of voices, notably in the wonderful intro. The similarities between the Earls and the Five Thrills are particularly close in "Gloria," a bona fide Thrills number, and "Darlene." Both share the same vocal arrangements, with the high tenor wailing, and the same songwriting approach. Gilbert Warren appears to have been the lead on all three sides.

The Five Thrills regularly played live dates in Chicago and the Midwest during 1953–54. "We did a package deal with Illinois Jacquet and we were traveling with him," Jenkins recalled. The group did two big shows at the Trianon Ballroom, first with sax man Wardell Grey and then with the supreme honker, Illinois Jacquet. The second show, held in March 1954, featured not only the Five Thrills but the El Rays (Dells), the Five Cs, and the Clouds. Other places where the Five Thrills performed were Ada's Juke Box Lounge (Fifty-first and Prairie), The Flame (Thirty-ninth and Drexel), and the Packinghouse (Forty-ninth and Wabash).

The downfall of the Five Thrills was a result of their live performance activity, according to Jenkins. He related it to an incident that occurred in January 1954: "We were supposed to have done a thing at the [Pershing Ballroom] for McKie Fitzhugh [another deejay]. He had a group playing there, the Drifters, who had just come out with 'Money Honey.' They had posters out and we were supposed to do the show with them as a 'battle of the groups' thing. This was McKie's thing, then he and Al Benson somehow had a spat. We were ready to do the show, and Al Benson called us at the hotel and told us don't do it. And that killed us." From that point on, the group was in conflict with Benson, which led to the dissolution of the Five Thrills before the end of 1954.

Some of the participants in the Five Thrills saga continued in the business. Andre Williams, whose appearance in the group was exceedingly brief, went on to greater success as a record producer and a maker of novelty records, such as "Jail Bait" and "Bacon Fat." Gilbert Warren organized a new group, the Orchids. Levi Jenkins, always the musician in the group, continued to play piano in various combos for many years after the Thrills broke up. He died sometime in the mid-1980s, but not before providing interviews to Bob Stallworth and to me, making possible the telling of the Five Thrills story.

The Orchids

The Orchids, in their few titles recorded for Parrot, must be considered one of the most splendid doowop groups to come out of Chicago. Members grew up on the city's South Side. Gilbert Warren was the principal lead and composer. Two other members were bass Buford Wright, who wrote and sang lead with the group, and second tenor Robert C. Nesbary, who also played piano for the group. There was just one other member, whom some recall as "Charles."[4]

Of all of Benson's groups, the Orchids had the most modern sound, generally less bluesy and more in the vein of the late-1950s "teenagy" approach. In other words, they had the new rock 'n' roll sound. "Newly Wed," a terrific tune written and led by Wright, is typical in its late-fifties feel. Its forceful background riffing gives it the most punch of all the group's sides. Many fans consider "You're Everything to Me" to be the Orchids' greatest song. Warren, who wrote it, possesses an appealing, carefully modulated tenor voice that is counterpointed cleanly by the chorus. Alternate leads by Wright and Warren are also effective, and Red Holloway provides a splendid sax break. This was in every respect a perfect record. Both sides were played in various regions of the country in the summer and fall of 1955, with "Newly Wed" doing particularly well in Philadelphia.

In November 1955, Parrot released "You Said You Loved Me," another Warren song that reprised the basic style of "You're Everything to Me"—low-key modulated singing counterpointed by chorusing. There is no Holloway sax, but the melody is nice and lingers on. The flip, "I Can't Refuse," led by Warren, is a change-of-style bluesy workout that in fact may have been an old Five Thrills recording. Levi Jenkins, never a member of the Orchids, recalled recording the song for Benson as a member of the Five Thrills. At any rate, it sounds more like the Thrills than the Orchids.

The Orchids played a number of dates, but their most notable appearance was on a Benson-sponsored package show at the Regal Theater in

September 1955, where they were billed as the Four Orchids. They shared the stage with LaVern Baker, the Spaniels, the Four Fellows, J. B. Lenoir, Lou Mac, and Buddy and Ella Johnson. In July, they had played an engagement at the Trianon Ballroom. On the bill with them were the El Dorados, the Diablos, Floyd Dixon, Billy Boy (Arnold), Dr. Jo-Jo Adams, Eddie "Cleanhead" Vinson, L. C. McKinley, and the Red Holloway Band. Acting as emcee was Al Benson. The deejay Herb Kent fondly recalled the Orchids. He exclaimed, "What a great group. They just all clumped together around a microphone and sang their asses off. And they absolutely looked dazzling in their purple suits. They wore purple because it was Al Benson's favorite color."[5] Besides playing in various clubs around the city, the group toured Canada for approximately two months. According to Sherman Nesbary, the younger brother of Robert Nesbary, "the Orchids were unhappy with Parrot. Benson beat them out of a quite of bit of change, and Parrot did a poor job of promoting the group even though they made good records."[6]

The Orchids continued to be valued for years among collectors and rock 'n' roll fans. It is instructive that when in the early 1960s Chess was putting out rock 'n' roll collections for Murray the K, the New York disc jockey, the albums included Orchids songs. And it was the slow ballads, not the jumps, that were selected. In the late 1960s, Lost Nite, a reissue label based in Philadelphia, put out the four Orchids songs, which were considered some of the choicest items in the company's extensive catalog.

In 1993 several more Orchids recordings surfaced. For some reason they had been in the Vee Jay vaults, possibly sent to that company by John Burton in order to audition the Orchids, after Burton purchased Parrot. The four sides featured three jumps, "Please Don't Leave Me," "Fine Sweet Woman," and "Met a Girl on the Corner." The last one harkens back to the style of the Five Thrills. "Fine Sweet Woman" and "Please Don't Leave Me" exhibit solid vocal-jump stylings with splendid sax breaks.

The exhilarating find was the ballad, "You Have Two (I Have None)," which exhibits the same understated flavor of "You Said You Loved Me" and "You're Everything to Me," complete with the languid lead and perfectly counterpointed chorusing. The singers keep the verses going to great length before creating a superb resolution at the choruses. The harmonized closer is stunning. "You Have Two (I Have None)" is a minor masterpiece and represents the highest art of doowop creativity.

The Orchids broke up after the collapse of Parrot in 1956. With regard to the subsequent history of the members, Sherman Nesbary said, "Buford Wright got in trouble with the law. He tried a strong arm robbery on someone with a baseball bat, and ended up in jail. My brother went into the service, where he played piano."[7] Members of the Orchids did not join later groups and were never heard on wax again. Gilbert Warren eventually married a cousin of Robert Nesbary and in the 1980s moved to Arizona and disappeared. Both Buford Wright and Robert C. Nesbary died sometime in the early 1980s.

The Fascinators

The Fascinators were one of those myriad vocal groups of the early 1950s who made a few recordings and then dropped out of sight. But twenty years or so later, as vocal group collectors proceeded to dig up ever more obscure and earlier vocal harmony recordings, the Fascinators were resurrected when bootleg recordings emerged, spreading their name among the public once again. Today they are perhaps better known than when they were originally active—ever so briefly—on the rhythm and blues scene.[8]

The Fascinators began in Detroit sometime around 1949 or 1950. Their genesis lay in the effort of Jerry Potter. As he recounted, "The original group was myself (I sang second tenor and lead); Donald Blackshear, lead baritone; Bob Rivers, bass; Clarence Smith, first tenor and main lead; Earl Richardson, lead baritone/tenor. The group started with me in high school. Earl and I went to Cass Technical together, and I got him interested in singing, along with Don Blackshear, who was in the neighborhood. I met Clarence Smith and Bob Rivers through Earl, who brought them into the group."[9]

The group first recorded on the Your Copy label, which was owned by Monroe Horn, the proprietor of Horn's Record Shop at 1135 Westminster Avenue in Detroit. Potter recalled, "Before Smokey Robinson got with the Miracles, he was with a group called the Chimes. They used to come up to the store during our rehearsals. Smokey was about twelve or thirteen years old then. They would come in and Mr. Horn had this little portable recorder and he would record them. The tapes may still exist today."

Horn put out two records on the Fascinators—"Sweet Baby" backed with "The Bells of My Heart," and "My Beauty, My Own" paired with "Don't Give It Away." Potter noted, "'Sweet Baby' was the A side that was getting all the play, and they had a disc jockey here—Ernie Durham—he was very popular in Detroit, he played the record. I wrote 'My Beauty, My Own' and 'The Bells of My Heart.' Blackshear wrote 'Sweet Baby' and 'Don't Give It Away.'"

The four sides were recorded in the rear of a record shop, Joe's Records, on Hastings Avenue. Other groups of the day also recorded there, according to Potter, who particularly mentioned the Serenaders. "Sweet Baby," led by Blackshear, is a jump number propelled by a Latin-sounding beat, but the recording is exceedingly thin—no audible piano, horns, or guitar. "Bells of My Heart" is a solid romantic ballad, but Potter's falsetto is far too weak and the song is undone by the primitive studio support. "Don't Give It Away," led by Blackshear, features the strongest vocal harmonizing; as a jump, though, it needs far more oomph in the instrumentation.

The best of the four is "My Beauty, My Own," a beautiful ballad led by Smith that best survived the thin and poor recording. "I thought the song had a lot of merit," Potter said. "It was just a matter of the way it was done originally. It really didn't have enough in it."

The next (and last) label the Fascinators found themselves on was Al Benson's Blue Lake. Benson released one record on the group and it was the result of one wild weekend in Chicago in 1955. Potter said:

> We went to Chicago on letters of recomendation from Horn. He couldn't continue to push his label, I guess financial problems. He was limited in what he could do, so he wanted to see us try to go make it. And we wanted to try to do something at that particular time. He suggested maybe we could try to go to Chicago and get with a label a little bigger. We went there on a weekend, left Friday, and got there the first thing Saturday morning.
>
> We went to Vee Jay, to United, and then Parrot. Al Benson was there. He had a lot of connections and he moved fast. He had his studio set up in his basement where he went over the air. He brought us down to his studio and told us to sing. So we auditioned right there in his studio. He liked us and said he would record us. That afternoon he brought us on his radio show and introduced us, and that evening had us sing at some nightclub he had some connection with in Chicago Heights. We recorded the next evening. It was kind of a whirlwind tour.
>
> Benson whipped us around pretty good and certainly gave us the Cook's tour of Chicago. Outside the Pershing Hotel, where he put us up, he had us in his car. He was driving the wrong way down a one-way street, drunk, with no license. And a policeman stopped us. Benson got out of the car and went back and talked to the cop. I don't know what he did, but he got back into his car and we drove off. I think we had a nice time.

The Fascinators' session at Universal Recording resulted in four sides, but the only two that have surfaced are two jumps, "Can't Stop" and "Don't Give My Love Away." The latter is a faster and more jumping remake of the Horn-recorded number "Don't Give It Away." Benson changed the title because he thought the word "It" sounded suggestive. "Can't Stop" is led by Richardson, and "Don't Give My Love Away" by Blackshear, and the group gets nice support from the good swinging combo of sessionmen. The sax breaks are terrific.

"They were obviously professional musicians," Potter pointed out. "They obviously had backed other groups. Now the original musicians were lousy on the first record. These guys were good. We did 'Don't Give My Love Away' originally for Benson the way we had arranged it originally, and he didn't like it. He was the one who set the tempo up on that."

The Fascinators waited for something to happen after the record was released, but they didn't hear it over the air in Detroit. "Richardson and Rivers," said Potter, "went back to Benson to find out why we weren't getting airplay. He gave them a lot of malarkey and promises of doing this and that. He gave them copies of our record and told them to take it to a record distributor in Detroit. I don't think he ever really pushed the record."

The failure of the Blue Lake record served to break up the Fascinators. None of the members ever joined any other group. Potter recognized that the Fascinators' story was pretty minor and said, "We didn't really get that big or that popular in Detroit. We were small, we were local, we didn't do anything"—anything, that is, except make some records that collectors still aspire to acquire in the 1990s.

The Five Chances

The Five Chances recorded for Art Sheridan's Chance label before their manager, Levi McKay, brought them to the Blue Lake label in 1955. With the change in labels there was a personnel change, and Johnny "Chubby" Jones replaced "Snooky." (Jones's first name was Hilliard but he preferred to be known as Johnny. He could have saved the concern; on the street he was always called "Chubby" because of his well-fed appearance.) The other members were Darnell Austell, Reggie Smith, Howard Pitman, and Harold Jones.[10]

Johnny Jones brought solid vocal group credentials to the Five Chances, having sung with the Daffodils, another group managed by McKay. "What it was," Jones said, "Levi McKay out of New York had a bunch of groups. He had the Fortunes (which was Donald Jenkins), the Fasinoles, the Daffodils, and the Five Chances. He had all them groups, but the main group was the Five Chances. He loved the Five Chances. You had to work your way up to the Five Chances. They were so conceited. They didn't want me at first because I was fat. They were always streamlined and had those good dance steps and stuff." But Jones won the group over. As he pointed out, "I sang good and when it came to the stage part they were amazed because I was so light on my feet."[11]

On Blue Lake, the Five Chances recorded the best single of their career, "All I Want." Without histrionics and exotic stylings and manner-isms, the group created a vocal harmony classic. Darnell Austell's evenly modulated lead is nicely echoed by fine chorusing, counterpointed by Jones's high tenor alternate lead on the bridge (which creates a dramatic tension in the song). The entire group was credited as writers, although the song was originally sung by the Five Thrills in an unreleased version a year or so earlier. The flip, "Shake a Link," is an appealing jump written and led by Jones. Released in the summer of 1955, the record, alas, never hit nationally.

In 1956 the Five Chances joined Leonard Allen's States label, and as usual there were some changes in personnel. Harold Jones and Darnell Austell were replaced with Jesse Stafford and Ronald Johnson. Smith explained the loss: "They dropped out for the simple reason they were always being late, didn't show up for certain dates when they were supposed to rehearse, and what have you. And we had strict discipline. That happens to all groups."[12]

And where did the Five Chances find Ronny Johnson and Jesse Stafford? "Ronny used to sing on the corners with various neighborhood groups," Smith said. "And Jesse was on our basketball team. We had a basketball team at the time, called the Whiz Kids. He went to DuSable High with us, and so we naturally thought of him."[13] The Five Chances' basketball team was more precisely called the Junior Whiz Kids. There was a Senior Whiz Kids team, whose members included Lou Rawls, another talent from the neighborhood.

The sides the Five Chances made for States, released in May 1956, were two of the best of their career. The ballad side, "Gloria," was written and led by Jones, who is both the regular lead and the high tenor wailing lead on the side. The song is unrelated to the more famous Cadillacs' number, but it is a delicious example of mid-fifties exotic vocal harmony, with loads of atmosphere. The jump side, "Sugar Lips," was written by Pitman and led by Jones. The chanting is forceful and magnetic, and "Sugar Lips" was one of the few jump sides of the day that equalled the ballad side in appeal. "Bashful Boy" was also recorded at the States session, in January 1956, but it remained on the shelf.

Despite the excellence of their recordings for States, the Five Chances were not retained by the company. The following year the group moved on to the Federal label, which was then under the aegis of Ralph Bass. "My Days Are Blue," written by Stafford and led by Jones, features exotic doo-wop warbling that warms the hearts of all vocal harmony fans. "Tell Me Why," led by Jones and written by Pitman, is, in its bluesy intensity, the stronger side. The short recitation with the chanting in the background adds to the song's appeal.

Despite not having a national hit, the Five Chances surprisingly got a lot of work and toured extensively. "We traveled half across the country,"

Smith said. "The only place we really didn't go was the West Coast and Washington, D.C. We covered practically every part of Illinois, Michigan, and Indiana. We played in Cincinnati, Philadelphia, Pittsburgh, many different places."[14] In Chicago, the Five Chances practically made their home at the Indiana Theater, playing midnight shows. (It didn't hurt that the theater's manager, Joe Clark, was Pitman's grandfather.) "That's where we got our start," said Smith. "We saw the Flamingos there and wanted to be like them."[15]

The key to the Five Chances' concert success was their dancing ability. "That's what carried us most of the time," Smith asserted, "the dance routines we had. We figured that we had to have something else to work with 'cause a lot of groups could really outsing us, as far as the harmony was concerned. For instance, you take a group like the Flamingos, their harmony would beat you to death. We knew we had to come up with something different and outstanding."[16]

"We used to rehearse eight hours a day dancing and the next day would rehearse singing eight hours a day. We learned a lot of dance steps from different shows we were on, like being with Butterbeans and Susie. We also got a lot of dance routines from different chorus girls that were on the shows. That's what got us on most of the package shows we were on."[17] Wesley Spraggins of the Ideals, a West Side group, said, "The Five Chances could dance their asses off; they were one of the first to have great choreography."[18]

The Five Chances had what they called "stage numbers," songs that did not come from their recordings but were specifically designed to be sung to their choreographed routines. One such stage number was "Wine," the same song recorded by another Levi McKay group, the Daffodils.

The stage act developed by the Five Chances took them into the supper clubs with major name entertainment. "Because we had such a heck of a dance act," said Reggie Smith, "we were on a lot of top shows with top artists. We were on shows with Ray Charles, Chuck Berry, Joe Williams and Count Basie, also Della Reese. We used to do a lot of road shows in places like that where blacks weren't allowed in except if you were on stage entertaining."[19]

Clearly the Five Chances were more than a teen rock 'n' roll act playing the package shows on the chitlin' theater circuit. They had developed into the type of act that did not have to depend on hit songs to get across to an audience, an act for the long haul reflecting the best traditions of show business.

The Flamingos

The best-known group in Benson's stable was undoubtedly the Flamingos. Their label, Chance, was going out of business, but when they were brought to Parrot by their manager, Ralph Leon, in late 1954, they were the hottest group in Chicago. They were coming off two years of sustained recording at Chance Records and regular appearances in Chicago clubs and theaters. Members of the group were the same as at Chance—Sollie McElroy (lead), Johnny Carter (first tenor and falsetto), Zeke Carey (second tenor), Paul Wilson (baritone), and Jake Carey (bass).[20]

The group's initial release by the company, in December 1954, was a classic love ballad, "Dream of a Lifetime." The lead by McElroy is sung with such great feeling that it captures all the romance of the title. The flip, "On My Merry Way," is a routine jump written by the ubiquitous Chicago nightclub entertainer Walter Spriggs.

Parrot followed "Dream of a Lifetime" with a revival of an Eddie Arnold country hit from the previous year called "I Really Don't Want to Know." The song uses alternate leads—McElroy and Carter—but the arrangement drags and sounds confused. The song was backed with the rousing "Get with It," a pure rock 'n' roll jump that the group made a standard in their stage shows to raise the excitement level. The song was from a second Parrot session that featured a new lead singer, Nate Nelson, the third "outsider" lead to join the group. Nelson was picked from another Chicago group, the Velvetones, which consisted of Lee Diamond, Donald Blackman, Roy Flagg, Winfred Veal, as well as Nelson. The group was based on the West Side and in December 1954 won an amateur contest called "Stars of Tomorrow" at the Club 34 (3417 West Roosevelt).

The last Parrot release was "Ko Ko Mo," which Benson had the group record in a hurry because the Gene and Eunice recording of the song, out of California, was making noise in early 1955 and Benson was sure he could grab some of the action with a cover. The record was issued in March 1955. The collector Bob Stallworth believes it probably came out at the same time as the group's previous release, "I Really Don't Want to Know."[21] "Ko Ko Mo" features Nelson and Carter in unison on lead and is a pleasing workout, but it was never able to steal the thunder from the Gene and Eunice version. The robust ballad flip, "I'm Yours," eventually became the oldie favorite. It is one of the few recordings that employs the "doowop" harmony riff, and the harmonies are breathtaking.

Surfacing years later, first on a 1976 reissue LP, were two other Flamingos cuts—the bluesy "If I Could Love You" and the splendid jump "I Found a New Baby." "If I Could Love You" was written by the great guitarist/vocalist Danny Overbea, who had won fame for "Forty Cups of Coffee" and "Train Train Train." He had recorded the song, but it remained in the can. "I Found a New Baby" was written by Walter Spriggs.

Although "Ko Ko Mo" got some play in various parts of the country, Ralph Leon was dissatisfied and began shopping for another label. He found it in the fast-rising Chess organization, where the Flamingos emerged among the stars of the early rock 'n' roll scene, with a body of music not appreciably different than when they recorded for Parrot.

Other Parrot Groups

The Parrots were the first group Benson ever recorded, in 1953. They seem to represent a transitional sound between the poplike black stylings of the forties and the emerging R&B sound. Their "Weep Weep Weep" is an excellent rhythm number with a driving, riveting vocal riff. Especially effective is the use of a switchoff lead that goes from baritone to a weird falsetto tenor (the bass recitation sounds like Benson himself). "Don't Leave Me" possesses a lead with a nice bluesy timbre and again makes superb use of the switchoff lead. This group was outstanding, and one wishes they were more than a mere name in this chronicle.

The identity of the Rockettes, another group recorded on the Parrot label, will probably forever remain a mystery. Their "I Can't Forget" was released on Parrot in 1953, so the sound in this lachrymose ballad is obviously early, but the recording possesses both a floating tenor and a burbling bass that captures the essence of classic R&B ensemble stylings of later years. It still has a nice bluesy flavor of the early fifties. The flip, "Nobody," is a jazzy jump with brassy flourishes and a cooking sax solo. The lead, however, sounds like a boy among men, for the rest of the singers provide solid support with a strong chanting bass and vigorous chorusing.

Another early Benson group was the Pelicans. The group was led by Roger Heard and came from Detroit. The Pelicans' two sides, released on Parrot in late 1953, were "Aurelia" and "White Cliffs of Dover." "Aurelia" was a deep-sounding ballad that got a few plays in Chicago, Detroit, and New York. There was a real person for whom the song was named, Aurelia Brown. Heard was dating her and apparently put his romantic inclinations into song. His efforts bore fruit, because they eventually got married.[22] The Pelicans became one of the earliest groups during the 1950s to turn "White Cliffs of Dover," a World War II pop icon, into an R&B tune. The group's deep vocal stylings to a bongo-driven Latin beat undoubtedly pioneered the R&B destruction of standards.

The Maples were a result of one ad hoc gathering of vocal group singers. The Five Chances started working with the singer Kenneth Childers, who was paying for his own sessions to get on record. Although Reggie Smith and Howard Pitman recalled that the Five Chances (using the name Maples) came out with a recording with Childers, Johnny Jones maintained that it never got that far. At the recording session, Jones arranged to back Childers with a group put together for the occasion, consisting of himself,

Albert Hunter (from the Clouds), and Andrew Smith (from the Fasinoles). The record was "I Must Forget You" backed with "Ninety-nine Guys" and was billed as by the Maples.[23] Smith said, "Al Benson played it for about a week, maybe not that long," which produced yet another rare obscurity for collectors years later.[24] Like most Benson-produced jump sides, "Ninety-nine Guys" gets a superb instrumental break, but the singing in the chorus, mostly in unison, has too little harmony for doowop fans.

A number of groups that Benson recorded never had sides released by Parrot. However, *Parrot Doowop,* a bootleg LP that included these unreleased Benson groups appeared in 1976, and legal releases of these groups appeared on LPs and CDs put out by Relic Records in the early 1990s. The Swans, whose identity is unknown, appeared for the first time on these releases. Their exotic warblings, with a youthful teenage sound, are what turned good music followers into fanatical R&B vocal group collectors. Doowop fans normally love the sound provided by the Swans—impassioned lead singing, deep bass bottom, and floating high tenor in the primitive balladry of "I Love You So" and the proto–rock 'n' roll jump styling of "Will You Be Mine." Transcending every standard measure of quality in music, the Swans inflame the passions.

*   *   *

The Parrot label went out of business just as rock 'n' roll was making its presence felt nationally. Most of its vocal group releases featured a deep rhythm and blues sound that reflected the early 1950s period. By 1954 and 1955, however, with the Flamingos and the Orchids, Al Benson was beginning to create genuine rock 'n' roll. The Flamingos enjoyed later success at Chess and at End Records, as rock 'n' roll stars, and the Orchids sides emerged in later rock 'n' roll anthologies. Both events demonstrate vividly that Parrot was present at the birth of rock 'n' roll.

Notes

1. Most primary sources on Al Benson have focused on his broadcasting success and made little reference to his recording activities. A solid secondary source on the label can be found in Rowe, *Chicago Breakdown,* pp. 120–25, which emphasizes the company's blues output.

2. Information about the Five Thrills comes from: Pruter, "The Five Thrills"; Stallworth, "Five Thrills"; Jenkins interview.

3. This and subsequent remarks by Jenkins that are quoted in this chapter are taken from the Jenkins interview.

4. Nesbary interview.

5. Kent interview, March 31, 1993.

6. Nesbary interview.

7. Ibid.

8. Information about the Fascinators comes from Pruter, "The Fascinators," pp. 28, 112; Potter interview.

9. This and subsequent remarks by Potter that are quoted in this chapter come from the interview with him.

10. Information about the Five Chances comes from: Pruter, "The Five Chances," pp. 18, 20, 33; and interviews with Hilliard Jones, Howard Pitman, and Reggie Smith.

11. Hilliard Jones interview, November 1, 1989.

12. Reggie Smith interview, September 28, 1989.

13. Ibid.

14. Ibid.

15. Reggie Smith interview, October 15, 1989.

16. Ibid.

17. Ibid.

18. Spraggins interview.

19. Reggie Smith Interview, October 15, 1989.

20. A complete list of Flamingos sources is given in chapter 1, n. 10.

21. Stallworth, "R&B Rarities."

22. Robert Stallworth, letter to author, March 16, 1994.

23. Information about the Maples comes from Pruter, "The Five Chances," p. 18; Hilliard Jones interview; Reggie Smith interviews.

24. Reggie Smith interview, September 28, 1989.

3

Chess Records

Chess Records was founded by Leonard and Philip Chess, two Jewish immigrants from Poland who came to Chicago in 1928. They got involved in the liquor business and by the 1940s owned a string of South Side bars, including the Macomba, a large nightclub at Thirty-ninth and Cottage Grove. Believing that the black talent they had seen at the Macamba was not being adequately recorded, the Chess brothers in 1947 entered into a partnership with Evelyn Aron, who, with her husband, had just started Aristocrat Records to record jazz, blues, and R&B. The Chess brothers bought out Aron in late 1949 and early the next year reorganized the company as Chess Records. The company grew, adding the Checker label in 1952 and the Argo label in 1956. Although Checker tended to concentrate on blues singers and Argo emphasized jazz, both labels had their share of vocal group acts.[1]

During Chess's early years, Leonard and Phil Chess were not just businessmen but were "record men" in every sense of the word. They lived, breathed, and loved the music they were recording. Because the brothers were intimately involved in the creative end of the company, there was little need to bring in A&R men and producers. Chess flourished during the 1950s with records in the blues, rock 'n' roll, and rhythm and blues markets, but historically it is best known for its blues artists, namely Muddy Waters, Howlin' Wolf, Little Walter, Jimmy Rogers, and Sonny Boy Williamson. This renown developed mainly because the guitar-dominated combo music that characterized Chicago bar-band blues was a major influence on rock bands after the mid-1960s.

The company's biggest successes in the 1950s were with Chuck Berry and Bo Diddley. These artists, who were steeped in the blues, emphasized the beat in the form and helped forge a new kind of music for teenagers called rock 'n' roll. Some of Chess's other solo rhythm and blues acts that did well for the company (not including leased records from other parts of the outfit) were Willie Mabon, Danny Overbea, and Andrew Tibbs.

When rock 'n' roll was discussed in the 1950s, conversation likely focused on the same sort of rhythm and blues vocal groups for which Chess was well known, principally the Moonglows and the Flamingos. Much of the company's vocal group output was actually on leased records that had been produced in other parts of the country. The vocal group acts that recorded elsewhere or that Chess picked up through leased arrangements will not be the concern of this chronicle. For the record, however, they included the Clefs, the Dream Kings, Lee Andrews and the Hearts, the Quintones, the Re-Vels, the Invincibles, and the Miracles, on Chess; the Blue Jays, the Teasers, the Tune Weavers, the Students, the Ideals, and the Sonics, on Checker; the Silva-tones, the Ravens, the Pastels, the Monotones, the Solitaires, and the Trends, on Argo.

The Flamingos

The Flamingos came to Chess after several years of recording activity that had yet to get them a full-blown national hit. With stints first at Chance and then at Parrot, the group produced some of the top vocal harmony of the postwar rhythm and blues era. But the singers were itching to achieve the prominence of national rock 'n' roll stars, a status they felt they merited. It would happen at Chess. The Flamingos' manager, Ralph Leon, died in early 1955 and the group learned that he had been in the process of negotiating the group's move to Checker. Phil and Leonard Chess approached the Flamingos and signed them.[2]

The Flamingos recorded their first Checker session in the company's office studio, coming out with their great ballad "I'll Be Home" and their first Checker release, "When." The songs were redone in a larger "professional" studio, but the Chess brothers thought the new versions sounded "plastic" and the company went with the office-recorded cuts on the released versions.

"When" was a very pleasing ballad that sounded like some of the Orioles' tunes. It was released in April 1955, but to little acclaim. The flip, "(Chica Boom) That's My Baby," was a mambo-beat jump written by Johnny Carter, which the group subsequently used in their stage routines. Neither side was able to launch the Flamingos for Chess, however. The company followed up with "I Want to Love You" backed with "Please Come Back Home," but these sides, too, had little to recommend them. The next release, however, would change everything, lifting the group from just another bird-group R&B act and elevating them to internationally famous rock 'n' roll stars.

"I'll Be Home" was released in January 1956 and became the Flamingos' biggest hit up to that time, garnering for the first time considerable cross-over coverage for the group. It's not hard to see why. The song has a beautiful melody, perfectly dramatized by Nelson's lead. After his long opening solo, the rest of the group chimes in with some exquisite tight harmony.

Although writing credits for "I'll Be Home" were given to the deejay Fats Washington and the record distributor Stan Lewis, Nate Nelson told the R&B historian Phil Groia that he should have gotten a solid part of the credit: "Leonard Chess came to me, all he had was the first line and the first line melody. I took the thing home and worked on it because I came out of the service myself. I came out of the Navy in June of 1953. I wrote the entire second verse, the bridge, the melody of the bridge, and the third verse. But I didn't know anything about copyrighting."[3]

"I'll Be Home" lasted eight weeks on *Billboard*'s R&B chart, where it peaked at position five in February 1956. The record never made it on the national pop chart despite heavy play on many top-forty stations. Pat Boone's cover version soaked up all of the pop chart action. "We got very hurt by that song," Zeke Carey said. "He sold many times more records than we did. We had worked so hard to get through and we knew that it was going to be a bona fide hit. We had done a show with Alan Freed in New York and Pat Boone was also on the show. Our song had been out about three weeks. About two weeks after that show, his record came out and swamped ours. It was a devastating, painful experience."[4] If it is any consolation for the Flamingos today, few recall Boone's version, while the group's original is fondly remembered.

"A Kiss from Your Lips," a great romantic ballad, served as an excellent follow-up to "I'll Be Home." On this tune, the group gives Nelson a magnificent haunting background chorus that makes it one of their outstanding efforts. The composing credits were given to "Davis and Fratto," but Zeke Carey contended he contributed the whole bridge and melody.[5] "Davis" refers to Billy Davis, a Detroit songwriter who brought the song (or much of the song) to Chess with him when he brought the Four Tops to the label. The Four Tops bombed with their Chess release, but the company had great success with "A Kiss from Your Lips," as well as with another Davis song, "See Saw," which the company used with the Moonglows. "A Kiss from Your Lips" made a two-week appearance on *Billboard*'s R&B chart, peaking at position twelve in June 1956.

"The Vow," also from 1956, was one of the Flamingos' most appealing songs. Besides having an engaging melody, it features simply wonderful chorusing. Especially effective is the part where the group answers Nelson's line "never to forget" with a most seraphic "oh ohhh," much in the style of the Platters. The record, however, failed to make the national charts.

"Would I Be Crying" followed. It was a beautiful song that got an extra push when the Flamingos performed it in the Alan Freed movie *Rock Rock Rock,* but it did not click with the public. (In the movie, Zeke Carey was not a part of the proceedings, having been drafted into the military.) *Rock Rock Rock* showed how far the Flamingos had come in the entertainment world. By virtue of their crossover success with "I'll Be Home," the group in 1956 had become a part of the rock 'n' roll revolution.

In 1958, the Flamingos appeared in another Alan Freed quickie, *Go Johnny Go.* It was not filmed until the group had moved to New York and was recording for End, but curiously the Flamingos chose to do a new, more rock 'n' roll–style version of their old Chance song, "Jump Children."

The Flamingos made their first tour of the South in 1956 as part of a big rock 'n' roll package show put together by the promoter Irvin Feld. "I think it had everyone who had a record in the top forty at the time," Nate Nelson recalled. "Everyone from Bill Haley to the Teen Queens. We had a lot of problems when we appeared in the South. There were also a couple of bomb scares where we had to clear out the auditorium. I would think that tour was our most exciting one."[6]

Most histories of the Flamingos assert that the group merely changed a couple of members in 1956, but according to Phil Groia, the group actually broke up at that time.[7] After Johnny Carter and Zeke Carey were drafted into the military, members went their separate ways, and Nelson signed as a solo artist with Chess. In 1957 the Flamingos regrouped, with Nelson, Paul Wilson, Jake Carey, and Tommy Hunt comprising the new lineup. Hunt was picked up from his hometown of Pittsburgh, although earlier he had lived and recorded in Chicago as a member of the Five Echoes.

The Flamingos then signed with Decca and were given a gala promotional party in Washington, D.C., which was attended by deejays, entertainment reporters, and the usual hangers-on. The group proceeded to record at least ten sides for the label in New York. The company's first release on the group was the fine Clint Ballard song "Ladder of Love," but it and subsequent Decca releases were virtually quashed by legal complications arising from Nelson's solo contract with Checker. In 1958, with the legal wrinkles presumably ironed out, the group added the guitarist Terry "Buzzy" Johnson and signed with End. The Flamingos moved to New York, but their Chicago days had essentially ended two years earlier with the initial break-up of the group.

The huge success the Flamingos enjoyed on End in 1959 with their distinctive remake of an old standard, "I Only Have Eyes for You," encouraged Chess personnel to search their vaults for suitable Flamingos material. The company then put out an LP called *The Flamingos* and a superb double-sided single—a Chess-recorded version of "Dream of a Lifetime" and "Whispering Stars," both with Nelson in the lead. Many collectors prefer this "Dream of a Lifetime," with a faster meter and Nelson's velvety vocals, over the Parrot version. "Whispering Stars," also a ballad, features an electrifying whispered opening and continues on a high plain throughout the rest of the song. Alas, for Checker, however, neither side charted.

The album was intended to promote "Dream of a Lifetime," where it was made the first cut on side A. And to avoid distracting the buyer, the company chose not to put "I'll Be Home" on this, the only LP it ever released on the group. Nonetheless, the album was excellent and included previously unissued ballad gems, "Stolen Love" and "Nobody's Love" (the latter a superior remake of their Chance song, "If I Can't Have You"). This last release on Checker was the final flicker of the Flamingos fabulous recording career in Chicago.

In subsequent years the Flamingos made many tour stops in their home town, but none so touched the public as the group's 1987 appearance at the Grand Ballroom, one of their old venues from their Chicago days. Amazingly, the show was under the auspices of Fletcher Weatherspoon, the same man who had discovered the group and launched them to stardom.

The Moonglows

By October 1954, the Moonglows, who had been recorded for Chance Records during the previous year—with only a modicum of success—were ready to move on. Chess Records was rising as fast as Chance was fading, and the Moonglows' mentor, Alan Freed, used his connections to get the group signed with Chess. The Chess brothers were familiar with the Moonglows' records and were eager to sign the singers. They bought the group's contract from Chance for five hundred dollars and took them into the studio immediately. By December that year, Chance had shut its doors.[8]

The members of the Moonglows were the same as those in the group during its Chance years—Bobby Lester (lead and tenor), Harvey Fuqua (lead and baritone), Pete Graves (tenor), and Prentiss Barnes (bass). Fuqua told the British journalist Cliff White, "We started off recording about twelve songs for Chess—on one track, mind you. It wasn't like they've got 32 and 64 tracks to play with today. They'd put the microphone right in the middle of the room and everybody stood around it, the band, the singers, everybody. If you wanted more of an instrument or a singer you'd have to either move back or forward."[9]

The first Chess disc for the Moonglows was their outstanding and best-known tune, "Sincerely," released in December 1954. Although separated from their Chance sides by only a couple of months, it seems to have been separated by years. The marvelous intro captures the essence of the song. It begins with the warbling of Barnes's classic bass riff, "bah, bah, bah-doh," followed after a few bars with a layered-on separate riff sung by tenor Graves and baritone Fuqua. Finally, after several more bars, comes Lester's impassioned lead. The song ends with what became a Moonglows' signature—the "ooh-wah" harmonized final note. That, in addition to the owl-like "vooit vooit" vocal riffing of the background, may have given rise to the Moonglows' "blow harmony" technique. (Both the Flamingos and Moonglows have used the "vooit vooit" riff, which probably came from some now-forgotten vocal harmony record of the 1940s.) The record shot to the number one position on *Billboard*'s R&B chart and lasted an outstanding twenty weeks there. It was the Moonglows' first national hit, a magnificent debut on Chess. The record was covered in the pop market by the McGuire Sisters, who also got a number one hit on the song with their soulless version.

Also released in November 1954 were two sides by the duo of Lester and Fuqua performing as the Moonlighters on the Checker label. Both the up-tempo and bluesy "So All Alone" and the more rock 'n' roll "Shoo Do Be Doo" picked up solid regional sales. "So All Alone" was written by Fuqua and Lester; "Shoo Do Be Doo" was by Fuqua and Freed. Regarding "Shoo Do Be Doo," Fuqua told the journalist Sue Cassidy Clark, "There was a record out called 'Sh-Boom' by the Chords. I wrote a song similar to that because that was what was *happening,* you know. 'Shoo Do Bee Doo' was such a great record, and anyway, they wanted to put that out before the trend died. So we put that out and it was a hit."[10] (The follow-up by the Moonlighters, "New Gal" backed with "Hug and a Kiss," however, failed to excite anyone and died without any airplay.)

On several of these early records, Freed and Fuqua are credited as co-writers. Fuqua said of Freed, "Actually he was not a great writer. In fact, he just put in a couple of lines every now and then. I hear on a lot of the other songs, on a couple of mine he put in a line or two . . . a word. Then he got fifty percent of the action. I can understand what the deal was in the early years."[11] The deal was that Freed's coauthorship theoretically helped get plays on his influential deejay shows.

The Moonglows, during the first months of their Chess association, were rapidly advancing up the ladder as a popular stage act. In October 1954 they played the prestigious Crown Propeller Lounge in Chicago, and by the following month they were touring with Lowell Fulson and Lynn Hope. From January through March they performed as one of the featured artists in the touring "Top 10 R&B Show," put on by the Shaw Agency. This prestigious chitlin' circuit revue package included the Clovers, Faye Adams, Fats Domino, Amos Milburn, Bill Doggett, and the Paul Williams Orchestra. During this most rugged of tours the Moonglows made forty-two one-nighter appearances in the East, the South, and the Midwest.

In January 1955, there was a crucial transition in the cultural understanding of the Moonglows' music. Previously, at all of Freed's shows and other venues, the Moonglows were billed as "rhythm and blues" performers. As part of Freed's invasion of the New York market, however, he staged a rhythm and blues show at the St. Nicholas Arena, and this time he dubbed it a "Rock 'n' Roll Ball." The group appeared as both the Moonglows and the Moonlighters and shared the stage with such stellar performers as the Drifters, Fats Domino, Joe Turner, the Harptones, Ruth Brown, and other acts supported by the Buddy Johnson Orchestra. Most notable about the show was that the audience was equally divided, black and white, and subsequent Freed shows would attract an ever greater percentage of white fans. In April the Moonglows played at Freed's Easter show at the Brooklyn Paramount, and the following month they appeared at a Freed show in Boston. In September they returned to the Brooklyn Paramount.

Many recording acts made most of their money at these live shows. The success of "Sincerely" was the first record that brought in the cash for the Moonglows. During their Chance years, Fuqua and Lester were even working in a coal yard to bring in the bread. Said Fuqua, "'Sincerely' sort of threw me in another frame of mind. We'd been struggling for a long time, we might make some money and have some fun." Asked whether they made money at Chess, Fuqua replied, "We all made money, probably didn't make the amount due us, but we all made money."[12]

Prentiss Barnes did not remember the situation the same way. "To be honest about it, now that the years have drifted by, we had no hotel money, we couldn't support ourselves. The money was just going under the table. Harvey in his interviews was mostly covering up that part. I can see his point to a certain extent. He doesn't want anybody to know of the group's ups and downs and hard-time years. He could go to Chess Records when he felt like it and come back in a car, buy clothes, watches, whatever. The rest of us didn't make shit. We just about starved to death. Harvey had a good education and he was a good producer. He could always get through doors that possibly would be closed if I tried to go through them."[13] Barnes also recalled that for a time in his association with the Moonglows, he and Graves were on salary, paid by Lester and Fuqua.[14]

There's probably a bit of truth in both stories. Fuqua was the businessman of the group and knew what kind of money was coming in, and undoubtedly the group made good money for those days. Barnes probably correctly recalled some hard times and that Fuqua got the most money, but it would not be going too far to speculate that, like many recording artists of the day, they would easily let the money they got slip through their hands.

Shortly after "Sincerely" became a hit, the Moonglows met the guitarist Wayne Bennett in the studio. Bennett had played on their second session at Chess. He was the same musician who years later built a legendary career backing the blues vocalist Bobby Bland, but in his early years was working in the Chess studio and for the house band at the Crown Propeller Lounge. "He was a good guitar player," remembered Barnes, "he was very tough and worked very very hard."[15] Bennett accompanied the group on one trip to the East Coast, to play at the Apollo Theatre in December 1955, but he then decided to return to his home in Texas.

"Most of All" followed in the spring of 1955. The ballad, which was also written by Freed and Fuqua, ranks as one of their best sides. Barnes opens the song with a descending bass that introduces Lester's emotional lead, which gets fantastic support with stop-time falsetto-edged chorusing by the group. And one can hear the great blow harmony again. The finale echoes a little more elaborately the harmonized close of "Sincerely." "Most of All" went to position five and lasted eleven weeks on *Billboard*'s R&B chart.

The summer of 1955 saw the release of "Foolish Me" backed with "Slow Down." The top-side ballad features a great emotional lead by Lester and some of the best harmony work ever produced by the Moonglows, yet the record never charted and achieved only a few regional sales. The group continued their commercial slump in the fall with "Starlite" backed with "In Love," but one listen to "Starlite" confirms that there was no artistic slump. The song opens with the "ooh-wah" Moonglows trademark and works an interesting arrangement, counterpointing Barnes's bass, Lester's emoting lead, and a three-voice alternate lead of Lester, Fuqua, and Graves.

The Moonglows' chart failures continued to the end of 1955 with the release of "In My Diary." Most collectors would probably be surprised to learn that this magnificent and well-remembered midtempo ballad failed to dent *Billboard*'s R&B chart upon its release. Fuqua fondly recalled, "It was one of the songs brought to us because we were doing a movie. There were several songs submitted to us. I grabbed that one because it had different changes from whatever else was happening. The words were so true, everybody then sort of had a diary. It was compatible."[16] The song's unusual changes and descending arpeggios do produce a distinctive, fresh sound. Perhaps the public was not ready for it.

With "We Go Together" the Moonglows finally returned to the charts in the summer of 1956. Featuring a duet lead by Lester and Fuqua, the song takes an up-tempo approach decidedly not in the manner of an "R&B jump." One should perhaps characterize it as a rock 'n' roll ballad. With this song, the Moonglows could be said to have joined the rock 'n' roll revolution. Despite its obvious strength, the song surprisingly made it no higher than position nine and lasted no longer than a paltry two weeks on the R&B chart.

Sometime in late 1955 the Moonglows, who had been without a guitarist since losing Bennett early in the year, picked up another fine guitarist who became an integral part of the group, Billy Johnson (born 1924), of Hartford, Connecticut. Barnes recalled, "We were on this tour, and when we got to Cincinnati we met Billy Johnson. He had been with the Sonny Thompson band but had gotten into some kind of trouble with drugs and ended up in Angola Prison. He had just gotten out and was looking to fit in somewhere. He came up to our hotel room and played his guitar. We liked his personality and his attitude, and we hired him. He rehearsed with us in this hotel and caught on to some of the songs before we continued on our tour. And he stayed with us until we broke up in 1959."[17]

In the fall of 1956 the Moonglows came out with a fine double-sided hit, "See Saw" backed with "When I'm with You." "See Saw" is a rocking fast number that again defined the Moonglows as a rock 'n' roll group, and the flip is a splendid ballad featuring delicious harmonies and a flavorful lead by Lester. The group used James Moody's rhythm section, the first time the Moonglows made use of a jazz group on one of their records. As mentioned earlier, the song also introduced a fine new songwriter into the Chess organization, Billy Davis. The ballad flip, "When I'm with You," was written by Jackie McCoy and Harvey Fuqua. "See Saw" peaked at number six on the *Billboard* R&B chart while "When I'm with You" scraped the bottom at number fifteen.

The Moonglows continued to ride the rock 'n' roll revolution, playing both on the "rock 'n' roll" stage shows put on by such deejays as Alan Freed and the rhythm and blues shows put on by black jocks. In April 1956, the group appeared on Dr. Jive Smalls' "Rhythm and Blues Review" at the Apollo Theatre. In September the Moonglows played on Freed's Labor Day show at the Brooklyn Paramount, which had a combination of black and white acts (noticeably weak white acts, such as Cirino and the Bow Ties, the Shepherd Sisters, and Jean Chappel). This was followed by other Freed shows at the Paramount, in December and July 1957. The Moonglows last stage show sponsored by Freed was at Loews' State during Christmas 1958.

Although not always on the charts during late 1956 and early 1957, the Moonglows were still consistent in releasing topnotch tunes. It seemed every release was an artistic winner. "Over and Over Again" backed with "I Knew from the Start" is a case in point, two superb sides that did not make the charts. They were performed in the Alan Freed film *Rock Rock Rock* (1956). The group—along with Chess's two other major acts, Chuck Berry and the Flamingos—was featured in two segments, singing each side of this record. Interestingly, there were two versions of "Over and Over Again," slow and fast, but the only one that later appeared on Chess anthologies was the vastly superior slow version. It was written by Ben Weisman, a Tin Pan Alley songcrafter who in his career penned such hits as "Let Me Go, Lover," "Wooden Heart," and "The Night Has a Thousand Eyes." "I Knew from the Start," which features the dual lead of Lester and Fuqua, is an extremely strong side.

The Moonglows appeared in one more Alan Freed film, *Mr. Rock and Roll* (1957), in which they sang a perfectly atrocious song, "Barcelona Rock." It was never released on wax. Strangely, the group never performed any of its hits in the movies. Fuqua remarked, somewhat fatalistically, "In order to get the movie shots, you had to do the songs. That was the real deal. Those songs were selected to be in the pictures. This is what you had to do. If not, they'd find somebody else to do it."[18]

Meanwhile, in December 1956, the Moonglows entered the Chess studios for a big album project, in which the instrumentation would be augmented with strings and flutes arranged by Mike Simpson. Songs recorded for the session included "Love Is a River," "Don't Say Goodbye," "Blue Velvet," "This Love," and "I'll Stop Wanting You." Only seven numbers were recorded with strings, however, and the album project was shelved. Over the next several years the company dribbled out songs from the session, five of which appeared on the *Look! It's the Moonglows* album released in early 1959. Most collectors contend that this session signaled the decline in the sound of the Moonglows, because on most of the numbers good old-fashioned vocal harmony was muted away or replaced by strings.

"Don't Say Goodbye," a noncharter from early 1957, was the first release from the strings session, and the ballad's poplike arrangement likely turned off disc jockeys. Harmony fans probably do not care for it, either, because very little of the group is used on the arrangement, which was essentially a Bobby Lester solo. But it is a beautiful tune. The flip featured Fuqua on lead with a jumped-up version of the standard "I'm Afraid the Masquerade Is Over," featuring, of all things, a "doowop" vocal riff, making it one of the few doowop songs that actually employed that nonsense syllable. The song got a little airplay.

"Please Send Me Someone to Love," a remake of an old Percy Mayfield tune, returned the Moonglows to the charts in the summer of 1957. Fuqua's lead is magnificent and group support is subdued—more subdued than harmony fans might have preferred. Master numbers indicate that the song appears to have been recorded for the strings session, but no strings were added to it. Fuqua's fondness for it was evident: "I liked it because it was a ballad. It was in my key, it was a wonderful song. I was vying for a song I could lead because I had to sing all the up-tempo songs. I wasn't a balladeer, Bobby Lester was the balladeer guy. I was vying to sing a ballad."[19]

The Moonglows followed with a superb double-sided record, "Confess

It to Your Heart" backed with "The Beating of My Heart." One of the Moonglows' least known releases that is of top quality, the record exhibits all the sparking elements that made the group successful, great blow harmony with terrific emoting leads by Lester. Alas, neither side charted. The next record, "Too Late" backed with "Here I Am," from late 1957, is a lamentable effort, and it deserved not to chart. Inexplicably left in the can from that session was a marvelous ballad, "What Are You Going to Do?" (it surfaced only in 1993 on a Moonglows retrospective).

The Moonglows' first release in 1958, "Soda Pop" backed with "In the Middle of the Night," is an eminently forgettable record. Yet top quality was evident in the very next release, the wonderful "Sweeter than Words," a record that was rarely heard but is absolutely lovely. Bobby Lester's performance on this record is one of his most sublime, but unfortunately it was also one of his last. He was hospitalized that year for what may have been an alcohol or drug problem (no one was forthcoming about what the problem was) and was being edged out of the group. To put this issue in context, Barnes did recall, "Lester was not too heavy on drugs when we were together, but he did have a problem. Once he got caught at the Apollo Theatre with drugs. This was about 1956–57. He just bought some marijuana. The drug was pretty notorious then, and he bought some from a detective who set him up. We had a week to play there, and I think we had to bail Bobby out to keep him from going to jail so we could play through the week at the Apollo. He could handle marijuana, so it didn't affect the group. After we broke up, however, Bobby started getting into heavy stuff with needles and all that."[20]

The Moonglows' next record, "Ten Commandments of Love," from the fall of 1958, was one of their biggest hits and helped immensely to immortalize their name in the history of rock 'n' roll as well as rhythm and blues. To my ears and to many other fans of vintage music it is one of the most dreadful things ever put on wax. Behind Fuqua's saccharine recitation of the "ten commandments of love" in a pseudobiblical style ("thou shalt never love another"), the rest of the group oohs and ahs in the background. The song is just one entire recitation. Yet this record went to position nine and lasted nine weeks on the R&B chart, and on the pop chart proved to be the group's biggest hit, lasting sixteen weeks and going to position twenty-two.

With "Ten Commandments," some shady business began concerning the song credits. The company credited as composer one "M. Paul," who in reality was sixteen-year-old Marshall Chess. He was not a songwriter but got the credit because he was the son of Leonard Chess. The first follow-up to "Ten Commandments" featured two more "M. Paul" songs, taken from the long-canned December 1956 strings session, "Love Is a River" backed with "I'll Stop Wanting You." They were both ballads led by Fuqua. The "River" side garnered some play in the latter part of 1959. Seven of the twelve cuts on the album called *Look! It's the Moonglows*—which was released in 1959 but contained cuts dating from between 1956 and 1958—featured "M. Paul" songs. (Chess people even put the name "M. Paul" under "When I'm with You," apparently forgetting that they had credited the song on the single to the real writers, Jackie McCoy and Harvey Fuqua.) Members of the Moonglows and other writers for Chess are still annoyed over the "M. Paul" shenanigans. It especially rankled Fuqua, who wrote "Ten Commandments of Love," which over the years has proved to be Marshall Chess's most valuable copyright.[21]

The Moonglows broke up in November 1958. Fuqua explained to Cliff White, "We had a problem with one of the fellas in the group." Reluctant to tell White who that was, Fuqua finally admitted it was Bobby Lester, "my good ole school buddy. He had a bad problem, which eventually led to him being hospitalized and I didn't like what was going on. It was detrimental to the group so I decided I didn't want to be there anymore. So I found four singers called the Marquees in Washington, D.C.—that's how I met Marvin Gaye."[22] (The other singers were Reese Palmer, James Nolan, and Chester Simmons.)

Recalling those days, Fuqua said,

> We were performing at the Howard Theater in Washington and Marvin was outside looking for autographs. He said he wanted to meet the guys who wrote most of the songs. Finally he got in to see me, he said my group could sing. We'll have to see you later. I sort of brushed him off, because I didn't want to hear anymore groups. I was still disturbed about what was happening about the group at present. At the half I heard him sing, he got his little guys together, and they sounded exactly like us, a little better. I said, "You guys have really done your homework." Right away it clicked, take this group, they're young guys, get rid of this trash situation that's happening.[23]

Fuqua took the group to Chicago in early 1959 and added to them the bass singer Chuck Barksdale, who had been a member of the recently disbanded Dells (a breakup that was only temporary, as it turned out). The Moonglows recorded under the auspices of Fuqua, who was getting more involved with the producing and writing side of the entertainment business. Fuqua recalled, "Leonard had offered me a production kind of deal—a weekly salary and points that whole trip."[24]

Most of the new Moonglows records were below par. In October 1959, Chess released "Mama Loocie" backed with "Unemployment," which sank with barely a trace—but that "trace" was a bunch of records that were grabbed up a few years later by record collectors wanting to complete their holdings. "Mama Loocie" has the distinction of being the only song in which Marvin Gaye led as a member of the Moonglows. The Moonglows record that was most difficult for collectors to find was the group's next new release, "Junior" backed with "Beatnik." By the mid-1990s it was a two-hundred-dollar collectible, but only for its paper and plastic, not for the sound in the grooves, which is truly wretched.

Meanwhile, Bobby Lester was left to his own devices. In 1959 he managed to get Chess to put out a single on him, "Am I the Man." Nothing came of the record, however, and Lester dropped out of the entertainment business and returned to Louisville, where he later managed a nightclub.

Fuqua was also recording on his own and in duets with Etta James at this time. He came out with a single, "I Want Somebody," which was a pleasant ballad but not something that could make the charts. The follow-up single paired two titles Fuqua recorded with the Moonglows but were released as by Harvey: "Don't Be Afraid to Love," recorded by the original group in 1958, and "Twelve Months a Year," recorded by the new Moonglows in 1959. The latter is a delight, a true vocal harmony record in which the group offers magnificent harmonized support behind Fuqua.

At this time, however, Fuqua was more interested in pursuing a solo career than continuing the group, so there was really no future for the new Moonglows, no matter how good they sounded. Another Fuqua solo record, "Ooh Ouch Stop!" (1959), is a poor record that evoked no interest from the public. During 1959 Fuqua was also playing solo dates, for example, billing himself as "Harvey of the Moonglows" at a gig at Chicago's Pershing Ballroom in February of that year. He also appeared alone in the movie *Go Johnny Go*, in which he lip-synched "Don't Be Afraid to Love."

The duets with Etta James were first recorded on the Bihari brothers' Kent label, on which James was recording in 1959. The pair recorded as Betty and Dupree. Their one release, "I Hope You're Satisfied" backed with "If It Ain't One Thing," is uninteresting. However, one of their unreleased numbers at the time, "We're in Love," is very enjoyable. In 1960 James moved to Chess and during her first year with the label recorded two duets with Fuqua, which were released as by Etta and Harvey. "If I Can't Have You" was a smash on the R&B charts during that summer, but the flip, "My Heart Cries," seems to have had more staying power. It is the one played years afterward as an oldie but goodie. Both songs were written by James and Fuqua. The second duet paired a Willie Dixon tune, "Spoonful," with another James and Fuqua original, "It's a Crying Shame." The Dixon tune proved to be a minor hit in late 1960.

The last Moonglows release put out by Chess was "Blue Velvet," recorded at the strings session of December 1956 but released on a single in 1962.

"Blue Velvet" was made famous as an R&B hit by the Clovers in 1955 and as a pop hit by Bobby Vinton in 1963, but the Moonglows' version should not go unnoticed. Especially notable is the "ooh wah" vocal riffs that open the song. The flip, "Penny Arcade," is a fine song recorded back in mid-1956 that first appeared on the *Look! It's the Moonglows* album in 1959. Despite the excellence of both sides, nobody was interested in 1962 and the record went largely unnoticed.

The new Moonglows continued to tour until the summer of 1960. Marvin Gaye recalled making a "triumphant return" then as a member of the Moonglows, performing at the Howard Theater.[25] Fuqua disbanded the group around this time, and he and Gaye went to Detroit and established themselves in the music scene there. Fuqua formed his Harvey and Tri-Phi labels, which began his long career as a behind-the-scenes force in the record business. He also recorded three more solo singles, but with no better success. Marvin Gaye, of course, went on to become one of the biggest Motown recording artists of the 1960s and 1970s. Like most famous, as well as not-so-famous, groups of the 1950s, the Moonglows went through periodic reunions and attempts at career revivals, none of which relate to the doowop era.

The Coronets

The Coronets were a Cleveland group, who, like the Moonglows, tried to grab the brass ring of success. Unlike their more famous Cleveland counterparts, however, they never became any more than one-hit-wonders. Their only hit, "Nadine," became a staple of Chess anthology albums and in 1970 was revived by the Dells for Chess Records, with great success.[26]

The Coronets originated in Cleveland's Thomas Edison High, where Sam Griggs sang in the school's glee club and made the acquaintance of Lester Russaw and George Lewis. Nothing happened immediately, but after his graduation and marriage, Griggs decided to form a vocal group. He had tried his hand at boxing and thought there must be a better way to make money in the entertainment world. Undoubtedly inspired by the wave of vocal groups then sweeping the charts, he contacted his former glee club compatriots, first-tenor Russaw and baritone Lewis, and, with himself as second tenor and his brother William as bass, he formed a group. The group became complete when Griggs added Charles Carruthers as lead and Tony King as guitarist. The group decided on the name Coronets.

The Coronets made their foray into the entertainment world in early 1953 with four songs in their repertoire. One was an original, "Nadine" (written by Carruthers). Another, "I'm All Alone," was supposed to be an original but really wasn't. When it was eventually released, there was no songwriter credit because the song was basically the chorus section of B. B.

King's "Woke Up This Morning," which the group undoubtedly heard when it came out in March 1953. The other two songs were musical versions of "The Lord's Prayer" and a frequently recorded solo number that the group adapted for vocal harmony, "Don't You Think I Ought to Know?"

After winning a few talent show contests, the Coronets presented themselves to the famed Orioles, who were appearing in Cleveland at the Ebony Club. The Orioles let the gatecrashers open for them, and in a backstage jam session the Coronets won the Orioles' appreciation for their version of "Don't You Think I Ought to Know?" The Coronets felt flattered but were devastated a month later when on the flip side of the Orioles' big hit, "Crying in the Chapel," there appeared "Don't You Think I Ought to Know?" sounding note for note like the Coronets' version.

The Coronets decided they had to make a serious attempt at getting their career in gear. As Sam Griggs analyzed the situation, "If the Orioles could pick up on our arrangements, I knew we were heading in the right direction."[27] The group went to one of the few recording studios in Cleveland, Snyder Recording, at Fourteenth and Prospect, and recorded a demo of "Nadine" backed with "I'm All Alone." And what better way to get the break they needed than to take the demo to the fast-rising Alan Freed. At his office in the city's Keith Building, Freed gave Griggs only "a quick minute," but Griggs got to talk to Freed's manager, Lew Platt, and Freed's wife, Jackie, and left them the demo.[28]

Freed gave a listen to the demo and, suitably impressed, sent it to the Chess brothers, who were likewise taken with it. Freed contacted the Coronets within two weeks, signed a managerial contract with them, and had them travel to Chicago for a recording session at Chess Records. In June 1953 the Coronets laid down the usual four tracks, but the session did not go smoothly. Griggs said, "The session and the musicians were totally disgusting to us 'cause we were so unorthodox. We ended up calling it our 'emetic' style because those musicians looked ready to throw up."[29] According to Griggs, the group's style and arrangement that so attracted Freed and the Chess brothers were tossed out during the session for a completely different approach. When the group finally heard the record on radio, they hated it and turned off the radio.

"Nadine" did extremely well upon its release in September 1953, lasting ten weeks on *Billboard*'s R&B chart and going to the number three position. The group's happiness over the record's success undoubtedly was tempered by having to give up writing credit for the song to Alan Freed. The Coronets were told that unless they gave Freed the credit, "nothing else would happen [with the song]."[30] One wonders what kind of tension was in the air in their one-time meeting with Freed, when they made an appearance at one of his shows, in Canton, Ohio.

The Coronets worked off the success of "Nadine" primarily in Ohio, but the group went on one extensive tour in the South, visiting Kentucky, Tennessee, Georgia, and Louisiana. The booking agency had them working with dancers and comedians.

The group's second session at Chess, on October 11, 1953, yielded the beautiful "It Would Be Heavenly" backed with "Baby's Coming Home," the latter led by Sam Griggs. The record sold few copies. Not long after, the Coronets became inactive, thanks to the military draft. Their lead, Carruthers, went into the service in late 1953, and Lester Russaw followed in March 1954.

The singers regrouped in the spring of 1954 with a new lead, Charles Brown. At a session on May 22, 1954, the Coronets recorded "Corbella" and "Beggin' and Pleadin'," but these sides remained unreleased. Chess Records apparently gave up on the group. The feeling was probably mutual; according to Griggs, each member made only about fifty dollars in royalties for their Chess recordings. Griggs laid much of the blame for the failure of the Coronets' career on their manager, Alan Freed, believing that he neglected them for other concerns, such as the Moonglows.[31]

The Coronets persevered and, with a new lead, Bobby Ward, in 1955 recorded a single for Irv Lief's Stirling label in Cleveland. Nothing happened with the two sides, but Lief sold four more Coronet sides to RCA, which released them on its Groove subsidiary in July 1955. Again, there was no success for the group, and the Coronets broke up, undoubtedly embittered by their recording experience.

When Charles Carruthers was discharged from the army, however, Sam Griggs was inspired to revive the Coronets yet again. Along with Carruthers, Griggs added Desious Willie Brooks as first tenor and Lucky Jordan as bass. In 1960 they recorded "Footsteps" backed with "Long John Silver" for Job, a Cleveland label, but when those sides did not do well, the group disbanded for good.

The Fortunes

The Fortunes go back to 1955, when each of the members was about twelve or thirteen years old and attending grade school on Chicago's South Side. Donald Jenkins as lead singer got together with Ronnie Strong (tenor), Walter Granger (baritone), and William Taylor (bass). Earlier, Strong had been a part of the Hambone Kids with Dee Clark and Sammy McGrier. After some months doowopping, the Fortunes established a considerable local reputation performing original material as well as the latest hits. They came under the management of Levi McKay, whose stable of groups included the Five Chances, the Fasinoles, and the Clouds.[32]

The Cats and the Fiddle, a typical vocal harmony–string band group of the 1940s, helped lay the foundation for the doowop groups that arose in the next decade. Top, left to right: Ernie Price, Chuck Barksdale, and Herbie Miles; bottom: Austin Powell. Courtesy of Peter Grendysa.

A doowop group appears on stage at the Club Delisa, an elite nightery on Chicago's South Side. This group is the Five Buddies (temporarily down to four members). Courtesy of Ularsee Manor.

Unless noted otherwise, all photographs are from the Robert Pruter Collection.

Boulevard Recording Studio. Here a Vee Jay vocal group, the Orioles, records some doowops in 1956. Seated at left is the famed session guitarist Lefty Bates. From the Scotty Piper Collection, courtesy of the Chicago Historical Society.

YWCA amateur shows conducted by the folk singer Ella Jenkins were important in nurturing doo-wop groups in the 1950s. The ensemble on stage is the Five Buddies. Courtesy of Ularsee Manor.

The Seward Park Field House, with its practice rooms, was an important near North Side center where doowop groups would hone their craft.

The Flamingos, 1954. The singers hit on Chance Records with "Golden Teardrops." Clockwise from top left: Paul Wilson, Sollie McElroy, Zeke Carey, Johnny Carter, and Jake Carey.

The Moonglows, 1954. Clockwise from top left: Prentiss Barnes, Harvey Fuqua, Pete Graves, and Bobby Lester.

The Five Echoes recorded first for Chance Records and later for Vee Jay. Left to right: Johnnie Taylor, Earl Lewis, Constant Sims, Jimmy Marshall, and Freddie Matthews. In the 1960s Johnnie Taylor emerged as a major soul star, recording for Memphis-based Stax Records.

Chance Records executives Art Sheridan (left) and Ewart Abner (standing) consult with Vee Jay co-owner James Bracken, 1954. Chance Records was highly instrumental in launching the Vee Jay label. Courtesy of Johnny Keyes.

The Maples, an ad hoc group formed from the Five Chances, recorded for Al Benson in 1955. Top: Reggie Smith; middle row, left to right: Harold Jones, Johnny Jones, Howard Pitman; bottom: Kenneth Childers. Courtesy of Howard Pitman.

The Five Chances, famed for the song "All I Want," recorded for Al Benson's Blue Lake label. Here the members are shown as the group was constituted in 1956. Left to right: Reggie Smith, Ronald Johnson, Johnny Jones, Jesse Stafford, and Howard Pitman. Courtesy of Robert Stallworth.

The Fascinators, 1954. This Detroit group recorded for Al Benson's Blue Lake label. Left to right: Bob Rivers, Jerry Potter, Earl Richardson, Clarence Smith, and Donald Blackshear.

The Flamingos, 1956. One of the exceptional doowop groups of the 1950s, the Flamingos had a big hit for Chess Records with "I'll Be Home." Left to right: Jake Carey, Nate Nelson, Johnny Carter, Zeke Carey, and Paul Wilson.

The Moonglows on stage at the Apollo Theatre. Left to right: Bobby Lester, Prentiss Barnes, Pete Graves, and Harvey Fuqua.

The Moonglows, 1957, on the set of the Alan Freed movie *Mr. Rock and Roll*. Left to right: Billy Johnson, Pete Graves, Bobby Lester, Prentiss Barnes, and Harvey Fuqua. Courtesy of Showtime Archives (Toronto).

The new Moonglows, 1959. Harvey Fuqua (bottom) recruited the new group in Washington, D.C. Top, left to right: Chester Simmons, Reese Palmer, James Nolan, Marvin Gaye, and Chuck Barksdale.

The Four Jewels provided some doowops harmonies behind Bo Diddley, record-ing in Washington, D.C. Left to right: Sandra Bears, Grace Ruffin, Margie Clark, and Carrie Mingo.

The Vibrations, shown in the early 1960s, had a major hit with "The Wa-tusi." This group got its start in Los Angeles in 1956, but beginning in 1960 the singers were re-cording doowops for Checker, a subsidiary la-bel of Chess Records.

The Five Cs, from Froebel High in Gary, Indiana, were the crosstown rival of the Spaniels. They recorded for Leonard Allan's United label. Courtesy of Johnny Keyes.

The Danderliers, 1957. The group had a big hit with "Chop Chop Boom" on the States label. Clockwise from top left: Bernard Dixon, James Campbell, Richard Thomas, Walter Stephenson, and Dallas Taylor. Courtesy of Richard Murray.

The Moroccos, 1955. Left to right: Ralph Vernon, Fred Martin, Sollie McElroy, Melvin Morrow, and George Prayer. Courtesy of Robert Stallworth.

The Pastels, ca. 1958. Left to right: Jerry Mills, Robert Randolph, Norman Palm, and Charles McKnight.

The Sheppards, 1955. This
was Bill Sheppard's first
namesake group. Top, left to
right: Oscar Boyd, James
Dennis Isaac, George Parker;
bottom, left to right: John
Pruitt and Nathaniel Tucker.
Courtesy of Richard Murray.

Vivian Carter at the mike of
radio station WWCA, Gary,
Indiana, ca. 1954. She presid-
ed there while running Vee Jay
Records. Courtesy of Johnny
Keyes.

The Spaniels, 1953, the original ensemble that recorded the group's signature tune, "Goodnite Sweetheart, Goodnite." Top, left to right: Pookie Hudson, Opal Courtney, Gerald Gregory, Junior Coleman (pianist), and Ernest Warren; bottom: Willis Jackson.

The Spaniels, 1955. Top, left to right: Willis Jackson, Gerald Gregory, Ernest Warren, and Pookie Hudson; bottom: Jerome Henderson.

The Spaniels, 1957. This second configuration of the group recorded such big hits as "You Gave Me Peace of Mind," "I Lost You," and "Everyone's Laughing." Left to right: Carl Rainge, James Cochran, Pookie Hudson, Donald Porter, and Gerald Gregory.

The El Dorados, 1954. Top: Louis Bradley; bottom, left to right: Jewel Jones, Pirkle Lee Moses, Richard Nickens, Arthur Bassett, and James Maddox.

The El Dorados, 1955. The group cut the classic rock 'n' roll hit "At My Front Door" for Vee Jay. Top, left to right: Richard Nickens, James Maddox, Jewel Jones, and Louis Bradley; bottom: Pirkle Lee Moses.

The El Dorados on tour in San Francisco. Top, left to right: James Maddox, Louis Bradley, Richard Nickens, and Jewel Jones; bottom: Pirkle Lee Moses. Courtesy of Rico T.

The Kool Gents at a club date in 1955. Top: Dee Clark; bottom, left to right: John McCall, John Carter, female fan, Teddy Long, and Doug Brown.

The Dells, ca. 1956. The group's big hit was "Oh What a Nite," for Vee Jay. Left to right: Marvin Junior, Verne Allison, Chuck Barksdale, Mickey McGill, and Johnny Funches (lead).

The Magnificents, 1956. This group hit on Vee Jay with "Up on the Mountain."
Left to right: Thurman Ramsey, Fred Rakestraw, Johnny Keyes, and Willie Myles.
Courtesy of Johnny Keyes.

The Rhythm Aces, 1955. Left to right: Billy Steward, Chuck Rowan, Clyde
Rhymes, and Vince House. Courtesy of Showtime Archives (Toronto).

The Goldenrods, 1957. Left to right: Charles Colquitt, Crosby Harris, Jesse Rodgers, and Hiawatha Burnett. Courtesy of Showtime Archives (Toronto).

The Orioles, 1956. Top: Sonny Til; bottom, left to right: Jerry Rodriguez, Albert Russell, Aaron Cornelius, and Billy Adams.

The Fortunes' break into recording came with a vocal group contest conducted by the deejay McKie Fitzhugh at the Pershing Ballroom in early 1955. Jenkins's group and the Clouds each won an opportunity to record after winning the contest.

The first two sides recorded by the Fortunes were apparently intended to be released on Parrot. The titles were "Bread" and "Love" and remained unreleased until they appeared on a bootleg LP in 1976 called *Parrot Doowop*. Both "Bread," a jump, and "Love," a ballad, are typical of the era, exhibiting a lot of youthful, amateurish vigor. Two other sides on the Fortunes were actually released on Checker in the summer of 1955, "Believe in Me," featuring the double lead of Jenkins and Strong, and "My Baby's Fine," featuring Jenkins as the sole lead. Both songs were written by McKay but were exceedingly weak, much weaker than the unreleased Parrot numbers.

The Fortunes broke up before the members of the group finished Dunbar High School. Jenkins went into the navy for a three-year hitch but kept his chops sharp by continuing to sing. After leaving the military in the early 1960s, he got together again with Ronnie Strong and recorded a number of records, billed as Rico and Ronnie on Checker in 1962 and as the Starr Brothers on Cortland in 1963. In 1963 Walter Granger rejoined the pair and the new group took the name Donald Jenkins and the Daylighters (later Delighters) and recorded a national hit, "Elephant Walk."

Bo Diddley

The conventional rock 'n' roll view of Bo Diddley is derived from such typical numbers as "Bo Diddley," "Who Do You Love," and "You Can't Judge a Book by Its Cover," all featuring a powerful, thick sound, and all based on a rhythmic figure now known as the "Bo Diddley beat." This "shave-and-a-haircut" beat has loomed so large over Bo Diddley's reputation that his career unfairly is noted for little else. He has been hailed as a pioneer "roots" artist by some critics and dismissed as a limited artist by others, but both opinions are based on the throbbing beat of his guitar. However, throughout his career, Diddley was looking for all kinds of sounds besides "the beat" to fill his musical palette. In an essay for the liner notes of the MCA boxed set on Diddley, the critic Robert Palmer masterfully made the case that, "far from being an artist with one great idea, Bo Diddley has created a whole musical rhythmical world." As Palmer astutely pointed out, the recorded evidence clearly shows that Diddley's music generally exhibited "fluid watery textures."[33] And among those textures could be found doowop harmonies.

Hand in hand with doowops come ballads, and Diddley was a master at writing ballads, such as "I'm Sorry," "No More Lovin'," and "Dearest Dar-ling." Two of Diddley's biggest ballad compositions were never recorded by him; instead, the team of Mickey and Sylvia went high on the charts with the immortal "Love Is Strange" and the almost equally good "Dearest."

Bo Diddley was born Ellas Bates McDaniel on December 30, 1928, in McComb, Mississippi. In 1935 the seven-year-old Ellas moved with his family (an aunt and her three children) to the South Side of Chicago. There he attended Ebenezer Baptist Church and began to take an interest in mu-sic. The congregation's musical director, Professor O. W. Frederick, taught the youngster violin and trombone. By the early 1940s Diddley had taken up guitar, and around 1945 he formed a street group called the Hipsters, a trio consisting of Diddley on guitar, Samuel Daniel as a singer and sand dancer, and Roosevelt Jackson on bass washtub. In 1951 Diddley got his first club job, at the 708 Club. By this time the Hipsters had evolved into the Langley Avenue Jive Cats, which, besides Bo and Jackson, now includ-ed Jerome Green on maracas and Billy Boy Arnold on harmonica.[34]

In 1955 Bo Diddley and his group auditioned at both Vee Jay and Unit-ed and were turned down at both. Leonard Allen at United rejected Did-dley after getting a report from one of his assistants that Diddley wasn't "worth shit."[35] He went to Chess, where the Chess brothers heard some-thing in his street-corner crude sound that people at the other companies did not.

Diddley created his musical world with marvelous use of doowop groups, notably members of the Moonglows, the Flamingos, the Marquees, and the Carnations. Most of the doowop backgrounds on Diddley records were creations of ad hoc groups, sometimes put together by Diddley's first female guitarist, Peggy Jones.[36] (In 1970, when she was known as Peggy Malone, Diddley gave her the tag "Lady Bo.") Diddley was an inventive musician, highly creative and eclectic in his approach, but he had to bor-row heavily from others and from his previous compositions the basic tunes on which to build new songs.

The earliest vocal group collaboration with Diddley was "Diddley Dad-dy," from 1955, which featured the Moonglows in the background. Did-dley cowrote the song with Harvey Fuqua. It is not truly a doowop but more of a blues than anything else, especially with the presence of Little Walter's harmonica on the track. The Moonglows simply chant two phrases through-out the song, "diddle diddle diddle diddle daddy" and "diddle diddle dum, dum dum di-diddle." The song is credited to Bo Diddley but Billy Boy Arnold has claimed to be the writer, and he came out with a variation on Vee Jay called "I Wish I Would."[37] The record made the *Billboard* R&B chart for four weeks in the summer of 1955. The Moonglows also supplied the "diddy wah" doowop chant for the number "Diddy Wah Diddy." These

Moonglows-backed numbers appeared on Bo Diddley's first album, *Bo Diddley,* released in 1958. Prentiss Barnes, the Moonglows' bass, recalled that Bo Diddley "liked the sound of vocal groups. When we were on tours with him, we would clown and jam with him on the bus or backstage, working out on doowops."[38]

In 1957 Peggy Jones, a guitarist and vocalist from New York, joined the Bo Diddley band as a replacement for Jody Williams, who had been drafted into the army. Jones brought doowop experience to her Diddley association. That year she sang on the third release by the New York-based Bop Chords, who the previous year had a rock 'n' roll hit with "Castle in the Sky." The single, "So Why" backed with "Baby," included Jones, Ernest Harriston, Ken "Butch" Hamilton, and Skip Boyd.

Diddley began using Jones on the choruses and for occasional guitar leads, and Jones was present on most of the vocal chanting and doowopping on Diddley records from 1957 to 1961. The usual chorus would consist of Bo; Jones; Bob Baskerville, Jones's husband at the time; Jerome Green, Diddley's longtime maracas player and alternate vocalist; and whoever was in the studio at the time. At the time of the recording it was usually decided when a chorus or a doowop harmony would be put into a song. Said Jones, "Sometimes somebody will have a thought, or Bo will have a thought. Once he's done the lead and the music is down, he'll say 'that's good enough, let's put some harmonies in there.' It's like it grows; he never preplanned a lot of things."[39] On the first records with which Jones was associated, "Hey Bo Diddley" and "Say Boss Man," the vocal supports were chants and not true doowops, even though Johnny Carter and some other top-notch voices were present. But that would soon change.

In December 1958, Diddley recorded one of his most famous doowop sessions, waxing "I'm Sorry," "Crackin' Up," and "Don't Let It Go (Hold on to What You Got)." Jones said, "I remember doing the vocals on them, but I think there were other vocals added later on."[40] These sides reveal the smooth expertise of a finely honed vocal harmony group, far beyond the usual ad hoc ensemble chanting that had been heard on earlier Diddley records. Although Jones has no recollection of the Carnations, the group listed as the background vocalists, members of the Carnations have claimed in two published accounts that they were on the session. While they were singing as the Teardrops, they went to Chicago and recorded the backgrounds to those songs. The Carnations are best known for their 1961 recording, "Long Tall Girl." The group came out of Bridgeport, Connecticut, and when they formed in 1954 as the Startones they consisted of Carl Hatton, Arthur Blackwell, Matthew Morales, Alan Mason, and Harvey Arrington. Hatton and Arrington were drafted into the service, but when they came out they re-formed the group as the Teardrops, with new members Tommy Blackwell and Edward Kennedy. It was this group that claimed to be on the December 1958 session with Bo Diddley.[41]

There is yet another claim for that session. The Magnificents' lead singer, Johnny Keyes, has asserted that "'I'm Sorry' was me, L. C. Cooke, and a fellow L. C. picked up in the pool room along the way. I don't recall this fellow's name, because I never met him before."[42] But Keyes's memory should be considered a bit suspect in this case, because he believed "Crackin' Up" was a separate session, in which he, Reggie Gordon, and Jerome Browne were the backing unit.

In any case, this historically confused session yielded two chart records for Diddley in 1959, "I'm Sorry" and "Crackin' Up." The haunting chanting by the chorus on "I'm Sorry" shows the value of doowop as an art form. The simple lyrics of Diddley would have sounded thin and hollow without the rich tapestry provided by the group. Some of the parentage of "I'm Sorry" can be heard in Don and Dewey's "When the Sun Has Begun to Shine," from 1955.

Yet it is "I'm Sorry" that becomes the parent of other songs, vaguely in Robert and Johnny's "Baby Baby," and more obviously in the Ohio Untouchables' "Forgive Me Darling." Diddley in his later years demonstrated his longtime appreciation for doowop when he reworked "I'm Sorry" into a more ambitious song, "Tribute to Rock 'n' Roll." In it he honored various doowop groups, such as Little Anthony and the Imperials, the Five Satins, and the Moonglows.[43]

The excellent "Crackin' Up," although not a doowop, provides good interaction between lead and the chorus. "Don't Let It Go (Hold on to What You Got)" is not a doowop either, but it comes alive because of the call-and-response in which the chorus sings "don't let it go" and then "whoo hoo hoo." All three of the songs came from Diddley's second LP, *Go Bo Diddley,* released in 1959. Another album cut, "Dearest Darling," was from a January 1958 session, and benefited from the addition of some good vocal harmonies. The song was strongly derived from a 1957 doowop, "I Do Believe," recorded by the Crystals for Aladdin.

In a 1959 session Diddley recorded two ballads that cried out for some doowop accompaniment, "Mama Mia" and "What Do You Know About Love." If they had had members of the Moonglows or Flamingos on them they would have been considered top doowops. Diddley had intended to add vocal harmonies at some point but it never happened, and both songs lay in the can for many years. "Mama Mia" surfaced on the *Bo Diddley & Company* album in 1962, and "What Do You Know About Love" appeared on an album of vintage material, *The Originator,* in 1966.

Diddley's third album, *Have Guitar, Will Travel,* from early 1960, featured a pure gospel call-and-response in "She's Alright," recorded in September 1959. It isn't a doowop but it does show Diddley's appreciation of vocal harmony fills and responses. The song was heavily derived from Little Anthony and the Imperials' "I'm Alright," a hit in the fall of 1959. Undoubtedly, the Imperials' version came from a common gospel routine in the black church.

More vocal harmony work can be found on Diddley's fourth album, *In the Spotlight,* from 1960, where doowop stylings can be heard on "Love Me" and "Walkin' and Talkin'." "Love Me" is a slow, dirgelike doowop that has a solid vocal backing with former Flamingos tenor Johnny Carter holding down the top. The song could have been better. "Walkin' and Talkin'" is obviously inspired from the Coasters' "Along Came Jones." On it the ensemble tries to chorus in a sassy way, but ultimately its support sounds uninteresting. These recordings, made in January 1960, were part of the first session recorded in Bo Diddley's new basement studio built in his home on Rhode Island Avenue in Washington, D.C. Again, overdubs were added in Chicago, where possibly Carter's and other vocals were added (Carter doesn't recall recording in D.C.). Keyes said that the backing on "Walkin' and Talkin'" was by him, Rufus Hunter, and Reggie Gordon. Also on the album some low-key chanting can be heard by a group on "Road Runner," which Keyes said was provided by him, Gordon, and Jerome Browne.[44]

Since the CD revolution of the late 1980s, record companies have been mining their vaults to get products into the stores. The benefit to music fans is the availability of previously unissued masters. On the Bo Diddley boxed set from 1990 there appeared a magnificent doowop, "You Know I Love You," which the compilers credited to the Flamingos, from the January 1960, session. Next to "I'm Sorry," it is the best doowop Diddley ever recorded, and one wonders about the wisdom of the company's never releasing it. Johnny Carter's falsetto top is most evident, which means that the Flamingos of 1960 were not involved, since Carter had left the group in 1956. Jones said that the group on the session was composed of herself, Carter, and members of Harvey Fuqua's new Moonglows, who were originally the Marquees, a D.C. group.[45]

The Marquees—Marvin Gaye, James Nolan, Chester Simmons, and Reese Palmer—were taken under the wing of Bo Diddley in 1957. He produced and arranged four sides on the group—two sides backing another Diddley protégé, Billy Stewart, "Billy's Heartache" and "You're My Only Love," and two sides on their own, "Wyatt Earp" and "Hey Little School Girl." The session was recorded in New York and released on OKeh Records. Bo Diddley claimed to his British biographer, George White, that he had no idea the records would come out on OKeh, since he was a Chess artist. He had given the tapes to his manager, Phil Landwehr, and the next thing he knew they were out on OKeh without the proper credits to Bo.[46] The Diddley origin is most evident on these songs, showing his doowop sensibility through and through.

There was one other song on the *In the Spotlight* album, "Deed I Deed I Do," that could have benefited from even more up-front doowop fills. The chorus—which consisted of Diddley, Jones, Baskerville, and Green—is too faint and far back, but the song features a great bass voice (Jones says it is Jerome Green) responding to Bo's lead. The song has a doowop character and again shows Diddley's sensibility in that area.

In the summer of 1960, over several sessions, Bo Diddley recorded his *Bo Diddley Is a Gunslinger* LP. Practically all the numbers had some sort of vocal support, usually shouted-type chanting by Diddley, Green, Baskerville, and Jones. The most spectacular doowop number on the album is "No More Lovin,'" a stylistically pure doowop with rich vocal harmonies that reflect the presence of some top doowoppers. The song appears to have Carter and Jones creating a splendid edge on the top. As Jones recalled, besides Johnny Carter, other background singers on the *Gunslinger* sessions were Nate Nelson (the famous Flamingos longtime lead), Harvey Fuqua (alternate lead of the Moonglows), and various members of the new Moonglows (probably including Marvin Gaye). Jones even thought Billy Stewart might have lent some vocal support on some numbers. She noted, "At that time, everyone was friends, and if Bo was cutting a session they were all welcome to jump in. It makes it really hard to determine who did what."[47]

Other vocal group treatments on *Gunslinger* are far less interesting. "Doing the Crawdaddy" features a childish-sounding female vocal chorus, responding to Bo Diddley's spoken directions for what presumably would be a great new dance, in Bo's mind at least. "Somewhere," like many of Diddley songs, is a derivation, in this case of the standard "Somewhere over the Rainbow." Diddley does it in the best doowop style, and the group supports him in a subdued yet effective doowop vocalizing. One can hear the burbling bass and tenor top, but doowop fans would probably have preferred to hear the vocal support given more prominence in the mix and arrangement.

When Diddley performed on stage he usually did not bring a vocal group to back him on his doowop songs—songs such as "I'm Sorry." What did he do in that case? As Jones explained, "the chorus on stage was me, Jerome Green, and Bo. When Bo was doing a lead, he always used to talk back and hit a third note with us. A lead singer is not always singing constantly. If you choose your harmonies carefully you don't need four or five voices. It's like a style you fall into."[48]

Diddley used a girl group in a March 1961 session, in three songs that appeared on the *Bo Diddley Is a Lover* LP, namely, the title track, "Not Guilty," and "Love Is a Secret." Only the last named can be considered a doowop. The girls provide some beautiful harmonies on the song, but it is not all that strong. Diddley used a girl group again in November of that year, for "Doin' the Jaguar." The song offers a bit of doowop but is of little interest, although one can tell that the girls have a great harmony sound. The song appeared in early 1962 on the album *Bo Diddley's a Twister.* The girls were joined by Jones in her last session work with Diddley. Jones said, "There was a situation in which Bo Diddley wrote a tune and he knew some little girls down the street who were starting out. They had a pretty good sound and he said I have a song for you. I used to come up from New York every two weeks to record, and when I got to Washington they were already there working on 'Jaguar.' "[49]

The girls on the above sessions were the Impalas, Sandra Bears, Margie Clark, Carrie Mingo, and Grace Ruffin (the last a first cousin to Billy Stewart). During the same sessions, Diddley recorded the Impalas on two songs, "I Need You So Much" and "For the Love of Mike." Using his clout with Chess, he got the company to put them out on the Checker label. After nothing happened on their first release, the girls began recording with a local D.C. label, Start, and with a new name, the Four Jewels. The group got some recognition with "Loaded with Goodies," which ironically was re-released on the Checker label in 1963. The group's one national hit was "Opportunity" (1964), recorded for Carole King's Dimension label in New York under the name Jewels. Later they recorded singles for James Brown and backed him in concerts.[50]

Diddley used one of the most respected vocal groups of the early sixties when he recruited the Vibrations for several tracks on two albums in 1962, *Bo Diddley's a Twister* and *Bo Diddley* (the latter distinguished by its black cover). The Vibrations had joined Chess in 1960 and struck it big the following year with their giant dance hit, "The Watusi."

When the Vibrations appeared on the Diddley sessions in January and July 1962, their career was already trending downward at Chess. On *Bo Diddley's a Twister,* the group was used on "Here 'Tis." The chorusing on the song is straightforward and offers nothing to the doowop fan. On *Bo Diddley,* the group appears on "Mr. Khrushchev," "You All Green," and "Babes in the Woods." "Mr. Khrushchev" offers nothing but simple chorusing, however, "You All Green" provides some aggressive doowopping and chorusing in the spirit of the Olympics vocal group. The unknown harpist adds some downhome funk to the proceedings. "Babes in the Woods" is an awful song; the simple choruses by the Vibrations have a top edge courtesy of the Duchess, a successor to Peggy Jones as Diddley's guitar accompaniment.

By 1966, Bo Diddley was no longer making doowops but was trying to get into the soul market with such songs as "We're Gonna Get Married" and "Wrecking My Love Life." He was done with his most fruitful and creative recording years.

To cover Bo Diddley as a doowopper alone may strike some readers as perverse. In the 1990s, the influence of doowop in the formation of rock 'n' roll has been minimized or denied, while the seminal role of the blues in creating rock 'n' roll has been increasingly emphasized. Many college and alternative radio stations in the land consider themselves hip for playing a blues-based Diddley track but they would never consider playing a doowop-influenced Diddley track, let alone any other doowop. Thus it is instructive to show that one of the great guitar heroes of the 1950s loved doowop and was obviously a doowopper himself. Bo Diddley never considered "doowop" something outside of his sense of rock 'n' roll.

The Vibrations

The Vibrations, who joined Chess in 1960, represented the company during the transitional era of vocal harmony, when doowop was evolving into soul, and their records with the company reflect that transition. The group began in Los Angeles, when Carl Fisher (lead), James Johnson (tenor), Dave Govan (baritone), and Carver Bunkum (bass) got together in 1956 at Jefferson High. Their original name was the Jayhawks.[51]

The Jayhawks hooked up with a man named Ted Brenson and recorded their first records in a garage. The record was released on the Flash label, an extension of a record store owned by Charles Reynolds. Their first release was the doowop ballad "Counting My Teardrops," in April 1956. It got them some local notices but not much more than that. With their next release, however, the group got a huge hit with a jump novelty, "Stranded in the Jungle," which went to R&B number nine and pop chart number eighteen in the summer of 1956. There then followed one more release on Flash. With a move to Aladdin, on which the Jayhawks recorded "Everyone Should Know" (1957), Carver Bunkum left and Ricky Owens (first tenor and lead) joined. A switch to the Eastman label in early 1959, when they recorded "Start the Fire," also brought the bass singer Don Bradley into the group.

In 1960 the Jayhawks changed their name to the Vibrations and put out "So Blue" on Bet, a label they partly owned. It is a haunting ballad with atmospheric high tenor wailing in the background, very much inspired by the Flamingos. Chess had enough interest in the song to buy the group's contract and put out "So Blue" on its Checker label. The song never got more than regional action but Chess stuck with them. The Vibrations' second release, "Cave Man" backed with "Feel So Bad," followed the pattern on all their releases by marrying a doowop ballad and a novelty or dance number. "Cave Man," featuring an appealing raunchy vocal riff, is a variation on "Stranded in the Jungle." As exciting as the song was, however, it sounded dated in 1960, as did "Feel So Bad," a song that harks back to the past in its doowoppy warbling.

In 1961, the Vibrations got a giant hit with "The Watusi." The song was a group original, written by Fisher, but discerning listeners will hear the melody of Hank Ballard's "Let's Go Let's Go Let's Go" in the song. "The Watusi" went to number six on the *Cash Box* R&B chart and number twenty on the pop chart. So big was the song, Checker even put out an album on the Vibrations, *Watusi!,* a rarity for Chess acts at the time. Besides featuring cuts of the group's earlier single sides, the album featured some impassioned ballads, notably "So Little Time," "Time after Time, "I Had a Dream," and "People Say." On the latter one, the singers try somewhat unsuccessfully to imitate the Platters' pause notes, "ah-ooh." "I Had a Dream" is the best ballad on the album and remains a Vibrations doowop masterpiece, although so far unrecognized. Another nice song was the "Serenade of the Bells." "So Little Time" and "Doing the Slop," a routine dance song from the LP, were paired for the next record, but for some reason Checker voided the release.

A rousing dance number, "Continental with Me Baby," was the next Vibrations release, in April 1961, but it did not do anything. The group was caught in a bit of moonlighting in June that year, when they recorded "Peanut Butter" as the Marathons for the Arvee label in Los Angeles. The moonlighting would probably have gone unnoticed had not the record, which was produced by H. B. Barnum, become a big hit. It went to number twenty-five on the R&B chart and became the group's second-biggest crossover hit when it went to number twenty on the *Billboard* pop chart. Chess negotiated a deal where the company picked up the release, and put it out on its Argo subsidiary, billing the artists as "The Vibrations Named by Others as the Marathons." The novelty song was very much in the Olympics mode, not surprising since Barnum was the Olympics' producer as well.

Also in the summer of 1961, Checker released a remake of "Stranded in the Jungle," but the song was dated by that time. Radio stations were still programming the original "Stranded in the Jungle" as a golden oldie, so the song offered nothing new. The flip featured a nice up-tempo version of the Moonglows' "Don't Say Goodbye." August 1961 saw the release of "All My Love Belongs to You," a Vibrations-styled version of the old 1940s rhythm and blues hit by Bullmoose Jackson. An appealing segment of the song comes when the group closes the song with a Moonglows-style blow-harmony riff.

Few people bought the record, however. "Let's Pony Again," from October 1961, tried to ride the Pony dance craze, and the throbbing fast-paced beat fits the dance perfectly. However, the record met with little success. Its flip, "What Made You Change Your Mind," is routine.

At the end of 1961 came "Oh Cindy," one of the most fondly remembered of all the Vibrations' songs. Not to be confused with Vince Martin's "Cindy, Oh Cindy," the ballad is done at midtempo pace and features a beautiful melody and luscious harmonizing. On the flip, "Over the Rainbow," the Vibrations deconstruct a standard as the group speeds up and rocks the song in their winning way. The next release, from March 1962, "The New Hully Gully," again tried to exploit a dance craze, unsuccessfully. The track, however, is identical to "Continental with Me Baby," except for the vocals, which employ slightly different lyrics. Following a barely released and routine "Hamburger on a Bun," the Vibrations came out with a fantastic rendition of the old 1940s standard "Since I Fell for You," turning the ballad into a scrumptious and exciting up-tempo raver. Unfortunately for the group, it didn't sell upon its release in March 1963. The Vibrations' last release on Checker was "Dancing Danny," and they sounded tired on it. They were ready to change labels.

During the Vibrations' association with Chess they emerged as one of the most exciting acts on the chitlin' circuit, wowing the crowds with their athletic choreography and beautiful harmonizing. In Chicago they became one of the Regal Theater's most popular acts. Their first Regal appearance was in June 1960, when they were billed as "The 'So Blue' Vibrations." On the bill were Jackie Wilson, Ruth McFadden, Elmore James, and Dion and the Belmonts. The group has mentioned this as the first big show they'd performed on. In February 1961 they were on the Regal with Roy Hamilton, Etta James, Etta Jones, the Shells, the Chimes, and Buddy and Ella Johnson. They came back in May 1961, billed with Jerry Lee Lewis, Bobby Bland, the Crests, and Ben E. King, among others. They were on the Regal bills in November 1961, March 1962, October 1962, and August 1963.

The Vibrations achieved much success during the soul era, first in New York on the Atlantic label with "My Girl Sloopy" (1964), in Chicago on the OKeh label with "Misty" (1965) and "And I Love Her" (1966), and in Philadelphia on the OKeh label with "Love in Them There Hills" (1968). The Vibrations are one of the great groups in rhythm and blues history but have too long gone unrecognized in the music press.

Other Chess Vocal Groups

Chess had a few other Chicago-based vocal group recordings that made a bit of an impact in a few markets, such as the Daps' "When You're Alone"

(1956) and the Blue Jays' take on the World War II goody, "White Cliffs of Dover" (1953). The company had notable success with the Five Notes' double-sided masterpiece from late 1955, "Park Your Love" backed with "Show Me the Way." With its relaxed lope, vigorous doowop chanting, and splendid work by the bass and the high tenor, "Park Your Love" was the side that got the most plays across the country. "Show Me the Way," the ballad side, likewise got strong doowoppy support from the chorus. These sides, which virtually define the doowop approach to music making, were played for years on oldies radio shows.

The Five Notes were a Milwaukee-based group that was originally formed in Dallas. It consisted of Al Braggs (lead), the brothers Cal Valentine (second lead) and Robert Lee Valentine, Jesse Floyd, and Billie Fred Thomas. After winning a few talent shows in Texas they attracted promotional interest and soon found themselves in Milwaukee, where a deejay, Chuck Dunaway, took them under his wing and featured them in all his stage shows. After going to Chicago and recording the Chess sides, the group moved on and made some sides elsewhere as the Five Masks on the Jan label and as the Five Stars on Blues Boy Kingdom (B. B. King's label). The group returned to Dallas and appeared in an obscure, locally produced rock 'n' roll film from 1957 called *Rock Baby Rock It*. Then the singers disbanded.

Braggs became a solo recording act on the Houston-based Duke label and developed a reputation as a crowd-rousing opening act for Bobby Bland. His moniker was suitably "Al 'TNT' Braggs." Cal Valentine took up guitar and with his brother, Robert, formed a blues and boogie combo called the Valentines, which recorded six sides for King Records. Later moving to Oakland, he made some records with another group, the Right Kind, for the Galaxy label, and in the 1990s emerged as a solo blues artist, recording an album in 1994.[52]

The Equadors came out with two jump sides on Argo in 1960, "Say You'll Be Mine" and "Let Me Sleep Woman." Both sides were written by Chuck Berry, who appeared to be their mentor. One can hear in these up-tempo sides the basic Berry songwriting approach, which has been adapted for a vocal harmony group. Berry used the Equadors as background chanters for his song "Do You Love Me," but the song lacked doowop flavor.[53] Berry was just not a natural-born doowopper like Bo Diddley.

*   *   *

Of all the Chicago record companies, Chess was most adept at exploiting the rock 'n' roll revolution. When Chess executives saw that the new rock 'n' roll sound was heavily dependent on doowop groups, they signed the Moonglows, the Flamingos, and the Coronets and worked with them in

close association with Alan Freed. Unlike any other Chicago groups, the
Moonglows and Flamingos appeared in Freed's rock 'n' roll movies. Later, before vocal group music would veer into soul, the Vibrations would
score big rock 'n' roll hits with "The Watusi" and "Peanut Butter." Both
of Chess's biggest solo rock 'n' rollers, Bo Diddley and Chuck Berry, also
made use of doowop groups in creating their brand of rock 'n' roll. The
events at Chess clearly show the symbiotic relationship between the record
companies, the doowop groups, and the radio deejays in developing rock
'n' roll as the new sound in popular music.

Notes

1. Chess Records has been more extensively documented than any other Chicago record company, largely because of its impressive blues output. The best resources on Chess's early years prior to the soul era can be found in Galkin, "Black
White and Blues," and Rowe, *Chicago Breakdown.*
2. The complete list of Flamingos sources is given in chapter 2, n. 10.
3. Groia, *They All Sang on the Corner,* p. 136.
4. Hoekstra, "Flamingos Return."
5. Tancredi, "The Flamingos," p. 5.
6. Jones, "Nate Nelson," p. 12.
7. Groia, *They All Sang on the Corner,* p. 137.
8. The complete list of Moonglows sources is given in chapter 1, n. 18.
9. White, "Harvey Fuqua." p. 24.
10. Sue Cassidy Clark, unpublished interview with Fuqua, transcript, Center
for Black Music Research, Columbia College, Chicago.
11. Propes, "The Moonglows," p. 12.
12. Ibid.
13. Barnes interview, September 26, 1992.
14. Barnes interview, September 27, 1992.
15. Barnes interview, July 27, 1994.
16. Propes, "The Moonglows," p. 12.
17. Barnes interview, September 26, 1992.
18. Propes, "The Moonglows," p. 12.
19. Ibid.
20. Barnes interview, September 26, 1992.
21. Confirmation that "M. Paul" was in fact Marshall Chess comes from Jay
Warner, "The Moonglows," *The Billboard Book,* p. 262.
22. White, "Harvey Fuqua," p. 24.
23. Propes, "The Moonglows," p. 13.
24. White, "Harvey Fuqua," p. 24.
25. Ritz, *Divided Soul,* p. 44. Ritz generously devoted two chapters to Gaye's
career in the new Moonglows, which yields a fascinating portrait of Harvey Fuqua and the Moonglows organization in their declining days.

26. Information about the Coronets comes from Goldberg, "Coronets' Smooth Style," and Jackson, *Big Beat Heat,* pp. 57–61.

27. Goldberg, "Coronets' Smooth Style," p. 12.

28. Jackson, *Big Beat Heat,* p. 57.

29. Goldberg, "Coronets' Smooth Style," p. 12.

30. Jackson, *Big Beat Heat,* p. 105.

31. Ibid., p. 61.

32. Information about the Fortunes comes from Pruter, "Donald Jenkins' Story," and the Jenkins interview.

33. Palmer, liner notes, "Bo Diddley," p. 18.

34. Information about Bo Diddley is extensive, as would befit one of the founders of rock 'n' roll. The most useful to this profile are: Braunstein, "Bo Diddley Bo Diddley"; Bo Diddley, liner notes, "Bo Diddley on Bo Diddley"; Loder, "Bo Diddley"; Palmer, liner notes, "Bo Diddley"; Pruter, "Bo Diddley."

35. Allen interview, 1976.

36. George R. White, letter to author, October 13, 1992.

37. Beauchamp, "Interview with Billy Boy Arnold," p. 14.

38. Barnes interview, January 12, 1993.

39. Malone interview.

40. Ibid.

41. Information about the carnations comes from Anderson, "The Carnations"; Jay Warner, "The Carnations," *The Billboard Book.*

42. Keyes interview.

43. George R. White, to author, April 15, 1993. I am indebted to Mr. White for information that enabled me to provide a context for Diddley's work and to make some connections between the Diddley style and that of other artists.

44. Keyes interview.

45. Malone interview.

46. White, letter to author.

47. Malone interview.

48. Ibid.

49. Ibid.

50. Information about the Four Jewels comes from Oates, liner notes, *Loaded with Goodies;* Pruter, "The Jewels."

51. Information about the Vibrations comes from Abbey, "The Vibrations," and Goldberg, "The Jayhawks/Vibrations."

52. Information about the Five Notes comes from Opal Lewis Nations, letter to author, March 1, 1994; Rainsford, "Doin' the Boogie Twist"; Schuller, "The Al Braggs Story."

53. Fred Rothwell, letter to author, May 28, 1993.

4

United Records

United Records was founded by Leonard Allen, a tailor by trade and a neophyte in the record business, and Lew Simpkins, an experienced record man. In the 1940s Simpkins had worked in A&R at Miracle and then at Premium, two labels owned by Lee Egalnick. Premium went bust in 1951, but Simpkins was still itching to stay in the record business. He talked his friend Allen into getting involved and providing the seed money for a new operation, to be called United Records. Early in the company's history, in May 1953, the thirty-five-year-old Simpkins became ill and died, leaving Allen in charge. Assisting Allen at the company were Samuel Smith (Smitty), his nephew by marriage, who did the A&R with the vocal groups, and a Miss Harris, the secretary, who was the administrative mainstay of the company. Also working with United's recording artists was Al Smith, but he was an independent contractor who had no formal position at the company. The company's headquarters were located at 5052 South Cottage Grove, in the heart of the South Side "record row."[1]

Allen kept United going until 1957, when a lack of hits did in the company. During its existence, however, United—and its subsidiary label, States—had national hits with Tab Smith's "Because of You," Jimmy Forrest's "Night Train," the Danderliers' "Chop Chop Boom," and the Four Blazes' "Mary Jo," but the company also subsisted on a regular diet of local and lesser hits by the Caravans, the Moroccos, the Staple Singers, and many blues acts.

Most of the blues artists had been signed by Lew Simpkins, because Allen knew nothing about the blues. The company recorded a large number of invaluable blues songs. Especially outstanding were the sides recorded by Robert Nighthawk, whose Delta blues slide guitar stylings represent one of the finest legacies in blues. Allen recorded the first sides, including

"Hoodoo Man," by Junior Wells, whose squalling harp blowing and gritty blues singing have always epitomized Chicago bar-band blues. Another of Allen's historic harmonica blues recordings was Big Walter Horton's "Hard Hearted Woman." The company had some minor successes with such veteran bluesmen as J. T. "Nature Boy" Brown ("Windy City Blues"), Memphis Slim ("The Comeback"), and Roosevelt Sykes ("Security Blues"). Other company blues artists recorded by Allen included Lefty Bates, Browley Guy, Dennis Binder, and Harold Burrage. It was this rich catalog of blues, as well as jazz, that prompted Delmark Records' Bob Koester to purchase the masters of the United operation from Allen in 1975.

But the catalog also contains a wealth of impressive vocal group recordings, notably those by the Danderliers and the Moroccos, but also those by the Palms, the Sheppards, the Pastels, the Hornets, and Five Cs. Few of United's vocal groups sold much beyond the confines of Chicago, if that far, and so many of the releases remain obscurities. Nonetheless, United recorded an interesting body of vocal group music, and among the earliest were sides by the Five Cs.

The Five Cs

Of special interest to vocal group fans are the Five Cs, on whom United released four sides during 1954. It is believed the group was brought to Allen by the local deejay Sam Evans. A relative of Evans, Clarence Anderson, was in the group, as were Curtis Nevils, Melvin Carr, and Carlos Tollerver. That leaves four, but nobody has been able to recall the fifth "C" (although, obviously, his first or last name must have started with "C"). The Five Cs came out of Gary, Indiana, and attended Gary Froebel High, the crosstown rival to the Spaniels' school, Roosevelt High. The two groups knew each other casually.[2]

The first recording session for United took place in December 1953 and produced "Tell Me" backed with "Whoo-ee Baby." "Tell Me" is a bouncy poplike doowop and it got the group its first notices during the first months of 1954. "Tell Me" received good play in Los Angeles. The *Chicago Defender*'s "Night Beat" columnist for the Gary edition said, "Gary has another reason to be proud, for we now have another recording group known as the Five Cs and they have come up with a tune that should be a hit. So get behind the boys."[3] In March the group played at the Pershing Ballroom, sharing the bill with Chuck Willis and Illinois Jacquet. In Gary, the group played a teen dance at the Majestic and with Muddy Waters at the Playdium Ballroom.

From the second session, in May 1954, the Five Cs produced another fine release with the poplike up-tempo tune "Goody Goody." It was backed by a nice ballad, "My Heart's Got the Blues." The record got little airplay outside of Chicago, however. Sam Evans claimed he could not keep enough copies of "Goody Goody" in his record stores, but that was typical promotional talk that publicists gave trade magazines in the fifties. In more promotional talk, Dave Clark reported that "Goody Goody" was voted a hit on the influential Peter Potter deejay show in New York. But unfortunately for the Five Cs, the record never took off.

In June the group got on a show promoted by Sam Evans at the Pershing Ballroom that featured Fats Domino, Joe Turner, Muddy Waters, and Eddie Boyd. In Gary, the Five Cs continued to make the local spots, for example, playing with the Spaniels at Roosevelt High in November.

In December 1954, the Five Cs and Eddie Chamblee were the acts that United Records sent down to the annual WDIA Goodwill Revue in Memphis, Tennessee. Radio station WDIA promoted an annual show to support education for disabled children, and record companies would provide free talent from their record stables, in part to keep the station playing their products. The other Chicago labels to send talent were Vee Jay, which sent the El Dorados, and Chess, which sent Eddie Boyd.

Meanwhile, the Five Cs had one more session, in July 1954, from which nothing was released. The unreleased Five Cs sides, as is true of much of United's group material, are as high in quality as the released songs. The second session yielded a jump version of the standard "There's No Tomorrow" (derived from the Italian "O Solo Mio") and a semi-jump of "I Long for You," both of which are most solid. The third session produced a superb droopy doowop, "Going My Way," and a pop-sounding jump in "I Want to Be Loved." On all the songs the group gets terrific support from saxophonist Eddie Chamblee.

From the evidence of their songs, the Five Cs were a typical transition group, who can be placed between the poplike 1940s groups and the R&B–related 1950s groups, with a slight tilt to the latter. They sang beautifully, but they also sang soulfully.

The Hornets

The Hornets became famous in the 1980s for just one thing: singing on the most expensive vocal group collectible of all time, "I Can't Believe" backed with "Lonesome Baby" on States, the only record the group ever made. In 1988 three 45rpm copies of their single surfaced, and a copy was sold by one collector to a more well heeled collector for the astronomical sum of $18,000—or it may have been that two copies were sold to the same collector for $9,000 each; no one knows for sure.[4] In any case, the Hornets' disc replaced the Five Sharps' legendary "Stormy Weather" in every collector's mind as the ultimate big-ticket item. But the Hornets should not be remembered merely as a group who put big bucks in the pocket of a lucky collector. Back in the early 1950s they were a group of young fellows who wanted to sing and who thought they had what it took to entertain people.[5]

The Hornets recorded in 1953 during the era of deep R&B harmony and bouncy jump tunes, and their recordings reflect the sounds of the day coming out of New York and Chicago. The Hornets' mournful balladry and peppy jumps remind one of the music of great street-corner pioneers such as the Five Chances, the Cardinals, and the Crows, who created some of the most wonderful sounds of the early 1950s. It is these groups to which the Hornets can be compared.

The Hornets got together around 1951 at Cleveland Central High. The members of the group were James "Sonny" Long (lead), Johnny Moore (tenor), Ben Iverson (baritone), and Gus Miller (bass). They originally called themselves the Mellotones but decided to change their name when they discovered its similarity to another group's name. The Hornets' first material was typical of the day, songs by the Dominoes, the Orioles, and the Drifters, and some pop standards.

The break for the Hornets, such as it was, came when an owner of a skating rink in Cleveland heard their performance and then took them to United Records in Chicago. The group recorded five sides on August 12, 1953. Two of them—"Lonesome Baby," a driving jump tune, and "I Can't Believe," an Atlantic Records–style ballad—were released in November on the States label. The record did nothing, and perhaps that is why Leonard Allen chose not to record the Hornets again or release the remaining material by the group. But the three unreleased songs showed considerable promise—"Big City Bounce," a jump with a nice bass lead by Gus Miller; "You Played the Game," a fine slow understated ballad; and "Reelin' and Rockin'," a rousing swinging jump—all of which might have done something if released.

The Hornets made appearances throughout the Midwest, in Cleveland, Cincinnati, Chicago, and Detroit, playing clubs, theaters, and gymnasiums. Around this time Bill Brent replaced Gus Miller as bass. But nothing was happening for the group, so when the Drifters asked Johnny Moore to join them, around Thanksgiving of 1954, he leaped at the opportunity. Sonny Long had a problem with timing, and Moore was being groomed for the lead, so his departure served to finish the Hornets. Moore went on to become a mainstay in the legendary Drifters for some thirty years.

Ben Iverson formed another Hornets group in the early 1960s. This group made at least two records for Lester Johnson's Way Out label, but without any success. Bass singer Bill Brent also saw the music world again

when in 1966 Moore brought him into the Drifters for about six months.
But the real legacy of the Hornets were the five sides they did for States.

The Danderliers

The Danderliers, with their typical Chicagoan soulful style of vocal harmonizing, rank as one of the best of the city's groups from the 1950s. With
two strong leads (Dallas Taylor on the jump and bluesy sides and James
Campbell on the romantic ballad sides), superb writing abilities, and excellent instrumental support (especially in the tenor saxophone work of Red
Holloway), the Danderliers were Leonard Allen's most compelling vocal
ensemble. They were also his most successful commercially, but given the
quality of the act, they should have been much bigger. Unfortunately for
the group, when they recorded for the States label, Leonard Allen's operation was already on the downside and incapable of pushing their records.[6]

The group began on the South Side in the Washington Park community
(one member, Bernard Dixon, says the youths lived between Sixtieth and
Sixty-eighth Streets and between Cottage Grove and South Parkway). When
originally formed, the members of the group attended two different high
schools. Dixon (first tenor), Taylor (tenor and lead), and Campbell (tenor
and lead) went to Chicago Vocational, and Richard Thomas (bass) and
Walter Stephenson (baritone) went to Englewood. Earlier, they had all attended the same grammar school.

The Danderliers had been singing only a few months before they were
"discovered" by United Records. Dixon said,

> We had been up there to United several times and had auditioned for
> them, but each time we had been turned down. And it was just this
> one day when we were in Washington Park, messing around with
> chords and stuff, that Smitty came by and saw us. I guess he was
> driving through the park and he heard us doing "Chop Chop Boom."
> The way that song got written, one day while we were rehearsing in
> the park, I had been doing "um chop chop boom, um chop chop
> boom," and Dallas said keep it going, and he had come in with the
> line, "Lord, lord, saw a man . . ." The song originated in the park,
> and as a matter of fact, we had just got it down, we were trying to
> make it perfect, when Smitty came by.[7]

The group was taken to Al Smith's basement where they rehearsed for
the recording, and not long after the Danderliers recorded their first sides.
The company released "My Autumn Love" backed with "Chop Chop
Boom" in March 1955. Both sides are superb, but the company thought
"My Autumn Love" would be the hit and made it the A side, and with good

reason. With Holloway's sax weaving throughout the group's nonsense-syllable refrain of a dozen "ho ahs," the record had all the marks of an instant classic. But the jocks instead began flipping the record for the catchy jump tune. "Chop Chop Boom" scored well enough to make the national charts in April, lasting three weeks and peaking at position ten on *Billboard*'s R&B survey.

Art Talmadge of Mercury was interested enough to have its best-selling vocal group, the Crewcuts, cover the record, and Allen was more than happy to give them the song to get the publishing royalties on it. Needless to say the Crewcuts' version easily outsold the Danderliers' original. As the writer, Taylor should have received a nice chunk of change for composing the song, but he didn't, and why he didn't is worth a digression into a long account by Allen:

> The record of course went pretty big. So then Smitty and I opened a tailor shop on Seventy-fifth Street. Smitty did the pressing and I did the tailoring. But I stayed in the record office all the time. Before "Chop Chop Boom" broke big, we had a meeting on the royalties situation. We used to rehearse groups in Al Smith's basement. And so Al says, "Allen, all you got to do is put me down as writer of the music." He said, "Then when the royalty come in we'll split it three ways." I said, "Sure Al, it's alright." So I told our secretary, Miss Harris, "Put Al's name down on every group we cut in the city as writer of the music." Later I remind Miss Harris, "You know Al Smith is writer of the music on 'Chop Chop Boom.'" So she says, "Ain't nobody the writer but Dallas Taylor." So I asked her why she didn't put Al's name down. She says she forgot. I know she lies. Smitty also told her to put his name there, but neither one had his name there.
>
> So Smitty went down to our publisher, Bud Brandom. Bud says to Smitty, "I tell you what, we better copyright this thing over again, because in about three or four years Art Talmadge is gonna claim it." So they copyright it over and Smitty just put his name down there as writer without me knowing it.
>
> The Danderliers called up and said, "Mr. Allen, what about our royalties?" I said to myself, oh, man, Smitty didn't say nothing about that. I'll see that he'll go down to Bud and get it. Then he went down there and came back with $1,100, take it or leave it. I say, "I'm not going to pay these four or five boys this little bit amount of money. I'm gonna go down to Bud and take an auditor in there." Smitty says, "Oh, man, don't do that, we might need Bud again." But the thing is, the sucker [Smitty] actually had two of them royalty checks. Bud wasn't cheating at all.

So I say, "How are you gonna pay them boys? One of them is a musician. He knows something about it. How are you gonna give them this?" Smitty says, "Well, we have a suit in there we made for a fellow, the man didn't come and get it, it's new. I'm gonna give it to Dallas!" I say, "I tell you what to do, buddy. When he comes, you take him out there, don't bring him in my office at all. I don't want to hear it. Close the door. I don't want to be in on it, screwing people like that, because it isn't right."

The Danderliers didn't like it, you know, so after a while they come again, hoping another check would come. I had called our accountant, "I want you to send me a copy of all the canceled checks that Smitty picked up." That's when I find out he's gotten two. So when the boys come in, I didn't tell them that. I don't think I even told Smitty.[8]

Today, the writer's credit on "Chop Chop Boom" shows "Taylor/Smith" even though Dallas Taylor was the sole writer of the song. The Danderliers' follow-up, later in 1955, was "My Loving Partner" backed with "Shu Wop," a pair of fine bluesy sides. According to Ralph Shurley who talked to Taylor for *Bim Bam Boom* magazine: "The title of 'Shu Wop' was originally intended to be 'New Way.' On the record the group backs Taylor with the line, 'Dally got a new way, Dally got a new way.' The record company [presumably Smitty, as its representative], asked, 'Dally got a new way to what?' After [he] found out, it was decided that 'New Way' was too suggestive, the title 'Shu Wop' was chosen."[9] The record, despite its excellence, did nothing.

After the first two releases, the Danderliers changed bass singers, replacing Richard Thomas with Louis Johnson. Dixon recalled,

At the time, Richard was trying to make us realize that things weren't right as far as the money situation was concerned. He was trying to get us to get some type of legal help and get them to look into the situation. We wouldn't go along with him, so he kind of started a little internal turmoil within the group. Richard was working, he was married at the time. He got married very young, at the age of sixteen. He had a job, a good job, and travel was interfering with his job. From that we came across Louie, what at the time was a better bass. He had a good voice, but as far as choreography was concerned, we had him just sit on the side and clap.[10]

The Danderliers' next release, in 1956, was a magnificent ballad, "May God Be with You," backed with a jump, "Little Man." The record seemingly failed to make any of the charts, but according to Eugene Record of the Chi-lites, "May God Be with You" was very big with teenagers in Chicago and he recalled the song with great fondness.

The group's last release, "My Love" backed with "She's Mine," in November 1956, was another fine effort. The ballad side, "My Love," might have had a different, more doowoppy sound if Allen, who supervised the session, had not interfered. On the master tapes, the group puts a lot of whoo-whoo-ing in the vocal mix, but after several bars Allen halts the take and yells at the group, "What's with this whoo whoo shit!" Thereafter, on subsequent takes, the Danderliers sing the song straight without any vocal background flourishes. Although "My Love" did well in Chicago, United Records simply lacked the ability to get the record off the ground nationally.

After "My Love" the Danderliers just faded away. They did some demos for Mercury, under an independent producer, but Mercury decided against using the songs. (The Danderliers at that time were still under contract to United, but Allen was not doing anything with them.) Eventually, some members went into the army and others drifted into other endeavors. Taylor became a member of an ad hoc group of Dells with Chuck Barksdale and Verne Allison on "Swinging Teens" backed with "Hold on to What You Got" in 1961 (there was a fourth member whose name no one can recall).

In 1967 Taylor got most of the Danderliers together to record "Walk on with Your Nose Up" backed with "All the Way" on George Leaner's Midas label. No one who hears the record would ever believe that this dreadful release was from the same group that recorded "Chop Chop Boom," "My Autumn Love," and "May God Be with You." James Campbell insisted that all the original members were on the record, but Bernard Dixon, for one, said he was away and in the army at the time. None of the Danderliers are still on the recording scene. Dallas Taylor passed away in 1986, and at his funeral some ex-members of the group got together to sing "May God Be with You."

The Danderliers made only eight sides for Leonard Allen, but none was less than good and most were exceptional. The group belongs in the pantheon of great R&B groups from Chicago.

The Moroccos

The Moroccos came out of the Englewood community on the South Side, the same area that produced the El Dorados and Dukays. The Moroccos got together around 1952, and like most neighborhood ensembles in their earliest days, they experienced an almost constant flux in personnel as guys floated in and out of the group. Eventually the Moroccos stabilized around Norman Bradford (lead), George Kemp (baritone), Fred Martin (bass),

Melvin Morrow (tenor), and Lawrence Johnson (tenor). The group worked
out mainly on mellow R&B and pop ballads.[11]

George Kemp, whose birth surname was Prayer but who used his step-
father's name as his stage name, generally acted as the group's spokesman
and leader. After more than a year of just messing around, the Moroccos
were perhaps more than ready to record. Prayer took the initiative in getting the group a session: "I had been over at Cottage Grove and Fifty-first
and had seen this record company, United," said Prayer. "So I go down to
United and I go and talk to Mr. Allen, and he said, 'Bring this group in and
I'll listen. I'm not promising you anything, but I'll listen.' I told the fellows, 'Hey, look, we got an appointment to talk to a man about a recording contract. I say let's go, let's try it.' So we went down there and he liked
us, and we got a contract."[12]

By this time Larry Johnson had already dropped out. (Years later
Johnson would become a member of an obscure seventies group, the Majestic Arrows.) In addition, just prior to the recording session for Leonard
Allen, Bradford had to make himself scarce in Chicago and joined the
armed services. At the last minute Prayer recruited Ralph Vernon, who was
then in another Englewood group.

The first session, in the fall of 1954, did not prove satisfactory. The
group, then calling itself the Four Chimes, did some average songs—"My
Easy Baby" and "When Was My Baby Born," the latter a reworking of the
old Negro religious folksong, "The Last Month of the Year." United shelved
the numbers, and Allen and the group agreed that what they needed was
not only a fifth member but also an additional lead.

The group got Sollie McElroy from the Flamingos as their new lead. As
Prayer reconstructed the event, "Our manager, Allen, knew the Flamingos'
manager. And at that time Sollie was having problems within the group.
They were trying to oust Sollie or something. Allen said to us, 'I know this
dude Sollie from the Flamingos; I'll have him come over.' Sollie showed
up. He was much older than us. We were kids, Sollie was a man. We were
all in the same age bracket, sixteen, seventeen, eighteen; Sollie was twen-
ty-something, you know. Anyway, that's how we got him, and we liked
him."

With McElroy as a member, the group went into session again in January 1955. One of the musicians in the studio had a set of maracas, which
inspired the group to adopt the name Moroccos. The first session yielded
a pretty ballad, "Pardon My Tears," and a dance tune, "Chicken," which
when paired became the Moroccos' first release. While the ballad is generally held in greater esteem by collectors, it was "Chicken" that got the
radio play. The record was not a hit but it did get the group noticed.

The next session, in May, produced the old Harold Arlen tune "Somewhere over the Rainbow" (led by McElroy), backed with a fine jump, "Red Hots and Chili Mac" (led by Vernon). Upon hearing the latter song one could almost taste the greasy dogs and spicy sauce. Released in October 1955, this record was a double-sided hit in Chicago and nationally it clicked on the ballad side. But the Moroccos could not exploit the record's popularity with live appearances, because some months earlier, on June 5, they had left for Australia.

The group had joined the famed Larry Steele's Smart Affairs road show, which during the 1950s was the preeminent black entertainment organization presenting a variety of black acts in one package tour. In Australia, the show billed itself as the Harlem Blackbirds. The Moroccos were chosen to audition for the road show at the Pershing Ballroom. Other Chicago groups such as the Sheppards, the Five Echoes, and the Pastels also tried out, but it was the Moroccos who got the contract, which should be indicative of the group's talent. Because Vernon was still attending high school, he was not permitted to make the trip.

Prayer said,

> We went truckin' off to Australia, bag in hand with nothing but hopes. And it was a hell of a show. There was Freddie and Flo, which was a comedy team . . . there was Pigmeat Markham . . . there was the Leonard and Leonard dancers, who did everything—African stuff, modern ballroom, tap, whatever. Peter Ray was a tap dancer . . . we had my man, Maurice Rocco, he was a pianist. That man could play piano. And there was Mabel Scott, who could sing anything. We went to stay eight weeks—it was an eight-week contract—and I think we stayed almost nine months. But it was an experience I'll never forget.

"We did a variety of songs," McElroy recalled. "I remember doing 'Money Honey,' also 'Unchained Melody,' which was done in such a way that we had a standing ovation. We did it practically a capella (we had a twenty-six-piece band backing us, but we didn't use all the instruments on this song.) We did another song, a spiritual called 'Go Down Moses.'"[13]

The Moroccos did not do any of their own R&B material, as McElroy explained: "The reasons we didn't do too many R&B numbers was because Australia was way behind the United States. If we did numbers that were current or popular in the United States, they would have no idea what we were singing. So we would do mainly things like what Nat King Cole would do."[14]

The Moroccos got back to Chicago in mid-February 1956 and resumed gigging around after Vernon rejoined the group. Prayer remembered playing at the Pershing Ballroom, the Trianon Ballroom, and the Club Delisa. Besides appearing in Chicago, the group also performed in Cleveland,

Cincinnati, Akron, and even at a roller rink in Madison, Wisconsin. The Moroccos shared bills with such groups as the Coasters, the Spaniels, the Flamingos, the Danderliers, and the Dells.

Sometime after the Moroccos' return, they recorded a session backing a singer called Lillian Brooks, on King Records. The handlers of Brooks had wanted to give her a vocal harmony background and got in touch with Allen, who in turn sent them the Moroccos. Although the group appreciated the gig, the session was not representative of the Moroccos. They did not care for the songs they were required to do.

In July the Moroccos had one more session with United. Some of the songs were written by Prayer, but shortly before the group was scheduled to go into the studio, he joined the marines. The Moroccos recruited a replacement, Calvin Baron. The session produced two releases for the group. The first paired Prayer's saccharine "What Is a Teenager's Prayer," in which McElroy gives a fine reading, with the excellent loping "Bang Goes My Heart." It came out in September, but as commercial as both songs were, neither made it. Prayer, however, remembered hearing the songs on the radio while walking his post on guard duty in California, so apparently the songs got some exposure.

The second release from the session and the last for United featured the lovely Prayer-penned "Sad Sad Hours," which had McElroy trading the lead with Vernon. The song was backed with "The Hex," a dreadful novelty jump. As with the previous release, the record had little sales action, but United was going down the tubes about this time and proved incapable of promoting and pushing the Moroccos.

The Moroccos did one other session, for Salem Records, which produced "Believe in Tomorrow," an obviously poor song. They then broke up, with Vernon and Martin following Prayer into the marines and Morrow later going into the army. Only McElroy and Baron immediately continued in the music business.

The Moroccos were not what one would call hitmakers, but they did make records that had some regional success. They also made some good songs. To a man, however, the group members felt they never got what they deserved, in recognition or in remuneration. To be fair, Prayer admitted that Allen was good to them in many ways and did give the group money out of his pocket. But Prayer, the group's fine songwriter, exclaimed when asked if he had ever got a royalty check, "A what? I have never seen a royalty check. What do they look like?"

Prayer also contended that where Allen was listed as songwriter on Moroccos' tunes, such as "Chicken," his own name belonged there. ("Allen didn't write nothing. He didn't know a C flat from a B flat.") There is confirmation of Prayer's claim. For example, on the original Moroccos' version of "What Is a Teenager's Prayer," Prayer's name is listed as composer, but on Joe Simon's 1966 hit version, Allen's name is there instead. Prayer recalled bitterly that when he heard the Simon song, "I say, man, somebody done did my tune. I got some money coming. And I went to check my stuff out, and I found out that Allen had copyrighted it in his name, and I couldn't collect a dime. And that's a song that helped make Joe Simon famous."

The most money the group made was the 150 dollars a week per member on their Australian tour. Many groups in the 1950s with bigger hits than the Moroccos failed to make even that minimal amount. The Moroccos, and especially Prayer, were undoubtedly burned, but probably no more than most groups of that era, sad to say.

The story of the ex-members of the Moroccos was mostly that of on-and-off careers in lesser ensembles. Near the end of the 1950s, Calvin Baron would join the Cosmic Rays, a doowop vocal group created and recorded by the avant-garde jazz artist Sun Ra. In the late 1960s Prayer and Morrow joined with the former El Dorados lead, Pirkle Lee Moses, to form the Major-Minors and put out an obscure record on the Scat label in Detroit. In 1970, when they recorded some tunes for Al Smith's Torrid label, Smith insisted on having their name changed to the recognizable El Dorados name. Shortly afterward the group broke up, but during the 1980s Moses and Prayer were part of yet another El Dorados revival group. Morrow died in 1982; Prayer, in 1992.

McElroy also continued intermittently in the music business. He had a brief association in the early 1960s with the Chaunteurs (a pre–Chi-lites Eugene Record group) and with the Nobles. Around 1982 McElroy joined with Larry Johnson (an original member of the Moroccos), Fred Martin, and Richard Nickens, a former El Dorados member, to form a new Moroccos group. No recording career developed and infrequent gigs paid poorly, so when Martin died in 1986, the group broke up. Johnson later joined a revived El Dorados group. McElroy retired from singing, and in 1995 he died.

Whatever their subsequent activities were or might have been, however, the original Moroccos need not have done anything else, for their legacy of fine music recorded during their early career was sufficient to establish their name in the annals of rhythm and blues.

The Pastels

The Pastels of this story are a Chicago group who have no relationship to an East Coast group of the same name who hit with "Been So Long" and "So Far Away." The Chicago Pastels were an earlier group who made one record for the United label in 1956. The sides were in the El Dorados style and did not make much of an impact upon their release, but their unreleased practice tapes reveal that the Pastels had a sound that could have taken them far. Why they never went far is the subject of this story.[15]

Fred Buckley, the group's first lead, organized the Pastels from among high school friends in his South Side neighborhood. The other members were Charles McKnight (baritone), Vernon Thomas (first tenor), Trey Clark (second tenor), and Pettis Williams (bass). Thomas, Clark, and Williams eventually dropped out of the group, and after a number of personnel changes, Norman Palm (first tenor), Robert Randolph (second tenor), and Charles Williams (bass and brother of Pettis) rounded out the group in its final form. The members all attended South Side high schools—McKnight and Randolph went to Corpus Christi; Williams, Hyde Park; Palm, Phillips; and Buckley, St. Elizabeth.

The Pastels auditioned at several local companies, including United, and were turned down. Their break came through Leona Lee, a teacher at McKnight's school. After school she worked in a recreation center, and one day she held auditions there to find a group she could manage. McKnight said, "She called some girls in for critics. So we do a couple of songs, and they got up and danced, and showed Miss Lee that they liked what we were doing. She stopped us halfway through a song and said she didn't have to hear anymore. Then she said if you sign with me I'll guarantee you that within a week's time you will have a recording contract. And so she did just that."[16]

McKnight said further, "We signed up with United and States, Mr. Allen. He put us on the United label. Within a week of our signing a contract, we had cut some songs." That was in October 1955, and the songs were "Bye Bye" and "Goodbye." Both songs were fairly good but the company for some reason chose not to release them. A month later the Pastels were recording again, putting on wax an average ballad, "Put Your Arms around Me," with a bouncy El Dorados–type jump tune, "Boom De De Boom." The latter song was originally intended for the El Dorados to record, but the group was out of town when the person who brought it arrived from New York, so he took it to United.

"Boom De De Boom" got its original airplay on local station WHFC, but then listener requests pushed "Put Your Arms around Me" on the playlist. Off the record, the group developed a considerable local reputation. Some of the venues they played included Club Delisa, Cotton Club, Casino, Park City Bowl, and Trianon Ballroom, all in Chicago. At Barbara's Playhouse, in Gary, Indiana, the group did a show with the Dells, the Spaniels, and a number of other groups.

After about a year, Buckley was replaced on lead by Julius Collins.

"Miss Lee heard Julius Collins sing," said McKnight, "and his voice was so clear and beautiful that she thought he ought to sing lead on our next recording. Everybody agreed and one evening at rehearsal we told Fred, and he accepted. He didn't like it too well, but what could he do. He was out. Leonard Allen went along with whatever Miss Lee said."

Judging from the practice tapes I've heard, Collins was some prize. The group was tremendous in their backup harmony work as well. The tapes are truly remarkable, but what is even more remarkable is that this new ensemble was never able to prove its worth to the public. The Pastels' only legacy was their one average release on United.

The group was ended because Miss Lee's possessive husband did not want his wife managing anymore. McKnight said, "He said to us, 'You'll gonna have to find yourselves another manager, and I'll tell you why, because it's breaking up our marriage. You're taking her away from me too much.'" Since Allen had been dealing with the Pastels through Miss Lee, her exit finished the group's recording career.

The Pastels continued on a few more years. They got a new lead, Claude McCrae, who surfaced some years later as lead for the Dukays. Also, their bass, Charles Williams, left the group to be replaced by Jerry Mills. The group, however, never was able to get another recording contract and, disgusted, they broke up around 1958.

Most of the Pastels did not continue in music. McKnight, however, served for many years as a gospel soloist for a traveling Pentecostal minister. Palm joined the Crystals, who recorded "Ring a Ring a Do" and "Left Front Row" for Delano Records, and in 1966 he penned a local hit for Evonne Gomez, "Ease the Pain." During the 1970s, 1980s, and 1990s Palm was part of a revived El Dorados oldies group.

The Sheppards

The Sheppards, who recorded for United and Theron in the mid-fifties, should not be confused with the later, more famous group that appeared on Apex and Vee Jay. Both groups, it is true, were namesakes of the same manager, Bill "Bunky" Sheppard, but each had a different history and personnel. The United/Theron Sheppards never achieved even a modicum of fame during their few years of existence, but like most quintessential streetcorner groups they established a considerable reputation at the local level. In the collector community, their records are highly prized and have been counterfeited.[17]

The group as originally formed was known as the Cavaliers. They got together in late 1953 and were organized by Andre Williams (who later won renown for his novelty numbers "Bacon Fat" and "Jail Bait" and for his work as a producer). The Flamingos, just off the success of "Golden Tear-drops," were big stars around this time and were having a profound influence in helping to generate a flourishing street-corner vocal group scene in Chicago. Williams formed the Cavaliers with the specific intent of patterning them after this famous group. A Detroit native, Williams was officially in the navy at this time, but as one of the former Sheppards put it, "he had gone over the hill and stayed away."[18] The rest of the group came out of DuSable and Tilden Tech high schools on the South Side and consisted of John Pruitt (first tenor and lead), Albert "Pee Wee" Bell (baritone), Nathaniel Tucker (bass), and James Dennis "Brother" Isaac (second tenor and lead). Williams sang baritone, but his principal contribution was to devise various choreographed routines for the group. He was considered the group's "clown."

The Cavaliers regularly got together at the corner of Fifty-second and Indiana to rehearse and to compete against other vocal groups. They sang Flamingos and Drifters hits and such songs as "Have Mercy Baby," made famous by the Dominoes, and "Crazy Crazy Crazy," as recorded by the Five Royales. This went on for more than a year, and then Williams left the group. He was replaced by Oscar Robinson, a baritone. Robinson had come out of another Chicago ensemble, the Five Thrills, who had already recorded for Parrot, cutting "Feel So Good" backed with "My Baby's Gone." Robinson, who had sung lead on "My Baby's Gone," brought some needed experience to the group and he was expected to help them in working out their harmony.

By 1955 the Cavaliers had graduated from being street-corner harmonizers to being real professionals. They were playing teenage hops and such clubs as Martin's Corner, Joe's Deluxe Club, the State Lounge, and the Trianon Ballroom. Eventually a relationship with the pianist Earl Washington and the independent producer Bill Sheppard was established. Then Albert Bell and Oscar Robinson were replaced with George "Sonny" Parker and Oscar Boyd, respectively, and the Sheppards were born. In 1955 they put out "Love" backed with "Cool Mambo" on Connie Toole's Theron label. "Love" featured Pruitt (lead), Isaac (first tenor), Tucker (bass), Parker (baritone), and Boyd (second tenor), while "Mambo," with the same personnel, had Parker on lead.

"Love" flopped, but a second opportunity for the Sheppards came in February 1956, when they recorded "Mozelle" and "Sherry" for United. Since the group's first session for Theron, Parker, who had gone in the service, was replaced with Kent McGhee. As it turned out, however, Parker was given leave by the army and participated at the last minute in the "Mozelle" recording. The personnel on "Mozelle" were Parker (first lead), Pruitt (second lead), Isaac (first tenor), Tucker (bass), McGhee (baritone), and Boyd (second tenor). On "Sherry" there were Isaac (lead), Pruitt (first tenor), Tucker (bass), McGhee (baritone), and Boyd (second tenor).

"Mozelle" garnered considerable local radio play, so the group enjoyed a degree of celebrity in the Midwest. "Sherry," which sounds equal if not better to contemporary ears, got only a few plays. The Sheppards translated their recording success, such as it was, into an engagement at Club Delisa. They also parlayed a tour from the songs, playing numerous cities in Indiana, Ohio, Kentucky, and Tennessee with a group of chorus girls and the blues singer Tiny Topsy.

Two other songs at the "Mozelle" session were recorded but not released. They were two aggressive jump tunes, "Pretty Little Girl" and "Just Let Me Love You," the latter featuring a marvelous sax break by Tommy Badger. Also in the group's catalog of unreleased numbers were "You're the Cream of My Coffee" and "Devil Eyes," the latter an undistinguished Latin-sounding jump blues. These were produced independently by Bill Sheppard.

Around 1957, after Pruitt and Tucker were drafted and Boyd dropped out because he was going blind from a cataract condition, the Sheppards broke up. Isaac eventually drifted into another South Side group called the Bel Aires, a group that did one record and then was forced to split. Three of the Bel Aires, including Isaac, then became a part of yet another group, in 1959. The group? It was the Sheppards, of "Island of Love" fame.

The Palms

The Palms were one of those unheralded groups that had a lot of talent but never truly received the opportunity to shine. They came out of the West Side and attended Creiger and Crane high schools. Members of the Palms were Wilbur Williams (lead), Willie Young (tenor), M. C. Ward (bass), O. C. Perkins (second tenor), and Murrie Eskridge (first tenor and sometime lead). Perkins, or "Perk," was the group's songwriter, and a talented one at that, so the Palms did not lack original material when they finally recorded.[19]

Reminiscing about how the group's recording break came about, Perkins said,

We used to play talent shows. They used to have a lot of talent shows around town. One night we happened to go out to Phoenix [a suburb south of Chicago]. We went out to a little club they called the White Room. One guy by the name of Bob heard us. He was scouting people to record but was unaffiliated with anyone. He was just doing it on his own free time. He happened to know people who were involved in recording companies, such as Chess and Vee Jay, when these people were all down south by Forty-seventh and Cottage Grove. So he and Al Benson were down there. So Benson got us a session to do background on a lady by the name of Lou Mac on his Blue Lake label. She did a tune called "Slow Down," and that was our first recording, just background work.[20]

Record collector fans of jump rhythm and blues stylings should not pass up "Slow Down." It is a gem, as is the flip, a superb urban blues that does not feature the Palms. The record was released in the summer of 1955 and got a few plays.

Perkins continued, "Then we started to write a little stuff and go around on Saturdays to record companies and audition. They would listen to you and tell you if you had it. So we stopped by United and there was Mr. Smith [Smitty]. He told us to come back next Saturday. And when we came back, Allen was there. We sang and they both said they liked our stuff. Then we recorded. They took a little time in doing it, but they did it. Anyway, that's how we got started."

The Palms had only two releases with Allen—"Edna" backed with "Teardrops" on United, and "Little Girl of Mine" backed with "Teardrops," which they recorded as the Five Palms on States. Both were released in early 1957, and despite some local airplay neither made it even as a local hit. The songs were not especially remarkable, and that was part of the problem. There was excellent material in the can, as I have heard, notably "Dianne," the one song that the group had hoped the company would release. It wasn't, and as Perkins explained, "the company was all wrapped up in the Danderliers." A more compelling explanation would be that the company was in the process of going out of business in 1957, undercutting the development of the Palms' career.

Leonard Allen was less interested in his own artists and more in getting ready cash. He sold "Little Girl of Mine" (or "Girl of Mine") to Mercury, which had the Diamonds record it on their 1957 album *America's Number One Song Stylists*. There were four Palms songs in the can, all better than the released sides, that never saw the light of day.

The Palms broke up and evolved into the Ballads, whose members were Perkins and Eskridge, O. C. Logan, Willie Logan, and Kermit Chandler. In late 1958 the Logan brothers left the group and the remaining three Ballads joined three members of the Bel Aires (of "My Yearbook" fame) to form the famous Sheppards (of "Island of Love" fame).

The Palms were a strong group at United, judging from their unreleased sides, but with two poorly distributed releases to their credit the opportunity to succeed was just not there. That two members eventually became a part of the excellent Sheppards group is indicative that there was plenty of talent in the Palms.

*   *   *

The group sides recorded by United are distinguished both by their quality and by their obscurity. Allen used the best session musicians, recorded
at the finest facilities (namely Universal Recording), got the most talented
groups, and used great production sense, yet he had few hits. The company was going downhill in 1955 but took a while to die, not reaching the
end until 1957. This was when the rock 'n' roll revolution was going full
throttle, and thus United was ineffective in properly exploiting its groups
as rock 'n' roll stars. The Danderliers, and perhaps the Moroccos and the
Palms, had what it took in the late 1950s to become a part of the rock 'n'
roll revolution, but their company did not.

Notes

1. Information about the United/States label complex comes from Grendysa,
"The United and State Labels"; Pruter and O'Neal, "Leonard Allen"; and the Allen
interviews.
2. Virtually nothing is known about the Five Cs. From late 1953 to late 1954
there were occasional mentions of the group in the Gary, Indiana, edition of the
Chicago Defender.
3. "Nite Beat," *Chicago Defender,* December 12, 1953.
4. Many collectors who pay thousands of dollars for records do not want their
names and dealings publicized. The collector in this case is known to me, but he
requests that his name be kept confidential. The lack of certainty about the price
of the record is due to the nature of such nonpublic transactions.
5. Information about the Hornets comes from Pruter and Goldberg, "The Hornets," and the Moore interview.
6. Information about the Danderliers comes from Pruter, "Danderliers Define";
S[h]urley, "The Danderliers"; Dixon interview; Allen interview, 1976.
7. Dixon interview.
8. Allen interview, 1976.
9. S[h]urley, "The Danderliers."
10. Dixon interview.
11. Moroccos sources include: Pruter, "Moroccos Career"; Sbarbori, "Sollie
McElroy"; and the Morrow, Prayer, Johnson, and McElroy interviews.
12. This and subsequent remarks by Prayer that are quoted in this chapter are
from the Prayer interview.
13. McElroy interview.
14. Ibid.
15. Information about the Pastels comes from Goldberg and Whitesell, "Fred
Buckley"; Pruter, "Pastels' Promise"; and the McKnight and Palm interviews.
16. This and subsequent remarks by McKnight that are quoted in this chapter
are from the McKnight Interview.

17. Information about the Sheppards I comes from Pruter, "Chicago's 'First'";
Bell, Isaac, Pruitt, and Tucker interviews.

18. Isaac interview, February 18, 1978.

19. Information about the Palms comes from Pruter, "Palms Undercut," and the
Perkins interviews.

20. This and subsequent remarks by Perkins that are quoted in this chapter are
from the Perkins interview, October 24, 1977.

5

Vee Jay Records

Vee Jay was one of Chicago's most successful labels, and until the advent of Motown during the early 1960s it was the country's largest black-owned record company. Four individuals were most responsible for the success of the label—James Bracken and Vivian Carter, who founded the company in mid-1953; Vivian's brother, Calvin Carter, who was the principal producer and A&R man; and Ewart Abner Jr., who, starting in December 1954, was the company's chief administrator.[1]

Bracken was born in Oklahoma on May 23, 1909; grew up in Kansas City, Kansas; and attended Western University in Quindaro, Kansas. He was living in Chicago when he met Vivian Carter in 1944, when she was working in the Signal Corps in the city. Carter had been born in Tunica, Mississippi, in 1920 and moved to Gary, Indiana, as a little girl. She graduated from Roosevelt High in 1939. In 1948, in Chicago, she won a talent contest for new deejays conducted by Al Benson of WGES. She worked three months at WGES and then moved to WJOB in her hometown of Gary. Carter and Bracken became business partners in 1950 when they founded Vivian's Record Shop in Gary. After three years of saving their money, in summer 1953 the couple decided to start a record label. Meanwhile, Vivian continued her deejaying in Gary, joining WGRY in 1952 and moving to WWCA in 1954, which was undoubtedly a significant factor in attracting talent to their label.

At this time two acts, a vocal group called the Spaniels and a blues singer by the name of Jimmy Reed, inquired at the store about recording opportunities. Both acts were to become two of Vee Jay's biggest recording stars during the 1950s. James and Vivian set up headquarters at the record shop, at 1640 Broadway. Since the couple was already tied by business interests, on December 16 they got married in the headquarters of Ernie and George

Leaner's United Distributors. In early 1954 the Brackens would move Vee Jay's headquarters to Forty-seventh Street in Chicago.

The first Spaniels and Reed records were released in the summer of 1953 and became strong local hits. The company was firmly established following the March 1954 release of the Spaniels' third single, "Goodnite Sweetheart, Goodnite," which became a top R&B hit and, as covered by the McGuire Sisters, a million seller.

Ewart Abner entered Vee Jay through his executive position at Art Sheridan's Chance Records. Vee Jay was experiencing explosive growth, and Sheridan and Abner were gradually becoming closely involved with the Brackens, helping them to run the company. In December 1954, Sheridan decided to close Chance. Ewart was appointed by the Brackens as general manager of Vee Jay, and eventually he was given a share of the company.[2] One of the musicians at Vee Jay, Red Holloway, said,

> Abner's role in Chance had been as administrator. In fact, he learned his tools of trade at Chance Record Company, he learned the business there. Vivian and Jimmy didn't really know all that much about business things when it got into the real paperwork, so since Abner had been doing that at Chance, they just made a deal with him and he went over there. Abner became pretty much the boss. Jimmy and Vivian still called the shots, because they owned the label, but when it came to the final details of making deals and stuff, that's where Abner was boss, because he knew more about it and had more insight into what was happening.[3]

Calvin Carter (born May 27, 1925) became the label's A&R man and principal producer. His first experience in the record business was when he joined his sister's and brother-in-law's firm in 1953. He found he was a natural for the business. By 1955, the Vee Jay house band had been established. The rhythm section usually included Lefty Bates (guitar), Quinn B. Wilson (bass), Paul Gusman and Al Duncan (drums), and Horace Palm (piano). Bates, who led the sessions, began his career in the mid-1940s as a member of the Hi De Ho Boys, a string quartet that played the Club Delisa. Around 1951 he formed the Lefty Bates Trio with Wilson and Palm in order to play the local clubs. The trio played regularly in the clubs throughout most of the 1950s while working sessions at Vee Jay.

The brass section usually included Red Holloway and Lucius Washington (tenor saxes), Vernel Fournier and McKinley "Mac" Easton (baritone saxes), and Harlan "Booby" Floyd (trombone). Al Smith was the band leader and was in charge of rehearsing and preparing Vee Jay acts for recording sessions. While Carter was nominally the producer, there was often a collective approach in producing the sessions. Said Holloway:

Calvin Carter was in charge of the recording sessions. Calvin was a singer, and when we recorded singers he would be saying things like, "Hey, you all didn't sing the do-do-wop right," or "you're out of tune with this one." When it came to the musicians' parts, certain fellows in the band, usually Lefty and I, would listen to the playback and take it upon ourselves to say, "let's take that over," or "you're not doing this or that," or "hey, that's not right, let's straighten that up." We in the band basically directed our part of it. When it came to vocals, though, Calvin Carter would do that. He had a good idea of what harmonies were supposed to sound like. Abner would come around to the sessions every once in a while, but he didn't usually have much to say. Musically, Abner wasn't that sharp, but he was good at making deals and doing things administratively.[4]

For its recording sessions, Vee Jay went to Universal Recording on the near North Side. As Pirkle Lee Moses noted, "Vee Jay always used Universal Studios—that's the way they did it—in three hour or six hour sessions. They would rent the studio for half of a day and they would cut maybe two or three artists."[5]

Abner formed Vee Jay's first subsidiary label, Falcon (which later changed its named to Abner), in 1957. Two years later he established the company's jazz line with such artists as Wynton Kelly, Wayne Shorter, Eddie Harris, and Lee Morgan. Early on, Vee Jay became involved in gospel music and recorded many of the top acts in the field, notably the Staple Singers, the Swan Silvertones, the Harmonizing Four, and the Highway QCs.

It was with the doowop groups and the blues singers that Vee Jay established itself as a hitmaker in the industry, however, and it was for the doowop groups that Vee Jay was first known as a producer of rock 'n' roll hits. The biggest groups on the label were the Spaniels, the El Dorados, and the Dells, but the label could boast of a host of lesser names, principally the Magnificents, the Kool Gents, the Prodigals, and the Rhythm Aces. Many group records released by Vee Jay were leased product from other parts of the country and not part of the Vee Jay story. These acts included the Hi-liters, Sherrif and the Ravels, and the Infatuators.

The Spaniels

The Spaniels are universally recognized by R&B fans as one of the great vocal harmony groups of the 1950s. They harmonized with superb tightness and expertise, and—unlike many fifties groups—they received fine, crisp production from their record company. Most remarkable was the group's lead vocalist, James "Pookie" Hudson. With his smooth tenor and just a touch of vibrato, Hudson ranks as one of the outstanding voices of the 1950s, along with Clyde McPhatter, Sam Cooke, and Willie Winfield (of the Harptones). If one were to describe tenors as either sweet or dry, one could say Hudson's was semisweet. Then there was the Spaniels' outstanding bass, Gerald Gregory, whose low-register vocalizing out front mimicked magnificently the sounds of the saxophone, and in the background provided a solid bottom. Surrounding the lead were the two tenors and the baritone; with a restrained falsetto top that comes from the diaphragm and not the nose, they created the classic Spaniels harmony sound. Their marvelous riffing both enhanced and ennobled the work of Hudson as well as Gregory. What the Spaniels did with a song lifted them from the level of fine craftsmen to the level of exceptional artists.

With deep feeling, the Spaniels managed to evoke the emotions and sensibilities of youth growing to adulthood in the fifties. Listening to the classic balladry of "Goodnite Sweetheart, Goodnite," the spiritualized sound of "You Gave Me Peace of Mind," the joyous rapture of "Everybody's Laughing," and the lilting Latin-beat of "I Know," one feels transported to that decade, to a basement party. The lights are dimmed, and you are dancing with your girl, closely. It is two o'clock in the morning and the Spaniels are closing the by-now quiet party as Pookie gently croons, "goodnight sweetheart, it's time to go . . ."[6]

The Spaniels were one of the earliest of the street-corner groups and hailed from Gary, Indiana, where they all attended Roosevelt High. The group was formed for the purpose of performing in a school talent show around Christmas 1952. Besides lead singer Hudson and bass singer Gregory, the other members were Willis C. Jackson (baritone), Opal Courtney (baritone), and Ernest Warren (first tenor). In an era of bird-named groups, the Spaniels' name was a bit different. Hudson told Alan Lee of *Yesterday's Memories* how the group got its name: "At one time our group was called Pookie Hudson and the Hudsonnaires, but I really did not like that. While we were thinking of a new name, Gerald Gregory's wife told us that we sounded like a bunch of dogs, so we named ourselves the Spaniels."[7]

The Spaniels auditioned at Vivian's Record Shop in the early spring of 1953 and within a matter of weeks were being recorded by the neophyte owners of Vee Jay. In this first session, in May, when the group was less than six months old, the Spaniels proved remarkably adept. The session yielded their delightful minor hit "Baby It's You." The record was Vee Jay's second release, but it proved too potent for the tiny company to handle it. Carter and Bracken leased the record to Chance Records for national distribution and it was on Chance that the record was heard throughout most of the country. In the fall of 1953, "Baby It's You" lasted two weeks on

Billboard's R&B chart and went to number ten. Both the Vee Jay and Chance discs are highly sought-after collector's items.

"Baby It's You" made the Spaniels a nationally known act, and in October the group signed with the Shaw Agency. Soon the bookings poured in. But before the first national engagements, the Spaniels played a few local venues; their first professional performance was at the Park City Bowl on Chicago's South Side. Before 1953 was out, the Spaniels also recorded a collector's favorite, "The Bells Ring Out," and what has become the group's signature tune and their biggest hit, "Goodnite Sweetheart, Goodnite." "The Bells Ring Out," pleasing to the record collector today, did nothing upon its release in November.

On the other hand, "Goodnite Sweetheart, Goodnite" swept the nation in the spring of 1954. The song lasted sixteen weeks on the *Billboard* R&B chart and went to number five. Considering the year, when it was extremely unusual for an R&B-oriented black act to make the pop charts, the song's pop success was remarkable, going to number twenty-four. But most radio stations and deejays playing pop music in 1954 were not quite ready to play a black-sounding record, and the McGuire Sisters, with their obviously whiter-sounding cover, garnered most of the pop air play and chart action. As Hudson pointed out, "White stations didn't play black records then. They played white artists, and we were limited to the black audience. And then there were only so many black radio stations. There are a lot of people who are under the impression that the McGuire Sisters first recorded 'Goodnite Sweetheart, Goodnite.' They never heard of the Spaniels."[8]

Decades later, the Spaniels' version is the one that gets the greater percentage of the radio play as a golden oldie. For good reason, the Spaniels' way with the song reflected a genuine and heartfelt involvement that was not so evident in the McGuires' rendition. Hudson said, "I used to have a girlfriend and used to go to her house. But you know you always have to be home at a certain time, so I was walking home one night from her house thinking about her and just put the song together in my head." Ironically, the group originally did not want to record the song, feeling slightly embarrassed by its street origin. "We thought it sounded dumb," confessed Hudson, "like someone singing on the corner, kinda childish. The company made us do it."[9]

In August 1954 the Spaniels began a big one-nighter package tour of the East, Midwest, South, and Southwest with Roy Hamilton, the Drifters, the Counts, Faye Adams, LaVern Baker, King Pleasure, the Erskine Hawkins Orchestra, and the Rusty Bryant Orchestra. The package was called the Rhythm and Blues Show and was put together by the Gale Agency. This tour was highly instrumental in helping to break rhythm and blues into the white market as rock 'n' roll music. The tour opened in Cleveland, where the show was promoted by Alan Freed. It pulled 9,400 fans, an impressive number at the time. Detroit, for example, attracted only 4,800 ticket buyers. The package swung east in September and played the Brooklyn Paramount, where the trades noted the mixed, white and black crowds.

Touring the South was an eye-opening experience for the group, and the crowds were decidedly less mixed. Courtney told the *Post-Tribune* writer Mark Taylor: "It was rough in the '50s. We can laugh now, but it was hard. We were pulled over and arrested in little towns in the South and thrown in jails no bigger than this room, just for being the wrong color. A couple times we even had to sing for state troopers."[10]

October 1954 saw the release of one of Hudson's favorite numbers, "Let's Make Up," a favorite became it had the same sort of genuineness as "Goodnite Sweetheart, Goodnite." He said, "It reminds me of the time of going with girlfriends and breaking up, and at the time I wrote it from that sort of situation. That is why I like it."[11] Perhaps Hudson also felt fondness for the tune because it provided him with his first substantial royalties when it appeared on the flip side of "The Ballad of Davy Crockett," on the Voices of Walter Schumann RCA release.

The flip on "Let's Make Up" was a terrific bluesy novelty featuring the rough-hewn voice of Willis C. Jackson. Using the brand names of two vices—booze and tobacco—Jackson goes through the lyrics while the group exuberantly moans vocal riffs in the background. In Chicago, "Play It Cool" became one of the most frequently played of the Spaniels' oldies, partly because it served as a standard accompaniment to a popular dance in the city called the Walk. The same session that produced "Let's Make Up" and "Play It Cool" also resulted in a fine rendition of "Danny Boy," a song that was a natural for the group. Vee Jay never released it, however, and it appeared on a reissue album in 1984.

The Spaniels played no big package tours in 1955, but they did appear at such venues as the Masonic Hall in St. Louis and the Orchid Room in Kansas City. A release in April of that year was "Don'cha Go," one of the group's less-inspiring efforts. The public was not very inspired to buy it. However, "You Painted Pictures" was an outstanding release in August, when for one week it made number thirteen on *Billboard*'s R&B chart. It should have done a lot better. Things were not going well for the Spaniels, so it was not surprising that the group began falling apart before the end of the year.

Opal Courtney was the first to leave when he quit to finish high school. Calvin Carter filled in on baritone for a few months before a permanent replacement was found in James "Dimples" Cochran. Then Ernest Warren was drafted into the military. No replacement was found for Warren, so the next session, in late 1955—in which the Spaniels recorded two low-key ballads, "Dear Heart" and "False Love"—featured only four voices.

Vee Jay made the truncated Spaniels a part of a package tour, the Cavalcade of Vee Jay Stars, in early 1956. With the El Dorados, Jimmy Reed, Joe Buckner, and Tommy Dean's Orchestra, the tour package followed an eight-week stint at the Trianon Ballroom in Chicago with appearances in Milwaukee, Dallas, Seattle, and other West Coast cities. While touring, the Spaniels pushed their latest releases, "False Love" and "Dear Heart," without much success. At the end of the tour, with record sales slow, the irreplaceable Hudson left, along with Willis C. Jackson. The group was kept going by Gerald Gregory and James Cochran, who proceeded to add second tenor Don Porter and Carl Rainge.

Since Hudson was unavailable to record, the company next put out an old song from the can. For its July 1956 release it chose "Since I Fell for You," an evergreen the Spaniels' had remade in 1953. As one could expect of a song recorded that early, this version had what collectors call a "deep" sound (very R&Bish and not at all poplike). Most peculiar is the way Hudson's lead is echoed by Willis C. Jackson, who talks each line with a bluesy slant. Some listeners interpret this call-and-response routine as being tongue in cheek, but others find it more irritating than anything.

In late 1956 Hudson rejoined the Spaniels, whose members now included an old member, Gerald Gregory (bass), and the three new members, James "Dimples" Cochran (baritone), Carl Rainge (first tenor), and Don Porter (second tenor). The group appeared on a big Christmastime Regal show on December 24 with Muddy Waters, the Kool Gents, and Al Smith's Orchestra.

The Spaniels proved to have lost none of their recording magic with their December 1956 release of "You Gave Me Peace of Mind," a tremendously moving and gospel-like ballad. The song is thoroughly doowop in its vocal conventions, yet it is deeply infused with that intangible quality called "soul," which rests in Hudson's heartfelt lead that's counterpointed magnificently by the high tenor–topped chorusing of the other members. Despite its lack of chart success at the time, the song is fondly recalled in Chicago, where it was played on oldies shows years afterward.

"You Gave Me Peace of Mind" was a superb exhibit of the vocal talents of the new group of background singers. Hudson was very fond of both groups and explained their differences to the group's historian, Richard Carter:

> The first group was a feelin' group. We felt our way through the harmonies, we felt our way through the songs and things and basically, we sang straight from the heart. The second group was more technical. They sang parts, everybody stayed on their part. I mean, they sang correctly, what can I say, and they were soulful. They had more vo-

cal talent, they were more harmony-oriented. The imagination wasn't there, but they didn't have to have as much imagination. All they had to do was the vocal truth. Whereas the first group, everything we did was through imagination.[12]

There was no letup in the spring when the new Spaniels recorded the delightful Latin-beat gem "Everyone's Laughing," which reached the lower rungs of the pop charts in June 1957. On the *Billboard* R&B chart it reached number thirteen and lasted two weeks. "You're Gonna Cry," released in August 1957, was another standout, but it was the jump side, "I Need Your Kisses," that got the big airplay, in Chicago anyway. Tour stops in 1957 included Chicago's Grand Ballroom, Civic Opera House, and Regal in April; Philadelphia's Liberty Theater in May; the Apollo in July; and the Regal again in August. Also in August the group went on a Gale Agency tour to Oklahoma.

"Crazee Babee" backed with "I Lost You" was released at the end of December with the expectation that the jump "Crazee Babee" would be the hit. However, it was the marvelous ballad, "I Lost You," that slowly gained favor, and it was the song the group sang when it appeared on Dick Clark's "American Bandstand" in March. "I Lost You" demonstrates perfectly how deep pain and emotion can be conveyed by subtle nuances in singing without resorting to histrionics and overemoting, tactics that were so fashionable during the soul era. The record has come down today as one of the Spaniels' classic releases.

The spring of 1958 saw the release of the song "Tina," a pleasing Latin-styled up-tempo number that lacked *gravitas*. Its flip was "Great Googley Moo," a jump that decades later would find favor with British fans of vocal groups. In the late summer, the Spaniels came out with "Stormy Weather," a smooth, excellent remake of the Harold Arlen standard. The flip, "Here Is Why I Love You," was particularly noteworthy. In it, the interplay of Gregory's bass, Pookie's romantic lead, and the haunting harmonies (the harmonies that one hears from deep down) is especially effective. The song remains one of the unheralded masterpieces in the group's song catalog. In December the group came out with a great rendition of "Heart and Soul," featuring Gregory as lead. The presumed A side was a remake of "Baby It's You," which did not improve on the original. Despite the quality of the 1958 songs, the Spaniels were getting few sales and their future looked bleak. But there was no letup in the touring, with the group playing on the eastern seaboard in March of that year.

The first release of 1959 was a lovely ballad rendition of the Joyce Kilmer poem "Trees," but it failed to excite the public. Having no national chart record since "Everyone's Laughing," in the summer of 1957, the

Spaniels saw concert engagements dry up by early 1959. The days of play-
ing on the chitlin' theater circuit appeared to be gone. For example, the
Spaniels were playing in May 1959 at an obscure Chicago club called the
Del Morocco, co-billed with "Afro Cuban" dancer Lola Lady Day and
Rickey "Hi Hi" Brown.

After one more session in 1959, the Spaniels disbanded. But what a
wonderful session it was, yielding a bunch of great songs, notably a September pairing of "These Three Words" and "100 Years from Today," and
a November release of "People Will Say We're in Love" (paired with "The
Bells Ring Out" from 1953). None of these songs became hits, but all were
fine examples of the Spaniels at their best. The most masterful song from
the session for many collectors was the group's rendition of "Red Sails in
the Sunset." The song appeared only on a Vee Jay anthology album from
1962 called *Unavailable 16*.

In 1960, Hudson and Gregory decided to give the Spaniels another
chance and got together with Andy Magruder, Billy Carey, Ernest Warren
(from the original group), and guitarist Pete Simmons to form a new ensemble. (Magruder, incidentally, had a long history in vocal harmony, having been a member of the Five Blue Notes on Sabre, a Chance subsidiary.)
The single session produced one of their all-time bests, "I Know," which
featured a light Latin-beat, dubbed "chalypso," typical of many R&B tunes
of the day. The song lasted six weeks and went to number twenty-three on
Billboard's R&B chart, and Vee Jay put out the group's second LP. Other
fine songs by this third group of Spaniels included "So Deep Within," featuring Gregory in the lead, and "Bus Fare Home," featuring the duet lead
of Hudson and Magruder. These songs appeared on the outstanding second LP, which included many of their past standouts, such as "I Lost You,"
"100 Years from Today," and "Everyone's Laughing." The Spaniels left Vee
Jay in 1961 and never again recorded a record equal to any of their 1950s
output.

The El Dorados (I)

One of the most significant vocal groups to come out of Chicago in the
1950s was the El Dorados, who sang the street-corner harmonies of the day
with a magical, soulful feeling that simply overwhelms one's emotional
circuits. They created a genuine folk art by composing songs that were in
tune to the rock 'n' roll revolution. As in any R&B form, the presumed
audience was a black one, but in the early days of rock 'n' roll the music—including that of the El Dorados—was of such popularity that it would
transcend ethnic categories and touch all youth. "At My Front Door," the
El Dorados' jump classic from 1955, is their main claim to fame, but such

outstanding songs as "Fallen Tear," "Lights Are Low," "I Began to Realize," and "I'll Be Forever Loving You" formed their solid musical legacy.[13]

Their story began on the South Side in the middle-class neighborhood of Englewood. It was late 1952, when vocal groups were becoming all the rage on the R&B charts and their impact was being felt in the black high schools of the city, as kids began forming groups to practice in the hallways, the parks, and the street corners. At Englewood High five kids got together and formed the Five Stars—Pirkle Lee Moses (lead), Louis Bradley (tenor), Jewel Jones (second tenor–baritone), James Maddox (baritone-bass), and Robert Glasper (bass). The school's custodian, Johnny Moore, heard them one day, liked what he heard, and became their manager.

"Mostly we sang songs by the Dominoes and Orioles," said Moses. "We did 'White Christmas,' 'Bells of Saint Mary's,' 'Don't Tell Her What's Happened to Me,' which was an Orioles song, things like that. We sang spirituals too. Not professionally, but several times we went to church and sang and went to the gospel shows at DuSable High. We did things by the Soul Stirrers, the Five Blind Boys, and the Pilgrim Travelers. Songs we used to do were 'The Lord's Prayer' and 'Trouble's in My Way.' And we came up with original songs also."[14]

After a while, Glasper and Moses went into the air force together. "I didn't stay but ninety days; it was a ninety-day active duty," asserted Moses. "Glasper stayed in. When I came back in 1954 two other guys were in the group, Arthur Bassett [tenor] and Richard Nickens [baritone-bass]. My place was already in there, because I had written a tune while in the air force called 'My Lovin' Baby.'" The group now had six members—Moses, Jones, Bradley, Maddox, Bassett, and Nickens—so a new name was necessary. The name "Cardinals" was considered but rejected in favor of the "El Dorados," which was taken from the name of a popular Cadillac model.

The El Dorados by 1954 had developed a considerable reputation in the city. They had already won one talent contest under the auspices of Al Benson when they were invited to participate in a contest at the Park City Bowl skating rink conducted by Vivian Carter. She had rented the rink and invited groups to challenge the Spaniels, her only group at the time. The El Dorados won. "She was impressed not only with our singing but also our showmanship," said Moses, "so she signed us up." That was in June 1954.

The group's first record for Vee Jay, cut at Universal Recording, was typical of the year 1954, kind of deep and bluesy—real street-corner style. The songs were "My Lovin' Baby," with Moses singing lead, and "Baby I Need You," with Bassett as lead, the latter song exhibiting excellent vocal arranging. The songs were not really commercial and they got sporadic play across the nation. Local coverage of the songs, however, was strong, and decades later collectors still adore them.

The next release, "Annie's Answer," teamed the El Dorados with Hazel McCollum, a young female singer who was a member of another Vee Jay act. "Annie's Answer" was the label's attempt—feeble, as it turned out—to exploit the tremendous popularity of the Midnighters' "Work with Me Annie" hit by coming out with an answer song (a composition of the same melody that responds to the theme of the original). The Vee Jay disc went virtually unheard.

"One More Time" backed with "Little Miss Love," both led by Moses, were recorded at the same August session as "Annie's Answer" and quickly followed in release. "One More Time" was a droopy ballad and "Little Miss Love" was an unexceptional jump, and both were substandard for the El Dorados. Nonetheless, the group put such craft in the singing that both songs are highly listenable.

During the fall of 1954, the El Dorados played venues throughout the Chicago area, but the most famous performance came in September at Corpus Christi High School. It was a giant bash sponsored by McKie Fitzhugh, which pitted the El Dorados against a fellow Vee Jay group, the Five Echoes, in a battle of groups. Other shows were a bill sponsored by Sam Evans and held on the West Side, at the Madison Rink, and another Fitzhugh bill, also on the West Side, at the Fifth Avenue Ballroom. In December the El Dorados were Vee Jay's representative act at the WDIA Goodwill Revue in Memphis. Early in 1955 Arthur Bassett left the group to complete his education, eventually going into the air force, the apparent service branch of choice for the El Dorados. In February the El Dorados made their first appearance at the famed Apollo in Harlem, which indicates that the group had developed a national name before their first national chart hit.

In the summer of 1955, the El Dorados achieved that national success when they hit for twelve weeks on *Billboard*'s R&B chart with "At My Front Door." The song's appeal is based on equal parts of El Dorados and backing band. The El Dorados, singing with natural ease and swing, pushed through the energetic number with great rock 'n' roll verve, especially in Moses's fine lead work and tenor squalling. Lefty Bates and his band created one of the most memorable opening riffs in rock 'n' roll, and without Al Duncan's propulsive drumming and the great sax break (by either Cliff Davis or Red Holloway) the song could have been far less successful. However, the flip, "What's Bugging You Baby," with Louis Bradley as lead, is nondescript.

Moses wrote "At My Front Door" by working on a derivation of the Spiders' "I Didn't Want to Do It," yet songwriter credit on the label is given to Johnny Moore and Ewart Abner. This intentional misattribution happened on many of the El Dorados compositions. Moses bitterly told journalist

Todd R. Baptista, "They had other guys' names as writers and fooled me, telling me, 'We needed to do it that way to help get it around and accepted,' but that wasn't the truth. I thought I was going to get paid and treated right but it didn't turn out that way. Moore got his name on [many of] them. Same thing with Abner."[15] This should be considered a crime, because in subsequent years "At My Front Door" has proved to be one of Vee Jay's all-time best copyrights, and one wonders how much income Moses never saw from it.

"At My Front Door," a number one record on the R&B charts, launched the El Dorados on an extensive touring career for the next several years. "We went to the East Coast, West Coast," said Moses, "and also the South—Nashville, Atlanta, all through there." Moses most remembers playing the Apollo. "It was great," he said, "there was no house in the country like that house at the time. The Apollo was a theater that was renowned for the talent, and the discovery of the talent, and it was thrilling to be a part of that. We played there maybe five, six times. We were scared the first time because it was a new experience for us all."

The record also introduced the El Dorados to the rock 'n' roll revolution, because the record was one of the key rhythm and blues records that year to cross over to the pop market and thereby launch rock 'n' roll. It became a rock 'n' roll standard and earned the group lasting fame. The year 1955 was the heaviest year for pop covers of R&B hits, and Dot Records rushed out a version of the song with its preeminent cover singer, Pat Boone. His version reached number seven on the *Billboard* pop top-forty chart, while the El Dorados' original peaked at seventeen, which was no small feat. As a result the El Dorados were invited to make an appearance on the "Ed Sullivan Show," which proved memorable.

The El Dorados' next record, "I'll Be Forever Loving You" backed with "I Began to Realize," released in December 1955, was the group's only other national chart record. "I'll Be Forever Loving You" made it to number eight on one of *Billboard*'s several hit lists, the jockey's chart. "Forever" was originally recorded by the Rip-Chords for Vee Jay when they were known as the Five Knights of Rhythm, but it never saw release. Leon Arnold, the lead of the Rip-Chords, was the writer of the song. Vee Jay thought it was ideal for the El Dorados, and indeed they do the song justice with their consummate professionalism. Despite the soulfulness of Moses's lead, however, the song lacks the deep feeling that best characterizes the El Dorados approach. "I Began to Realize" is another matter. It ranks as perhaps the most beautiful and richly soulful of the group's songs. Not surprisingly it is Moses's all-time favorite, and he explained, "I realize the group is best known for up-tempo songs, but personally my favorite were ballads. I have time and room to stretch out with them. I don't have to do a lot of hollering, and can just stand back and express myself. 'I Began to Realize' allows me that." Both sides got substantial air play and survive as two of the El Dorados' most memorable performances. After the release of the two, Richard Nickens left the group, to enlist in, not the air force, but the army.

The El Dorados' major live dates in early 1956 were a part of the Vee Jay label's Cavalcade of Vee Jay Stars tour, which started out at the Trianon in Chicago and then went to Milwaukee, Dallas, Tucson, and the West Coast. The El Dorados shared the stage with the Spaniels, Jimmy Reed, Joe Buckner, and other Vee Jay acts. The group on tour undoubtedly pushed its latest release, "Now that You're Gone" backed with "Rock 'n' Roll's for Me," a typical ballad/jump combo of the era in which both sides were led by Moses. It was a decided letdown artistically and the record flopped. The El Dorados returned to form spectacularly in the summer of 1956 with "A Fallen Tear." The use of a duet lead of Bradley and Maddox, a switch-off lead, and echoing tenor counterpointing, combined with some sweet harmonizing, demonstrated superbly the creative abilities of the group in vocal arranging. A fair jump, "Chop Ling Soon," led by Moses, was the flip. In August the group returned to the Apollo, capping a heavy schedule of one-nighters during the previous six months.

Although "A Fallen Tear" did well in a number of markets, it was still not a national hit. So in perhaps a desperate move, the El Dorados came out with a soundalike jump, "Bim Bam Boom," in September 1956. Unlike a lot of contrived follow-up attempts, however, the song is a solid number and ranks as one of the group's best jumps. ("Bim Bam Boom" later served as a title for an East Coast doowop fanzine.) Paired with "Bim Bam Boom" was a fine soulful ballad, "There in the Night." Both sides were led by Moses.

The winter of 1957 saw the El Dorados still vigorously touring, making a one-nighter tour through Pennsylvania and playing the prestigious Regal in Chicago. They were considered a strong visual act that could draw an audience whether or not they had a hit on the charts. The summer introduced two lesser El Dorados songs, "Tears on My Pillow" (not the Little Anthony song) backed with "A Rose for My Darling." Both sides were written by Moses and featured him as lead. Compared to their early rough and bluesy efforts for Vee Jay back in 1954, these polished and romantic sides show how much the group's members had grown as singers. Vee Jay, however, was not pleased, because throughout the summer the label limited release of the record to the Chicago area.

It did not matter much, as the group was in disarray. Jewel Jones, James Maddox, and Louis Bradley had decided to split from Moses and left Vee Jay. Moses said, "They wanted to go on to new management that I didn't approve of and under conditions I did not approve of. They wanted to be managed by some attorney and they tried to force me to go along with it, and I wouldn't. Aside from that fact, Vee Jay had me under a separate contract and they held me to it. I wanted to leave also and go to RCA or something, but I didn't want the management that the rest of the group wanted. But Vee Jay would not let me go."

Seemingly the story of the El Dorados should end with their breakup at this point, but it did not, as the following Kool Gents account will make clear. A second El Dorados group emerged from the ashes of both the Kool Gents and the first El Dorados.

The Kool Gents

The original Kool Gents were formed in 1952 by Cicero Blake from among his classmates at Marshall High. He recalled, "I started the group, I'm responsible for it. What happened, a friend of mine was also at Marshall on the football team with me. His name was Howard McClain. Howard and I got to be real good friends and I found out that he was interested in singing. So then we met another fellow, James Harper, and from there we added Teddy Long and Johnny Carter. We called ourselves the Goldentones then." Their lineup thus was as follows: Blake (lead), McClain (second tenor), Harper (first tenor/baritone), Long (second tenor/baritone), and Carter (bass).[16]

The Goldentones sang the usual hits of the period by such stellar groups as the Clovers, the Dominoes, and the Five Royales, as well as some gospel material by the Highway QC's. "We also had a few originals we got together," said Blake. "We would always name them after some girl or something."[17]

After high school, Blake joined the air force. This was around the latter part of 1954 and James Harper had already left the group. The group recruited a new lead in Dee Clark, who two years earlier had been a member of the Hambone Kids of "Hambone" fame. Blake said, "Dee took my place because he used to go to most all the rehearsals with us. He had a nice tenor voice. As a matter of fact, I didn't really expect Dee to remain in the group. I thought maybe he would do it for awhile and then just kind of drop out, because I didn't think at that time he was really interested in singing."

Shortly after Clark joined the Goldentones, Doug Brown (second tenor) and John McCall (first tenor) came into the group as Howard McClain left. With Clark, Long, Brown, Carter, and McCall now comprising the group, the Goldentones soon jelled to the point where they had become one of the crack groups on the West Side. Blake said, "I can never forget, I came home from the air force that same year [1954]—it was the Christmas holidays—I went by one of the rehearsals and Dee was singing lead. They had really gotten it together, man! I never forget he was doing a tune by the Diablos called 'The Wind.'" (Readers who know of the song can imagine how Clark's warm lilting tenor would have handled the "The Wind." It would have been scrumptious.)

The Goldentones worked awhile before their break came in the recording scene. Clark made it a habit to hang around the studios of WGES, which was in his neighborhood. There he struck up an acquaintance with the legendary deejay Herb Kent, who designated himself the "Kool Gent." Clark persuaded Kent to give a listen to the Goldentones. Kent was impressed with the group's talent enough to become their mentor, but he refused their request to act as manager. The group also adopted a new name, the Kool Gents. Most important, Kent got the group an audition with Vee Jay Records. The singers demonstrated their talents in front of Jimmy Bracken, Vivian Carter, and Calvin Carter. Passing that hurdle, they signed a contract and then began some hard practice to prepare for recording.

When the Kool Gents returned to Calvin Carter, their material was polished enough for Al Smith to work on the arrangements. Their first session, at Universal Recording, included "This Is the Night" and "You Know" (two ballads led by McCall), and "Do Ya Do" (a jump led by Long). "This Is the Night" and "Do Ya Do" were paired and released in 1955. Frankly, these numbers were not exceptional R&B, although pleasing enough to the average doowop collector. The record died.

Nonetheless, the Kool Gents were becoming established in Chicago. They began working at a major club on the West Side. Clark recalled:

> They had this guy Danny Overbea, who had "Forty Cups Of Coffee," and we had to really beg for that job. The club's manager was Herb somebody. I said, "We sure would like to come play your club. We got three different changes of uniform." He said, "Hey kid, look, we got Danny Overbea and blah, blah, blah . . ." I came back a couple nights later and talked to him some more. I said, "Look, why don't we just come in and do your freebie shot. We'll come in on your best night, sing a few tunes." He said, "OK, fine, it won't cost me anything, come in." Well, the people liked us so much, he said, "Why don't you guys put a few more tunes together and play regularly." Johnny McCall would do tunes like James Brown's "Please Please Please" and I would do "The Great Pretender" and Clyde McPhatter and the Drifters' tunes. We stayed there for about three months."[18]

Later Kool Gents' recording sessions at Vee Jay yielded "I'm Gonna Be Glad," led by McCall, and "I Just Can't Help Myself," "Just Like a Fool," and "When I Call On You," all led by Clark. "Just Like a Fool" was never released as a single but appeared on a Dee Clark album several years later. Likewise, "When I Call on You," a beautiful, ethereal ballad that is one of the Kool Gents' better songs, surfaced on a Dee Clark reissue LP in 1980. (This version of the song should not be confused with a later solo version done by Clark.)

By 1956 Clark had taken over the majority of the lead chores from McCall. "It was kind of weird the way it went down," Clark remembered, "because McCall had a hell of a lead voice, but he couldn't harmonize. So it took me from the lead, you know, to back him up on first tenor. Then I taught him later how to harmonize, which then gave us two lead singers."

"I Just Can't Help Myself," an excellent ballad, was paired with "You Know," which had been recorded earlier. As with the group's previous release, this record did poorly. But there are hit records and then there are records that get enough air play to give a group enough notice to get them performing in the clubs. The Kool Gents did not lack for work, playing most of the clubs in the Chicago area as well as venues in Gary, Indiana, and Ypsilanti, Michigan.

Also in 1956 the group got together with whoever happened to be in the studio at the time and recorded a novelty number called "The Convention," on which they were billed as the Delegates. The theme was a rock 'n' roll convention, a takeoff on the political conventions of that year.

Clark was clearly the dominant talent in the Kool Gents, and by 1957 he was ready to leave. When the Kool Gents recorded "Mother's Son" (a cover of an earlier release by the Chicago group the Debonairs), "Gloria," and "Kangaroo Hop" in 1956, the latter two were released the following year under the name of Dee Clark rather than under the Kool Gents name. "Mother's Son" was paired with the previously recorded "I'm Gonna Be Glad" and released under the Delegates name. "The group and I," said Clark, "weren't getting along too well, different things came about and I came around to the company and asked Calvin Carter and Ewart Abner if they would record me as a single. Calvin said, 'I'm glad you asked because we have been wanting to do that anyway.' So it wasn't much longer after that I told the fellows I was leaving to go it alone." When Clark left, that ended the Kool Gents as an act on the Vee Jay label.

The El Dorados (II)

As the foregoing two stories make evident, Vee Jay in 1956 was stuck with a lead, Pirkle Lee Moses, who had just lost his group, and a group, the Kool Gents, who had just lost its lead. With evident approval of all parties, Vee Jay thus teamed Moses up with the remaining Kool Gents to form a new

El Dorados group, which besides Moses consisted of Johnny Carter (bass), John McCall (tenor), Douglas Brown (second tenor), and Teddy Long (second tenor/baritone).

This new El Dorados ensemble came out with two more releases for Vee Jay during 1958. The first, "Three Reasons Why," was a respectable ballad backed by "Boom Diddle Boom," a forgettable jump. The record did virtually nothing upon release, but collectors today would probably give it fairly high marks. The second release, "Lights Are Low" backed with "Oh What a Girl," was strong on both sides. "Lights," written by Leon Arnold, ranks as an El Dorados all-time classic. Moses was at his soulful best and, in backing him, the group came up with a splendid arrangement that puts Carter's bass wonderfully out front. "Oh What a Girl," written by Long, is generally unrecognized, but R&B fans should give this fine jump a hearing.

Since neither of the El Dorados' 1958 records hit, Vee Jay finally gave up on the group and released them from the label. Not long afterward the El Dorados broke up, probably in 1959. As with the Drifters, the Five Satins, and a number of other classic R&B groups, the El Dorados' story became in later years a story of competing groups and a dizzying array of personnel changes.

For a fan of 1950s vocal harmony, only one strand of the story is worth following, and that is the subsequent effort of the original El Dorados to continue without Moses. After they left Vee Jay in 1957, Jewel Jones, James Maddox, and Louis Bradley picked up a new lead, Marvin Smith, who came out of a West Side gospel group. The Smith-led El Dorados then released "A Lonely Boy," an excellent song Smith composed, on Frank McGovern's Academy label in 1958. For legal reasons, the group billed itself as the Four El Dorados. Unfortunately for the group, the record got no exposure and died.

"We went out to California in 1958," said Smith, "I guess trying to get business deals, make business contacts, as well as work to keep us going. Jewel, he had gotten married and all that and he was going to live there. So the rest of the group—all of us were single—decided to go also. You know, we just took a chance. But it got so bad there. Just wasn't nothing happening. I was going to night school out there, trying to get a diploma."[19] While in California the group, under the name Tempos, came out with a song called "Promise Me" on the Rhythm label. But as with "A Lonely Boy," it did nothing for the group. They returned to Chicago broken down and then broke up.

The Dells

"I don't know whether or not we came to our singing natural, or what it was, but maybe because we were so together, we never really had to do hard drawn-out practice on songs. It just always seemed to fall into place for us. We never had to plan that much for a recording session. What we would do was learn the melody to get the right background, then we would go into the studio and that was the magic."[20] So said the great baritone lead Marvin Junior of the Dells, one of the most heralded groups of the 1950s, explaining what most observers have always assumed about this exceptionally talented group. The Dells in the mid-1990s were still together and were still singing the same great harmonies that originally brought them in the spotlight in the 1950s with such songs as "Oh What a Nite," "Dreams of Contentment," and "Dry Your Eyes."[21]

Like most of Vee Jay's groups, the Dells were native to the Chicago area. Junior recalled,

> We were living in Harvey, a suburb of Chicago, and for some reason we were all interested in the live shows that appeared in Chicago. And the other guys around Harvey weren't, so we ended up together— the five of us—by going to shows together. We went to such places as the Regal Theater, Crown Propeller Lounge, and Trianon Ballroom. Well, we loved singing, so we decided to form a group. At this particular time, Chuck Barksdale was just coming out of the air force. When he came home he fell right in with us, myself, Chuck, Mickey McGill, his brother Lucius, Verne Allison, and Johnny Funches, who was our lead. Johnny had a great voice. When he was in the group I was second lead, but I led on the fast songs.

The two McGills, Allison, and Funches were tenors; Junior, a baritone; and Barksdale, a bass.

This was in 1953, and by 1954 the singers, then calling themselves the El Rays, had made a recording for Chess Records, "Darling I Know" backed with "Christine." Lucius McGill said, "I remember going down to Chess Records on South Cottage Grove and talking to them, and right away after hearing us they were very enthused. We recorded for them within days."[22] Despite the enthusiasm of the Chess people, the amateurishness of the group is telling on the record, and members of the Dells readily admitted years later that they didn't quite know what they were doing at first.

"It was the Moonglows who helped us become a good singing group," Barksdale told the journalist Mike Lenehan, "they took us under their wings as personal friends, and they used to come out and spend their time rehearsing us and telling us about the things we could expect on the road. We looked up to them as more or less big brothers in show business."[23] Added Junior, "They actually set us down and voiced us correctly. Like they would sing 'wooo,' then say, now you sing it—'woo.' What we were doing before that, we were singing two or three parts. Two guys would be singing the same note."[24] Mickey McGill interjected, "they call that fish—you're fishing it, gang banging. By the time we made 'Oh What a Nite' we were beginning to sing correct R&B."[25]

"In those days," said Junior, "we were singing plain everyday stand-on-the-corner doowop. We didn't have a lot of music behind us. We were accompanied by four or five pieces, so we had to fill up all those holes with a lot of background vocalizing, a lot of bass, and a lot of tenor."

The El Rays were playing gigs in the Chicago area, at first singing at "little neighborhood functions," according to Lucius McGill. They did play two major jobs for shows promoted by WOPA deejay McKie Fitzhugh, who had the group play at the Pershing Ballroom and at Corpus Christi High School. After four of the group finished school at Thornton High in June of 1954, Lucius McGill dropped out to get a job in the post office. He conceded, "I just didn't have that feeling for show business. The thrill and excitement of being on stage and having a lot of young people screaming at you, it just wasn't for me. I needed a job, we all did."[26]

By 1955 the group was sounding good enough to fill a thousand holes and signed with Vee Jay. The first release for the group, now called the Dells, was "Tell the World," and it became a modest local hit. The next release was "Dreams of Contentment," which established the classic fifties Dells sound of Funches's plaintive lead answered by the rest of the group with pristine chorusing harmonies, all of it undergirded by Barksdale's wonderful bass work. Mickey McGill attested, "I Love it. When I hear it, it reminds me when we were kids. A beautiful song, before its time." The record never hit the national charts, but "Dreams" got some regional action early in 1956 along with the quality jump on the flip, "Zing Zing Zing."[27] The jump got good crossover action in Pittsburgh and was the group's first action as a rock 'n' roll act.

So far so good, but it was the Dells' next release, "Oh What a Nite," that established the group as a national act. Junior explained the song's origin:

We were playing in a place near Harvey called Boots and Saddles, a combined nightclub and rodeo, and we were singing there every weekend. We were getting two dollars a night and a hamburger. Some girls came in to see our show. They enjoyed it and said we want to do something for you guys, how would you like to come to a party? We'll have food and the whole bit. We said sure. When we arrived, it wasn't a party really, only the five girls and us, and a bowl of chicken. We were expecting a lot of people. But we really had a lot of fun; boy, we partied and danced and sang all night.

So the next day we were at rehearsal and started talking about the party. We said, "What a party, what a night!" So Johnny sing-songs "Oh what a night." I said, "Wait do that again!" He did and I came back with "to love you dear," and we sat down and wrote the song. "Oh What a Nite" was really about the party we had the previous night.

As Junior fleshed out his account, "In those days we were working on songs like crazy in the studio, because we only had one track to work with. The rehearsal we did was with the band. There was no charts, so you had to rehearse with the band. When we got into the studio, a lot of ideas developed in there. Like on 'Oh What a Nite,' we were doing it, but it just wasn't coming off right. Vivian Carter was there and she suggested that we express ourselves more on the 'oh,' bring out the 'oh.' And that's the one thing that made the song!"

"Oh What a Nite" became an R&B hit in October 1956, going to number four position and lasting eleven weeks on *Billboard*'s chart. This success probably surprised many of the record distributors who at a preview meeting with Vee Jay executive Ewart Abner Jr. picked the nice flip, "Jo Jo," as the potential hit. Most surprised of all were the Dells. The group at the time was not even together, and Barksdale was not on the record. He had gone to Cincinnati to join Otis Williams and the Charms of "Ivory Tower" fame. His place on "Oh What a Nite" was taken by Calvin Carter. Junior explained:

We had just got tired. We had no traveling jobs and we were just singing around town. Everybody had gotten bored and tired. Then one day at where we were hanging out on a basketball court, the Moonglows came by. They pulled up in this big Cadillac they had just bought, and got out and sat up on the hood wearing nice silk suits and diamond rings. Oh man, were we in awe, because when they had left Chicago on their first big tour they had been something like us, struggling. Only they could sing better. They told us they heard "Oh What a Nite" in New York. We said you got to be kidding. They said you got a hit, man! We're smalltown boys, so to get a record played in New York was unheard of. So that got us back together again. And about two weeks later in runs Chuck! Of course we welcomed him back.

A deejay, Dr. Jive—Tommy Smalls—put us on his stage show. We had been doing shows around Chicago, but that was our first big thing. We left Chicago and went straight to the Apollo Theatre. That was the biggest thing in the world for us.

That was in October 1956, and at the same time the group signed with Smalls to represent them as their personal manager and with the famed Gale Agency to do their booking. The Dells during the 1950s never had a hit to equal the success of "Oh What a Nite," but they managed to continue to record fine songs that had scattered success throughout the country. Especially good were the Funches-led ballads—"Why Do You Have to Go" (1957), "Pain in My Heart" (l957), and "Dry Your Eyes" (1959).

"Why Do You Have to Go," a gentle ballad, should have returned the Dells to the charts upon its release in March 1957, but it didn't. The record best typified the Dells' approach to ballad harmony in the 1950s. Funches establishes the tone of the song with his plaintive-sounding lead, and the rest of the group answers with chorusing, either with short phases or words or with doowop syllables. Throughout the song Barksdale supplies a bottom, filling the holes with his bass vocal work. The flip, "Dance Dance Dance," ranks as one of the group's lesser jumps, but it does reflect the influence of the rock 'n' roll revolution because it was written as a rock 'n' roller, down to the obligatory sax break and the appeal to dancing.

"A Distant Love," from August 1957, is a wonderful midtempo number that never achieved more than a few local airplays. The song features dual leads of Junior and Funches. The flip, "Q-Bop She-Bop," is a poor Dells jump.

"Pain in My Heart" (November l957) was another great plaintive ballad and like its predecessors failed to ignite the public. Again the dual lead of Funches and Junior is featured. McGill cited it as his favorite fifties Dells song. Throughout, one can hear Barksdale working the bottom with his great bass singing. The flip was a McGill-penned midtempo number, "Time Makes You Change." McGill rewrote slightly this very solid number as "Oh What a Day" in 1969 and got a moderate national hit out of the tune, even though it did not come through the first time for the group. The Dells were writing most of their material at this time, and McGill explained why: "When we were younger, in a younger frame of mind, we used to write our own material. When you're kids you think entirely differently than when you're older and have more problems and things. We used to write a lot of great tunes."

"Dry Your Eyes," released in September 1959, was the Dells' last great Funches-led ballad, and typically it combines bittersweet sadness with a feeling of romance. Especially effective is the way the group augments the lead with two styles of chorusing support—high-end crying response (ahh-aah) and lower-end doowop riffing (wee-ooh). With a great bottom supplied by Barksdale's bass, all the holes are filled in what should be considered a classic approach to vocal harmony.

In the last decade or so, there have been various reissues of Dells 1950s material, in which some real gems have been unearthed, notably "She's Just an Angel," "You're Still in My Heart," "My Best Girl," "Now I Pray," "Rain," and "Restless Days." The latter tune was written by McGill and Allison and surfaced in a version sung by a girl group, the Opals, in 1965. The Dells had taken the girls under their wings as mentors, and the upshot was one of the group's best songs.

If anyone is under the illusion that show business in the 1950s was all glitter and glamour, some of the Dells' bitter experiences would set them straight. Junior attested:

> We had done dances down South like it was just in a cowboy movie, fight and the whole bit. But we were used to rough nights; the bad shows weren't so bad. What really turned me off, the real traumatic experience, was we couldn't quite adjust to the racial thing. Among entertainers there was no color. When we worked the Apollo, white acts would work right along with us. We worked the Alan Freed show with its white and black acts. Also, we grew up in Harvey, which had always been an integrated area.
>
> But then we would go South and there would be black downstairs and white upstairs, and we would see signs on the road, "Colored Motel," "Colored Guesthouse," and white and colored water faucets and bathrooms. That kind of hurt us. I remember when the first time we went to Miami Beach, which we all had heard and read so much about. I ran down to the beach with my shorts on to swim, the guy there stopped me and said, nope, the colored beach is ten miles down the road. Things like that kind of turned me off, kind of made me feel inferior for awhile, until we kind of saw that's the way it was and we had to accept it. The funny thing is that those areas are now great. The segregation and stuff is almost completely forgotten down there.

But, a cynic might ask, did the money take away some of the pain? There was very little of it in the 1950s, according to the Dells. Royalties from the record company were practically nonexistent, but money from radio play was forthcoming, partly due to the writers royalties that also accrued to the group. "When we were with Vee Jay," McGill said, "whatever we wrote, we only got BMI money [royalties for radio play]. That was in the era that whenever you wrote and recorded songs they would apply that to whatever debt you owned the company. We were lucky that someone told us about BMI. But there was no record label royalties, not for us."

The lack of money for the Dells precipitated Funches's not staying with the Dells into the next decade. Junior pointed out, "He always had the problem of not wanting to pay the dues. He wanted everything to jump off really great from the get-go and start making money. You know it was a little hard in them days. You didn't make much money."

In late 1958 the Dells' career was temporary halted. As McGill recalled:

We were in a bad automobile accident on the Ohio Turnpike. I broke my leg badly in three places, in the thigh. When I got back from the hospital, I was kind of disenchanted as far as going on the road and traveling, and being in show business anymore. We were traveling around the country like a bunch of kids, and not making any real money. I just said, well, I'm going to give it up and get married, and I did. We all got other jobs. I went to Kaiser Aluminum. Marvin was working in a steel mill as was Johnny Funches. Verne had just taken off and gone to New York. Chuck had gone with the new Moonglows.

Barksdale added, "We stayed in contact from day to day, but I think everybody was a little shell-shocked."[28]

It took a while before the group could get reunited, which happened in 1960. Funches, however, could not be persuaded to come back. The group then obtained the tenor Johnny Carter, who had dropped out of the Flamingos sometime earlier. The new Dells ensemble soon worked into what became the patented Dells style of the soul era, using the tradeoff leads of Junior's gruff baritone and Johnny Carter's mewling tenor. But that is another story.

The Rhythm Aces

The Rhythm Aces were not a rhythm and blues group as such. Their style actually hearkened back to the 1940s and could be considered a type of vocal jazz. They aspired to follow in the footsteps of the Ink Spots, the Mills Brothers, and the Four Freshmen. The rhythm and blues groups in the city knew the Rhythm Aces as a "modern harmony" group who would play in the fancy jazz nightclubs, such as the Crown Propeller Lounge. Chuck Barksdale, of the Dells, said, "The Rhythm Aces were one of your more sophisticated vocal groups. They didn't sing the ding ding dong type changes, the doowop things. They were singing things like 'Moonlight in Vermont' and your real Modernaires-type songs."[29] On most of the group's Vee Jay output it is the "modern harmony" sound that predominates rather than the rhythm and blues sound.

The Rhythm Aces was formed in Germany around 1950, when the members were stationed as soldiers in the United States Army. Members were Billy Steward (first tenor), Chuck Rowan (second tenor), Clyde Rhymes (baritone), and Vic House (baritone/bass). House and Rowan were cousins. The group won a Special Services talent contest and as a result made an appearance on the "Ed Sullivan Show." Their Special Services activities got them on several entertainment tours in which they performed on the same bill with such entertainers as Vic Damone and Eddie Fisher.[30]

Upon their discharge in 1954, the Rhythm Aces decided to make a go of it in the entertainment world and started a tour in the Midwest. When they hit Chicago, they went to the famed Crown Propeller Lounge to see the blues singer Prince Big Miller perform. He asked them to get on stage to sing, and the group so impressed the audience that they were put on the bill, replacing the Moonglows. This was in October 1954. Ewart Abner, who was making the transition from Chance to Vee Jay, saw the group at the show and got them signed to Vee Jay.

The first release on the group was "I Wonder Why" backed with "Get Lost." Both sides were led by Steward. "I Wonder Why" is the best example of the Rhythm Aces' modern harmony approach, a beautiful ballad where the emphasis is on the entire group singing in harmony, as opposed to the R&B style of lead vocals backed by doowop riffing of the other members. Most atypical for the Rhythm Aces is the up-tempo "Get Lost," which is a basic blues speeded up to achieve a nice jump rhythm.

The next release, in 1955, was "Whisper to Me" backed with "Olly, Olly, Atsen Free." "Whisper to Me," lead by Steward and House, is a fantastic example of fine R&B, featuring a sweet-sound lead tenor and answering deep bass typical of the R&B formula. The flip, led by House, was a novelty based on the children's schoolyard game.

The last release by the Rhythm Aces for Vee Jay was "That's My Sugar" backed with "Flippety Flop." "That's My Sugar" is a peppy up-tempo number with no lead work at all, but it is surprisingly distinguished by a fierce sax break. It is the sort of thing that the Modernaires could have done in the 1940s. The flip, led by House, is not as inspired. Left in the can was "I Realize Now," a slow modern harmony led by House that had much the flavor of "I Wonder Why." It appeared on a Solid Smoke reissue album in 1984.

The Rhythm Aces presented a problem for Vee Jay. They were too adult and sophisticated for Vee Jay to market to the emerging rhythm and blues and rock 'n' roll fields, and as a result the company just could not score a hit on them. The group could play only in supper clubs, which limited their exposure to the market Vee Jay was targeting. The group was released from the label before the end of 1955. After a tour of Canada in late 1955, the Rhythm Aces broke up.

In 1956, however, Rowan, House, and Steward got together again and, with a new member, tenor Jimmy Brunson, formed a new group in California. This group recorded in California from 1956 through 1958, under the various names of the Rockets, the Rocketeers, or the Planets. They backed Johnny Otis on "Willie and the Hand Jive" and his album on Capitol. In the first half of the 1990s Rowan was still working in California, playing piano in a combo that included the famed Midnighters' guitarist Cal Green, Sammy Dee on sax, and Roscoe Riley on drums.

In 1961 Vee Jay released some rhythm and blues numbers by a group it called "Rhythm Aces," but it was a group that had nothing to do with the earlier Rhythm Aces. From the first listen to the songs, it is evident that there is no relationship between the two groups. One of the songs, "Be Mine," is a gritty, greasy-sounding doowop, with weird warblings forming the background for intensely felt lead vocalizing. The song is nicely ended by one of those ultradramatic recitations that make so many doowop songs fun. "Joni," with its shouting lead and bouncing background, typifies the rock 'n' roll vocal group sound of the late 1950s and early 1960s, loose and aggressive.

The Magnificents

The Magnificents never achieved the fame and extensive recording history of other Vee Jay groups, but that does not mean the music they produced was any less interesting. They are a classic street-corner group, because even though they did not possess an outstanding lead, they made up for it with a splendid ensemble sound that allows one to feel the sense of fun and excitement these fellows must have had in putting their songs together.[31]

The original members of the Magnificents—Johnny Keyes (tenor lead), Thurman "Ray" Ramsey (tenor), Fred Rakestraw (tenor), and Willie Myles (bass)—came together as the Tams to perform at an annual amateur show at Hyde Park High School on the South Side. At the performance was a local deejay who called himself the Magnificent Montague. He liked what he heard, became the group's manager, redubbed them "The Magnificents," and, most important, got them a contract with Vee Jay.

The Magnificents' first session in 1956 yielded the group's only hit, "Up on the Mountain," which in its earliest form was nothing more than the bass-line part of a street-corner song called "Newborn Square." Said Keyes, "The only part of 'Newborn Square' that made sense to Montague was the bass line."[32] With some lyrics added, and some pruning and polishing by Montague, who was producing the session, the finished song emerged with the exact ingredients needed to become a rock 'n' roll classic. In Willie Myles's burbling bass and Johnny Keyes's rapid-fire lead, the group exhibited a real street-corner genius for creating a great rhythmic tune. That this was no accident is shown by the previously unreleased gem, "Yes, She's My Baby," which appeared in 1984 on a reissue LP. With equal zest, the group created another "magnificently" bouncing number wonderfully enhanced by a terrific sax break. "Why Did She Go," also from the first session, is a thoroughly solid ballad number that enhanced the Magnificents' capabilities as a group able to do far more than jump tunes.

With the success of "Up on the Mountain," the Magnificents went on a whirlwind of gigs and tours during the summer and winter of 1956 to exploit the record's popularity. In June, in Chicago, the group performed on Jim Lounsbury's "Bandstand Matinee," a teen dance show on television. They followed that appearance with a tour that included shows in Milwaukee, Cincinnati, and Pittsburgh.

Following the first session, Thurman Ramsey was replaced by L. C. Cooke (Sam Cooke's brother), and Barbara Arrington was added to make the Magnificents a five-person ensemble. The new lineup recorded "Caddy Bo" and "Hiccup," both led by Arrington, but neither side did anything upon release in August 1956. The use of Arrington on the leads was ill-advised; the group had developed a recognizable and superb style, and the new releases diverted the singers from what they did best. The group thus chose to return to the hit sound of their first record with "Off the Mountain." The song was done with the same sense of fun and same sparkling vocalizing, so it does not pale next to "Up on the Mountain." The session also produced "This Old Love of Mine," a song not released at the time but appearing on a 1984 reissue. It is a moody-sounding ballad effort featuring Arrington as lead, and it captured a late-night romantic atmosphere.

In October 1956 the Magnificents played in New York and Washington, D.C., and the following month were back in Chicago to play a Thanksgiving dance at the Trianon with the Calvaes, the Kool Gents, the Clouds, Otis Rush, the Five Echoes, Harold Burrage, Lil "Upstairs" Mason, Big Walter Horton, and G. L. Crockett, among others. In April 1957 the Magnificents returned triumphantly to Hyde Park to play on a show sponsored and emceed by Herb Kent that featured an imposing array of doowop groups, notably the Moroccos, the Danderliers, the Dells, the Debonairs, and the Kings Men.

The Magnificents around this time had a falling out with Vee Jay and Montague, over money. Said Keyes, "What happened, we got a lawyer and sued Vee Jay. The word was out and Montague got pissed off. So Abner says we're going to have a meeting, and you guys don't say anything to Montague. Don't blow your top, just keep your cool. That was the meeting in which what I call the 'infamous ten dollar royalty check' was given to us. We didn't touch it on the advice of our lawyer. What then happened, they started giving whatever group they had that wasn't working our gigs. People would call the agency or our company and they would send them the El Dorados."[33]

Meanwhile in June 1957, with things in disarray, Keyes and Rakestraw formed a touring Magnificents group with tenor Reggie Gordon (who came out of the Five Frenchmen) and bass Rufus Hunter (who came out of the Five Bells) to work their latest record, "Off the Mountain." Gordon was the best lead vocalist the Magnificents ever had. But in Philadelphia, bereft of funds, the group broke up. Gordon joined the Rays (who were coming off their "Silhouettes" hit) and Hunter joined the Cameos. Keyes and Rakestraw also hustled a bit and became members of Thurston Harris's backup group.

Montague then formed still another Magnificents group (whose members' identities remain unknown) to record another batch of songs in 1958. The best of them was the rousingly energetic "Don't Leave Me," a nicely melodious rock 'n' roll jump. The song was paired with "Ozeta," a revamp of the El Dorados' earlier song "My Lovin' Baby." Also recorded at the session but not appearing on wax until 1984 was "Rosebud," a great doowoppy number sung with a cha-cha beat.

Back in Chicago in 1958, Keyes became a part of a dizzying whirl of groups, most formed from ex-members of various groups from the Ida B. Wells projects—the Five Frenchmen, the Five Bells, and the Five Buddies. In the fall of 1958, Keyes, Gordon, Rakestraw, and L. C. Cooke made some sides for Checker, but instead of being credited as "L. C. Cooke and the Magnificents," only Cooke got billing. Also during the year, Keyes and Gordon, with a former Five Frenchmen member, Glen Phillips, and the Dells bass, Chuck Barksdale, made a recording for United Artists that apparently never saw release.

In either late 1958 or early 1959, a group billed as Johnny and the Keys, consisting of Keyes, Gordon, former Five Bells Jerome Browne, and former El Dorados lead Pirkle Lee Moses, came out with a record on Mercury called "Tuscumscari" backed with "Lost Teen-ager." In 1959, a group consisting of Keyes and Gordon and the brothers Jimmy Hawkins (from the Five Buddies) and Julius Hawkins (from the Five Bells) backed Beverly Ann Gibson on some sides for King records. Keyes, Gordon, and the Hawkins brothers also backed L. C. Cooke on a record in 1964, but by that time doowop was history.

Keyes's later involvements in music were as a member of the touring group of Packers, who hit in 1965 with the instrumental "Hole in the Wall," and as a co-composer for Clarence Carter's "Too Weak to Fight." Thurman Ramsey led a local Chicago nightclub group called the Magnificents during the 1960s, and in the 1980s he briefly resurrected the group for oldies concerts. In 1991, Keyes began performing in a revived Magnificents group that included his singing partners from 1957–60, Reggie Gordon, Rufus Hunter, and Julius Hawkins. Keyes also has made himself a historian and general observer of the doowop scene with his self-published book

Du-Wop, an evocative recreation of the doowop era as experienced by one group.

The Prodigals

The Prodigals were not what they seemed. Listening to their Vee Jay records, one pictured a vocal group from the streets of the big city, and an African American one to boot, given the label's stable of artists. Most readers would be surprised to learn that the group, which was racially mixed, played instruments and thus was a self-contained ensemble. Moreover, it started in Clarksburg, West Virginia, around 1956 as the Jumping Jacks, an all-black group. But in 1957 the musicians changed their name to the Chords and began their transformation with the addition of a white guitarist, Gerald Folio, who had come to the United States from France in 1949. Besides Folio, the Chords came to include Billy Smith on keyboards, Roy Davis on saxophone, Maurice Davis on bass guitar, Eddie Gayles on drums, Billy Gayles as bass vocalist, Chuck Collins as lead singer, and a singer recalled only as "Theme Song," who performed as alto vocalist.[34]

The Chords would play at dances throughout the central West Virginia area and were eventually approached by some gentlemen from Cleveland who were friends of the Brackens. The contact resulted in the Chords' being signed to the Falcon label in the late spring of 1958. The eight-member group and its manager then made the trip to Chicago in two 1956 Chevrolets. Finding themselves lost in Chicago, they poured out of their cars and into LaSalle National Bank to ask for directions. Police soon swarmed around them, but the group managed to persuade the nervous officers that they were merely asking for directions and weren't bank robbers.

After the Chords found Vee Jay on South Michigan, they met with Calvin Carter, who would supervise their session. Carter told them that their name was already taken by a recording group and they needed a new name. They came up with the "Prodigals." The session lasted two hours, and as usual, four sides were cut—"Marsha," "Judy," "Vangie," and "Won't You Believe." "Marsha," a jump tune, was paired with "Judy," a ballad, for the group's first release, in March 1958. "Marsha" became a strong regional hit in the Prodigals' home territory of West Virginia and in the neighboring states of Ohio and Pennsylvania (particularly in Pittsburgh).

Most appealing is Folio's guitar work, especially on "Marsha," in which he modifies the famous riff from Mickey and Sylvia's "Love Is Strange" to come up with something original that sounds tasty throughout the number. "Judy" is a standard "doowop" ballad that has more appeal today among rhythm and blues collectors. The lead, Collins, with his sad-sounding soulful voice, dominates the proceedings. The chorus work is barely heard, as one might expect from a self-contained group, but it is there, making the record in essence a vocal group record.

The Prodigals parlayed a lot of work from the record, appearing in numerous country clubs, universities, and colleges. The group also started appearing in black nightclubs, such as the Off Shore Club in Blythedale, Pennsylvania. They appeared on a bill with Bo Diddley in Morgantown, West Virginia, and with the Chantels in Pittsburgh. Being a self-contained band, the group frequently would be used to back the vocalists and vocal groups who would appear with them.

In September 1958, Vee Jay released "Vangie" and "Won't You Believe" on the Abner label (renamed from Falcon). Although it appeared that "Vangie" would continue to keep the Prodigals in the spotlight, the group began unraveling. The member known as "Theme Song" had left just after the recording session. Then the group lost its manager when, after a local concert in Fairmont, West Virginia, he disappeared with the Prodigals' share of the receipts. In short order, the lead vocalist, Chuck Collins, left and was replaced by Phil Lightfoot; drummer Eddie Gayles also left, to be replaced by Michael Forte. The new alignment of Prodigals stayed together until 1961, but without any more recording opportunities.

Gerald Folio would continue throughout the 1960s with various permutations of groups, some using the Prodigals name and some not. One such group put out two records on the Raven label out of Clarksburg. In 1969 the last Prodigals group broke up.

Other Vee Jay Groups

The story of the Vee Jay groups is far from complete without a mention of the Orioles, whose pioneering new style in the late 1940s signaled the emergence of teen-oriented rhythm and blues. Without the Orioles there could not be rock 'n' roll. When they came to Vee Jay in 1956, all that remained from the original group was the Orioles lead, Sonny Til. The original Orioles had broken up in 1955, and Til recruited a new supporting cast from the Regals, another group that had just lost its lead. The new members were Albert Russell (baritone), Billy Adams (baritone), Aaron Cornelius (tenor), Jerry Rodriguez (tenor/baritone), and Paul Griffin (piano). The group was capable of singing modern harmony, which was the attraction for Til.

The Orioles recorded eight songs for Vee Jay, six of which were released. Two of the released up-tempo songs, "Sugar Girl" and "I Just Got Lucky," were led by Russell and sounded like rock 'n' roll, rather than R&B or modern harmony. They did not go over, and neither did the ballads, led by Til. The best of them, "For All We Know," was lovely but it sank without a trace. Before 1956 was over the Orioles were no longer recording for Vee Jay—or anybody else for that matter. They dissolved the group.[35]

A Vee Jay group that made a brief splash was the Goldenrods—Crosby Harris (lead tenor), Hiawatha Burnett (tenor), Cleve Denham (tenor), Jesse Rodgers (baritone), and Charles Kolquitt (bass)—out of Roosevelt High School in Gary, Indiana. In 1958 they hit locally with "Color Cartoon," a comedic novelty like those the Coasters were putting out at the time. In later years collectors would prefer the flip side, "Wish I Was Back in School." Like the Spaniels five years earlier, the Goldenrods got on Vee Jay by walking into Vivian's Record Shop in Gary and auditioning for the contract on the spot.[36]

Vee Jay produced other outstanding releases (but not hits, sadly) on a half dozen minor acts whose stories have yet to surface. The nicest sides came from a rare entity, a "girl" doowop group, the Capers. The preteen family group from New York consisted of three sisters and a brother. Their "Miss You My Dear" (1958) and "High School Diploma" (1959) are worth searching out on reissues. Another fine group, the Lyrics, produced "Come On Home," a fine 1958 release. They also recorded as the Falcons on Vee Jay's subsidiary Falcon label and cut a terrific song, "Now that It's Over." Early in the 1990s more group sides surfaced on reissue CDs, showing the richness of the holdings of the Vee Jay vaults. Some notable discoveries were Miss Mello and Heavy Drama ("Send Me"), the Dornells ("Raindrops"), and El Cincos ("Kiss Me").

*   *   *

Vee Jay was enormously successful in recording top-notch material on its three principal groups—the Spaniels, El Dorados, and Dells. Each made an impact on the rock 'n' roll revolution with a durable rock 'n' roll hit—namely, "Goodnite Sweetheart, Goodnite," "Oh What a Nite," and "At My Front Door." More important, each created a substantial body of terrific music that makes the Vee Jay catalog one of the greatest of the 1950s. Of the lesser groups, the Magnificents made the biggest impact in rock 'n' roll with "Up on the Mountain." Vee Jay, like many companies in the 1950s, tried to spin off lead singers from groups to promote as a solo act. They did that most notably with the Kool Gents, from whom they spun off Dee Clark, who became one of Vee Jay's biggest rock 'n' roll/rhythm and blues stars. Vee Jay must be considered one of the biggest Chicago players in forging the rock 'n' roll revolution, and, what is most significant, the company played its role largely with its doowop acts.

Notes

1. Information about Vee Jay comes from Callahan, "Vee Jay Story." For a

discussion of Vee Jay in the soul era, until its demise in 1965, see Pruter, *Chicago Soul.*

2. Biographical sources on the Vee Jay executives include: Hep, "Night Beat"; Southern, "James ('Jim') Bracken," *Biographical Dictionary,* pp. 43–44; "Vivian Bracken, 69," *Chicago Sun-Times,* June 15, 1989; "Vivian Carter, Disc Jockey, Moves to WWCA."

3. Callahan, "Vee Jay Story," p. 7.

4. Ibid., p. 8.

5. McGarvey, "Knocking at the El Dorados' Front Door," p. 15.

6. Information about the Spaniels comes from Carter, *Goodnight, Sweetheart, Goodnight: The Story of the Spaniels;* Hopkins, "Wax and Needle"; Horlick, "The Spaniels" and "Spaniels—Revisited"; Italiano, "The Splendid Spaniels"; Lee and Hennings, "The Spaniels"; Marchesani, "Time Capsule"; Pruter, "The Spaniels"; Taylor, "Smithsonian Tunes"; Hudson interviews.

7. Lee and Hennings, "The Spaniels," p. 4.

8. Hudson interview, February 8, 1984.

9. Ibid.

10. Taylor, "Smithsonian Tunes into the Spaniels."

11. Hudson interview, February 8, 1984.

12. Carter, *Goodnight, Sweetheart, Goodnight,* p. 171.

13. Information about the El Dorados comes from Baptista, "The El Dorados"; Galgano, "El Dorados & Kool Gents"; Hinkley [with Goldberg], "The El Dorados"; McGarvey, "Knocking at the El Dorados' Front Door"; Pruter, "El Dorados Make Rock-and-Roll History"; Moses interview.

14. This and subsequent remarks by Moses quoted in this chapter are from the Moses interview, 1982.

15. Baptista, "The El Dorados," p. 70.

16. Kool Gents sources are virtually identical to those for the El Dorados sources; see Galgano, "El Dorados & Kool Gents"; Hinkley [with Goldberg], "The El Dorados"; McGarvey, "Knocking at the El Dorados' Front Door"; and Pruter, "El Dorados Make Rock-and-Roll History"; and the Blake and Clark interviews.

17. This and subsequent remarks by Blake quoted in this chapter are from the Blake interview.

18. This and subsequent remarks by Clark quoted in this chapter are from the Clark interview.

19. Marvin Smith interview.

20. This and subsequent remarks by Junior quoted in this chapter are from the Junior interview, 1984.

21. Information about the Dells early years comes from Lenehan, "Conversations with the Dells"; Pruter, "The Early Dells"; Richardson, "The Dells"; Sbarbori, "The Dells . . . 23 Years Later"; and the Barksdale, Junior, Lucius McGill, and Michael McGill interviews.

22. Lucius McGill interview.

23. Lenehan, "Conversations with the Dells," p. 32.

24. Ibid.

25. Ibid.

26. Lucius McGill interview.

27. This and subsequent remarks by Michael McGill quoted in this chapter are from the McGill interview.

28. Barksdale interview.

29. Ibid.

30. Information about the Rhythm Aces comes from Goldberg, "The Rhythm Aces."

31. Information about the Magnificents comes from Keyes, *Du-Wop;* Greggs, "Lead Singer"; Whitesell [with Goldberg], "The Magnificents"; Keyes interview.

32. Keyes interview.

33. Ibid.

34. Information about the Prodigals comes from Janusek, "Prodigals."

35. Information about the Orioles comes from Goldberg, "The Orioles."

36. Information about the Goldenrods comes from the Burnett interview.

Small Entrepreneurs—
Citywide

OKeh Records

OKeh, which made a small mark in Chicago during the 1950s, was a Columbia Records subsidiary label and based in New York. The label had a long and rich history, having begun in 1916 as an independent that recorded all kinds of music. In 1920 it launched the black-music recording industry with the release of Mamie Smith's "Crazy Blues," and in the following decade OKeh made a name for itself recording blues and jazz discs, most notably the seminal sides of Louis Armstrong's Hot Five and Hot Seven combos. Columbia picked up the label in 1926 but during the Depression let the imprint lapse. Following a revival of OKeh in 1940, the label was retired again in 1942 because of a wartime shellac shortage.

In the postwar years, major companies such as Columbia saw their control of the rhythm and blues market taken away by a host of new small independent labels, which in Chicago included Miracle, Chess, and Chance. In 1951, the company revived OKeh as a specialist R&B label and placed a go-getting young man in his twenties, Danny Kessler, in charge.[1] In late 1952 OKeh's distribution was changed from company branches to independent operators, so as to get better penetration in the rhythm and blues market.[2] It did not help much because the label remained a minor player throughout much of the 1950s, despite notable success with two New York–based artists, Chuck Willis and Big Maybelle. Because OKeh was such a small player in Chicago's rhythm and blues market, however, it is appropriate to discuss it in the present chapter, on the small entrepreneurs, despite its connection with the huge Columbia organization.

Among Kessler's first signings for OKeh in 1951 was the veteran Chicago musician, drummer, and orchestra leader Theodore "Red" Saunders.

He was born in Memphis, March 2, 1912, and moved to Chicago with his older sister while still a child, temporarily in 1921 and permanently in 1923. In the 1920s he briefly lived with friends of his sister, Lil and Louis Armstrong. He attended Tilden Tech but left to join a band led by Stomp King. After touring extensively with several bands, notably the Walk-a-Thon Band, Saunders joined the house band at the Annex Club in Chicago in 1935. He stayed there a year. He then worked with the Albert Ammons band, which in early 1937 was hired as the house band by the newly opened Club Delisa. In November 1937 Saunders took over as the house bandleader, a position he held until the club closed in 1958.[3]

After Saunders signed with OKeh in 1951, he released three records without notable success. That Saunders represented the past rather than the future was most evident in the recordings. One other notable Chicago act of Kessler's likewise looked to the past, the Big Three Trio, led by Willie Dixon. The act was rapidly winding down as the harder blues sounds and doowop groups were growing in popularity. The combo (bassist Willie Dixon, guitarist Ollie Crawford, and pianist Leonard "Baby Doo" Caston) sounded much as it did as when it was formed in 1946—it was a lounge combo that mixed jazz, vocal harmonies, boogie-woogie, and a touch of blues—a sound established by Dixon's predecessor groups, The Five Breezes, in 1939, and the Four Jumps of Jive, in 1945.[4]

Kessler signed another group of Chicago artists in late 1951, adding to the stable the Fritz Jones Trio, June Davis (a vocalist for Red Saunders), balladeer Ray Orlando, and another archaic-sounding group, the Dozier Boys. Of all the Chicago-based acts brought to the label by Kessler, he had only one notable success—with one of the oldest sounds in black music, the Hambone, conveyed by the record "Hambone," put out by the Red Saunders Orchestra with Dolores Hawkins and the Hambone Kids in early 1952.

In a passage in *Life on the Mississippi,* which described customs on the river in the 1840s, Mark Twain tells of some raftsmen entertaining themselves: "Next they got out an old fiddle, and one played, and another patted juba, and the rest turned themselves loose on a regular old-fashioned keelboat breakdown."[5] "Patted juba" is one of the earliest references to the patting juba routine of slapping the hands, knees, thighs, and torso to create a dancing rhythm. The routine developed among the slaves because their masters had forbidden the use of drums for fear they would be used as signaling devices in revolts. Slapping had to substitute for drums.

What Twain knew as patting juba we know today as the Hambone. In 1952 a trio of kids from Chicago—eleven-year-old Sammy McGrier, thirteen-year-old Delecta Clark [Dee Clark], and fourteen-year-old Ronnie Strong—launched a nationwide revival of interest in the Hambone with their record of the same name done with Red Saunders. "Hambone" is an archaic sound, one from the streets, befitting OKeh's reputation in the market, but it succeeded on its novelty value.[6] Sammy McGrier told how the whole Hambone phenomenon came about:

> When I was in Evanston [a suburb north of Chicago], a kid came from the South, from Mississippi, and he brought the Hambone with him. It became a kind of novelty around the school. At the Foster School in Evanston, I say maybe 10 percent of the kids had picked up the Hambone. When my family relocated to Chicago, I attended Calhoun School and there I was the only kid who really knew how to do the routine. Then what happened was that a neighbor across the street, who worked for the "Morris B. Sachs Amateur Hour," a local television show, submitted my name in audition. I then appeared on the show and sure enough, Red Saunders saw me. He contacted my father and wanted to know whether my father would be interested in a rhythm-novelty record.
>
> Red Saunders suggested we bring three other people besides myself down. We only knew of two other people that could do the Hambone good enough—Delecta Clark and a step-cousin, Ronnie Strong. Delecta had picked up the Hambone quite readily, but he had one little ingredient that just made a world of difference. He patted the heel of his foot on the second and fourth beat just to give it that extra little rhythm. Ronnie Strong lived on Forty-third Street, on the South Side, but because of the family ties he knew how to do the Hambone.[7]

Horace McGrier Sr., Sammy's father, helped the group polish the routine and added two other verses to follow the first, which was derived from an old English folk rhyme. After the record was released, McGrier Sr. was surprised to hear from a fellow steelworker at his plant, who remembered doing the Hambone and singing the rhyme nearly thirty years earlier in the South.

"Hambone" became a hit in early 1952, and the boys became local celebrities. "The first thing we did in a kind of promotional effort," said McGrier, "we went around to many of the radio stations and appeared on various disc jockeys' shows—Howard Miller, Norman Ross, Marty Faye, Norm Spaulding, and Sam Evans. We had some tour arrangements set up—we were suppose to make a tour of the East (Philadelphia, Baltimore, Washington, D.C., New York, some of the southern cities on the eastern seaboard), but Red Saunders could not break his contract and get away from the Club Delisa." The Hambone Kids were able to appear at the Indiana Theater in March 1952, performing with Red Saunders on the theater's famed midnight show.

McGrier recalled reading in *Billboard* that the record sold 50,000 copies in its first two weeks of release. An *Ebony* magazine article from June 10, 1952, said that the record had sold 150,000 copies and sales were still "going strong."[8] Nobody will know absolutely for sure how many copies "Hambone" sold, but what is significant is that a number of cover versions came out to take away sales from the original—notably records by Jo Stafford and Frankie Laine, and Tennessee Ernie Ford. The Stafford/Laine record went as high as fifteen on the pop charts and lasted many weeks. The Hambone Kids release lasted one week and went as high as twenty on the *Billboard* chart. McGrier pointed out that the Hambone Kids used genuine Hambone while all the imitators had to rely on sound effects.

The Hambone Kids were more than Hamboners. "Delecta could imitate the hell out of Johnnie Ray," claimed McGrier, "he had a *very* good voice. Strong probably could sing better than Delecta. We expected Delecta and Ronnie to do the song bit. I demonstrated a fondness for drums, so while they would be out there doing their little solo on the singing, I was going to get behind the drums and spell Red Saunders. Then we had picked up a few tap dancing steps. We had a whole act."

The Hambone Kids made two other records in 1952 to keep their name in prominence. The first was "Zeke'l Zeke'l," which McGrier asserted "was a much better record than 'Hambone.' It had more rhythm; it was a more listenable record." The other was "Piece a Puddin'," which with its "hambone, hambone" refrain was essentially a remake of "Hambone." The two follow-ups failed to connect in the market—the fad had died—and the Hambone Kids broke up not long after.

The Hambone Kids personally never made any money from their short-lived success. (Perhaps, the most they made was from a chicken commercial they did, which McGrier said was the best number they ever recorded.) "We didn't mind," said McGrier, "because that period was a fun time for us. My father did get two royalty checks, one of which was large enough to use as a down payment for a flat. It wasn't all for naught. And I feel I became a better individual because of the experience. I have to think, Delecta benefited from it; Ronnie, I'm not quite so sure about."

McGrier, after spending his high school years playing drums in a jazz combo, left the music scene. He eventually became a successful business executive. Delecta Clark and Ronnie Strong both became doowoppers, Delecta, as Dee Clark, in the Kool Gents and Ronnie Strong in the Fortunes (later Donald Jenkins and the Delighters). Had OKeh built a doowop group around Dee Clark, perhaps the label could have sustained itself better in Chicago's R&B arena. In 1963, "Hambone" was revived as a theme for a children's television show in New York and OKeh re-released the record, thinking that there might be a chance to revive interest in it. It didn't happen.

Theron Records

Theron Records was owned by Connie Toole, an employee for the Santa Fe Railroad who had always loved music and at the rather late age of forty-three got into the record business. Toole was born August 2, 1909, in Coffeyville, Kansas, the son of two well-educated parents. He named the company after a son, Theron. His other son, Cornelius Toole, an attorney, said, "After the First World War Chicago became a mecca for blacks. A lot of people came here to work in the stockyards. And his mother and father came here. His mother was a concert pianist who had graduated from Chicago Musical College. His father was a lawyer. He had been a bugle player in the Spanish-American War. They divorced in 1925, when he was still a teenager and he grew up in that era during the 1920s. I guess he would be the male version of the flapper."[9]

Toole worked various jobs, such as at United Cigar Company, at the stockyards, and as a messenger for the post office. In 1929, when the Regal Theater opened, he was one of the first ushers there. Cornelius Toole recalled,

> It was a beautiful theater. I can remember when I was five years old getting into the Regal free. Of course, it was loaded with visiting bands. I remember seeing Fats Waller there when I was young. Then my father went on the railroad, the Santa Fe, as a waiter in 1939. My father was extremely interested in the music world. My father played the trumpet and the piano. These musicians used to come by the house all the time and play. I remember Art Tatum coming by our house. He had a passion for the music and for musicians, and the sporting life. He liked that environment, always liked nightclubbing and music.

The elder Toole made the record company his life work, after establishing the company in 1952. His first address was 500 East Thirty-third Street; a later one was further south in the heart of the nightclub district, at 6306 South Cottage Grove. Cornelius Toole said, "He produced all the records for the company, using money he made on the railroad to do it. He put every penny back into the company. That caused conflict in his family, and his wife divorced him. The railroad industry went down after the end of the Second World War, and he couldn't count on that and he lost that job. Fortunately through the grace of Congressman Dawson he got a job in the traffic court as a clerk."

The first records Toole put out were by the pianist/vocalist Byllye Williams ("Salty Simple Fool") and Bobby Anderson ("S'posin'"), and they got enough response for him to continue. He worked a lot with the jazz musicians Leon and Earl Washington. The first group he recorded was the

Ebony Moods in early 1955, but the sound was in an archaic 1940s style and could not sell.

In the summer of 1955 Toole put out an appealing ballad on the Sheppards, "Love," but it was a bit deep for that year and didn't do anything. The record featured John Pruitt (lead), James Dennis Isaac (first tenor), Nathaniel Tucker (bass), George Parker (baritone), and Oscar Boyd (second tenor). "Cool Mambo," the flip, featured Parker on lead. By the end of 1955, the Sheppards had moved to Leonard Allen's United label.

Toole pushed a female singer, Connie Allen ("I Haven't Got the Heart"), and another vocal group, the Marvellos ("You're a Dream"), at the end of 1955 and the beginning of 1956. Connie Allen played the local clubs regularly, including the Delisa. Toole apparently spent a lot of his railroad money grooming the Marvellos, a quartet that included two brothers, because he had them go on a promotional tour in early 1956. According to a trade publication, "Connie Toole of Theron Records is lending his group, the Marvellos, to Eastern distribs, for promotional stunts. Connie thinks the boys' waxing of 'You're a Dream' can make it big."[10] The flip was "Calypso Mama." Alas, as with all of Toole's acts, his dreams were not fulfilled with the record.

The Marvellos in 1958 recorded for Norman Forgue's Stepheny label (based in Evanston), on which they did much better with "Come Back My Love" and "Boycee Young." In 1961 the Marvellos launched and gave their name to the Marvello label, which was owned by a musician, James P. Johnson. They recorded two sides for Johnson—"I Need a Girl," a nice bouncy number that is a bit thinly produced, and "Red Hot Mama," a boring jump with good bass work. Both were one-sided releases, with the other side on each featuring a number by songbird Dottie Tillman. Neither release on the Marvellos did anything, as both sounded dated in 1961 (some sources say these sides were released in the mid-1950s).

Toole's last activity in the recording business also came in 1961, when he recorded the Vals on "The Song of a Lover" backed with "Compensation Blues." The record was released on Val Hutchinson's Unique Laboratories label, but the label shows it was produced by Theron Records. Reportedly, only two hundred copies were pressed, apparently to test the waters. When nothing happened, the record was dead. The mid-1950s doowop sound of the record made it too dated for 1961. Only five copies of this record are known to exist. The Vals—Billy Gibson (lead), David Wilkerson Jr., Clarence Green, Ernie Morris, and William Taylor (bass)—were used on one other Unique Laboratories release to back a singer named Vicki Johnson, but their support is anemic and of little interest to doowop fans.[11] Toole continued to try to make it in the record business until the end of his life in 1968. Asked if any records came out during that period, Cornelius Toole sadly and bitterly said,

I don't remember and I doubt it. He was still struggling though. My father tried desperately to maintain the company but he just didn't have the business know-how. Many a problem with black entrepreneurs was that they didn't know how to work a company up to something. And then of course there was a tremendous amount of racial prejudice. It amounted to outright thievery. I'm especially concerned about the thievery. I do know a lot of things he should have had credit for and he should have made money on. I heard stuff over the radio. His stuff was being played by Benson and other people. He didn't get the money.

Club 51

Club 51 was owned by a South Side entrepreneur, Jimmy Davis, and was operated as part of his Savoy Record Mart store at 527 East Sixty-third Street. It was not his only business interest. Two blocks west was his principal enterprise, the Park City Bowl, a skating rink at 345 East Sixty-third, on the corner of Sixty-third and South Parkway Boulevard. From 1947 to 1958 he served as manager (and later, owner) of the rink, where the local deejays, mainly McKie Fitzhugh, held many vocal group concerts and competitions. Up until 1947 Davis was assistant manager of the skating operation at the Savoy Ballroom at Forty-seventh and South Parkway. Through these connections Davis, as well as his wife, Lillian, kept their fingers on the pulse of the black entertainment scene. Because the skating rink served as a rhythm and blues venue and was the home of frequent amateur contests, he could easily find talent.

Davis soon built a small rehearsal studio in the back of his record store and started a label. He appears to have begun the label sometime in 1955, as nearly all of his releases came from the period 1955–57. By the time Davis closed the Park Bowl in 1958, he was out of the record business as well.[12] His was such a small operation that almost all of his acts—performers such as Prince Cooper, Rudy Greene, Bobbie James, Honey Brown, Sunnyland Slim, the Five Buddies, and the Kings Men—were obscure when he recorded them.

Lefty Bates and his combo would be used as accompaniment on most of the sessions. As Jimmy Hawkins of the Five Buddies described the operation, "Davis would record a lot of our stuff in his practice studio first. Then we would go to Universal and have a regular session, but he was always having a hard time getting money for the sessions. I don't know how he recorded as many people as he did. He did have a successful record shop, so maybe the money came from that as well as the skating rink."[13]

The practice studio was used by many groups in the community to make audition dubs to take to other companies. Davis charged $2.00 an hour for studio time and $2.50 a dub, and other Chicago companies, particularly Vee Jay, had aspiring groups cut their audition dubs at Davis's studio to save time. Davis reportedly made hundreds of such dubs.

The Five Buddies is the best known of Club 51's acts. The group was formed in the Ida B. Wells housing project around 1952. The original group was called the Four Buddies and consisted of lead Ularsee Manor, tenor Jimmy Hawkins, tenor Nathaniel "Sam" Hawkins (Jimmy's cousin), and bass/baritone Willie Bryant. The later addition of baritone/bass Dickie Umbra made the group the Five Buddies. Most of the members attended Tilden or Phillips high schools. Sam Hawkins was soon replaced by Donald Ventors, but when Ventors moved back to his home in Texas he was replaced by Irving Hunter. The Five Buddies also sang in church as the Mount Moriah Quintet.[14] Manor recalled, "The clubs around town would hire us and we would perform for them on Saturday and Fridays. On Saturday nights, we'd stay up working all night long, go over get some breakfast, and go sing on Sunday morning at Mount Moriah Baptist Church."[15]

The Five Buddies practiced their craft with the songs made famous by such contemporary groups as the Clovers and the Drifters. For two years they made the local amateur circuit of talent contests conducted in such clubs as the Flame and the Crown Propeller Lounge, competing against such groups as the Five Echoes and the Five Chances. In September 1954 the group got its break and did a radio show with McKie Fitzhugh as part of the promotion for the deejay's big show at Corpus Christi, which featured a host of acts. Hawkins said, "We did the show as a guest group who was up and coming. Sammy Davis Jr. preceded us on the show. We sang that day, I don't recall whether it was an original or not. Jimmy Davis happen to hear us. He was interested and asked us if we wanted to record. We said yes, quite naturally, because we hadn't recorded with anybody."[16]

Davis used the Five Buddies initially as backup session singers, first on a 1955 release by Rudy Greene, a blues singer who had recorded for the Bullet label in Nashville in 1946 and later for Chance Records. On the one side on which the Five Buddies supported Greene, "You Mean Everything to Me," they do a nice low-key job that enhances the singer admirably. The other singer the Five Buddies supported was Bobbie James (Bobbie Mitchell), and on her "I Need You So," a release from the spring of 1955, they do a terrific job. In May 1955 in a Fitzhugh-promoted show at the Park City Bowl, the Five Buddies appeared with Bobbie James (billed as "Bobbie James and Her Buddies"), Amos Milburn, the Danderliers, and the Clouds.

The following year, the group got its first opportunity to record under its name alone, and the result was "Delores" backed with "Look Out." Actually, it was the name "Four Buddies" that appeared on the label, despite the fact that five singers recorded. Apparently Davis hoped to garner some sales by propagating confusion with a better-known earlier group, the Four Buddies, who recorded for the Savoy label. Members on the sides were lead Ularsee Manor, Jimmy Hawkins (who was alternate lead on "Delores"), Irving Hunter, William Bryant, and Dickie Umbra. In 1957, when the break the group was looking for still eluded them, the Five Buddies broke up. Except for Jimmy Hawkins, who sang briefly in a group with Johnny Keyes of the Magnificents, the other members of the Five Buddies never sang in any other groups.

Almost nothing is known of the Kings Men. Their sole record, "Don't Say You're Sorry" backed with "Kickin'," was released in 1957, and shortly afterward two of the five members were taken into the service. Writers listed for their songs—presumably members of the group—were Theodore J. Twiggs and Eugene R. Smith. Ularsee Manor recalled, "Davis signed them because he thought they had potential, but he used them as a way to tighten us up from time to time. One time we had problems with Davis during rehearsals and he didn't like the way we were performing and our attitude so he pulled the Kings Men in."[17]

In March 1957 the Kings Men appeared at the Grand Ballroom on a Herb Kent–sponsored show that included the Spaniels, the Dream Kings, J. B. Lenore, and the Willie Dixon Orchestra. Their record was released that month and the concert was a great way to kick off their recording career. In April the group appeared at Herb Kent's spectacular concert at Hyde Park High and shared the stage with the Danderliers, the Moroccos, the Debonairs, the Debs, the Dells, the Magnificents, and Dee Clark, among others. Presumably it was downhill for the group after that.[18]

The Five Chimes likewise made a recording in Jimmy Davis's studio, but they never had their record released. They were a South Side group and their genesis can be traced to one man, Maurice Simpkins.[19] When he was thirteen and attending Douglas Grammar School, at Thirty-second and Calumet, Simpkins and some of his classmates formed a group called the Sparrows. After some personnel changes, the group evolved into the Five Chimes. Besides Simpkins (first tenor/lead), there were Clarence Seymour (baritone), Joseph Miller (tenor), Lonnie Powe (baritone), and Donald Jenkins (tenor/lead). Jenkins soon left to form his own group, the Fortunes.

The Five Chimes replaced Jenkins with a terrific bass singer, Rufus Hunter. "He had come from those gospel groups," Simpkins said, "so he had been singing different types of stuff than we were singing, which was ballads, the pretty stuff. Rufus started with that blues-type stuff. We kind of liked the way he sang with that background in that church stuff, so we started bending a little his way."[20]

By the time the group was attending Phillips High, the young men had graduated from the street corner and were playing area clubs, garnering a considerable local following. The Chimes were discovered by a jitney cab driver on South Parkway, who had them record two sides in Davis's studio, "Penny" and "Baby." On the songs were Simpkins (lead on "Penny"), Joseph Miller (lead on "Baby"), Clarence Seymour, and Rufus Hunter. Unfortunately, for the Chimes, Davis was not interested enough in the recording to release it, and neither was any other company.

Not long after their recording, the Five Chimes broke up, and the members went their separate ways. Hunter eventually became a member of a touring Magnificents group, later recording with the Cameos in Philadelphia and backing Billy Williams for six months in Los Vegas. Simpkins continued more or less as an ad hoc vocal coach for other groups. He also appeared in a backing group on a Harvey (Fuqua) record in 1961, "The First Time" backed with "Mama." Besides Simpkins, that group included Marvin Gaye, Chuck Barksdale of the Dells, Bobby Walker of the Clouds, and John Miller of the Five Echoes. During the 1960s Simpkins developed a reputation as a songwriter, composing songs for Mighty Joe Young, Darrow Fletcher, Willie Mabon, JoAnn Garrett, Bobby Jones, and the Congenial Four.

Ronel Records

Ronel Records was an imprint of Boulevard Recording Studio, at 306 South Wabash, which was owned by Hal and Eleanor Kaichuck. They founded the label in 1955 and hired a promotion man, Dave Clark, to work A&R and promote the records. The Ronel label did not last more than a few releases, the principal act being a vocal group out of Cleveland called the Hepsters, who had two releases.[21]

The Hepsters got together in early 1954 as the Five Stars and had been formed by Joe Williams, a student at East Technical High. Other members were Art Kirkpatrick, Raymond Harvey, Carl Brown, and Woody Woodall. Like many inner-city youth, the group practiced at a settlement house, the Friendly Inn Settlement House, and paid their dues playing talent shows and teen benefit affairs. The group's break into the recording business came when they auditioned for Estrella Young, who was working for a local booking agency. Young had the group change its name to the Hepsters and worked with the singers in honing their talents for the recording studio and developing original material. Dave Clark, through nationwide contacts he developed for years as a promotion man, found the group via Young and brought them to Chicago to record.[22]

The first release by the Hepsters was "Rock 'n' Rollin' with Santa Claus" backed with "I Had to Let You Go." Released in November 1955, the "Santa Claus" side, a bouncy jump, was the one pushed by Clark. It was also the side he composed, but despite the expertise of the group at putting the song across, it fell flat. The combining of the new rock 'n' roll trend with a Christmas theme was too gimmicky. The other side, a midtempo ballad written by Young, was the A side in terms of artistry. With excellent work at both the bottom and the top, which created an exotic melange of vocal sounds, it represents what quality doowop is all about. Reportedly Clark traveled five thousand miles, pushing the group, yet the record never did much more than get a few plays in a few regions. Meanwhile, the Hepsters largely cooled their heels in Cleveland, playing local gigs when they could, such as stints at the Club Congo.

The Hepsters' second release was "This-a-Way" backed with "I Gotta Sing the Blues." "This-a-Way" was written by the leader, Williams, and the flip was written by Clark. "This-a-Way" opens with a splendid vocal arpeggio in which each member in succession sings a note of the chord (groups called this a bell-tone). It then becomes a routine jump, but it was not routine in its execution. "I Gotta Sing the Blues" is a midtempo workout that is pleasant but not memorable. It was a delayed release, since Ronel did not get the record out until December 1956. The Hepsters were a talented group but never had the opportunity to demonstrate their abilities with a top-flight hit song. Meanwhile, by early 1957 the Kaichucks found how easy it is to lose money in the record business and folded Ronel and returned to their true love, the recording studio business.

C.J. Records

C.J. Records was owned by Carl Jones, who otherwise worked in liquor distribution. He was born Morris Jones on June 9, 1913, in Waxahachie, Texas. As a teenager he took up the banjo and eventually added trumpet and trombone to his instrumental repertoire. He got a show on the local radio station, WXA, singing and playing. Jones soon joined the Carolina Cotton Pickers, the first of many groups to which he belonged. With one such group, Herman Flower's Melody Boys, he played at the Century of Progress Exposition in Chicago in 1933, returning to the city to stay in 1937. In 1945 he recorded two sides for Mercury, "Trouble in Mind" backed with "Mitzy," backed by Bob Shaffner and His Harlem Hotshots.

In 1956 Jones founded the C.J. label, eventually followed by two more, the Colt and Firma labels. He is best known for his output in the blues field, having recorded Earl Hooker, Mack Simmons, Hound Dog Taylor, Homesick James, and Detroit Junior. His vocal group material was almost nil, recording just two sides with the Daffodils and two with the Daylighters.[23]

Jones's record company was never more than a boutique operation, and in its last two decades of existence, during the 1970s and 1980s, he had no distribution. He maintained his nine-to-five job in the liquor distribution business and worked on Sundays as a bartender at a famed South Side blues bar, Theresa's. When Jones died, on September 24, 1985, he was still operating his record company.

Jones's first release, in April 1956, had featured a group called the Daffodils managed by Levi McKay. One side, "Wine," is only an adequate jump, and its lack of success in the marketplace is no surprise. The Five Chances recalled singing "Wine" in some of their live shows, but they never recorded it. The flip side, "These Kissable Lips," is a lovely cocktail lounge type of ballad by Phyllis Smiley, a vocalist who had worked with Duke Ellington. The Daffodils back her unobtrusively with "oohs" and "ahhs." The second release by Jones also featured the Daffodils, who sang the song "Walk." The flip, "Ike's Boogie," is an instrumental jump by the Ike Perkins Band, which played on all the previous sides. Jones claimed "These Kissable Lips" was his first hit record. By this time the group had come under the management of George Hill, who unlike McKay made the group his number one priority. Despite his efforts, however, Hill was not able to get the group into the big time.

The Daffodils were just one of the groups managed by Levi McKay, who also had the Five Chances, Fasinoles, and Fortunes. McKay's practice was to switch members from group to group, and he used the Daffodils as a training group for his other groups. Johnny Jones began his career in the Daffodils before he moved up to the Five Chances. Supposedly Edgar Sampson founded the Daffodils, but nothing is known of the group's other personnel. Like many groups of the early 1950s, the Daffodils were thoroughly at home in the world of nightclubs. On a series of one-nighters in 1956, the group was described as having "an unusual act which even includes some numbers sung in Yiddish."[24]

Another of McKay's groups, the Fasinoles, who emerged around 1954, is worth a mention. They played for a couple of months at Martin's Corner, sharing the bill with the blues singer George Crockett (later known as G. L. Crockett) and an exotic dancer, Rosemary Watts. During that time they took part in the huge McKie Fitzhugh extravaganza at Corpus Christi High that featured more than twenty blues, gospel, and doowop acts. Besides the Fasinoles, that bill included the Five Echoes, the El Dorados, the Kingslettes, the Five Chances, and the Five Buddies, in what was described as a "battle of the singing groups."

Two years later the group, identified as consisting of Eddie Stillwell, George Smith Jr., Andrew Smith, and Thurman King, presumably got on record. The titles reported in the *Chicago Defender* in September 1956 were "Day Break and Night Fall" and "Jewel of My Heart," but they have not been seen by collectors nor have they appeared in any discographies. It is possible that the group merely backed up a solo singer, whose name on the record disguised the participation of the Fasinoles. It is also possible that these were sides that were recorded but never released.[25] In any case, nothing was heard of the Fasinoles after 1956, when the group made an appearance at the Trianon Ballroom at a *Chicago Defender* show.

The Daylighters were recorded by Carl Jones in 1959, near the end of the doowop era. Their most significant recordings were made for the Nike and Tip Top labels.

Cobra Records

The founder and owner of Cobra Records was Elias P. Toscano, who was known in the business as Eli Toscano. He was reportedly of Italian and Mexican extraction, and lived on the West Side at 2910 West Fillmore. A few blocks away, at 2854 West Roosevelt, he ran his business, AB Television and Record Sales, which was a television sales and service outfit, a retail record store, and a one-stop record distributorship. Toscano's wife, Archie, worked in the shop. He had a second store at 3737 West Sixteenth. Another aggressive go-getting young man from the neighborhood, Howard Bedno, developed a friendship with Toscano, and together they would go nightclubbing at the West Side blues joints. Toscano probably got into the record business at the urging of Joe Brown, who provided blues talent for Toscano to record, just as he had for Art Sheridan at Chance. Toscano and Brown started a label in partnership, called Abco. Toscano set up a studio behind the store at 2854 West Roosevelt. His friend Bedno, who in a "handshake deal" worked promotion for the label and helped operate the AB one-stop, was also involved.[26]

The concentration for Abco was blues. There were only seven releases—two bar-band blues, one Louis Myers and the other by Morris Pejoe, and four blues with a more up-town sound, two by Arbee Stidham, one by Herby Joe, and one by Freddie Hall. There was one vocal group release, by the Rip-Chords.

Brown dropped out of the operation during the summer of 1956, and Toscano and Bedno reorganized the firm as Cobra Records in August. They brought in Willie Dixon from Chess Records to act as producer and signed such West Side artists as Harold Burrage, Magic Sam, Otis Rush, and Betty Everett. In the summer of 1957 the label relocated to 3346 West Roosevelt Road and, as at the old address, set up a studio in the back. Bedno left the operation in late 1957 to work promotion for George Goldner, eventually ending up at All-State Record Distributing and becoming one of the area's top promotion men.

Toscano soldiered on and in 1958 set up a subsidiary label, Artistic, on which he put out Buddy Guy and Shakey Jake releases. The company recorded the vast majority of its output at its own studios, but it also made use of Boulevard and Universal.

Toscano's labels probably went out of business before Toscano died, around 1959, presumably in a boating accident. For years, blues researchers quoted various Cobra artists who said that the record owner died in a gangland slaying. Toscano had a bad gambling habit and reputedly borrowed money from the mob to pay gambling debts. As the story goes, his harsh rebuff to a loan-shark collector caused his murder in a gangland hit. Bedno, however, who attended the funeral, asserts that there is nothing to that story.[27]

Cobra, during its three-year existence, got only one national R&B hit, Otis Rush's powerful "I Can't Quit You Baby," in October 1956. It was the company's very first release, and it established the recording strategy for Cobra. The company became best known for the powerful sides it made on the guitarists Otis Rush, Magic Sam, and Buddy Guy. Because the company made its guitar lead work so vital to the recordings, these artists had a tremendous influence in shaping the guitar style of later rockers (mostly British). But the tamer rhythm and blues stylings by Betty Everett and Harold Burrage should not be overlooked.

Cobra was less successful, artistically, in recording vocal groups. Given the talent it had on hand and its predilection for recording blues, the company probably should never have attempted it. Besides the Rip-Chords, the only vocal groups connected with Toscano's operations were the Calvaes and the Clouds. None of their records can be considered close to even local hit potential, but these groups did make something of an impact on the vocal group scene, mainly in live performances.

The Rip-Chords made only one record in their career, and that was for the Abco label in 1956.[28] The group began as the Five Knights of Rhythm around 1955. Members were Leon Arnold (lead), John Gillespie (alto), George Vinyard (first tenor), David Hargrove (second tenor), and Lester Martin (bass), and apparently they were signed with Vee Jay for a time. Arnold wrote a song for the group, "I'll Be Forever Loving You," but Vee Jay, having heard it, decided to place it with one of the company's most popular groups, the El Dorados. As luck would have it, the El Dorados got a hit with the song, and in 1956 the Five Knights of Rhythm left Vee Jay, changing their name to the Rip-Chords (maybe a play on "rip-off").

As was true of most groups of the day, the Rip-Chords worked on songs that were then popular, particularly those of the Moonglows and Flamingos. Arnold, however, contended that most of their repertoire was original material. To get a recording contract, the Rip-Chords auditioned for

Toscano, who accepted them and quickly put them on wax. The two less-than-stellar sides were, typically, a ballad ("I Love You the Most") and a jump ("Let's Do the Razzle Dazzle"). Not long after the record was released and bombed in the marketplace, the Rip-Chords broke up. Arnold blamed poor management.

The Rip-Chords made the usual appearances in local venues but even had a few gigs outside of Chicago. In September 1956, in Chicago, they played at a Jim Lounsbury promotion at the Memorial Auditorium with the El Dorados, the Dells, and two fellow Cobra acts, the Clouds and Otis Rush. After the group broke up, Leon Arnold joined the Calvaes but was not on any of the group's recordings. He did a solo record for Bunky Sheppard's Wes label in 1961, coming out with "But (Goodbye)" backed with "Here's to the Girl," but that record was his last effort in the music business.

The Clouds, though managed by Levi McKay, were promoted and mentored by the deejay McKie Fitzhugh. They regularly recorded doowop commercials for Fitzhugh and did his theme song for his WOPA radio show. The group first came to notice in January 1955, after they won a talent contest at the Pershing Ballroom.[29] Their reward was a recording contract, which apparently was for Al Benson's Parrot label. An unreleased side, "Say You Love Me," first surfaced in 1976 on a bootleg album called *Parrot Doowop* and later was legally released on a Relic album in 1990. It is an especially fine lost gem. The lead, presumably Sherrard Jones, is magnificent, and the vocal arrangement exciting. The song is distinguished by a recitation break that made it sound like a typical L.A. doowop record. Albert Hunter may have been on the Parrot sides, because in 1955 it's known that Five Chances member Johnny Jones pulled him out of the Clouds to sing in an ad hoc Maples session for Benson.

Fitzhugh had his own personal group, as did every disc jockey of the day, and his was the Clouds, which he booked at every show he produced. In May 1955 they played an engagement at the Park City Bowl that included Amos Milburn, the Danderliers, Bobbie James and Her Buddies, and Roy Eldridge. In September they played the Crown Propeller Lounge with T-Bone Walker, and on January 1 they opened the new year with another Fitzhugh promotion at the Park Bowl, which also featured Jimmy Witherspoon, Etta James, and Miles Davis.

In 1956 the Clouds joined the Cobra label, and at this time the lead was Sherrard Jones, with a supporting cast that seems to have been Al Butler, William English, and Bobby Walker. Cobra released just two sides on the group, "I Do" and "Rock and Roll Boogie." "I Do" was the ballad side, written by Butler, and is a fairly decent outing, but the recording done at Boulevard lacked production flair. With minimal piano accompaniment, the singers sounded as though they were on their own. "Rock and Roll Boogie," in which the company gave Howard Bedno writing credit, is something of a mess, with choruses coming in at the wrong time and other flaws.

Despite the weakness of the record, the Clouds were extremely busy with live appearances, thanks to their tie-in with Fitzhugh. In March the group played the Park City Bowl with Bo Diddley, the Pastels (the United group), the Drifters, and the Clovers. In the next month the group played a low-budget teen dance at the Trianon and shared the stage with a bunch of no-names—the Vi-Counts, the Teen Sweethearts, and the Enchanters. Also in April the group played with Billie Holiday at the Trianon. In September the group was in the Jim Lounsbury promotion at the Memorial Auditorium, but in November, on Thanksgiving Day, they participated in what the newspaper called a "McKie Fitzhugh rock 'n' roll package" at the Trianon, but what looked more like a Cobra Records promotion. Besides the Clouds, the bill included Cobra labelmates the Calvaes, Otis Rush, and Harold Burrage. Other acts on the bill were the Five Echoes, the Kool Gents, the Magnificents, G. L. Crockett, and Lil "Upstairs" Mason. The Clouds' last notable appearance was at the Mambo Easter Dance show in April 1957, sponsored by McKie Fitzhugh and Big Bill Hill.

The Calvaes, having not gotten more than a few local plays on their records, are not well known.[30] Clifton Carter, of the Five Cliffs of Dover, said, "The Calvaes was a little young group out of the Dearborn Homes, on the Twenty-ninth and Thirtieth blocks of State Street."[31] They came under the management of Ted Daniels, one of the top guys then working with groups. Toscano chose to release four sides on the group, whose members may have been James "Zeke" Brown (lead), Donald Handley, James Bailey, Donald "Duck" Coles, and Paul Morgan. The first pairing was two jumps, "Fine Girl" and "Mambo Fiesta," in which the group sing well on routine material. The bass and tenor work is outstanding, but the lead lacks distinction. Bedno was given songwriting credit for "Fine Girl" and Brown for "Mambo Fiesta."

The Calvaes were not so fortunate as the Clouds in getting work in the city, not having a deejay behind them who doubled as a promoter. They played the Jim Lounsbury Memorial Auditorium show in September 1956 and the Fitzhugh Thanksgiving show at the Trianon that year, sharing the stage with the other Cobra acts. They were able to play at two Sam Evans promotions: in September 1956, at a prestigious show at the Trianon, where they were on the bill with Ray Charles, Chuck Willis, J. B. Lenore, and Nate Nelson (who was attempting a solo from the Flamingos), and in February 1957, at a midnight show at the Central Park Theater, sharing the bill with Andre Williams, Jimmy Rogers, John Lee Hooker, Kool Gents, and Otis Rush. In July, Cobra released a second pairing, again two jumps, "Born with Rhythm" and "Lonely Lonely Village," both sides written by Daniels.

"Born with Rhythm" is uninteresting but, worse, the Latinish "Lonely Lonely Village" is unlistenable.

The Calvaes were able to linger for a couple more years, and they got a record out on Chess in 1958, "Anna Macora" backed by "So Bad." "Anna Macora" made the Cobra sides sound like masterpieces, and "So Bad," in which the artists were billed as "Oscar Boyd and the Calvaes," is thoroughly described by its title. The Calvaes, like the Clouds, should best be remembered as an outstanding live act, whose talents were never properly represented on records.

Bea and Baby Records

Narvel Eatmon, who went by the name of Cadillac Baby, ranks as one of Chicago's most colorful record men. Born in 1914 in Cayuga, Mississippi, a small hamlet near the town of Utica, Eatmon hitchhiked his way to Chicago in the early 1930s. In the 1940s he established his Cadillac Baby's Club at 4708 South Dearborn, which survived up through the 1950s. In 1959 he established his Bea and Baby label, which he named after himself and his wife, Bea. Subsidiary labels were Key, Keyhole, and Miss. With Ted Daniels he also operated the Ronald label. Most of his recordings were of bluesmen, notably Eddie Boyd, Little Mac, and Detroit Junior. His biggest record was Bobby Saxton's "Tryin' to Make a Livin'," which was a local hit in 1960. Eatmon only recorded three vocal groups, the Daylighters, Faith Taylor and the Sweet Teens, and the Chances (the latter a girl group consisting of his stepdaughters). In his later years Eatmon operated a candy and variety store at 4405 South State, where one could purchase some of his old records. After it burned down he opened another shop, at Fifty-eighth and State, which he operated until he died in 1991.[32]

Eatmon's recording of Faith Taylor and the Sweet Teens was something of an anomaly, as the adolescent voices of their recordings contrasted greatly with his label's usual gritty city blues fare. But he undoubtedly was familiar with Frankie Lymon and the Teenagers, saw how many records the thirteen-year-old Lymon sold, and thought he could sell a few with that sound as well.[33]

Fans of 1950s vocal harmony groups have over the years delineated various subgenres of doowop, and one favorite subgenre is made up of "teen tenor lead" groups. These ensembles generally patterned their sound after the tremendously successful Frankie Lymon and the Teenagers, who introduced it to rhythm and blues and rock 'n' roll. But the term "teen tenor lead" is not an accurate one, because the sound of the lead is that of a juvenile high-tenor, the voice of a middle-school boy before his voice has changed. The voice also has an ambiguous sexual identity and on recordings could easily be that of a female or male. Many females have been involved in the sound, even though twelve-to-fourteen-year-old males predominate. Notable females who have that sound are Pearl McKinnon of the Kodaks and, more recently, a revived Teenagers group; Ronnie Bennett of the Ronettes; and from Chicago, Faith Taylor of the Sweet Teens.[34]

Faith Taylor was born in Dumas, Arkansas, in 1948. She began performing at the age of four and won her first amateur contest in Little Rock. She came to Chicago with her family in 1957 and continued her music career by singing at small club affairs. She also worked in a few combos, including that of Muddy Waters. In June 1957 she entered and won the "Morris B. Sachs Amateur Hour" on WGN-TV. The following year a friend of Taylor, Charles Jones, was assembling a vocal group and brought her in as the lead. Other members of this group were alto Yvonne Waddell (age seventeen), tenor Saundra Long (sixteen), soprano Mary Collins (seventeen), and bass Curtis Burrell (seventeen). Most of the group came from two South Side high schools, DuSable and Dunbar. Faith Taylor and the Sweet Teens were unlike most "teen tenor lead" groups in being mostly comprised of females.

From that start, the group was not going to be a "girl group" but one patterned after Frankie Lymon and the Teenagers. Taylor said to a *Chicago Defender* reporter, "People say I sing very much like Frankie, but I don't care. I think Frankie Lymon is one of the greatest [performers in] rock 'n' roll, which is what I sing."[35]

The group made its first recordings in August 1958, recording "Your Candy Kisses" and "Won't Someone Tell Me Why," released back to back on the Federal label. Both were written by Charles Jones. "Your Candy Kisses" opens with a sax flourish, followed by Taylor doing a patented Frankie Lymon "oh oh ooh oh oh ooh." However, she sounds a tad too young, like the ten-year-old she was (although newspaper reports at the time stated she was nine). The vocal support is a bit weak, but Curtis Burrell's bass work is good. "Won't Someone Tell Me Why" opens with an impact, a vocal arpeggio, or bell-tone, and young Taylor goes into her "oh oh ooh" thing again. After that it sounds a bit ragged. They return to the "bell-tone" just before the bridge, again with good effect, and Burrell again distinguishes himself. Central to the appeal of both songs is Faith Taylor, who knew at a tender age exactly how she was supposed to sing them, but with all her talent she is still a bit raw. Despite the record's evident flaws, it is a terrific rock 'n' roll pairing that deserves to belong in anyone's record collection.

The two songs were paired on a single and released in September 1958. The record made a bit of a stir in Chicago and several other markets but never managed to crack the national charts. Faith Taylor and the Sweet

Teens appeared on Jim Lounsbury's record hop on WBKB-TV in October and played a few clubs in the Chicago area, notably Budland in the Pershing Hotel. The Budland date would seem strange today as the group shared the bill with a bluesman (Dr. Jo Jo Adams), a jazz combo (Prince James Combo), and an avant-garde group (Sun Ra).

In late 1959 Faith Taylor and the Sweet Teens joined Narvel Eatmon's Bea and Baby label. Members of the Bea and Baby group, besides Faith Taylor, were Curtis Burrell and Mary Collins from the original group, and two new members, Elizabeth Shelby and Ernestine Fisher. The Bea and Baby release, "I Need Him to Love Me" backed with "I Love You Darling," featured two outstanding sides in the Frankie Lymon mode. "I Need Him to Love Me," the ballad side written by Bernice Williams, is sublime, with chorusing by the rest of the group that sounded angelic. Faith Taylor now had the depth of expression to come across with a terrific soulful feeling. The flip is a rousing jump written by Charles Jones, and again the chorusing is terrific. Noticeably absent on both sides is the good bass work of Burrell.

The group was gone by the summer of 1960, when Faith Taylor appeared by herself at the annual Bud Billiken Picnic Show in August. She appeared again on the next year's picnic show as part of a youth package of performers, Paula Greer and Eddie Purrell among them. She was heard last in December 1961, when she performed for patients at a veterans hospital. Except for Curtis Burrell, who became a member of the Daylighters in 1964, nothing further is known about Faith Taylor and the remainder of the Sweet Teens.

Formal Records

The story of Formal Records is mostly the story of independent record entrepreneur Don Talty, who made his mark during the early 1960s with such acts as Willie Mabon, Young Guitar Red, the Philip Upchurch Combo, and Jan Bradley. But before he scored with those acts, he made his entrance into the record business in 1959 working with doowop groups, namely the Trinidads and the Masquerades. Talty never achieved anything with either group, partly because he was a neophyte at the time and was still learning how to make records. Talty was born August 16, 1911, in downstate Illinois, and by the late 1940s was the owner of his own excavating business in the Chicago area. His real passion was music, especially jazz and blues.

In the spring of 1959 Talty took over the operation but not the ownership of Formal Records, a label started in 1956 by an owner of a formal-wear shop, Angelo Giardini. Gradually he withdrew from his excavating business to become a full-time record entrepreneur. Talty operated out of his home at 5801 South Harlem in the southwestern suburb of Oak Lawn with the help of his wife, Zelda, and his two teenage daughters, Janice and Joanne.[36]

Curiously, Talty never seemed to own a label, yet for various labels that his productions appeared on—such as Formal, Boyd, Night Owl, and Adanti—he had logos designed, labels printed up, and records pressed. Regarding the Formal situation, Giardini said, "Talty contacted me. He decided he wanted to promote some songs of his, or material he had. And he wanted to use the label. I could never understand at the time why he couldn't just form a label of his own, which is so simple—it's just a matter of doing it."[37] Talty preferred to work with acts, and the first act he pushed was the Trinidads.

The Trinidads, a vocal group of five fellows, was the first act Talty ever released on record. The members of the group were all in their late teens and from the southwestern suburbs, mainly Argo and LaGrange. They were Charles Davis (lead and tenor), Hosea Brown (lead and tenor), Charles Colbert Jr. (first tenor), Norman Price (baritone), and Claude Forch (bass). Davis and Colbert were cousins. The history of the group was short, lasting only from early 1958 to 1961. During this time Talty released two unimpressive records on the group and had them play local dates at high schools and similar places.[38]

The Trinidads were obviously talented singers but the talent was not translated well on wax. Talty depended on an old high school friend, Frank Derrick, a big-band saxophone player, to arrange the records, and he was apparently as much a neophyte as Talty was. The first release coupled "Don't Say Goodbye," a mess of a ballad with a horrible instrumental arrangement done in a different key than the vocals, with "On My Happy Way," a bouncy Latin-rhythm number with an intrusive sax by Derrick. The record met with massive indifference upon its release in April 1959. The follow-up was mildly better. It paired "When We're Together," a droopy ballad with Derrick's intrusive sax, and "One Lonely Night," a jump tune with an oddly under-recorded lead vocal that seems overwhelmed by the background chanting. Fortunately, Talty would do better on subsequent releases.

The Trinidads replaced lead Hosea Brown with a gentleman who is recalled only by his last name, Kitchen. But no matter, the group fell apart in 1961, and Chuck Colbert Jr. joined another group, the Daylighters, who were originally from Alabama and had already recorded on Bea and Baby and on C.J. Records. Colbert stayed with the Daylighters until 1964, and then became a big rock star as a member of the American Breed, of "Bend Me, Shape Me" fame. Meanwhile, Charles Davis continued as a solo act for a while, and in 1962 joined the Dukays, replacing Gene Chandler as the group's lead. He made several fine records with the Dukays, then joined the Artistics for a short spell. During 1964–65, he recorded two superb songs for Constellation as Nolan Chance, "She's Gone" and "Just Like the Weather." The Trinidads owe their fame to the talents they produced rather than to any of the records they made.

The Daylighters, with Colbert and another new member, guitarist Gerald Sims, were coming on strong with dynamic new material. They recorded a few sides for Talty at the RCA Studio, but he was apparently losing interest in vocal groups and refused to pay for the session. The Daylighters paid for the sessions with money from Colbert's father, retrieved the tapes, and began issuing records on Nike and Tip Top, with good local success. I have heard practice tapes that were in the possession of Talty which included tremendous versions of two Daylighters' hits, "Cool Breeze" and "Oh What a Way to Be Loved." It appeared he made a mistake when he let the group go.

The Masquerades did absolutely nothing for Talty saleswise, but some of the best music he ever recorded was done with this group. They recorded nine songs, four of which eventually appeared on wax. The outstanding released side from the collector's standpoint is the group's second release from 1961, "Fanessa," a beautiful ballad. But the unreleased titles I have heard are three equally magnificent ballads—"Portia," "That's When Your Heartaches Begin," and "These Foolish Things"—and a slowed-down version of Little Richard's "Good Golly Miss Molly." The style of these songs evokes that of an adult harmony group from the 1940s—classy, smooth, and richly atmospheric—rather than a teenage doowop group. That the world never heard these songs at the time of their recording in 1960 was a real shame.

And who were the Masquerades?[39] None other than the Scott Brothers, before they became a self-contained band. The Scott Brothers Band was a Chicago institution during the 1960s and 1970s, backing innumerable soul artists in clubs and concert stages. But as the Masquerades they were a doowop vocal group. The brothers, who grew up on the near South Side, came from a musical family involving the mother, father, and grandfather, in particular. Their uncle, Cecil Perkins, used to play with Muddy Waters, Little Walter, and Memphis Slim. Robert Scott recalled, "All those old-time blues players used to be at our house every day."[40] Howard (or Cephus), one of the older brothers, was singing bass in gospel groups in the early 1950s, most notably with the Jackson Golden Bells.

The Masquerades were formed in 1957 as the Elpeccios and originally consisted of Howard, Charles, and Robert Scott, and cousin Jesse "Chico" Golden. Golden and Robert Scott soon dropped out, and in early 1958 the group reorganized as the Masquerades, consisting of Howard, Charles, and Tommie Scott, Jimmy Thompson, and Ike Hickman. Robert Scott entered the professional boxing ranks as a welterweight, fighting in the same stable as world junior welterweight champion Eddie Perkins.

The Masquerades were discovered by Talty in 1960 singing in a North Side nightclub. At the time of the first recordings for Talty, the group consisted of Howard, Walter, Charles, and Tommie Scott, plus Ike Hickman and guitarist Howard Taylor. Jimmy Thompson had left the group to take up guitar, and years later would emerge as a well-respected Chicago blues performer Jimmy Johnson. Thompson changed his name to "Johnson" after his brother Syl had achieved fame as a soul singer under the name "Syl Johnson." The Masquerades released "Mister Man" backed with "These Red Roses" in 1960 on the Formal label, which was not the best of debuts. The following year Buddy Scott replaced Taylor on guitar and the group came out with "The Whip" backed with "Fanessa" on the Boyd label. "The Whip" was intended to promote a dance and was considered the A side. Talty even had artwork done to show the dance steps, but nothing came of the record. The few collectors in possession of the record (there are about ten records in existence) highly prize the ballad side.

No more records by the Masquerades were released for Talty, but the group later went down to St. Louis to record two sides for Ike Turner on the Joyce label, "Summer Sunrise" backed with "Nature's Beauty." Again nothing happened for the group. They continued on, and guitarists who worked for them in the following years included their old vocal mate, Jimmy Johnson, and his brother, Syl Johnson. Around 1963–64, the Masquerades called it quits as a vocal group, and like a phoenix rising from the ashes re-emerged as the Scott Brothers Band. Said Howard, "We just got together and just sat down and said why don't we learn some instruments? That's how we got started."[41] The story of the Scott Brothers does signal a new beginning and thus another story, well deserving of a telling some day.

Lucky Four Records

Lenny LaCour has operated probably a dozen labels in his lifetime, working out of both Chicago and Milwaukee, but it is from 1960 to 1964, when he ran first the Lucky Four then the Six-Twenty, that he heavily recorded vocal groups. Among his acts were the Swinging Hearts, the Del Prados, the Uniques, and the Tides, along with solo rhythm and blues, country and western, and rockabilly performers. It was a one-man operation, in which LaCour was the chief songwriter, the arranger, and the producer. He usually recorded at Hall Studio.[42]

LaCour, a man of Cajun heritage, was born April 27, 1932, in Bayou

Bredelle, a community near New Orleans, Louisiana. When he was attending Saint James High, in Alexandria, Louisiana, he formed a band that played in the southern roadhouses and honky-tonks, specializing in what might be called country boogie; that is, country music with a rock 'n' roll beat. LaCour went up to Chicago in 1950 but was soon back again in Louisiana. Upon his return north in 1952, he brought a demo of a blues recording, "Alligator Man" backed with "My Baby She's Gone." Chess turned it down, and according to LaCour, Leonard Chess commented, "I promote black blues singers. The market is not ready yet for you; nor do I think whites will ever gain popularity singing the blues."[43] The recording came out on a small label called All American. LaCour was billing himself as King Creole at this time, a name he later trademarked. By 1953—showing his versatility—he was fronting the Al Peterson Big Band, singing pop tunes, and made two records with the band on the Spin and the Meteor labels. Then he went back home to Louisiana.

Around 1955, LaCour returned to Chicago to enter a talent contest that Orange Crush was conducting. The company was trying to find a singer to hawk their soda using the new rock 'n' roll sound to reach the teenagers. LaCour won the contest and as King Creole made a series of television commercials in which he sang about Orange Crush with a rock 'n' roll beat. A record by LaCour, "Rock 'n' Roll Romance," was hung on the side of each carton of Orange Crush. This project was tied into a contract with Frank McGovern's Academy label, recording under his given name, Lenny LaCour. The standout of the several records released on Academy was the highly esteemed "Rockin' Rosalie" in 1957.

Unhappiness with the Academy contract, which garnered him no royalties yet tied him to Academy for years, forced LaCour to become an entrepreneur. He first established his own publishing company at 3330 North Lake Shore Drive in 1957. The following year, in association with construction engineer Arnold Lauer (who provided the office space at 5400 West Diversey), he founded his own recording company. The Lucky Four label was launched in 1960. Eventually Lauer dropped out and LaCour became sole owner. He recorded himself under a pseudonym, the "Big Rocker," and also started to look for other acts, beginning with the rock 'n' roll band Eddie Bell and the Belaires. LaCour had some local success with this group with "The Masked Man" (which was leased to Mercury) and the "Great Great Pumpkin." At LaCour's suggestion and under his early sponsorship, Bell later left the rock 'n' roll world to become a huge polka star under his given name, Eddie Blazonczyk. Another notable act of LaCour's was a white rhythm and blues performer by the name of Bobby Oliver. He had some local success with "Where Do Dreams Go" on WGES, but not on any white outlet.

By 1961 LaCour was concentrating his energies almost exclusively on vocal groups. The Swinging Hearts were a five-man group from Robbins, in the south Chicago suburbs, featuring the excellent lead of Morris Spearmon and the outstanding bass of Roscoe Brown. Other members were Ernest Lemon, Jerry Williams, and Lee Brown (a cousin or brother of Roscoe). The four, minus Lee Brown, had attended Blue Island High and had sung in the Passions, a group with female lead Addie Bradley. Record entrepreneur Don Talty discovered the group but wanted only Bradley. He rechristened her Jan Bradley and she went on to fame with "Mama Didn't Lie." The remaining Passions added Lee and refocused their career with Spearmon as lead under the name Swinging Hearts.[44] Said LaCour, "I thought the Swinging Hearts had an exceptional amount of talent. Their dancing ability, their choreography, was unbelievable."

LaCour proceeded to record one of the best group records of his career, "Please Say It Isn't So," a rendition that was doowop but with strong gospel overtones. Spearmon's lead is highly flavorful and appealing and Brown's bass recitation in the song is riveting. LaCour sold about twenty thousand copies of "Please Say It Isn't So" after its release in 1961. But LaCour worked the record and it continued to garner sales across the country long after that. In 1965 Diamond Records in New York picked it up for national distribution. "Whenever a record started doing something I was concerned to try to cover my expenses. Then if someone was interested in picking it up I would let it go," said LaCour. "My deals were very difficult and very bad with these other record companies. I don't think I ever received one check from Diamond Records after they picked that record up."

The Swinging Hearts recorded doowops in a more traditional vein with their next release from 1963, on Six-Twenty, the Spearmon-composed "Spanish Love," a Latin-style song with a perky beat, backed with a droopy ballad, "How Can I Love You." The group's last release with the company was "You Speak of Love" (a pleasant but unmemorable ballad that featured superb singing) backed with "I've Got It" (which marvelously married street-corner doowopping with gospel call-and-response). But the record upon release in 1964 did not sell as LaCour expected.

LaCour had difficulty promoting the group, he said: "They were all working jobs and the difficulty was to get them out on the road touring to where they could have been appreciated. I believe they could have been one of the biggest groups in the business, but it wasn't possible because they were all working and had families."

The Uniques were a fabulously talented group, but destined to end up in obscurity. "I had picked them up as a background group," recalled LaCour. "I had advertised in the newspaper and they responded. They came from the West Side. I think they did three or four sessions background for me, and I thought it was so great so I said let's do a session on the group as a whole and get their names on the label."

The Uniques' first release, "Silvery Moon" backed with "Chocolate Bar," was on the Lucky Four label in 1962. "Silvery Moon" was typical of the period in that the doowop stylings were highly baroque, as though it was doowop commenting on a doowop. The record jumps out of the gate with fast vocal riffing and then surprises the listener by turning into a highly appealing romantic ballad. This is one of LaCour's best group recordings. "Chocolate Bar" is a typical rock 'n' roll doowop, with a fast-paced beat, strong vocal riffing, and a great sax solo at the break—a solid record representing doowop as a form of rock 'n' roll.

The next release on the Uniques, on Six-Twenty in 1963, featured "Saturday Night Walk," an eerie dirgelike dance tune meant to promote the Walk, a dance popular at African American teen dances in Chicago in the early 1960s. Alas, it failed to replace Martin Denny's "Quiet Village" and the Diablos' "The Way You Dog Me Around" as the music of choice by which to do the Walk. The flip, "Pretty Baby," was another story in which the group's falsetto lead performs most beautifully to produce an outstanding side. The Uniques followed in 1964 with another dance record, "Chicken (Yeah)," which was meant to create a chicken dance fad. But this routine side could hardly match the B side, called "Cry, Cry, Cry." With its baroque doowop stylings, prominent bass work, and smooth tenor lead, it perfectly captures the style of Italian-American doowop popular at that time.

LaCour also recorded the Uniques as the Tides, having them do the Sam Cooke song "Bring It Home to Me" in 1964 on his Six-Twenty label. It was anemic, but the flip, written by member Willie Sullivan, "Who Told You," features a nice chanting riff and ends with good falsetto work. According to LaCour, he changed the name of the group because "one of the fellows in the Uniques had gotten brisk with one of the popular disc jockeys. He said some bad things because they had to do a freebie for the disc jockey. It sort of cast a reflection so that the deejay was going to make sure nobody else would play their records also. So then we put the next record out under the name of the Tides. They never knew the difference and we did get a lot of pop play."

The Del Prados were not a LaCour discovery; their association with the company was a result of LaCour's ties with a disc jockey. LaCour recalled, "They had one record. It was sort of arranged for me by Jim Lounsbury, who had scouted the group. He worked with the group, rehearsed them and everything. It was just a matter of me walking into the studio, almost picking up the master, and walking out and going to work on it."[45] The Del

Prados' record, "Oh Baby" backed with "The Skip," released in late 1962, was not a winning effort. "Oh Baby" sounded so ancient that it could have been recorded in 1954 for Chance Records. "The Skip" sounded better but did not catch on as a new dance craze.

In 1964 LaCour moved to Milwaukee and had better success recording Milwaukee acts on the Magic Touch label, most notably Harvey Scales and the Seven Sounds (known for "Get Down" and "Love-Itis"). By the late 1970s LaCour was back in Chicago and releasing disco records, with less success. "I spent a very large sum of my life earnings producing records. After you figure all things that go into producing, mix down, and mastering a record, your costs will run sky high. My whole theory was to be independent, and to be independent costs a lot of money. I had offers on many occasions to go produce with major record companies. Now that I think about it might have been a great idea. Because a lot of times I would have to make deals. Once I had the records moving, major labels would be interested in taking the record and moving on with it. I would always have to stir up the interest. Then the outcome, I never got paid!" On a pensive note, LaCour added, "If I brought as much happiness to the groups and their families as I enjoyed working with them then 'God Bless.' It was worth every hour I spent down to perfecting a mixdown."[46]

Notes

1. Information about OKeh comes from Grendysa [company history essay] and Marshall [artists biographies essay], liner notes, *OKeh.*

2. "OKeh Handled by 20 Indies."

3. Information about Red Saunders comes primarily from Calloway, "Entertainment World" and "Red Saunders."

4. Willie Dixon sources include Bernholm, liner notes, Big Three Trio, and Grendysa, "The Four Jumps."

5. Twain, *Life on the Mississippi,* p. 23. I am indebted to the late Marshall Stearns for this quote; it was through his groundbreaking book *Jazz Dance* that I first became aware of the passage.

6. Information about the Hambone Kids comes from Pruter, "The Hambone Kids"; "Hambone Kids," *Ebony.*

7. This and subsequent remarks by McGrier quoted in this chapter are from the McGrier interview.

8. "Hambone Kids," *Ebony.*

9. This and subsequent remarks by Cornelius Toole quoted in this chapter are from the Toole interview.

10. Gart, *First Pressings: History of Rhythm and Blues,* vol. 6, 1956, p. 23.

11. Stallworth, "Vals."

12. Information about Club 51 comes from Fileti, liner notes, *Golden Groups.*

13. Hawkins interview.

14. Information about the Four Buddies comes from Hinckley [with Goldberg], "The Other Four Buddies"; Hawkins and Manor interviews.

15. Manor interview.

16. Hawkins interview.

17. Manor interview.

18. Fileti, liner notes, *Golden Groups.*

19. Information about the Five Chimes comes from Pruter, "Early Chicago Groups"; Simpkins and Hunter interviews.

20. Simpkins interview, August 7, 1977.

21. Information about Ronel comes from Gart, *First Pressings: History of Rhythm and Blues,* vol. 5, 1955, and vol. 6, 1956.

22. Information about the Five Hepsters comes from "Five Hepsters," p. 22.

23. Information about C. J. Records comes from Baker, "The C.J. Records Story."

24. The Daffodils have defied attempts to track them down, and there are no published sources on their career.

25. "The Well-Known Fascinoles."

26. Information about Toscano's labels comes from Haig and Snowden, liner notes, *The Cobra Records Story;* Rowe, *Chicago Breakdown,* pp. 175–83.

27. Bedno's only extensive interview regarding Cobra was with Diane Reid Haig and was published in the *Cobra Record Story* liner notes. He may not have been entirely forthcoming regarding the circumstances of Toscano's death, because his account was strongly disputed in a private conversation I had with a one-time prominent deejay who was a personal friend of Toscano.

28. Information about the Rip-Chords comes from Goldberg, "The Rip-Chords."

29. This profile of the Clouds has been pieced together from a myriad of small published items and interview comments.

30. This profile of the Calvaes has been pieced together from a myriad of small published items and interview comments.

31. Clifton Carter interview.

32. Information about Bea and Baby Records comes from O'Neal, "You Must Be" and "Narvel Eatmon (Cadillac Baby)."

33. Information about Faith Taylor and the Sweet Teens comes from "Faith Taylor, Nine Stars On Video"; "Faith Taylor Cited"; Roy, "Meet Faith Taylor."

34. Beckman, "Teenage Tenor Leads."

35. Roy, "Meet Faith Taylor."

36. Information about Formal Records comes from Pruter, "Don Talty" and "Formal"; information for this account also came from the private papers of Don Talty, held by Janice McVickers, Sandwich, Illinois. See also Giardini and McVickers interviews.

37. Giardini interview.

38. Information about the Trinidads comes from Pruter, "Don Talty"; idem, "Nolan Chance"; Colbert Jr. and Charles Davis interviews.

39. For information about the Masquerades, see Pruter, "Don Talty"; "The Masquerades" [caption]; "Six of a Kind" [caption]; Howard and Robert Scott interviews.

40. Robert Scott interview.

41. Howard Scott interview.

42. There are no published accounts of LaCour's operations. See LaCour interviews.

43. Unless otherwise noted, this and subsequent remarks by LaCour quoted in this chapter are from the 1993 LaCour interview.

44. Jan Bradley interview.

45. LaCour interview, June 22, 1984.

46. LaCour interview, June 6, 1984.

The Savoy Record Shop, shown in the early 1950s, was the headquarters of Jimmy Davis's Club 51 label. Courtesy of Relic Records.

The Five Buddies, 1956. Left to right: William Bryant, Irving Hunter, Jimmy Hawkins, Dickie Umbra, and Ularsee Manor.

The Kings Men, 1957. This group recorded for the Club 51 label. Courtesy of Relic Records.

The Clouds, ca. 1956. One of several groups sponsored by the Chicago deejay McKie Fitzhugh, the Clouds performed at Fitzhugh's promoted shows and sang his theme song for his radio show. Courtesy of the Chicago Historical Society.

The Calvaes, 1956. These singers made a much bigger impact with their live performances than with their recordings for Cobra.

Faith Taylor and the Sweet Teens, 1958. This was the first Chicago group to make doowop records in the preteen style of Frankie Lymon and the Teenagers.

The Trinidads, 1960. Left to right: Claude Forch, Charles Davis, Chuck Colbert Jr., and Norman Price. Courtesy of Janice McVickers.

The Masquerades, 1961. Top, left to right: Buddy Scott, Ike Hickman, and Howard Scott; bottom, left to right: Tommy Scott, Walter Scott, and Charlie Scott. Courtesy of Janice McVickers.

Lenny LaCour, whose label complex, Lucky Four/Six Twenty, concentrated on recording doowop groups—the Swinging Hearts, the Del Prados, the Uniques—during the early 1960s. Courtesy of Lenny LaCour.

The Swinging Hearts grew out of this earlier group, the Passions. When Jan Bradley (center) left the Passions in 1960, the remaining members—(left to right) Ernest Lemon, Morris Spearmon, Jerry Williams, and Roscoe Brown—reorganized as the Swinging Hearts. Courtesy of Janice McVickers.

The Four Gents, 1957. This group came from Chicago's Altgeld Gardens housing project. Left to right: Eddie Sullivan, Waymon Bryant, John Staple, and Louis Pritchett. Courtesy of Eddie Sullivan.

The Gems, 1955. Left to right: Rip Reed, Wilson Jones, Ray Pettis (with record), Bobby Robinson, and David Taylor. Courtesy of Marv Goldberg.

The Duvals, 1962. Left to right: Joseph Woolridge, Charles Perry, Andrew Thomas, Carlton Black, and Arthur Cox. Courtesy of Charles Perry.

The Von Gayles, 1956. Left to right: Stacey Steele, Jimmy Washington, and Joe Brackenridge. Courtesy of Joe Brackenridge.

The Cascades, 1964. This group was the soul-era successor to the Von Gayles. Top, left to right: Charles Johnson, Henry Brackenridge, Stacey Steele, and Willie C. Robinson; bottom: Joe Brackenridge. Courtesy of Joe Brackenridge.

The Players, 1964. These singers, who recorded the Vietnam War lament "He'll Be Back," had a long history in doowop. Left to right: John Thomas, Herbert Butler, and Otha Lee Givens. Courtesy of Herbert Butler.

7

Small Entrepreneurs—
Neighborhood Scenes

Altgeld Gardens Vocal Groups

The Altgeld Gardens housing project on the far South Side was the home of a small collection of vocal groups. The Gardens was miles away from Chicago's large black community, and as a result, the R&B scene there took on a localism not present elsewhere in the city. Few of the major acts ever ventured down to the project, so the neighborhood created its own acts, around personal followings developed. Such acts were the Four Gents, the Quintones, the Debonairs, the Nobles, the Belvederes, and the Junior Kingsmen, and most members attended George Washington Carver High School, which served Altgeld Gardens.

The center of vocal group activity was a recreation center in a nearby park that everyone called the "Children's Building." Stanley Vanorsby of the Junior Kingsmen explained, "It was like a center, and we used to call it the 'Children's Building' because that's where we had our activities when we were young. They had these doors where they could partition off the rooms and whatnot. And you'd have a group in this room, a group in that room, who would be rehearsing. It was nice, it was beautiful."[1]

Howard Denton, a woodshop teacher at the Children's Building, started a label called Park to record the vocal groups he had seen at Carver High and from the Altgeld Gardens housing project. He operated the label out of his home in the nearby Morgan Park community in Chicago. The two Altgeld Gardens groups he recorded were the Four Gents and the Quintones.[2]

The origin of the Four Gents can be traced back to Eddie Sullivan (born Albert Sullivan, January 31, 1942, in Chicago). Around 1954, while in grade school, Sullivan formed the Four Gents, the first of many groups with which he was associated. Besides Sullivan, its members were Louis Pritchett, Waymon Bryant, and John Staple. The group was together some four years, and while at Carver High School the Four Gents came out with one record, "On Bended Knee" backed with "Linda," typical doowops from that period.[3]

"We used to rehearse in the Children's Building," said Sullivan, "periodically on a weekly basis. A teacher from the building, Howard Denton, used to listen to us and he wanted to get into the record business, so he wanted us to be the first record for him. And that's how we got the record. I sang lead on both sides."[4] The record was released on Denton's Park label in 1957, but the record was never heard outside the Chicago area.

"Herb Kent played it quite a bit. Vivian Carter played it. It didn't get us too much recognition, but it did get us a costarring billing with Lee Andrews and the Hearts in a show held at the Children's Building. We thought we were somebody! That was actually my first big engagement. Under us, there was just three artists from Altgeld Gardens. They had a really packed house that night too. That was the peak of our popularity with the record 'Linda' and everything."[5] The Pastels, of "Been So Long" fame, and two other Altgeld Gardens groups, the Quintones and the Debonairs, were also on the bill.

"On Bended Knee," the ballad side, was weighed down by a rudimentary musical accompaniment and amateurish production. Sullivan, however, could write a solid melody even if the lyrics were simplistic, so the vocal arrangement and tune were carrying the record. "Linda," also written by Sullivan, sported a Latin tempo, as did so many doowops of the era. Again one gets primitive production and musical accompaniment, and one must appreciate the record for its vocal arrangement alone.

Around 1958, the Four Gents split in half. Eddie Sullivan and John Staples joined with Willie Crowley, and brothers Jerry and Kenneth Brown left to form the Belvederes. The latter group lasted one year before breaking up. Louis Pritchett and Waymon Bryant joined Matthew Perkins and Calvin Baron to form the Twi-lites. Baron also had previous experience in groups, having sung with the Moroccos and with a Sun Ra doowop group, the Cosmic Rays. The Twi-lites recorded two sides for George Leaner's M-Pac label in 1963. The record is one of the rarest releases from the Onederful operation.

Meanwhile, Sullivan had gone on to Chicago's Hyde Park High during his junior and senior years. The school was an integrated school, and as far as vocal group history is concerned, it was the home of the Magnificents, of "Up on the Mountain" fame. There Sullivan got into a group called the Enchanters. Besides Sullivan, who did the tenor work, the group had

Charles Middleton (lead), Del Brown (tenor), Johnny Nance (baritone), and Creadel Jones (bass). The last name may be familiar to fans of soul music as belonging to one of the members of the superstar group, the Chi-lites.

The Enchanters proved to be an extremely popular act at Hyde Park, but the group evolved into another ensemble called the Desideros when they lost Middleton and Nance picked up Marshall Thompson and Joe Manual. The Desideros came to the attention of the record man Leo Austell, who had the group record "I Pledge My Love" backed with "Flat Foot Charlie." (On "Flat Foot Charlie," another singer, Robert Goley, was in the group.) The record did nothing, but the Desideros under Thompson's direction became an outstanding choreographed live act. The group broke up when Thompson and Jones joined Eugene Record, Clarence Johnson, and Squirrel Lester of the Chaunteurs to form the Chi-lites in 1962.

From 1964 to 1966 Sullivan's music career was put on ice by the great interrupter of musicians' lives, the U.S. Army. But after his discharge, he dived back into his first love, music, performing by himself as Eddie Sull. He recorded a poor single, "I'm Looking for My Baby," on Leo Austell's Marc label. Far more successful was Sullivan's writing career. He seemed to be especially talented at writing songs for young female sopranos, conveying very effectively the sensibilities and concerns of teenage girls in love. His notable successes in this area were Diane Cunningham's "Someday Baby" (1967), Sunday Williams's "That's What You Want" (ca. 1969), and Candace Love's "Uh Uh Boy, That's a No No" (1969).

In the early 1970s Sullivan formed a vocal group with his two sisters, Barbara and Lorraine, called the Classic Sullivans. The best and most successful of their songs was "Paint Yourself in a Corner," in February 1973. The Classic Sullivans became the Sullivans when Eddie's sisters left the group and were replaced with his wife, Liz, and daughter, Judy. With various personnel changes, the group played in area clubs during the 1970s and 1980s without getting on record. During the 1980s Eddie and Liz Sullivan sponsored the Sullivan Awards, a Chicago awards show dedicated to recognizing the city's local talent.

Howard Denton likewise discovered the Quintones from his position in the Children's Building, releasing one record on them, "South Sea Island" backed with "More Than a Notion." The lead singer was Donald Burrows, and he was supported by first tenor Clifford Sutherland, second tenor Freddie Williams, baritone Ralph Fulham, and bass Bill McDonald. Another vocalist in the area, Willie Crowley, was often recalled as a member of the Quintones, but Williams says he wasn't on the record but occasionally sang with the group. Burrows wrote both songs.[6] "South Sea Island" is a Latin-sounding song with a midtempo lope, more distinguished by the group's bass and chorus support than the quality of the song or the thin instrumental support. The production is atrocious. "More Than a Notion" is a ballad that was even more poorly executed and produced.

The harmonies of the Quintones were exquisite, but without direction and solid musical support the talent was wasted. Williams recalled, "We were all talented, but we made that record in a studio on Wacker Drive, around State Street. It was not a top-notch studio; it looked like a rent-a-place." But as Williams fondly noted, "at that time it was just a thrill to have anything out."[7]

The Quintones were featured in two big shows. One was the Herb Kent–promoted show in the Children's Building with Lee Andrews and the Hearts, the Pastels, and other Altgeld Gardens groups. "The other show was out in Harvey, some school out there," said Williams. "Herb Kent promoted it. The Dells were on the show and the fellows who did 'Cherry Pie,' Marvin and Johnny. Those acts got top billing and everything. We were just a throw-in." The Quintones were not together very long. They were still attending Carver High when they made the record, and six months after recording it they had disbanded, disappointed on their evident lack of good fortune in the music business. Regarding their heritage on one obscure record, Williams said, "In the city it was unknown, but most people from the Gardens remember the record."

Another group from Altgeld Gardens, which Sullivan described as the Four Gents' strongest competition, was the Debonairs, whom the Four Gents regularly engaged in song battles. The Debonairs came out with "Mother's Son" in late 1956 on the Ping label. Homer Talbert said, "The strongest groups out there were really ourselves and the Four Gents."[8] The Ping label was owned by Frank Evans and was located in his record shop in the heart of record row, at 4648 South Cottage Grove. Evans established a rehearsal studio in the back of the shop, where his acts could prepare for recording sessions. Besides the Debonairs, he recorded instrumental acts like the Andrew Hill Combo and Porter Kilbert. The label lasted only during 1956–57 and was essentially started by Evans at the urging of the Debonairs' manager, Lawrence "Legree" Cox.[9]

The Debonairs were formed around 1953 and consisted of lead Ralph Johnson, first tenor Virgil Talbert, second tenor William "Sonny" Nelson, baritone Earl Vanorsby, and bass Edward Johnson (no relation). They all attended Carver High.[10] As Ralph Johnson told it, "Edward Johnson and I decided to start a group, hand pick some cats and audition them. Altgeld Gardens had a lot of talent. We just hand picked the cats we wanted to sing with us. We got at least ten guys who were exquisite. We couldn't turn them down so we made them substitutes in case someone else couldn't make it at any time. We rehearsed in the Children's Building. We were just as bad as we were 'cause we hand picked the cream of the crop so to speak."[11]

Johnson prided himself on casting the group with a distinct vocal harmony approach. "The true sound of the Debonairs was what was then called 'horn harmony,'" he said. "The baritone, Vanorsby, wouldn't move, he would just hold that key with Johnson the bass on the bottom. The other keys, second tenor Sonny and first tenor Virgil would make the changes plus the lead. The blend was 'horn harmony,' an original sound."[12]

The Debonairs around 1955 decided they needed an agent to advance their careers. As Johnson explained, "We were trying to get Herb Kent. He was at that particular time broadcasting from next door to the Trianon Ballroom. He had just started deejaying on WBEE. He was in the storefront and we walked in and started singing, interrupting his day I imagine. We just walked in; we were forceful. He said he couldn't manage us, but he would introduce us to someone and he introduced us to Larry 'Legree' Cox, who became our manager." Cox got the group on the Ping label.

While hooking up with the tiny Ping label may not be the greatest achievement, the group did get good facilities by recording at the Chess Records studio. "You should have seen some of the musicians that he had," said Talbert. "Andrew Hill, who played piano, being one of them." "Mother's Son" was a bluesy ballad with terrific interaction between the impassioned lead by Johnson and the chorusing of the rest of the group. Cox is credited as the writer on the label, but Johnson said he should get cowriter credit. He said, "Cox helped me straighten out the lyrics. It was 'Mama's Son' at first. He put his two cents in and cleaned it up a bit, and slowed it down, because it was faster. We were young guys at the time, teenagers, and we were popping with it." The flip was "Lanky Linda," led by Edward Johnson, and it seems to be the preferable side, with its nice midtempo lope. "Mother's Son" made so much noise locally when it came out in November 1956 that Vee Jay re-recorded "Mother's Son" by one of its own groups, the Kool Gents (who took the name "Delegates" for the release).

The Debonairs quickly followed up with "Say a Prayer for Me" backed with "Cracker-Jack Daddy," in December 1956. Both were led by Johnson. It did not do anything. In April of the next year, the Debonairs were part of a big vocal group show presented by Herb Kent at Hyde Park High. The groups in the show were the Danderliers, the Moroccos, the Debs, the Dells, the Kings Men, and Hyde Park's own Magnificents.

Around 1958 Homer Talbert joined the group, adding not only good vocals but piano skills as well. He replaced bass singer Edward Johnson, and another singer, Richard James, replaced Vanorsby as baritone. The group impressed Rob Roy of the *Chicago Defender*, who saw them performing at the paper's annual Bud Billiken celebration in August 1959 and wrote a story about them.[13]

Nothing much happened with the Debonairs until they ran into Billy

"The Kid" Emerson and he recorded them on the B&F label in 1961, the A side being a bluesy ballad written by Cox called "Fool's Love." It was led by Johnson. It was backed with the William-led "Ah La La," a Latin jump written by Emerson and Cox. Both sides are routine and didn't have a chance in the market.

The Debonairs did not break up abruptly but gradually fell apart as various members pursued other interests. By 1964 the group was history. They never made any real money and never had a national or even a local hit. But Talbert said, "We had a very nice time. We sang on the Jim Lounsbury show, 'Time for Teens'; we were regulars there. We even sang at Ciro's [a big upscale nightclub at 816 North Wabash] along with Tony Bennett." Nelson recalled the group's playing also at the Club Delisa, London House, and the Colonial Theater in Milwaukee, sharing a bill in the latter venue with the Spaniels and El Dorados.

Around 1966–67 Ralph Johnson joined a group with his sister, Betty Stamps, Andrea Jones, and Clarence Johnson. The group was called the Ti-Chauns and in 1964 recorded one single for Leo Austell's Sonar label, "I Don't Wanna" backed with "What You Wanna Say." In 1971 Johnson made a single for the Master Key label, "Have Your Fun," and after that gradually weaned himself away from the music business.

Homer Talbert worked during the mid-1960s in a production company with Zona Sago and James Porter, and in the early 1970s he started a songwriting partnership with Hersholt Polk. Their biggest hit was the million-selling "Ain't Understanding Mellow," which was recorded by Jerry Butler and Brenda Lee Eager. Talbert and Polk moved to California and wrote quite a few songs for various artists. Talbert produced several albums for Jerry Butler, the best of which was *Suite for a Single Girl.*

The Debonairs took the name Kingmen when they were first formed, and their formation inspired the creation of a group called the Junior Kingsmen by some of the younger brothers of the Debonairs and other kids in Altgeld Gardens. The younger group's members were Stanley Vanorsby, Reggie Johnson, Donald Smith, and "Curtis." While the Junior Kingsmen never got on record, Stanley Vanorsby would later make a record with Sherman Nesbary and former Debonairs Ralph Johnson, Virgil Talbert, and William Johnson. The group's name is not recalled today, but the song was titled "Why Pick on Me" and was recorded for James Porter and Zona Sago's Sago label.

Another Altgeld Gardens group was the Nobles, who consisted of lead singer LeRoy Kennard, Joseph "Cool Breeze" Jones, Horace Noble, Wilbur Foster, and Wayne Morris.[14] They were highly respected by the area's other groups. Homer Talbert said, "Joe Jones was a hell of a piano player at the time. I think they were a little bit older than us. These guys sang kind of advance harmony at the time." Freddie Williams of the Quintones noted, "LeRoy Kennard had a real pretty voice and he was what you called the spark of the group. Three of the guys were from what we called 'in the city' and not from the Garden, and would come here to rehearse with LeRoy. Wilbur Foster was from here, because he was in a group earlier called the Suedes. They were a real nice group, older than we were." Eddie Sullivan said, "At one time we had a battle between my group (the Four Gents), Debonairs, Nobles, and a real popular group out of Morgan Park. The Nobles won that one, because they were more up in modern harmony than anyone. They had a smoother sound."[15]

The Nobles recorded "Do You Love Me" backed with "Who's Been Riding My Mule" on Sapphire in the summer of 1956, and their use of smooth modern harmony is most evident on these up-tempo recordings. "Who's Been Riding My Mule," which got the radio play, featured a bass lead—a technique used by the Dominoes on their famous hit "Sixty Minute Man"—and a blues guitar break. Otherwise the song was 1940s in style. "Do You Love Me" likewise sounds like a cross between 1950s R&B and 1940s pop vocal harmony. The song exhibits doowop background chanting, but the Nobles sound so polished and crisp in their harmonies it seems more like pop. Because the Nobles brought so much expertise to their singing, their recordings hold up better than those of other Altgeld Gardens groups. John Burton, who had recently taken over Parrot from Al Benson, was the owner of Sapphire, which he operated out of 32 North State. The label probably had no more than a half-dozen releases and probably existed only during the year 1956. Other artists on the label, Earl Forniss and Terry Rae, were likewise obscurities.

When various members of the Altgeld Gardens groups discuss their careers, they all recall not only their time singing in the groups but also their fondness for their old turf, Altgeld Gardens. Most have moved "in the city" but many make return visits to keep in touch. All would agree with the sentiment expressed by former Debonairs member William Nelson, who said, "Altgeld Gardens will always be my home."[16]

Evanston Vocal Groups

Evanston, an upscale suburb on the northern border of Chicago, is known primarily as the home of Northwestern University and other institutions of higher learning. Of all the North Shore elite suburbs, the community is distinguished by having a great variation in material wealth and social standing among its citizens. Its working-class population has traditionally included a sizable number of blacks, and where there was a black population in the 1950s, there were vocal groups. Evanston produced a few. The city was also the home of some small record labels, but local groups recorded for companies in both Evanston and Chicago.

The Drexel label was Chicago-based and was formed in June 1954 by Paul King, Les Caldwell, and a third partner as yet unidentified. The company never actually opened offices and the company's business was conducted in King's home at 7319 South Vernon Ave. Caldwell, who had been a salesman for King Records, was the general manager and A&R head. The company in its eighteen releases recorded two vocal groups, six releases by the Gems and one by the Gay Notes. Its other releases were by solo singers, notably several by uptown blues singer Roy Wright. The company made all its recordings at Universal Recording. Drexel went out of business in 1958, having never gotten more than a little local play and sales for a few records in its four years of existence. Its legacy was its output on one of the finest groups to come out of the Midwest, the Gems.[17]

The Gems made marvelous records throughout their careers yet were fated to remain in nearly total obscurity. Their records have become highly sought-after collector's items both for their rarity and their undeniable quality. The Gems had one of the smoothest sounds ever heard, typically sublime rhythm and blues, which neophytes confuse with a pop sound. Although clearly singing in the contemporary R&B style, the Gems strongly evoked the more poplike sounds of their 1940s predecessors, such as the Charioteers, the Ink Spots, and the Four Vagabonds.[18]

The Gems came together in Evanston around 1952. Members were Ray Pettis (lead), Bobby "Pee-Wee" Robinson (first tenor and guitar), David "Moose" Taylor (second tenor), Wilson James (baritone and bass), and Rip Reed (bass). The group practiced on the usual hits of the day, such as the Orioles' "Crying in the Chapel," the Spaniels' "Goodnite Sweetheart," and the Moonglows' "I Was Wrong." The group was the first act signed by Drexel, and their first record, "Let's Talk about the Weather" backed with "Deed I Do," was the company's initial release. "Talk" is a midtempo ballad and "Deed I Do" was deeper and slower, but both were typical of the group's low-keyed style that hints of the forties era. The record got solid play in Chicago and could be considered a local R&B hit.

The Gems shared their next release with an Evanston chanteuse, Dorothy Logan. On the A side, "Small Town Man," she sang alone, and on the flip, a remake of "Since I Fell for You," she was backed by the Gems. The *Cash Box* reviewer was not enthused about either side and gave each only two stars.

Another release appeared in February 1955, featuring a superb jump, "Kitty from New York City," backed with a flavorful ballad, "I Thought You'd Care." Both sides again exhibit a certain deep rhythm and blues style, yet there is more than a whisper of the earlier 1940s pop-style groups.

Despite their excellence the sides did nothing. The virtue of the material was evident as years later another vocal group, the Skyscrapers, put out a remake of "I Thought You'd Care."

The fourth release by the Gems, also in 1955, paired "Ol' Man River" and "You're Tired of Love," both excellent sides, yet neither sold. The Jerome Kern and Oscar Hammerstein classic was a perfect vehicle for the Gems, with a tremendously evocative lead by Pettis and magnificent choral support by the rest. "You're Tired of Love" is a ballad that sounds straight out of the 1940s or like something out of Joe Davis's operation in New York, but the excellent saxophone work places the record in the 1950s.

In 1956 the Gems were back in the studio, producing four solo sides by Ray Pettis and four by the group. Two Pettis sides were put out first, "Please Tell Me When" backed with "Ow, You're So Fine." It did nothing, but that is not the end of its story. In the 1980s, record collectors decided that a great doowop release could be made from the recording, so a "contrived" doowop was created. By putting a 1980s group, the Sparrows, behind Pettis, and having them sing in the style of the Gems, the doowop fan would then have a great new "Gems" release to collect. The bootleg release was given the number 700, preceding Drexel's 701 release, and the ballad was renamed "I Can't Believe."

The Gems finally had a little luck with a change-of-style release, "One Woman Man" backed with "The Darkest Night." In November 1956 "One Woman Man," a most bluesy side, went to number thirteen on the WGES radio survey. "The Darkest Night" is a routine midtempo ballad that is considerably more rough sounding than previous Gems songs. The year ended with two Christmas titles by Pettis, "Does It Have to Be Christmas" backed with "Christmas Here, Christmas There." It definitely was not Christmas for the Gems. They never received any money for their recordings, except after the "One Woman Man" record when King gave each member a five-dollar advance on the next record.

The Gems' final record, "Till the Day I Die" backed with "Monkey Face Baby," was released in July 1957, perhaps after the group's dissolution. The Gems had found the offer of five dollars so insulting that they could no longer play the entertainment game and broke up. But the bluesy ballad side, "Till the Day I Die," was a mighty fine way to go out a winner, with a solid hook and tremendous work by the group. It got good play locally and is a superior record in every respect.

Pettis went on to become a member of another Evanston-based group, the Foster Brothers, who actually predated the rhythm and blues tradition and went back to the jubilee days, in the late 1930s.[19] Donald Clay formed the group as a gospel quartet in his native Evanston. Clay said, "The Four Harmonizers were what we were in the beginning. Then we went and studied voice and got sophisticated and became the Ebony Esquires. Then we studied some more and got even more sophisticated and became the Foster Brothers. I was an adopted child and I did have some foster brothers, one who was one of our singers, LaVerne Gayles."[20]

The Foster Brothers took a long time to get on record and were middle-aged men when they first recorded in 1957 for John Burton's El Bee label, located on Chicago's near South Side. Members at that time were Ray Johnson, Lindsay "Pop" Langston, George Lattimore, Don Clay, and LaVerne "Les" Gayles. A small write-up in the *Chicago Defender* indicated that the Foster Brothers were hardly a kid rhythm and blues group: "The Foster Brothers have been singing together for over 20 years. Well known in the concert field, the group sings a program of specially arranged music, consisting of Negro spirituals, westerns, classics and popular hits."[21] The El Bee release features "I Said She Wouldn't Go," a rousing rhythm and blues jump with a blasting sax, but one could tell that the Foster Brothers were basically a pop group who were simply "getting down." The flip, "Tell Me Who," is a pure pop number and less effective.

The group then lost Les Gayles, but Ray Pettis took his place, just in time to get the Foster Brothers some success. They finally achieved recorded recognition in 1958 when they got a crossover local hit with "If You Want My Heart," released on Mercury. The song, written by Don Clay, is a marvelous pop number like the ones the Four Knights were putting out at the time. "Show Me" is an up-tempo number equally pop in approach.

Following a dispute between Mercury and the group's manager, Eddie Valentine, the Foster Brothers recorded for Mel London's Profile label, coming out with "Trust in Me" backed with "Why-Yi-Yi" in February 1959. "Trust in Me," the old standard, was perfect for the Foster Brothers' approach, but the record lacks excitement and sparkle. "Why-Yi-Yi" was an original by Clay but thoroughly pop in sensibility. Neither side was suitable fare for the late 1950s and hardly could have been expected to return the group to the charts.

In 1960 the Foster Brothers found themselves recorded twice, on two small labels. On Bud Brandom's and Leonard Allen's B&F label they came out with "Revenge" backed with "Pretty, Fickle Woman." "Revenge" is a pop ballad that featured an Ink Spots–style recitation, strictly 1940s in conception, but "Pretty, Fickle Woman" has the Foster Brothers doing up-tempo rock 'n' roll, unfortunately with uninteresting material. On the Dillie label, out of New York, they came out with "Land of Love" backed with "Let's Jam." "Let's Jam," written by Clay, is a dated-sounding up-tempo number, and "Land of Love" is a pop-style number with a gentle lope that has its charms (although not for everyone).

Sometime during the previous four years, the group also came out with a record on the Hi Mi label, pairing "I Could Cry" with "Never Again." By 1961 the Foster Brothers called it quits. They were not the kind of group that makes the heart of a doowop collector flutter, but they are interesting because they represent an older vocal tradition that goes back to the nineteenth century.

Following the dissolution of the Foster Brothers, Clay joined with a former Gems member, R. C. "Bobby" Robinson, to form the Boss label. The two neophyte record men put out about ten releases on Boss, by such artists as Ray Pettis and Perk Lee (of the El Dorados), but nothing happened except for some local action on "Cotton" by the Duvals.

"Cotton" should be considered a neo-doowop, because it had a dated sound upon its release in late 1962. The group was formed by tenor and lead Charles Perry from among his friends in Evanston when he got out of the air force in the summer of 1961. Originally the other members consisted of second tenor Charles Woodridge, baritone Arthur Cox, and bass Andrew Thomas. In early 1962 Perry felt the group needed another member and added Carlton Black, who soon proved himself as the group's lead and principal songwriter. Perry led on "Cotton," but during 1964 the Duvals, under the name Naturals and with Black as lead, got on the local charts with an Impressions' soundalike, "Let Love Be True." They disbanded in 1965 when follow-ups failed.[22]

Meanwhile, Clay and Robinson had dissolved Boss in 1963 and had gone their separate ways. Robinson formed Dee Dee Records and under the name David Rockingham Trio (Robinson, the producer and writer, on guitar; David Rockingham on organ; and Shante Hamilton on drums) he recorded an instrumental called "Dawn," which he put out on Dee Dee. "Dawn" became a national hit after it was leased to New York based-Josie in 1963. Other Dee Dee releases, mainly by Ray Pettis, did little. Clay became heavily involved in the Chicago music scene, forming such labels as Dawn, Wise World, and Flash and working for such companies as St. Lawrence and Chess.

Near North Groups

The near North Side is the forgotten section of Chicago when it comes to being recognized as a fount of black talent. Yet during the 1950s, within the Cabrini-Green housing projects, there were a number of groups who emerged and made records for Chicago companies. The best known of these groups was the Impressions, out of which came Jerry Butler and Curtis Mayfield, but other near North Side groups during the soul era included Billy Butler and the Enchanters, the Cascades, the Pace Setters, the Players, and the Admirations. But these soul groups built on the foundation established by the area doowop groups that preceded them.

The story behind such 1950s groups as the Von Gayles, the Medallion-aires, the Serenades, and the Players—all from the near North Side—seems to involve a common thread of personnel, perhaps due to the close-knit quality of the community. Herbert Butler, a former member of the Players, recalled, "At that time everybody sang. You know that Major Lance lived right down the street, and Curtis Mayfield right on the next street."[23] Said Billy Butler, "We were all into trying to sing. That was the only thing to do really . . . the area didn't have street gangs at the time. Everyone would form a group and go into Seward Park, which had a recreation building and club rooms, in which everyone would practice."[24]

Regarding Seward Park, Herb Butler said, "Everybody who was anybody would rehearse there. In one room you would have the Von Gayles, in another room you would have the Serenades, in another room would be my first group, and in another the Capris would be in there. They had like seven rooms and you could come in and tell which room which group was gonna be in, because people would be hanging around the doors or rooms would be full and they would not be letting anybody in."[25] Tommie Johnson of the Serenades noted, "That's where most of the groups practiced. We primarily practiced there and at Lower North Center, 1000 North Sedgewick. It was called Chicago Youth Center, but we called it Lower North, because of the name up there on the building."

The Olivet Community Center at 1441 North Cleveland, a health and social center, also served as place where the area's youth could practice their music, but the building had a gym and was primarily used for basketball tournaments.

The Von Gayles got their start around 1956. The members of the group were lead singer Joe Brackenridge; his nephew, Stacy Steele Jr., first tenor; baritone Jimmy Washington; second tenor Willie C. Robinson; and bass Charles Johnson. Several schools picked up students from the area, so some youngsters in the group went to Wells, others went to Washburne Trade, and one went to Waller. The group never got into singing the hit songs of the day and instead concentrated on original material written by Brackenridge.[26]

The Von Gayles eventually made contact with Woodtate Anderson, a go-getter in the music business, and he brought the group under the management of the Impressions' manager, Eddie Thomas. Anderson and Thomas were instrumental in getting the group on record, having them sign with the USA label. The label was owned by a Milwaukee pop deejay, Lee Rothman, but apparently he was in some sort of alliance with Chicago-based All-State Record Distributing company, headed by Paul Glass.[27] (The USA label in later years was owned by Glass and fully based in Chicago.) Following the pattern of most groups of the era, the Von Gayles recorded four sides during their first session, held at Universal Recording. But as it turned out, the Von Gayles who performed on the records were more of an ad hoc group. Charles Johnson was temporarily separated from the group due to a spat and Jimmy Washington was working on the day of the session. So Joe Brackenridge, the lead, and Stacy Steele, first tenor, were joined by second tenor Willie Dial (Willie Wright), baritone Willie Daniels, and bass James "Doolaby" Wright. The three ad hoc members had actually been a part of an earlier group from the near North Side, the Serenades.

USA put out only two sides, "Loneliness" and "The Twirl," probably around 1959. "Loneliness" is something of a "For Your Precious Love" soundalike, and Brackenridge with his evocative gospelized lead made the song a standout. "The Twirl" is a dance number made appealing by Brackenridge's lead work and the "Love Is Strange" guitar riffs. Prior to its recording, the song had already made a big impression at Seward Park, according to Herbert Butler: "Joe and the guys would never do their song until everybody in the other rooms had stopped singing, when there was a moment's silence. Then you could hear them start that song, 'ah hoo' . . . and everybody would leave whatever they were doing and go up to the door and hear them guys do that song, because that was a super song."[28] It must have been super apparently only at Seward Park, because neither side did anything and the record has become rare. In 1960 Dore Records, owned by Lou Bedell and headquartered in Hollywood, California, picked up two Von Gayles sides, "The Twirl" and "Crazy Dance," but achieved no better luck. The group played a few gigs in Chicago and even appeared on a television show in Milwaukee—via the Rothman connection—but their fame, such as it was, was fleeting.

Joe Brackenridge and company cooled their heels for a while before appearing again on record. In 1964 the group, now calling themselves the Cascades, met a small-time entrepreneur in their neighborhood, Robert Plumber, who went by the name of Bobby Stone. He had some songs and wanted to start up a label, which he called McCormick. For his first and apparently only release he put out the Cascades singing "Pains in My Heart" backed with "One that I Can Spare." The group now consisted of Joe Brackenridge (lead); his brother, Henry Brackenridge (baritone); Stacy Steele Jr. (first tenor); Willie C. Robinson (second tenor); and Charles Johnson (bass).

"Pains in My Heart," which has the same kind of hypnotic deep drive as the Miracles song "I Need a Change," went to number seventeen on the local WVON chart in the summer of 1964. The rousing flip, "One that I Can Spare," was another worthy original from the group, although it bore a faint resemblance to the Miracles song "Happy Landing." Leo Austell saw the action on the record and picked it up for his Renee label. After the record ran its course, he put out another release by the group, "Sandra My Love" backed with "Will You Love Me (When I'm Old)." It didn't do anything.

The Cascades continued on and, as they were to do several times, adopted another name, the Pace Setters, but with no change in personnel from their Cascades days. They soon hooked up deejay Al Benson, who had a small record company on Record Row. Among his several labels was Mica, on which the Pace Setters had a single—a ballad "My Ship Is Coming In (Tomorrow)" backed with a midtempo workout called "Victim of Loneliness." It was the ballad side that got the play in the fall of 1966. Like another record from the summer, the Players' "He'll Be Back," the song deals with the highly topical theme of a serviceman returning home from the Vietnam War. Not so coincidentally, Joe Brackenridge was involved in the Players, another near North Side group. The Pace Setters failed to get much going for themselves, and after one more personnel switch, Andrew Robertson for Willie C. Robinson, they broke up.

A late 1950s rival to the Von Gayles were the Serenades. Their story goes back to Jenner Grade School, where Tommie Johnson, Otha Lee Givens, Terry Collier, Bryan Barlow, and Napoleon Hall formed a group. Tommie Johnson was the brother of Charles Johnson, the bass singer of the Von Gayles. The group graduated to Wells High and soon were playing at parties and talent contests. Johnson then met Willie Wright (aka Willie Dial), who had a group of his own, the Quails.

The story of the Quails goes back to the famed soul singer Jerry Butler, before he was a part of the Impressions. While still attending Washburne Trade, he and his classmates formed a group called the Quails. The other members were Willie Wright; his brother, James "Doolaby" Wright; and Ronald Sherman, the latter who used to fill in for missing members of the Von Gayles. Butler left the group when he had to drop out of school to go to work.

The Quails reorganized and became the Serenades. Members of the Serenades were lead singer Willie Wright, James "Doolaby" Wright, Willie Daniels, Tommie Johnson, and Ronald Sherman. The Serenades got a contract with Mel London's Chief label in early 1957. The two sides released by the group in March that year were a ballad, "A Sinner in Love," and a jump, "The Pajama Song." The ballad got played on the deejay Sam Evans's show but did little else.[29]

Butler vividly remembered "A Sinner in Love" because it credits "Wright" and "Snave" as the writers. "It was my first composition," said Butler. "After I left the group, they recorded it and didn't even put my name on the record. I remember Sam Evans playing it one night, and I said, 'That's my song!' I called the guys up but they were all covering their eyes and feeling ashamed."[30] The Serenades got a bit of recognition in April

1957 when they appeared on the big Mambo Easter Dance sponsored by three local deejays, McKie Fitzhugh, Big Bill Hill, and Richard Stamz. Other acts on the bill included Paul Bascomb, Tommy "Madman" Jones, Harold Burrage, the Clouds, the Gay Tones, and the Five Echoes. Willie Wright soon left the Serenades, and from the remains of the group Tommie Johnson and his old friend from Jenner, Otha Lee Givens, formed a trio with a brother-in-law of Givens named Herbert Butler (no relation to Jerry Butler).

Not all the best groups on the near North Side got to record. For example, the Capris were highly respected in the area. Bryan Barlow, after leaving Tommie Johnson's first group, joined the Capris led by "Budgie" Henry. They were known by their first names or street names—Budgie, Nolan, Barlow, and Blake. Herb Butler said, "They were a super group," and Tommie Johnson agreed, saying, "They were one of the groups that were always in competition with us, a very talented group."[31] But the Capris could never get it together enough to get on record. Joe Brackenridge confided, "They could sing real good, but most of what they did was drink a lot of alcohol. They're deceased now."[32] Johnson remembered their having "a drug problem later on."

In 1958 Willie Wright formed another group from the Cabrini-Green neighborhood called the Medallionaires, consisting of Wright as lead, tenor Earnest Montgomery, and two brothers, baritone David Anderson and bass Ronald Anderson. They were yet another group managed by Woodtate Anderson and Eddie Thomas.[33] In May 1958 the Medallionaires came out with a single that featured two Wright originals, "Magic Moonlight" backed with "Teen-age Caravan." The ballad side was "Magic Moonlight," which opens with a "bell-tone" separation of the harmony and has the exaggerated melodramatic lead and full vocal group support of the period, with burbling bass and such. The record is highly appealing. The jump flip, on the other hand, is uninteresting and sounds like a folksong, even though it deals with the subject of rock 'n' roll. This folk aspect will surface again in association with Wright. Today's collectors of vocal group records may find it hard to believe, but it was "Teen-Age Caravan" that got played on local R&B radio—but not enough to make it a hit.

Having not succeeded in three successive doowop groups, Wright finally must have thought that there had to be a better way. Since folk music had become all the rage, with the remarkable success of the Kingston Trio, and the emergence of black performers such as Harry Belafonte, Josh White, Odetta, and John Lee Hooker singing folk music in coffeehouses and folk nightclubs, Wright decided he would become a folk singer too. The genesis of that decision came from Chloe Hoffman, a staff member at the Olivet Community Center. Hoffman was much impressed with Willie

Wright's voice and, according to the *Chicago Defender,* "she suggested he try folk music. She provided him with a guitar and albums of folk songs. Willie returned three months later—a folk singer. Night after night he had listened to the records and practiced until he could play and sing each song. Miss Hoffman obtained more records. Olivet gave Willie a practice room and he began developing a style, a repertoire, and a new dream."[34]

Wright enrolled in the Old Town School of Folk Music, near his neighborhood, and soon was working regularly in folk spots in the city. He even got an album out on Chess Record's Argo label in 1963, called *I'm on My Way.*

Showing absolutely no awareness of his true folk roots in doowop, Wright came out with an album of mostly traditional material, such as "Cotton Eyed Joe," "House of the Rising Sun," and "Wayfaring Stranger," all of which he adapted and arranged.

Tommie Johnson went into the army in 1960, but when he returned to the near North Side in 1963 he formed a group with his grade-school friend Terry Collier and rounded it out with Carolyn Johnson and Phyllis Braxton. They took the name Saharas and recorded a couple sides for Gerald. Sims at Columbia Records, where Carl Davis was recently ensconced as a producer and A&R man. The sides were never released, however. Collier left and later became a noted singer-songwriter in the city, and Johnson settled down with a regular job. In 1966, however, Johnson was drawn into another group, the Players.

The story of the Players, who were well known for "He'll Be Back," is a complicated one that involved many different personalities and talents, among them several veterans of the near North scene. According to lead singer Herbert Butler, "The Players were originally Collis Gordon and John Thomas. They formed the group, just the two of them in 1966. I became involved when I got out of the army, February 22, 1966, and returned home to the neighborhood in which we all lived. They had seen me and known that I had always sang with another group, which consisted of myself, Tommie Johnson, and Otha Lee Givens."[35] Butler continued:

> Collis and John had written the song "He'll Be Back," and they had taken it to various record companies. The companies liked the song, but they didn't like their voices. Collis and John wanted to record the song, but A&R men like Calvin Carter at Vee Jay and Carl Davis wanted to buy the song. At that point they said, hey Herb, sing the song for us. So I went down to Calvin Carter and I did sing the song, and he was ecstatic and he wanted to sign us up. He assigned to us a manager, which was Al Smith, and it was Al's job to get us ready to record and to get other material to us so that they could take us into the studio.

What we have are the three of us under the tutelage of Al Smith rehearsing at his place on Seventy-fifth and Cottage Grove. At some point he decides this group, us, just will not work, because we're not good enough as a unit. But when he makes this decision he doesn't tell us. He just proceeds along like everything is alright and we go into the studio to record. When we get there that night we enter the studio and we meet the world-famous Dells. And Cal takes John under one arm and Collis under the other, walks them down the hall, and somebody I don't recall introduces me to the Dells and instructs me to fill them in on how the background goes. And we proceed to do the recording.

The Dells did not include their lead, Marvin Junior, in this session. The members here were bass Chuck Barksdale, falsetto tenor Johnny Carter, baritone Mickey McGill, and tenor Verne Allison.

Whatever the shortcomings of Gordon and Thomas in the studio, they were still a talented duo, as evidenced when they composed an incredible and timely song, "He'll Be Back," which was about the plight of a girl whose boyfriend is fighting in the jungles of Vietnam. Butler said, "It was altered a great deal by myself after I started singing it. But they wouldn't give me writer's royalties. However, they did compromise by naming me as writer on the reverse side." It was undoubtedly rough on Gordon and Thomas to be told that they would not be on the recording, especially after it became a national hit. The song went to twenty-four on the *Billboard* R&B chart in the summer of 1966 and lasted sixteen weeks.

Thomas was able to continue with the Players on their first tour, however. Butler recalled, "It was further determined that just as they had other voices do the singing, they needed other people for the image and to do the singing in person. That's where Tommie Johnson and Otha Lee Givens comes in. At this time Collis was pushed out of the group. John Thomas would have been out also, but the reason he was not out was because Tommie Johnson had a very good job, had a child, and was also married. So the first touring group was Herb Butler, Otha Lee Givens, and John Thomas."

After the tour, Thomas was likewise pushed out, and Tommie Johnson and Joe Brackenridge (of Von Gayles fame) joined Butler and Givens to record the group's album. It turned out to be a peculiar affair. Butler has a beautiful sweet voice but it belongs in a group setting. Yet on five of the numbers, only guest vocalist Chuck Barksdale appears. Such songs as "Since I Don't Have You" and the group's follow-up, "I'm Glad I Waited," therefore sound empty without voices. Half of the numbers, including three originals written by the group, sound much better with the group chorusing. Butler said that on much of "I'm Glad I Waited" the vocal chorus was removed by Calvin Carter, who clearly erred in not allowing Johnson, Givens, and Brackenridge to make their presence felt. On the strength of "He'll Be Back," "I'm Glad I Waited" charted for five weeks in late 1966.

The Players during 1966 and 1967 played many big dates, notably on the big Northeast chitlin' circuit, appearing at the Howard in Washington, D.C., the Apollo in Harlem, and the Regal in Chicago. The group also made a one-nighter tour with other Imperial/Minit artists—the O'Jays, the Diplomats, and Jimmy Holiday, playing such clubs as the 20 Grand in Detroit and Leo's Casino in Cleveland.

Subsequent singles by the Players were unsuccessful. Before 1967 was over, the group and Minit parted company, probably by mutual consent. Butler recalled that each member of the Players was promised an advance of three thousand dollars for making the *He'll Be Back* album, but when it came time deliver the cash Calvin Carter did not have it. The Players were thus disenchanted enough not to put much faith in making a career in the recording industry.

Butler astutely summed up the Players in the following comment: "The brains of the Players were Collis Gordon and John Thomas. They had the insight to come up with a timely song in an era that got the group in the door. I would like to think of Tommie Johnson, Otha Lee Givens, and Joe Brackenridge as the talent. Those guys could sing, had stage presence, and all the rest. And in all my immodesty, I was just a natural. I had the gift. It was through no effort of mine, no ingenuity of mine. The other guys had all the stuff."

Butler and Johnson went on to manage two more Near North groups, the Ambitions and the Admirations. Three brothers formed the core of the Admirations, lead singer Kenneth Childs, Bruce Childs, and Ralph Childs, all of whom lived at 852 North Sedgewick. Other members are recalled only as "Myles" and "Smith." In 1968 they had a fine local hit called "Wait Until I Get to Know You," released on George Leaner's One-derful. It is a nice, typically Chicagoan midtempo number, featuring a dry lead reminiscent of that of the Five Stairsteps. The other record of note by the group is "You Left Me" on the Peaches label, which in England is considered a northern soul collectible.

It is instructive to learn that Chicago's near North Side had such a rich and flourishing music scene, and that such a group as Curtis Mayfield and the Impressions did not arise out of a vacuum. The groups of the 1950s— the Von Gayles, the Serenades, the Capris, and the Medallionaires—created a wonderful music scene that helped engender the marvelous soul acts that followed them.

Notes

1. Vanorsby interview.
2. Information about the Park label comes from the Pritchett and Sullivan interviews.
3. Information about the Four Gents comes from Pruter, "The Eddie Sullivan Story"; Pritchett and Sullivan interviews.
4. Sullivan interview, August 16, 1980.
5. Ibid.
6. Williams interview.
7. This and subsequent remarks by Williams quoted in this chapter are from the Williams interview.
8. This and subsequent remarks by Talbert quoted in this chapter are from the Talbert interview.
9. Information about Ping Records comes from Gart, *First Pressings: Volume 6;* Johnson and Talbert interviews.
10. Information about the Debonairs comes from Roy, "Call Debonairs"; Ralph Johnson, Talbert, and Nelson interviews.
11. Ralph Johnson interview, February 28, 1993.
12. This and subsequent remarks by Ralph Johnson quoted in this chapter are from the February 21, 1993, interview with him.
13. Roy, "Call Debonairs."
14. Information about the Nobles comes from Gart, *First Pressings: Volume 6;* and Talbert and Vanorsby interviews.
15. Sullivan interview.
16. Nelson interview.
17. Information about Drexel comes from Gart, *First Pressings: Volume 4;* idem., *First Pressings: Volume 7;* Stallworth, "The Gems."
18. Information about the Gems comes from Stallworth, "The Gems"; R. C. Robinson and Clay interviews.
19. Information about the Foster Brothers comes from Stallworth, "The Gems"; "Foster Brothers" [caption]; Clay interview.
20. Clay interview.
21. "Foster Brothers" [caption].
22. Information about the Duvals comes from Pruter, "Evanston Soul"; Black and Perry interviews.
23. Herbert Butler interview, October 5, 1992.
24. Billy Butler interview.
25. Herbert Butler interview, October 25, 1992.
26. Information about the Von Gayles comes from Brackenridge and Steele Jr. interviews.
27. Peter Grendysa, letter to author, September 29, 1993.
28. Herbert Butler interview, October 25, 1992.
29. Information about the Serenades comes from the Tommie Johnson, Brackenridge, and Jerry Butler interviews.
30. Jerry Butler interview.

31. Herbert Butler interview, October 25, 1992, and Johnson interview.

32. Brackenridge interview, October 25, 1992.

33. Information about the Medallionaires comes from "Medallionaires" [caption]; "Willie Wright Makes Long Trip."

34. "Willie Wright Makes Long Trip."

35. This and subsequent remarks by Herbert Butler quoted in this chapter are from the October 5, 1992, interview with him.

8

Nike and Erman

The early 1960s were transitional years for African American music. The older sounds of rhythm and blues and rock 'n' roll, such as doowop and saxophone instrumentals, were fading and the soul era was coming on. The record companies in Chicago reflected this transition, coming out with music—much of it from vocal groups—that seemed to partake of the past yet looked to the future. While doowop vocal techniques were much in evidence on the recordings, there was something more gospel-like, more urgent, in the sound of the vocals, and that would become the sound of soul in the coming years. With such groups as the Daylighters, Donald and the Delighters, the Blenders, the Ideals, and the Versalettes, two small companies, Nike and Erman, came out with a worthwhile catalog of this transitional vocal-harmony rock 'n' roll.

Nike Records

Nike Records was formed in 1961 by Charles Colbert Sr., a musician and restaurant owner. His son, Charles Colbert Jr., had just joined a vocal group, the Daylighters, who had recorded some sides for Don Talty at the RCA Studio. Talty had lost interest in the Daylighters, and the members of the group did not have the money to pay the studio costs to retrieve the masters. They went to the elder Colbert, who not only gave them the money but set up a company to put out the record on the Nike label.[1]

The main partners in CaCoOl Productions, as the operation was first called, were the junior and senior Colberts, Bob Catron (a musician married to the elder Colbert's daughter, Claudette), and Doc Oliver (a songwriter). Colbert Jr. (born August 30, 1939, in Argo) was the principal producer and songwriter, and Catron and Tony Gideon (a founding member of the Daylighters) were the initial promotion men. Band leader Burgess Gardner and bassist Johnny Pate did the arranging. The company's offices were at the Colbert home at 8956 South Wallace. Recording was carried out at various studios, but a lot of woodshedding was done at a place at 800 East Sixty-third Street, where many South Side R&B acts would write songs, rehearse, and work up material.

The company reorganized in 1962. Oliver and Catron left, the latter to work A&R and produce for the Witch/Cortland label group. The reorganized Nike company introduced new subsidiary labels, Tip Top and Jive. Catron, who was still in the family, retained a small stake in the company and as a result there was a bit of cross-fertilization between Witch/Cortland and Nike/Tip Top/Jive. For example, the Nike vocal group called the Candles recorded as the Blenders on Witch. In 1966 Colbert Jr. added the Mellow label to the operation, but by that time doowop was just a memory.

The Colbert labels specialized in vocal groups, specifically the Daylighters, of course, but also the Dolphins, the Salvadores, and the Guys and Dolls. The only group that achieved any measure of success was the Daylighters, however.

The Daylighters were not originally from Chicago, but hailed from Birmingham, Alabama. The idea for the group first germinated in the mind of Tony Gideon, then a student at Hooper City High in the city. One summer in 1956, while visiting relatives in Chicago, he made the acquaintance of the El Dorados' Pirkle Lee Moses, who lived down the block on Fifty-ninth Street. This association inspired him to start a group of his own, and when he returned to school that fall he got one together for a talent show. The group called itself the Five Sparrows and sang the Moonglows' "Sincerely" to their schoolmates in assembly. The members at this time were Dorsey Wood (tenor and lead), his brother George (baritone), Charles "Sparrow" Boyd (baritone), Eddie Thomas (bass), and Tony Gideon (second tenor and lead). Not long after the group's formation, Boyd left and was replaced with Levi Moreland, who took over the lead chores of the group from Dorsey Wood.[2]

The Five Sparrows changed their name to the Velvetiers and began doing high school hops, assembly programs, and similar modest engagements. Their material, remarkably varied, included classic doowops such as "Oh What a Nite" and "I'll Be Home," but also aggressive and raunchy numbers like "Please Please Please," "There Is Something on Your Mind," and "Work with Me Annie." The group also did upbeat blues, such as B. B. King's "Woke Up This Morning."

The Velvetiers were also busy trying to get a record contract, sending tapes to any company they thought would be interested, but getting nowhere. In desperation they took off one Saturday in 1957 to Nashville to see what they could do. The group succeeded in recording a couple of songs for deejay Hoss Allen of WLAC, but Gideon doesn't know whether or not they were put on a label. The group returned to Birmingham without expectations.

As the Velvetiers became more and more involved in the music business, it became apparent changes were needed—starting with their name, which seemed to be similar to a half dozen different groups. They chose the Daylighters as their new name, a sort of counterpart to Hank Ballard's Midnighters. They also determined that Birmingham was no place to launch a music career, and when the Wood brothers' parents moved to Chicago, the whole group decided to do likewise, in May 1958.

The group that came to Chicago consisted of Gideon, Levi Moreland, Eddie Thomas, and brothers Dorsey and George Wood. The Daylighters searched around the city for a record company, but met with no success. Leonard Chess kept them cooling their heels in his office all day, only to turn them down. A session with Ralph Bass at Federal fell through when Moreland lost his voice from rehearsing too hard. Moreland was the only member of the group without any relations in the area, and after about two months of growing homesickness and discouragement he returned to Alabama.

Things began looking up after the Daylighters obtained the managerial services of a local deejay, George "G.G." Graves, then the morning man at WBEE. He brought the group to Cadillac Baby (Narvel Eatmon), the owner of Bea and Baby record company. The Daylighters did backup work as well as coming out with "Mad House Jump," their first record, in September 1959.

Shortly after "Mad House Jump," the group found itself in need of a guitarist. Graves worked his magic again and brought in a highly talented musician and creative songwriter from Kalamazoo, Michigan—Gerald Sims. About the same time, the group started an association with Betty Everett. Graves thought the trend was toward male groups headed by female leads, so Everett was teamed up with the Daylighters for gigs around the city. They recorded together on one record, "Please Come Back," on Carl Jones's C.J. label.

Until 1961, nothing was happening with the Daylighters. The association with Everett did not work out and she departed. Lesser groups struggling in the business with as many years as the Daylighters under their belts probably would have packed it in, but the group was made of sterner stuff and was unusually persistent and enterprising. The turnabout came when the group joined Nike.

The Daylighters' first Nike release was "This Heart of Mine," a doo-wop ballad that perhaps because of its dated sound did not do much. The flip was an Olympics-styled rock 'n' roll dance record, "Bear Mash Stomp."

Dorsey Wood took the leads on both sides. Gideon was not on the record, having earlier been forced out of the group over creative differences and replaced with Colbert Jr. Gideon worked briefly as promotion man, and while promoting "This Heart of Mine" in September 1961 was drafted into the service.

The Daylighters' next effort was an independent endeavor. In early 1961 they recorded two songs, the bluesy "No One's Gonna Help You" and the Vibrations-styled "War Hoss Mash." The same members who sang on "This Heart of Mine" were involved, with Dorsey once again taking the leads. After remaining unissued for a while, these sides surfaced in 1963 on the Checker label. They should have remained on the shelf.

The next two records reflected the ascendancy of Gerald Sims, who contributed significantly to a modern soul style in the group. The first was the beautiful "Oh What a Way to Be Loved," which combined a super-club feel with haunting vocal-group harmonies. Sims, who wrote the song and sang lead, had bridged the doowop and soul eras by creating a magnificent transitional tune (which, however, was a thinly disguised remake of Percy Mayfield's "Please Send Me Someone to Love").

The second Sims-led record, "Cool Breeze," was a sensational local hit in September 1962. It even got a little bit of pop play on the top-forty stations, reaching as high as seventeen on WLS. "Cool Breeze" was a genuine soul record, the first real break from the group's 1950s stylings. As with most records of the soul era, it owed as much to the arrangement and production as to the vocal artistry. Pate did the imaginative string arrangements that conveyed a blowing wind effect.

The flip, "Baby I Love You," written by Bob Catron and Colbert Jr. with the lead by Sims, is a fine, aggressively sung doowop blues—a good demonstration of the group's raunchier side. The "Cool Breeze"/"Baby I Love You" record is another transitional record—one side hearkens back to a previous era, the other suggests the sound of the future.

After achieving two successive hits with the Daylighters, Sims's talents did not go unnoticed. In 1962 Sims left to join Carl Davis at OKeh Records. The Daylighters' next record was slow in coming out; in fact, the group was drifting apart. The Wood brothers, Thomas, and Colbert were together again on only one more session, in the summer of 1963. They recorded four songs—four Colbert compositions—"Bottomless Pit" and "I Can't Stop Crying," in which Colbert took the leads, and two others in which Dorsey took the leads. But before these records came out, some records from Catron were released using the Daylighters' name.

With the Daylighters assumed to be inactive, Catron decided to push a new record in the summer of 1963, "Elephant Walk," by Donald Jenkins and a group consisting of Ronnie Strong, Walter Granger, and some members of the Daylighters. The record, released on Cortland, was billed as being by "Donald and the Daylighters." "Elephant Walk" became a national hit and Colbert Sr. protested the use of the Daylighters' name. When the record was peaking, Catron changed the name on the label to the "Delighters." The dispute arose the next year when Catron again put the "Daylighters" name on a Jenkins record, "I've Settled Down."

In October, Gideon had finished his army commitment and returned to Chicago at the tail end of the "Elephant Walk" brouhaha. The Wood brothers had left the group, and the decision was made to reform the Daylighters with Gideon, Thomas, Colbert, and two new members, baritone Curtis Burrell and tenor Ulysses McDonald (both of whom had been in the Dolphins, another Tip Top group).

Meanwhile, "Bottomless Pit" and the flip, "I Can't Stop Crying," released on Tip Top, broke in November. Throughout the winter both sides got substantial airplay. Both were solid songs in the soul idiom and rank among the group's best. The group's other success during the winter was "Oh Mom (Teach Me How to Uncle Willie)," which swept the city in early 1964. Colbert wrote and sang lead on the song. The flip to "Oh Mom" was "Hard-Headed Girl," with Colbert again in the lead. The backing musicians on it were a local rock combo, Gary and the Knight Lites. Earlier in 1963, Colbert, who played bass, had teamed up with the band and during the next three years Gary and the Knight Lites emerged as one of the leading dance-hall bands in the city. One of the more popular halls was the Embassy Ballroom (Fullerton and Pulaski on the North Side), where the Daylighters made frequent appearances with the Knight Lites.

The Daylighters' next release, "Magic Touch," was recorded at the same session as "Hard-Headed Girl" and featured the Knight Lites as well. Gideon and Colbert shared the leads on this Colbert-penned tune. "I Can't Stop Crying" was put on the back as insurance in case "Magic Touch" failed to break. Neither side created any kind of a stir.

Much more successful was "Whisper of the Wind" in December 1964. Originally released in 1963 with the Dorsey Wood–led ensemble of Daylighters in a more doowop version, "Wind" was redone with new vocal tracks by the new group over instrumental tracks from the earlier session. Fans of doowop usually warm up to the first version and consider the second too much in the soul style. "Here Alone," the flip, got the same revamping. Gideon sang lead on both songs, and was backed by Thomas, Colbert, and McDonald (Burrell having left the group). "Wind" featured a light wispy beat that presaged the similar reggae beat of the 1970s. The record was leased to Vee Jay, which put it out on its Tollie subsidiary.

The group had another local success in June 1965 with the vocally intense "For My Baby," again with lead work by Gideon. There was one more

Daylighters record, "Tell Me before I Go," released on the Smash label. It got a few local plays in September 1966. The song was penned by Gideon and Thomas, and featured the pair on the disc as a duet, even though the record label said "Daylighters."

Based on their rather modest recording successes, the Daylighters were able to get a few gigs, mostly locally, such as at Budland, the Trianon Ballroom, and the Gary Armory. During the Christmas season of 1964 the group made a tour of Alabama and Mississippi, but the Daylighters essentially broke up after "For My Baby." Colbert was more interested in the Knight Lites, who were metamorphosing into the American Breed (in 1967 the group had a million-selling hit, "Bend Me, Shape Me").

Erman Records

The success of Erman Record Company was fueled by equal amounts of enthusiasm for soft soul and for hard black coal. Bill Erman was the owner of Diamond Coal Company, at 1501 West Cortland on the North Side. He made his money from coal and oil, but his real love was music. Erman was born in Chicago on December 26, 1930, and inherited the coal business from his family. While in college he started his own band in which he played saxophone and clarinet, and the group played in Ivy League schools. Erman eventually graduated to songwriting, composing a couple of songs for Johnny Desmond along the way. He soon established his own publishing firm, Venetia Music, and from there it was no great leap to forming his own record firm.

Erman founded the company in 1961 and operated it from the offices of his coal company. His labels were Witch and Cortland for R&B music and Ermine for rock 'n' roll and country music. He produced most of the rock 'n' roll records and wrote many of the songs for the acts, including the black ones. He handled A&R for Ermine but had a black musician, Bob Catron, do the A&R producing work for Witch/Cortland. Catron usually did the arranging, but sometimes brought in Johnny Pate.[3]

Catron had a long career in music before his association with Nike and Witch/Cortland. He was born August 28, 1934, in Memphis, where he was raised. He was a music major in college, but while still in school he began gigging in R&B bands in the city's flourishing music scene. During the early 1950s he played in the Beale Streeters Band—both on tour and on record. Catron played saxophone and other brass instruments in the band. For the next decade, he worked in bands, and around 1960 ended up in Chicago, where he was drawn into the recording scene.

The company had some success on Ermine with rock 'n' roll, getting local hits with Johnny Cooper's "Bonnie Do" (January 1963) and Angelo's Angels' "Spring Cleaning" (April 1964) and "I Don't Believe It" (July 1964). The biggest hits were on the R&B end and were usually produced by Catron. Although the company edges into the soul era, there was something retrograde about its output. Just about every black act signed by the company had deep roots in the 1950s club and doowop scenes, and although Catron came from Memphis, with its hard-driving southern-style music, the one characteristic of the Witch/Cortland sound, for better or worse, is it's lack of fullness and drive in the music. As in 1950s music, the vocals are up front and vaguely evoke the era of doowop. Witch/Cortland seemed to be a transition from doowop to the point when soul became a full-bodied and full-flavored music. Many of the Witch/Cortland releases may have sounded dated during the 1962–64 period, but it was period when the music was rapidly making its transition to soul. Records looking both forward and backward were coming out simultaneously, making for an exciting mixture in the charts.

The company's first release was an R&B record produced by Erman called "Son-in-Law," an answer song to Ernie K-Doe's "Mother-in-Law." It was performed by a Chicago lounge pianist/singer, Louise Brown, who had been playing in South Side clubs since the early 1950s. The record made it on *Billboard*'s pop chart for five weeks in the spring of 1961. After that record, however, Catron took over A&R for R&B and concentrated his efforts on soft-soul groups. "Groups were the thing then" was his explanation.[4]

Much of Catron's work was with a veteran doowopper from the 1950s, Donald Jenkins, who had gotten on record as early as 1955 with the Fortunes. Jenkins came back to the recording scene in the early 1960s and rejoined one of his pals from the Fortunes, Ronnie Strong, to form a duo called Rico and Ronnie. They put a record out in 1962 on the Checker label called "It Takes a Long Time" backed with "A Losing Game" that probably wasn't distributed outside the confines of the city.[5]

That same year Jenkins and Strong moved over to Witch/Cortland to join Bob Catron. Under the name the Starr Brothers, the duo recorded three singles—"Don Juan," "Mr. Auctioneer," and "Mother Goose"—all in a soft neo-doowop style. None of these songs made any real noise, but "Don Juan" got some play in Pittsburgh and Chicago in the spring of 1963. "Mr. Auctioneer" got some play in Chicago during that same season.

Walter Granger, another member of the Fortunes, rejoined Jenkins and Strong in mid-1963, and the new group faced a conflict on their name. Catron insisted on calling the group "Daylighters" to cash in on an established name, that of the Daylighters who presumably had broken up. Jenkins explained: "Well, at first we were going to be the Fortunes over again, but well, the Daylighters idea was Catron's thing, you know. He did that."[6]

The first record by Donald and the Daylighters, as the group was first called, was the imaginative "(Native Girl) Elephant Walk." It typified the sound of the period—evoking a past era of doowop yet sounding modern enough to herald the emerging soul era. The song tells about an "American boy from the South Side of Chicago," who in a dream is enchanted by a "native girl from darkest Africa" doing a dance called the Elephant Walk. Jenkins's haunting lead vocals, the fine use of background vocals, the clashing cymbals, plus the addition of jungle sound effects, all contribute to a song that evokes the atmosphere of its subject. The record has the character and personality of a group record not overwhelmed by instrumentation.

"Elephant Walk" entered *Billboard*'s Top 100 chart on September 14, 1963, and left the chart after November 2 at position sixty-four. With more aggressive distribution the record could have done much better. In some markets the song was not played at all, while in other areas it was a top five record.

The later releases, "Adios (My Secret Love)" and "I've Settled Down," were superb sounds that never became hits. Jenkins went on the Dick Clark show and sang "Adios" to a national audience, but then Cortland backed off the record. The problem was that the song was a rewrite of a Nolan Strong and Diablos doowop oldie that made noise in Detroit nine years earlier under the title "Adios My Desert Love." It was written by Devora Brown, who headed Fortune Records, the label that released the song. The Jenkins version was credited to Jenkins and Catron. Brown said, "When we found out about it, our attorney wrote them a strong letter. They apologized and they said that we could even use their master. I thought it was a good master, better than Nolan Strong's version. But Cortland apparently quit plugging it, because I guess they couldn't keep their name on it. It seemed to be going real good, too."[7] "Adios" made its noise in December 1963.

The "Adios" fiasco could have been avoided, according to Catron, had he listened to the advice proffered by Chess's A&R director, Billy Davis, a native of Detroit. Catron said, "Billy Davis heard it and said 'Man, I've heard that song somewhere before.' I said, 'Oh no, Donald wrote this. In fact, he hummed this to me, and I wrote the music down for it.' He said, 'No Bob, I've heard that. If I were you I'd find out where the guy got that song. He's changed it around a little, but I have heard that song.' I went ahead and put it out and it got a beautiful reception. It seemed about every time we got something started we ran into legal problems."[8] The company should have pushed the flip, the superb "Somebody Help Me," with "I've Settled Down," the follow-up single, which captured the same compelling atmospherics as "Elephant Walk."

The Delighters did a few live gigs—mainly high-school lip-sync engagements. They did, however, play some Chicago nightclubs and tour on Dick

Clark's Caravan of Stars. After the Catron association ended, the group made records only sporadically. By the early 1970s they were no longer together. Ronnie Strong died in about 1983.

Donald Jenkins and his groups made records for more than twenty years, and at no time did the sales of their records ever reflect the artistry that went into them. The world of popular music can be terribly unfair, as dedicated followers of rhythm and blues music know. Good records are not always hit records, and Donald Jenkins, Ronnie Strong, and Walter Granger made good records.

The early 1960s were the heyday of girl groups, most of which were recorded on the East Coast. Chicago produced only a few, such as the Gems (featuring Minnie Riperton), the Opals, and the Starlets. Most never achieved more than regional success, because their sound was either not commercial enough or the company was too small to push the records nationally. Yet these groups produced some of the prettiest and most satisfying records to come out of the early 1960s. The story of the Versalettes, who recorded for Witch/Cortland, was typical of that of most Chicago girl groups.[9]

The Versalettes were formed in the summer of 1961, after the original members, Theresa "Therese" Legg, Viola "Vi" Floyd, Kathleen "Kat" Spates, and Vera Regulus, graduated from junior high. The leads were interchanged frequently among Legg, Floyd, and Spates. Vera Regulus Wallace recalled, "We had known each other since about nine years old. We knew each other from church and went to school together. Kat, Vi, and myself went to Grant elementary school, then McKinley Upper Grade Center. Therese went to Manley Upper Grade Center. All four of us went to Marshall High."[10]

Kathleen Spates Robinson said: "We wanted to be in this big talent show at Marshall High, the Jamboree, which was always right after the mid-year graduation. I remember when we went on stage, nobody applauded when the curtain came up. We did 'My Last Cry' [which was a Starlets song]. When we did that song it brought the house down. Reynard Minor, who played piano for another Marshall group, the Gems, wanted to play for us. He played for us briefly, but he didn't have enough time to devote to us and the Gems too."[11]

The real professionalism of the group began when they met fellow Marshall student and upperclassman Bobby Mason. He was the manager of another Marshall group, the Constellations, and decided to take the Versalettes under his wing. He teamed them with Elmore Nunn on guitar, Bernard Reed on bass, Kenneth Hollis on drums, and Frank McCoy on piano, and basically had the group play around various dates until they could get a contract.

Robinson said, "We were doing a lot of local shows, like at the Chicago Housing Authority. They would have different talent shows all over the city of Chicago. We were too good, apparently, because we were eliminated from contesting and they just made us guests. Bobby also got us into doing a lot of things at the Marillac House on the West Side. It was a teen center and it would have dances every weekend."

The key to getting a contract, however, was a show the young women did at the Century of Negro Progress Exposition held at McCormick Place in the summer of 1963. Robinson, who recalled the event as a "Black Centennial," said:

> We were doing this as students for the 4–H Club. We had won their talent contest. The 4–H contest was held at different places all over the city and suburbs, and then it climaxed in a particular suburb. We won first place, and as a result the 4–H had a booth, an exhibit at this Black Centennial, showing its activities in the inner cities, where nobody even thought it existed. We did a song called "Stop the Wedding" by Etta James. We did an actual wedding; that's how we won. We had a bride, bridegroom, the whole ceremony. The Versalettes were the bridesmaids, and I was in the audience. So when the minister got to the part where he said, "is there anyone here who . . . ," then I get up and start singing.
>
> While we were there we had to perform every hour, from ten o'clock in the morning to nine o'clock at night. Larry Steele, who had his revue in another part of McCormick Place, saw us and brought us to the attention of Lucky Cordell, who was a deejay at W-YNR at the time. So the next thing we know Lucky Cordell told the guys at Witch/Cortland about us. They came to hear us sing and we signed a contract.

In order to get the Versalettes ready for recording, A&R man Bob Catron put them in the hands of Donald Jenkins. Robinson noted, "Donald did most of the work with us. He started writing for us, our voices. Then we started practicing." The problem with this arrangement was that Jenkins, a doowopper at heart, favored soft delicate harmonies, and the Versalettes, with their gospel background and their ears attuned to the soul sounds coming out of Motown, were more attuned to hard-driving beat-driven songs. When Catron put the group on record he gave them a delicate-young-thing type of sound, completely at odds with their aggressive live performances.

Sometime before going into the studio in August 1963, the Versalettes added a fifth member, Helen Greenfield. Robinson explained, "Bobby said we could really use her when Viola is doing the lead because she had this real high voice that would blend in well. She had a beautiful voice, she had a very beautiful voice."

The local fans must have been very surprised in the fall of 1963 when they started hearing Versalettes songs on the local radio and the material sounded so unrepresentative of the singers' live performances. The group's first record featured two ballads, "Shining Armor" backed with "True Love Is a Treasure," which was released in the early fall on the Witch label. "Shining Armor," written by Catron and Jenkins, was something of a local hit, and for good reason. The song has an appealing young soprano lead, courtesy of Therese Legg, that made it especially attractive to high schoolers then.

The Versalettes did not like the record, however. Nor did they like most of the records they made for Catron. Wallace said, "It didn't seem they were geared to the market. 'Shining Armor' was a nice tune but it didn't have that funky beat. The backgrounds were so low you could hardly hear it. Basically that's what it was. We liked it to a certain extent because it was ours." Robinson observed, "I wasn't even in sync with it then, and we were young."

"True Love Is a Treasure" was written by Bill Erman, who the previous year had the Blenders record it. The version by the Blenders was very appealing, but it did not hit and Erman tried his luck again with the Versalettes, who with Kat Spates on the lead did a wonderful job on the song. Alas, it did not get played either. The girls parlayed "Shining Armor" into a few gigs, however. Wallace said, "Herb Kent would have us come to these teenage parties and we would lip sync to it and stuff like that."

The Versalettes did another song, "Don Juan in Town," composed by Donald Jenkins, but it was a dismal answer to "Don Juan," a song recorded the previous year by Jenkins and Ronnie Strong billed as the Starr Brothers. It never received a regular release, however, and only deejay copies are in existence. "We had another song that Donald had written," said Robinson, "it was 'House Divided.' We fooled around in the studio with it, but we never recorded it. It was a beautiful song."

The company also tried releasing the group as the Trinkets on the Cortland label, at the same time as the "Shining Armor" record in the fall of 1963. The record was "The Fisherman" backed with "Nobody But You." On "The Fisherman," a collaboration of Catron, Erman, and Jenkins, the girls sing with such passion it was almost camp. It has the strident sound of the classic girl-group sound. The recitation by the lead, Therese Legg, which opens the song, is especially neat. The Blenders had done the song earlier, but with no better success than the Versalettes. Erman's "Nobody But You" is a nice bluesy ballad, led by Kat Spates, although it certainly was not lively enough for radio play. Kathleen Spates Robinson said, "We never thought they recorded that, because we were just playing around with it."

The Versalettes were still something like local heroes to their fans. Robinson said, "Lucky Cordell was like our mentor. Once he invited us to his house for dinner, and every time there was a sock hop, we were always invited. When our music came out, he always played it a lot. Then there was a man called Mr. Taylor who had a record shop on Madison Street. He had taken a picture of us, and he was giving our picture out with our record. It freaked us out, because we couldn't stand the music."

The Versalettes' recording career was halted in 1964, when Witch/Cortland basically went out of business. Helen Greenfield was also removed from the group. "We saw that even though her voice was pretty it just wasn't going to work," said Robinson, "We would do a show and she would disappear, and she wasn't going to school. Her background did not fit in with us, as young ladies during that time."

The Versalettes continued to tear up Chicago with live appearances through 1964. The girls' most eventful performance was on a public television special, called "Teens with Talent," which was intended to display young talent in the city. The Versalettes appeared on the show with Fontella Bass, the Constellations, Jimmy Hudson, and the Baby Miracles (who later recorded "Joey" as the Young Folk). "We did a song by the Marvelettes, who were our favorites anyway," said Robinson, "called 'Locking Up My Heart.'" The Versalettes also became known for their searing version of the Martha and the Vandellas 1963 hit, "Heat Wave." Robinson added, "as popular as 'Heat Wave' was, people thought the Versalettes made 'Heat Wave,' because everywhere we go people would ask for 'Heat Wave.'"

The Versalettes graduated from Marshall in 1965, but in 1966 a teacher at the school, John Vanderheiden, took an interest in the girls' career. He got the girls a recording contract with Columbia but the experience was not a good one. They went to Detroit in the summer of 1967 to record with producer Mike Terry, and sang "So Glad Your Love Don't Change" and "Love Made to Order," both led by Viola Floyd. The songs are exceedingly weak, and one wonders what possessed Columbia to release them. The Versalettes were obviously ill-served by the company, who should have been able to do better. Also the company forced the girls to take a new name, the Little Foxes, which they detested.

The Versalettes broke up in the fall of 1967, when Vera went back to college. In the spring of 1968, Columbia put out on their OKeh label the two titles the group had recorded under the name Little Foxes. Members of the group never learned whether the record was actually released or not until I contacted them in 1992.

Wallace concluded, "We were talented and we were nice girls. That was one of the images we wanted to maintain. We were nice girls, we had vocal training, and we weren't just standing up there and shaking our butts. We sang in four-part harmony and we were coordinated. And we were good wholesome clean girls." Robinson said, "Bob Catron said he always wanted his daughters to be like us."

Two other acts on Witch/Cortland, the Ideals and the Blenders, owe their recordings with the company to a veteran doowop group, the Five Chances, which by the late 1950s had basically ceased to be an intact group. Members Reggie Smith, Johnny Jones, and Howard Pitman, however, continued to dabble in the music business, mainly by acting as mentors and songwriters for new and upcoming talent. Smith noted, "We tried to develop other groups; we had several—male groups, girl groups, something of everything going on."[12]

The P.S. and Corina recordings under the Five Chances name from 1960 were a result of just such mentoring. Newcomers Frank Simms and his cousin (whose name is not remembered) joined Smith, Jones, and Pitman in the recording of "Need Your Love." Smith said, "Simms and his cousin who played guitar came from Fortieth and Drexel. I was going over there to see a girl one day and they were just singing by themselves on the corner. The cousin was playing the guitar, and I liked the sound they were making; 'Need Your Love,' they wrote that song. I got the idea to try to put it together and record it. So I got my group to work with them on the number, and then we decided to cut that on our own label."[13]

"Need Your Love" was released on P.S., which stands for Pitman and Smith, and was paired with "Is This Love?" Neither side exhibits the classic deep, harmonized sound of the Five Chances, but the music was changing and obviously Smith and Pitman were trying to come out with something that would appeal to the contemporary market.

The P.S. record was barely released and the Five Chances looked elsewhere to get it out. "We sold the sides to Corina," Smith said. "We had lack of capital, and when you're undercapitalized you can't get much done." The people at Corina matched "Need Your Love" with "Land of Love," which was not a recording by the Five Chances (despite its being credited as such). Rather it was a recording by another group with whom the Five Chances were working, whose name Smith didn't recall.

In 1962 Jones and Pitman brought to Witch/Cortland a group called the Blenders. The group consisted of Jones, Albert Hunter (from the Clouds and Maples years earlier), and three young women—Goldie Coates, Delores Johnson, and Gail Mapp. The Blenders, ironically, achieved something the Five Chances never did—they made the national charts, the pop charts no less, scoring with "Daughter," a song penned by Jones and led by Coates, which had the flavor of both soul and doowop. It lasted eight weeks on *Billboard*'s pop chart in the summer of 1963, peaking at position sixty-one. Curiously, the record did not make the R&B charts. The song also took the group to the Apollo Theatre, something the Five Chances never experienced.[14]

The Blenders recorded other terrific transitional songs, such as Jones's "Boys Think" (led by Coates) and Erman's "Love Is a Treasure" (led in unison by the three female singers in the group). Neither of these deserving songs became hits, however. Another Blenders recording was "Junior," which like "Boys Think" was an answer song to "Daughter." With "Junior" the group recorded as the Candles on Colbert's Nike label. There was a prototype song that gave birth to all three of these songs. Smith recalled rehearsing "Junior" a couple of years earlier with other members of the Five Chances, but with a slightly different set of lyrics.

Jones also recorded for Bill Erman two singles on himself, under his real name, Hilliard Jones. The first, "Prison of Love" backed with "What Have You Got," was released on Cortland in 1962 but was so poorly distributed that few copies, if any, remain. The second, "Wish I Were the Wind" (flip unknown), was released the following year on Ermine. It is a pleasing number, but nothing that could become a hit. Other obscure records from this time are two releases by the Blenders on the Witch label—"You Trimmed My Christmas Tree" (led by Mapp) and "One Time," both from 1963. The flips are unknown, which means both were two-sided deejay releases only.

The only member of the Five Chances to work with the Ideals was Howard Pitman. The group made its name with an aggressive dance tune called "The Gorilla" in 1963 and was commonly thought of as a soul-era group. But long before the Ideals had ever made their name on wax, they had established their reputation during the 1950s as one of the best West Side doowop ensembles.[15]

The Ideals were formed about 1952 when the singers were freshmen in high school. The original members were Frank Cowan (lead), Leonard Mitchell (first tenor), Wes Spraggins (second tenor), Robert Tharp (baritone), and Clifford Clayborn (bass). Spraggins attended St. Malachy, the local Catholic high school, and the others attended Crane High. The group sang the popular tunes of the day, the Vocaleers' "Is It a Dream?" being one of their favorites. After about a year, the personnel had changed so that Reggie Jackson had replaced Frank Cowan as one of the group's leads and Sam Steward had taken the place of Clifford Clayborn on bass. The group for a time was known as the Mel-tones but decided to change the name after messing up at a benefit concert. They chose their new name, the Ideals, from a sign on a local factory, the Ideal Metal Company.

The Ideals started out doing just high school get-togethers, parties, wedding receptions, and little local appearances. As they got better, they began playing the clubs, for the most part not for pay but for the exposure. They played such nighteries as the Trianon Ballroom, the Pershing Ballroom, Sylvio's, the Cotton Club (in west suburban Argo), and the Skins (in south suburban Robbins). The Ideals even played at the Regal, where they shared the bill with Big Maybelle, Screamin' Jay Hawkins, the El Dorados, and the Five Chances.

"The Five Chances wouldn't follow us on stage," Spraggins contended. "We gave the Spaniels hell. They were in their heyday so they were just super, astronomical. The Del Vikings, we ate them alive, in a hall on Sacramento and Adams. The Del Vikings had just made their record, 'Come Go with Me,' and we performed against them, and it was no contest. Our group was so tight, we had been together for so long, and we rehearsed every single day.

"We were so versatile we sang the Spaniels, the Moonglows, and even the Kool Gents. I remember a show at Crane High where the Kool Gents had come out with—I forget the name of the song—and we sang their song before them. And they wouldn't sing it!"[16] Johnny Carter of the Kool Gents remembered the group from a different slant: "The Ideals were good," he said, "they put on a good show, very entertaining. The talent was there but they lacked a good lead singer to put them across vocally."[17]

Naturally, a question arises: If the Ideals were as good as Spraggins claimed, why weren't they recorded? He explained, "In those days we weren't aware that we had to come up with our own material. They weren't looking for voices, they had the Spaniels, the Moonglows, and such. We were good imitators. This was the thing that hurt us. When you heard the Ideals do 'My Prayer,' you heard the Platters. The thing we specialized in were the Moonglows. When you heard us sing, you thought the Moonglows were singing their own records."

About 1956 Reggie Jackson left the Ideals to go into the service, and his place as lead was taken over by Fred Pettis. Spraggins felt that with Pettis the group was at its very best. "The man was gifted," said Spraggins, "he could sing soprano and yet could sing baritone; he had a fantastic range." Major Lance was also in the Ideals for a short spell. Lance, a dancer on the Jim Lounsbury's "Time for Teens" television dance show, brought the Ideals on the show and sang lead with them as part of the group.

By 1958 Pettis was drifting away from the group, not showing up for engagements and generally becoming undependable. Likewise, Spraggins also left and went into the service in November of that year. But at this point Jackson was back from his military commitment and rejoined the group to form a four-man ensemble with Mitchell, Tharp, and Stewart. This group continued to knock around the city for several years, and finally, the Ideals got their opportunity to record in 1961, some nine years after their first formation.

Deejay Richard Stamz had a record label called Paso. The Ideals approached him and he gave them a contract, the first effort being "What's the Matter with You Sam," backed with "Together." "Sam" is an Olympics-styled mediocre jump that is distinguished by Stewart's marvelous bass, and "Together," a ballad, is notable because it sounds exactly like a New York Italianate doowop group of the same era, something like the work of the Roommates. "Sam" got a little local airplay but not much else. A follow-up, "Magic," was a bluesy ballad backed with "Teens," a jump in the similar vein as "Sam." Neither side showed any promise.

The Ideals cooled their heels for a while before their next opportunity to record presented itself, in 1963. By that time they had added a new lead, Eddie Williams. Howard Pitman had started a record company, Concord, and chose the Ideals to record "The Gorilla," a song he composed. He was also working with another group at the same time, the Candidates, and put out their "Hypnotize" backed with "Space and Time" on his Concord label. But unlike his experience with the Ideals, he had no success with them.

In recording "The Gorilla," the Ideals broke with their doowop past. Williams's rough-hewn, aggressive lead gave the record a decidedly soul sound. The record was brilliant in its conception. Pitman set out to make an utterly savage-sounding record and succeeded admirably with the weird background humming of the Ideals, the wild riffing of the saxophonist (in the wrong key, probably intentionally so), and the bottom-heavy beat of the accompaniment.

"The Gorilla," released in September 1963, near the end of the Monkey dance-fad, proved to be the Ideals' biggest hit. Jackson said that Herb Kent would take the group around to all the high schools, along with a guy in a gorilla suit, to promote the record. With the powerful influence of Kent, the record sold like crazy. It quickly proved beyond the capabilities of Pitman, who had sold some twenty thousand copies out of his car, shopping it around the city. Pitman sold it to Cortland, along with the Ideals' contract, receiving a thousand dollars up front for the publishing rights and 10 percent of future royalties. He never saw another cent.

Cortland put out "The Gorilla" and it became a national hit, selling some ninety thousand copies in Chicago alone. In December 1963 the Ideals were rewarded with their most prestigious date of their careers, the annual Christmas show at the Regal. They shared the bill with Maxine Brown, Roy Hamilton, Percy Mayfield, Pigmeat Markham, and fellow Chicago acts, the Impressions, Bobby Miller, and Betty Everett.

The Ideals were national stars and soon were playing dates across the country. "We played Pittsburgh several times," said Tharp, adding, laughingly, "That's where Reggie fell in love."[18] "Patti Labelle and the Bluebelles were playing on the date," explained Jackson. "I met Nona Hendrix and we had a good time. We played the Apollo. Before we went on stage they warned us that the audience would throw tomatoes and anything they could get their hands on if we weren't good. Fortunately, 'The Gorilla' was real big just as we were coming in from New Jersey—so we didn't have any trouble the seven days we were there. We were also on a local television show in Washington, D.C."[19] Tharp added, "We owned Wisconsin, we played there lots of times."[20]

The Ideals' follow-ups, which tried to capitalized on "The Gorilla" sound, failed both commercially and artistically. "Mojo Hanna" was a remake of Motown's Henry Lumpkin's song of a year earlier, and "Mo Gorilla" was a forceful but uninteresting remake of "The Gorilla." "Local Boy" continued the same uneventful trend.

The group's move to St. Lawrence/Satellite brought a modification in their sound, generally less harsh and aggressive and more melodic than in their doowop days. Before the move to the new operation there were some key personnel changes. Williams was drafted and Jackson dropped out when the exigencies of marriage required something a little more stable. The group then remained at three, with just Mitchell, Tharp, and Stewart for a spell. By the time the group began recording for St. Lawrence, however, Jackson had returned and Tharp had dropped out to join Jerry Murray to form a dance duo called Tom and Jerrio, specializing in boogaloo records. Tharp took the professional name of Tommy Dark.

Tharp, however, joined in on the Ideals' first session with St. Lawrence even though he wasn't under contract with the group. The first release, in June 1965, was "Go Get a Wig," an average novelty made interesting by Stewart's bass, paired with an intriguing version of the Everly Brothers' "Cathy's Clown." The three-member Ideals had several more releases on St. Lawrence/Satellite, their biggest being "Kissin'," which managed to make *Billboard*'s national R&B chart in February 1966. Their best number was "You Lost and I Won," which is the one that even doowop collectors often go for.

Unfortunately, the Ideals were attracting little interest among the record buyers during 1966–67 and they were forced to call it quits, after being together for fifteen years. None of the members of the Ideals held any regrets about their longtime involvement in entertainment, except that they expressed a desire to have been more successful. "Those were good years," said Spraggins. "They brought a lot of joy and happiness in my life; that we were able to perform and do things for people and yet try to do something for ourselves."

"It was an enjoyable experience up until the end," Jackson said. "The best experience was with the audience. There is nothing like having the audience behind you. You don't worry about being nervous up there, because when the audience is cheering for you, you forget about nervousness and just entertain."[21] Entertainment was what the Ideals were all about, and if the audience brought joy to the Ideals it was certainly reciprocated.

Only Leonard Mitchell continued to record by getting together with Jerome Johnson and Robert Thomas to form the Channel 3. With their guitarist, Larry Blasingale, the group had one release in 1973, "The Sweetest Thing" backed with "Someone Else's Arms." Soon after, however, Mitchell left the music business when he converted to a sanctified religious faith. Except for Tharp, who in the 1990s was working as Gene Chandler's road manager, the Ideals absented themselves from the music business, but they should not be forgotten. They were one of the longest-lived and most interesting of Chicago doowop groups.

*   *   *

The Nike and Erman operations were handicapped in that most of the principals involved in the companies were products of the doowop era trying to make records for the up-and-coming soul era. They were destined to fail, but because of their situation they produced a marvelous transitional style of rock 'n' roll that straddled the doowop and soul eras. The Daylighters in their best recordings could produce pure soul as well as pure doowop. Donald Jenkins, who recorded both his group and the Versalettes, was constitutionally incapable of putting out soul records, unless they had a strong doowop element. The Ideals were likewise a transitional act, and like all of the above mentioned acts, they could be described as post–rock 'n' roll and proto-soul.

Notes

1. Information about Nike comes from the Catron, Colbert, Jr., and Gideon interviews.

2. Information about the Daylighters comes from Pruter, "The Daylighters"; Colbert Jr. and Gideon interviews.

3. Information about Erman comes from the Catron, Erman, and Gideon interviews.

4. Catron interview.

5. Information about Donald Jenkins comes from Pruter, "Donald Jenkins Story"; Jenkins interview.

6. Jenkins interview.

7. Brown interview.

8. Catron interview.

9. Information about Versalettes comes from the Wallace, Frank, and Kathleen Spates Robinson interviews.

10. This and subsequent remarks by Vera Regulus Wallace quoted in this chapter come from the Wallace interview.

11. This and subsequent remarks by Kathleen Spates Robinson quoted in this chapter come from the Robinson interview.

12. Reggie Smith interview, October 15, 1989.

13. This and subsequent remarks by Reggie Smith quoted in this chapter come from the September 28, 1989, interview with him.

14. Information about the Blenders comes from Pruter, "The Five Chances"; the Hilliard Jones interviews; and the Gail Mapp interview.

15. Information about the Ideals comes from Pruter, "Windy City Soul"; and the Jackson, Pitman, Tharp, Spraggins, and Mitchell interviews.

16. This and subsequent remarks by Wesley Spraggins quoted in this chapter come from the Spraggins interview.

17. Johnny Carter interview.

18. Tharp interview.

19. Jackson interview.

20. Tharp interview.

21. Jackson interview.

9

The Bill Sheppard Groups

In the late 1950s and early 1960s there were many vocal groups working across the country who are highly regarded today by those who specialize in the popular music of the era. Yet these same groups remain largely unknown to the majority of rhythm and blues and rock 'n' roll fans. Such groups include the Martinels, the Volumes, and, from Chicago, the Sheppards, the Dukays, the Blenders, Donald and the Delighters, the Daylighters, and the Radiants. Their relative obscurity perhaps can be attributed to the fact that they were popular during the long-denigrated 1959–63 period, when doowop was fast becoming a memory and soul had a few years to go before it would make its impact. Only a few of their songs crossed over to the pop charts to become rock 'n' roll hits. But these vocal groups deserve wider recognition. They are the artists who helped to redeem the early 1960s by creating a marvelous transitional style of R&B distinctive to the period. It was a music that drew much of its character from the earlier doowop, yet it incorporated instrumentation and vocal stylings that in later years would inform soul music.

The success of the Sheppards, the Dukays, the Bel Aires, the Equallos, and other such transitional groups discussed in this chapter was due mostly to the efforts of the colorful Bill "Bunky" Sheppard, a record man in every sense of the word. He lived and breathed the business every day of his life. Sheppard was born in New Orleans on March 20, 1922. The early 1950s found him in Chicago working at the Favor Ruhl art supply store in the city's downtown.[1] He began his music career as a protégé of Ted Daniels, one of the preeminent vocal group managers in the 1950s. Maurice Simpkins, once a vocal group member, said, "Bill Sheppard didn't know anything at the time; he hung around Ted. He's black but he looks white. He wore sunglasses then; it was one of his trademarks."[2]

Sheppard would work as an independent manager and producer of vocal groups and would shop his groups around to various record labels (his mid-1950s work with an early Sheppards group on Theron and United was discussed earlier). In 1959 Sheppard took the plunge and started his own label, Apex. In establishing Apex he cemented an alliance with two music business veterans, Tommy "Madman" Jones and Dempsey Nelson. With Jones's Mad label and Nelson's Dempsey label, the three set up an operation at 951 East Forty-seventh Street.[3]

The Mad/Dempsey/Apex complex had its beginning in November 1957, when Jones, a tenor sax player, established his Mad and M&M imprints. His operation was at 1207 East Fifty-third Street. Jones was born October 19, 1922, in Chicago, and attended DuSable High in the late 1930s. He started blowing sax when he was about eight or nine, and by his early twenties he was making an impression on the city's club scene. His exuberant persona and wild playing soon earned him a following. Jones recalled, "I used to walk the bars, blowing my sax. I sang a lot, told jokes, that kind of stuff, and they just started calling me 'Madman.'"[4]

Although a perennial club favorite, Jones had limited recording opportunities. He started his labels mainly to get himself on wax. He also recorded other performers, but most were dated acts that reflected his own background. His roster included Tony Smith and the Aristocrats, the Four Shades of Rhythm, Lefty Bates and His Band, and Rudy Robinson, all acts that had been on record in the 1940s. Jones recorded two vocal groups reflecting the newer trend in music, the Equallos and Freddie and the Freeloaders. Regarding the latter group, he said, "I thought they were a real good group, but I couldn't get anything going with them."

Jones could not get anything going with any of his releases and found himself increasingly angry and embittered by the experience. He said,

> I took all the money I made and put it into the record business. I gave distribution to Ernie Leaner to handle, and for some stupid reason I trusted the guy. I've never been a businessman, and I took my releases to him and he didn't do a doggone thing with my stuff. Deejays were taking money then, and I remember saving up three hundred dollars and gave it to a disc jockey. He played my record twice, and I just got disgusted completely. It was horrible. I remember sitting at the back of my third-floor apartment and just taking records and sailing them into the alley, because they weren't selling.

Jones's Mad label lingered on into the 1960s but never got even a local hit.

Dempsey Nelson's label, Dempsey, was the weakest and most short-lived of the Mad/Dempsey/Apex trio. His Ed Redding sides came from Jones, and he recorded his Jim Conley Combo sides on his own. The Jim

Conley Combo consisted of Jim Conley, a tenor sax player who was once a Memphis Slim sideman; guitarist Phil Upchurch; pianist John Young; organist Dave Green; bassist Richard Evans; and drummer Marshall Thompson. Of the four released sides, a number called "Nite Lite" did well locally. But because of tax problems in the early 1960s, Nelson fled to Africa to escape prosecution,[5] and the Dempsey label closed down.

Bill Sheppard, with his Apex label, had the biggest success of the three imprints, recording mostly his namesake group, the Sheppards. He also released recordings supplied by Jones on older-style acts, namely the Lefty Bates Trio, the Floyd Morris Trio, and the Four Shades of Rhythm. Sheppard, however, was most attuned to recording vocal groups. The Sheppards group on Apex represented a second configuration of Sheppards. The first configuration had broken up in 1957.

In 1958 Sheppard met Carl Davis while trying to promote one of his groups, the Bel Aires. Davis, who was working for the deejay Al Benson at the time, told how the meeting came about:

> He had a group called the Bel Aires, and he was trying to do something with their record, "Rockin' an' Strollin'." I remember he brought the record over to Al Benson. He came upstairs and he had a fifth of gin. His intent was to give Al this fifth of gin to play his record. I don't know why, I just took a liking to him. I said, "Don't go offer that man no gin 'cause I know Al. He don't want no gin." I said, "Let me hear your record." I listened to it. I didn't think it was a hit, but I thought it was good enough to be played on radio. So I told him, "Let me take it in and see if I can get it played for you." Al played it and the record did all right. The important thing, it brought Bunky and I together.[6]

While at Columbia Record Distributors, Davis began to get an itch to make records on his own. Sheppard was getting some success on a new group, the Sheppards, so Davis teamed him up to form Pam Productions in 1961. They set up their operation on the near West Side, at 2400 West Madison. Three labels were established—Nat, named after an accountant for the firm; Pam, named after one of Davis's daughters; and Wes, the initials of William E. Sheppard.[7] To trace the complicated story of Sheppard's various groups on various company labels, it is best to start with the Bel Aires.

The Bel Aires

The Bel Aires, known for "My Yearbook" backed with "Rockin' an' Strollin'," were not even a one-hit group; they were a one-record group. But what a fine record it was. "My Yearbook" is a delightful midtempo ballad with a compelling tenor lead complemented by an echoing falsetto and great chorusing in the background. The song has a nice romantic feel to it. "Rockin' an' Strollin'" is an up-tempo bouncy type of rock 'n' roll number with marvelous harmony that features a sharply etched falsetto providing a subtle edge to the sound.[8]

The record was released by Decca in the summer of 1958 but it was never much of a hit. It had some regional success in Chicago (where Benson had it in his top ten) and a few other markets. Years later, as it attained status as a recording well worth including in doowop collections, many doowop fans mistakenly assumed that the Bel Aires were an East Coast group and that they were white (there is something of a "white" sound to the disc).

The Bel Aires called themselves the Del Rios when they first got together in 1957. They were typical of those myriad street-corner groups that graced the urban landscape during the 1950s. The members came from various high schools on the South Side—Millard Edwards (lead and bass) from Englewood; his brother, Jimmy Allen (baritone), from Chicago Vocational; Ezell Williams (first tenor) from Tilden; Frank Taylor (second tenor) and James Dennis Isaac (bass and top) from DuSable. Only Isaac had any previous recording experience, having recorded with the Sheppards on the Theron and United labels. Edwards had dabbled in group singing early in his high school days when he would join the Five Stars in impromptu harmonizing sessions in the hallways of Englewood High. (The Five Stars would later go on to great fame as the El Dorados.)

The Del Ricos at first sang without pay at innumerable parties and high school hops, but after Edwards joined, the group became more professional. Edwards had a regular job and was able to buy the group's members their first uniforms as well as to lead the singers to higher aspirations. The Del Ricos' first memorable show was at Hyde Park High. "It was a big show for us," Edwards said. "I went to one of the local disc jockeys, Herb Kent, and he put us on the show with the El Dorados and the Spaniels. We sang a song by the Del Vikings, 'Come Go with Me,' and everybody thought we were the Del Vikings."[9] One wonders how the emcee introduced them.

Eventually the Del Ricos hooked up with Bunky Sheppard, who got the group the two excellent songs from the composing team of Marie Dell and Nick Jovan, "My Yearbook" and "Rockin' an' Strollin'," along with an excellent arrangement and production and a release on a major label, Decca. He also gave the group a new name, the Bel Aires, after the name of his publishing company, Bel Aire Music.

The record generated brisk sales locally on both the R&B and the pop stations. Edwards noted, "It was selling at a pace of five thousand a day, and most people at the time thought we were a white group." But the record, like so many terrific disks from the rock 'n' roll era, never took off. Edwards recalled, "We got a few pennies as far as royalties were concerned, but one of the misfortunes of being with a big company is you get lost."[10]

The Bel Aires did more than get lost; they fell apart just as they were working on another recording date with Sheppard. Ezell Williams had written a superb ballad called "Island of Love," but he and Frank Taylor got their draft notices and the Bel Aires were left shorthanded.

About this time, the Ballads, a Sheppard-managed group from the West Side, were coming unglued as well. The group consisted of O. C. Logan, Willie Logan (brother of O. C.), Kermit Chandler, O. C. Perkins, and Murrie Eskridge (the latter two had earlier recorded as members of the Palms on United Records). The Logan brothers dropped out and the Ballards were also short of vocalists. By a series of circumstances, however, Perkins got in touch with James Dennis Isaac of the Bel Aires and they arranged a joint practice session of the remnants of their two groups. The practice worked to everyone's satisfaction and it was agreed that they should merge. The combined group took the name Sheppards, after their mutual manager and producer.

The Sheppards

To fans of rock 'n' roll and rhythm and blues, the Sheppards are known for just one record, the doowop classic "Island of Love," from 1959 on the Apex label. But, more important, the group built a substantial career during the early 1960s with a series of blues ballads and jump tunes sung in a part-doowop and part-soul style that contributed to bridging earlier and later eras. The formation of the Sheppards took place in 1959. The lineup consisted of Millard Edwards (lead and bass), Jimmy Allen (baritone), James Dennis Isaac (bass and fifth tenor), O. C. Perkins (second tenor), Murrie Eskridge (lead and top tenor), and Kermit Chandler (guitar). The group featured two first-rate leads—the smooth ballad voice of Edwards and the sharper-edged, gospel-like vocals of Eskridge. The Sheppards were also blessed with excellent songwriters; virtually all of their material was written by group members. Perkins and Chandler teamed up on nearly a third of the songs and created most of the hits, and Edwards proved prolific with the pen as well. The Sheppards, in short, combined the strengths of two groups. Bunky Sheppard made the group his main focus on his Apex label.[11]

The Sheppards' first Apex release paired "Island of Love," which came from the Bel Aires, and "Never Felt Like This Before," which came from the Ballads. The latter song, with the strong, soulful lead by Eskridge, got a lot of play on the East Coast, but it was the enchanting and romantic Edwards-led "Island of Love" that became a national hit. The song was not a chart success, but after its release in the spring of 1959 it sold strongly and steadily for almost a full year and became the group's trademark tune. While "Never Felt Like This Before" seemed to be a harbinger of the coming soul era, "Island of Love" seemed to hark back to the glories of doowop.

Because of their initial recording success, the Sheppards were given the opportunity to tour the chitlin' theater circuit in the summer and fall of 1959. In their first show, at the Tivoli Theater, the group was billed behind LaVern Baker, Roy Hamilton, and Huey Smith and the Clowns. In their second show, at an auditorium in Calumet City (a suburb south of Chicago), the Sheppards and the Skyliners were first-billed and it was that show that proved most memorable to the group. Perkins remembered:

> That was the first time I really saw our name up in lights. They had it in some kind of sequins or something. It was just dynamite for me to see this. After we got in, we worked the auditorium. Like four or five thousand kids were in there. The crowd was excited, and it was really exciting to see them excited, because I've never seen this in nowhere but the movies and I thought it was bullshit. Then you get to see it with your own eyes, and then you realize this is for real and its happening to you. . . . And all those kids—I actually saw this one girl just faint when we hit "Island of Love."[12]

Nothing much happened for the Sheppards on the next few releases, but their fifth one, "Come Home, Come Home," had some pop success in the fall of 1960. The group's next release, "Tragic," proved even more successful. It got substantial play on the R&B outlets in early 1961 and was the song that the group sang on the Dick Clark show. Because of the peculiar procedures on the show, however, only four of the Sheppards could be shown and Chandler and Isaac were excluded from the telecast.

The Sheppards left Apex after "Tragic," but there was one more release for the label, "So in Need for Love," a fine bluesy ballad. It was released under the name "Murrie Eskridge" for legal reasons. The group joined Pam, Bunky Sheppard's new label owned in conjunction with Carl Davis, and the first release for it was a fine double-sided effort, "Never Let Me Go" paired with "Give a Hug to Me." The latter side made some noise in the Midwest but turned out to be only a "turntable hit" with few record sales. Two other fine songs from the Pam session, "Queen of Hearts" and "Forgotten," later came out on the Sheppards' first album released on Constellation in 1964 as part of an oldies series.

With the release of "The Glitter in Your Eyes," in December 1961 (first on Wes, then on Vee Jay after a move to that label), the Sheppards were rewarded with their first national hit since "Island of Love." The song features exotic but splendid warbling that sounds somewhat like doowop, but it has a certain degree of soul styling to place it between eras. The Sheppards, still on Vee Jay, then re-recorded "Tragic" with an unsuitable echo effect. The song came out in the spring of 1962 and proved to be another national hit for the group. The flip, "Come to Me," an equally wonderful song, somehow never achieved any popularity.

The year 1962 also saw the release of the group's "Elevator Operator," an aggressive jump tune, backed with "Loving You," a superb example of the group's way with a blues ballad. The members of the Sheppards felt that all their releases on Vee Jay could have been much bigger with proper handling, so the group left the company in protest.

Throughout the early 1960s the Sheppards did an extensive number of live dates, especially in the Midwest, where they played just about every large or medium-size city. They also made a tour of the East Coast from New York to North Carolina, highlights being dates at the Howard in Washington, D.C., and the Royal in Baltimore. At home in Chicago, they appeared at the Regal twice, in November 1960 and in December 1961. The latter date featured a great show that included Lloyd Price, Dukays, Mitty Collier, and Erma Franklin.

The Sheppards played the local clubs regularly, the most prestigious being Robert's Show Club. One club in the western suburbs proved particularly memorable for the group. It turned out to be a front for a gambling operation of the mob. While the Sheppards were performing in the downstairs lounge, cards were being shuffled, dice were being thrown, and a lot of money was changing hands on the upper floor. One night the group had the "honor" of entertaining the Chicago don himself, Sam "Momo" Giancana.

After Vee Jay, the Sheppards never had a hit and their career went into a decline. In 1963 Sheppard got Davis to release on OKeh "Pretend You're Still Mine," a fine doowoppy ballad. The song never caught on, however, perhaps because it sounded dated. Following that release, Edwards left the group to go it alone as a single under the name Mill Evans.

The Sheppards continued as best they could without Edwards on a number of records, but they hadn't any success. Most of their records after 1964 featured an earlier recorded side in hopes that if the new side failed to click the old side might work out. In 1966 the group did four sides for ABC–Paramount Records. Only three of the members participated in those sessions—Eskridge, Perk, and Chandler. Chandler sang for the first time and took the lead on one of the songs, "Little Girl Lost." That song plus "Let Yourself Go" came out in early 1966 but did nothing. The other two songs, "Stubborn Heart" and "How Do You Like It," were assumed by the group to have been unreleased, but the sides did surface on a California label, Mirwood, late in 1966 (probably from a deal Sheppard made).

The Daylighters, 1961.
Clockwise from top left:
Eddie Thomas, George
Wood, Dorsey Wood, and
Chuck Colbert Jr.

Donald Jenkins recorded his group,
the Delighters, and the Versalettes
for the Witch/Cortland label group in
the doowop vein.

The Versalettes are shown recording "Shining Armor" in August 1963. Standing, left to right, the young women are: Kat Spates, Helen Greenfield, Theresa Legg, Vera Regulus, and Viola Floyd. Lower left, Witch/Cortland A&R director, Bob Catron. Courtesy of Bob Catron.

The Versalettes, 1966. Top: Theresa Legg; bottom, left to right: Vera Regulus, Viola Floyd, and Kat Spates.

The Blenders, 1963. The group got a national hit with "Daughter." Top, left to right: Albert Hunter and Johnny Jones; bottom, left to right: Delores Johnson, Goldie Coates, and Gail Mapp. Courtesy of Gail Mapp.

The Ideals, 1955. Left to right: Wes Spraggins, Sam Stewart, Reggie Jackson, Robert Tharp, and Leonard Mitchell.

The Ideals, 1966. Left to right: Sam Stewart, Reggie Jackson, and Leonard Mitchell.

The Sheppards, 1961. The Sheppards made their mark with "Island of Love." Top, left to right: Jimmy Allen, James Dennis Isaac, and Murrie Eskridge; bottom, left to right: O. C. Perkins, Kermit Chandler, and Millard Edwards.

The Dukays, 1961. When the group recorded "Duke of Earl," a million-selling doowop, the artist was billed as "Gene Chandler." Top: Eugene Dixon (Gene Chandler); center: Ben Broyles; bottom, left to right: James Lowe, Shirley Johnson, and Earl Edwards.

The Dukays, 1962. Left to right: Charles Davis, Earl Edwards, James Lowe, and Margaret "Cookie" Stone.

The Dukays, 1964. Left to right: Claude McCrae, James Lowe, Earl Edwards, and Richard Dixon.

Al Benson, Chicago's most powerful disc jockey, could make or break any doowop group by choosing to play or not play its record. Courtesy of the Chicago Defender.

Deejay Sam Evans, with his nightly show on WGES and his local concert promotions, was Al Benson's biggest competitor through much of the 1950s. Courtesy of the Chicago Defender.

Deejay McKie Fitzhugh, who broadcasted over WOPA and operated McKie's Disc Jockey Lounge, was an important promoter of doowop groups but was best known as a supporter of jazz. Courtesy of the Chicago Defender.

Herb Kent, who was heard over WBEE, replaced Al Benson as the city's top R&B deejay. Kent had a teen-appeal approach and a strong identification with doowop groups. Here he is shown during a rare appearance in the Chicago suburbs. Courtesy of Janice McVickers.

In late 1968, the entire group, minus Edwards, began recording again. A release on Bunky Sheppard's Sharp label, "What's the Name of the Game," made it as a chart record in Chicago in January 1969. In July of the same year, a release on the Bunky label, the old Jimmy Hughes secular-gospel song "Steal Away," achieved moderate local success as well. The song featured Isaac on lead vocals for the first time.

Bunky Sheppard was heavily involved with the career of the Esquires in the late 1960s and was giving little attention to the Sheppards. The group decided to break up in 1969, because as Perkins put it, "They had to do something with their lives."

It is sad that the Sheppards as a group could not "do something with their lives" as singers. They were a much better group than the modest success of their records indicated. The performers had such talent that they could have made it to the big time, as did the Dells and the Temptations, but they did not. Perkins explained why: "The most unfortunate thing that ever happened to the Sheppards was that they didn't ever get someone to take the act and really polish it and produce it to what it could have been. No one took us and said, 'I'm going to make you an act instead of a record.'" Notwithstanding Perkins's remarks, the Sheppards have made an indelible mark on the history of rhythm and blues and soul. This was evidenced by a *Time* magazine profile of the group in January 1981, some nineteen years after the group's last hit record. The profile was prompted by *Time*'s selection of *The Sheppards,* a Solid Smoke reissue LP, as one of the top ten pop records of 1980.[13] The Sheppards made music that had staying power.

What happened to the various members of the Bel Aires, Ballads, and Sheppards after 1969 was uneventful for most of the members. Millard Edwards was the only one to continue successfully in the music business, having joined the Esquires, of "Get on Up" fame, in 1967. Later, he achieved much success in the jewelry business. James Dennis Isaac sang in a group called the Satagons in the early 1970s and the group came out with one nondescript single. Kermit Chandler also continued in the music field, getting work—sometimes regularly, and at other times not so regularly—as a session guitarist and performing in live gigs. But he drank himself to death in 1981 at the age of thirty-seven. Jimmy Allen had died the previous year.

The Logan brothers of the Ballads, the group that gave rise to the Sheppards, also continued to sing in a vocal group, forming the Equallos with Arthur Ford and Dave Hoskin. Their first release was on Tommy Jones's Mad label in 1959. They recorded two ordinary numbers, "Yodeling" backed with "Patty-Patty." It failed to generate any response. Much better was a follow-up in 1960, "Underneath the Sun" backed with "In between

Tears." "Underneath the Sun" is particularly noteworthy for its exaggerations in both the screaming falsetto and the comic bass work. Going baroque did not generate any sales, and in 1962 the group signed with George Leaner's One-derful label. Much to the Equallos' dismay, however, he never put anything out on them.[14]

In 1963 the Equallos, billed as Willie Logan and the Plaids, recorded a two-sided neo-doowop featuring "You Conquered Me" backed with "Say That You Care," which appeared on Jerry Murray's Jerry O label. The two thinly produced sides with exotic, slightly off-key warbling sounded dated next to the soul sounds that were developing in the recording industry. The record did not do anything, but doowop fans treasure the record today as one of the late products of the golden age of doowop. (The same recording of "Say That You Care" was recycled on a Dukays' record a year later credited to the Dukays.)

The Dukays

The Dukays were known for a few moderately successful transitional soul-doowop hits, but few followers of popular music realized in the early 1960s that they also recorded one of the best known early rock 'n' roll records, "Duke of Earl." The song was made famous by Gene Chandler. Eugene Dixon, to use Chandler's birth name, was the Dukays' first lead singer, and as lead he recorded the song with the entire group. Due to a marketing decision and record company politics, however, he alone was credited on the record. Chandler became the "Duke of Earl" and went on to national fame, while the rest of the group continued on a few more years with only intermittent, modest success.[15]

The Dukays came out of the Englewood neighborhood of Chicago and got together when they were high schoolers, about 1957. Earl Edwards—the Dukays' spokesman, leader, founder, and self-confessed "daddy" of the group—told how it was formed:

> I met one of the fellows when he was robbing a bus, Ben Broyles. I decided I would be a good guy and make a nice guy out of him. I found out he liked to sing, so every chance I got I had him come around to sing to keep him out of trouble. With the other fellows, we used to get together on the corner, Fifty-ninth and May, and sing and choose sides. Then, nobody wanted to choose me because I was new in Chicago, and they didn't think I could sing. I had to take what was left, and it turned out that the fellows I chose were better than any of those other guys.[16]

Edwards next added bass singer Motee Thurston to the group, and later, through a barbershop connection, brought in lead vocalist Gene Chandler. Edwards explained, "A man had a barbershop in the neighborhood and his name was Cooper. He picked the name for us, and said he was going to call us the 'Dukays.' We would go into his shop and rehearse and have little contests. That's the way Gene Chandler joined my group. He liked the way we did things so he decided to leave his group, the Gaytones, and sing with us."

Dixon soon left the Dukays to join the army. While he was stationed with the 101st Airborne Division in Germany, he did some performing with the Special Services. The Dukays continued to stay together in his absence, and when Dixon got out in 1960 he reclaimed his place as lead. He also brought along his cousin, Shirley Johnson, who the group felt would be an attraction because it was not common for females to be in doowop groups. At this juncture, the group consisted of lead vocalist Eugene Dixon, baritone Earl Edwards, second tenor Ben Broyles, bass Motee Thurston, and Shirley Johnson, who did the customary male part of first tenor. The Dukays were now ready to go beyond street-corner harmonizing to making records, but they were weak on original material and sought the help of Bernice Williams, the Englewood songwriter who worked with vocal groups in the area.

Williams worked with the Dukays, polished their act, and developed some songs for them. During this time James Lowe replaced Motee Thurston as bass. After some months the group was ready for the recording studio and, especially, to record with Carl Davis and Bunky Sheppard. The sessions resulted in the following songs: "The Big Lie," "Festival of Love," "Kissin' in the Kitchen," "Girl Is a Devil," "Nite Owl," and "Duke of Earl." These songs were typical of the period—partly in the group-harmony tradition and partly in the soul style. The vocal parts were allowed to assert themselves well in front of the few instruments employed in the mix, but despite this 1950s complexion there is a subtle soul element in the hard-edge vocals.

"Girl Is a Devil," the first release, came out on the Nat label in the spring of 1961. After the record entered *Billboard*'s pop Top 100 on May 15, it lasted a relatively long thirteen weeks on the chart, going as high as sixty-four. The song, written by Williams, has a terrific urban flavor well conveyed by Dixon's soulful and perfectly enunciated delivery. The follow-up to that song was the equally masterful "Nite Owl," another Williams composition thoroughly evocative of the ghetto streets of Chicago. "Nite Owl" broke into the Top 100 chart on January 20, 1962, slipped off the chart on February 24, but returned for one week on March 31. On the *Cash Box* R&B chart the record went to number fifteen.

The Dukays' next record, "Duke of Earl," was released in November 1961, only weeks after "Nite Owl." The song was a product of street-cor-

ner harmonizing. The usual routine was to "open the vocal cords" by singing the scales, using some nonsense syllables. Usually it would be something like "ah, ah, ah, ahh," but this time someone in the group started
working with "du, du, duu," which soon evolved into the compelling
"Duke, Duke, Duke of Earl" chant (which involved nothing more than
going up and down the scale). Chandler and Edwards started working in
some lyrics, but the song remained incomplete when they went into their
second recording session for Nat to record "Nite Owl."

Davis told how the "Duke of Earl" got to be recorded. It was a typical
seven-hundred-dollar, four-songs-per-session deal, as was customary of the
period:

> We listened to the Dukays and they had a song called "Nite Owl." I
> said that "Nite Owl" sounds like it would be a smash. So Bunky and
> I, we were trying to find the money to cut it. I remember I went to
> this girl I was dating. I went to her and told her I needed seven hun-
> dred dollars. Between her and her mother, they came up with the
> seven hundred dollars. I got my brother Clifford to write out the chord
> changes. We got the musicians in there, in those days I think it was
> only two-track; the music's on one, the singing is on the other.
>
> The night before the session the Dukays were in our office, and
> they were rehearsing the songs they were going to record the next day.
> When they got through rehearsing, I was in my office, and they were
> in this outer office, and through the door I kept hearing—I thought
> they were singing "do cover"—the "Duke of Earl." I thought it was
> something else man, I said, "What is that!" They said, "We're just
> rehearsing our next session. We haven't even written all the lyrics to
> this song yet." And I said, "Run it down, let's hear it." They started
> and the song just knocked me. I said, "Let me tell you something, if
> you don't cut this song tomorrow, there ain't no session."[17]

The Dukays trudged back to Bernice Williams's house and she worked with
Edwards and Chandler in helping them flesh out their "Duke of Earl" chant
into a complete song. The next day the group was ready to make recording history.

Following the session, Davis sent both "Nite Owl" and "Duke of Earl"
to their New York-based distributor, Lesgal Productions, to pick which one
it wanted. Lesgal, which consisted basically of owner Bill Lasley, preferred
"Nite Owl" over "Duke of Earl" and released the record on Nat. Davis then
had something of an option for taking "Duke of Earl" to someone else. Carl
Davis said, "We took the 'Duke of Earl' record to Calvin Carter, the A&R
guy for Vee Jay Records, and he just went ape, just as I thought he would.
Ewart Abner, who made all the decisions, was in Europe, and Carter put a

call into Europe and told him, 'Listen, Carl and Bunky came up with a smash, and I'm gonna by it from them.' He said go on and get it. That was somewhere around the first week of November of 1961, and by Christmas it was a million seller."

After Vee Jay purchased "Duke of Earl," Davis and Sheppard began trying to determine what artist would be on the record. At the same time, O. C. Perkins—a member of the Sheppards—was attending a show in Gary, Indiana, where a young singer by the name of Charles Davis was performing. Charles Davis recalled, "Perkins heard me sing and said, 'Sheppard needs a singer; you're a single artist and I like the show so come on down.' So I met with Bill Sheppard and Carl Davis and auditioned. It was just about all set and I was going to be 'Gene Chandler.'"[18]

Carl Davis, however, then presented Dixon with a choice: Dixon could either stay with the group and let Charles Davis become the solo artist for the "Duke of Earl" record, or Dixon could be the solo artist for record. "When I got in touch with Eugene and brought up the idea of his going solo," Davis said, "he was like 'oh yeah!' But [the name] Eugene Dixon just did not set right, so it had to be changed. My favorite actor was Jeff Chandler, and so we came up with the name 'Gene Chandler.'" Davis and Chandler had the pop market in mind and considered that "Chandler" also seemed like a "white" name.

When this move was made, "Nite Owl" was already high on the charts, and "Duke of Earl" had not happened yet, so it was not easy for Chandler to decide to go solo. Chandler characterized it as taking a chance.[19] "I told him that the song wasn't going to make it," Edwards confessed, "This is what I thought, you know. I told him, 'You make your couple of bucks and come right on back to the Dukays.' It didn't work out that way."

On January 13, "Duke of Earl" began what became a fifteen-week stay on *Billboard*'s pop chart, including three weeks in the number one position. The record launched Chandler, who would become one of the mainstays of the flourishing Chicago soul scene during the 1960s and 1970s, with more than thirty hits to his credit.

Asked what it was that struck him about "Duke of Earl," Carl Davis replied, "It was really that haunting chant, 'Duke, Duke, Duke of Earl.' They didn't have a song written at the time. But they had that vamp, that haunting thing, and this is what sold me. I didn't care what the lyrics were. It was just a giant record, and Gene Chandler was immediately a pop act. It had to be one of the first black records to be a million seller. A million seller was hard to come by in those days, especially on black product."

Meanwhile, the Dukays were left with no credit and no glory from the song, although they collected royalties on the record. But with Charles Davis as their new lead, they did obtain a contract to reap rewards on their past hits as well as on their later, more modest successes. Before the first Vee Jay session dates, however, Shirley Johnson left the group and was replaced with Margaret "Cookie" Stone.

The first record for the Dukays under Charles Davis's leadership was "Please Help," a novelty number, backed with "I'm Gonna Love You So," a ballad. In the spring of 1962 both songs got a lot of play on a regional basis in Chicago, Philadelphia, and Indianapolis but did virtually nothing nationally. "Please Help" even went pop in Chicago on the powerful WLS station. The next record, "I Feel Good All Over" backed with "I Never Knew," came out later in the year and sold even less. "I Never Knew," an emotionally sung but quiet ballad, deserved a better reception because it ranks as one of the Dukays' best sides.

About this time the Dukays made a tour on the black theater circuit. The touring group consisted of Earl Edwards, James Lowe, Richard Dixon, and James Brown. Dixon mentioned some of the songs they performed; "'Please Help' was like a novelty number that got the audience up; 'I'm Gonna Love You So' was like a rest number—we did it slower than the recording. We were still putting all our prestige on 'Duke of Earl.' We'd go with 'Duke of Earl' and 'Nite Owl.' Once in a while we would do 'Girl Is a Devil,' but the audience would prefer 'Nite Owl,' 'Curfew Time' they would call it."[20]

The Dukays did two more sides for Vee Jay, "Combination" backed with "Every Step," which were released in January 1963. The record was the weakest of the Dukays up to that time and bombed. Davis, Broyles, and Stone then left the group. Davis explained what happened:

> We fell into a lull. I always relate it back to the money the group got from "Duke of Earl." It seemed as if the group kind of lost its enthusiasm at that time. The record was a top record and the Dukays never got that much credit for it. Locally, everybody knew the group did the record, but from a national standpoint, nothing. They received substantial royalties from the record, and when that happened, I think Ben Broyles was the first to kind of drift away. They received close to seven grand apiece all at one time. Earl was always the stabilizing force—he really kind of kept it together—but then after he bought a building, the group started drifting away and stopped rehearsing. They just sort of lost motivation.[21]

The Dukays continued with some new members—Claude McCrae as a new lead and Richard Dixon as permanent replacement—and lasted a few more years. (McCrae, incidentally, sang for some time with the Pastels, who did "Put Your Arms around Me" on United.) The Dukays went over to George Leaner's One-derful organization, but the company failed to come up with a release for them. A backing track from Motown had somehow been obtained, illegally as it turned out, but the group recorded a song on it. The company, after some internal bickering about whether to release the record or not, decided to shelve it. The group then moved to Chess, but Edwards said they "didn't do anything there, mostly hung around."

Jerry T. Murray (known as Jerry O), who was writing and arranging for One-derful at the time, finally gave the group a chance to record again in 1964, on his own Jerry O label. Murray had them do two songs, "The Jerk" and "Mellow-Feznecky." On these records, Donald "Doncie" Rudolph replaced McCrae. Rudolph sang lead on "The Jerk," Edwards on "Mellow-Feznecky." "The Jerk" preceded the Larks' considerably different song by the same name and had substantial sales in Chicago. The record also made much noise in Philadelphia and Cleveland, where it was number one for two weeks. After the Larks' "Jerk" came out, the Dukays' effort died, as far as national success was concerned.

"Mellow-Feznecky," released in 1965, was inspired by the term a local deejay, Herb Kent, coined for attractive females. The Dukays appeared at all the Kent record hops to push the record, but the song never made it. The group, despondent over their declining fortunes, broke up. The big success they had all hoped for was all too elusive.

For the most part the various members of the Dukays remained in music only peripherally after they left the group, although Gene Chandler was the notable exception to this. Charles Davis was able to continue in a part-time capacity under the name Nolan Chance, but without any real success. Richard Dixon joined a new aggregation of Magnificents, whose other members were Ray Ramsey of the original group, James Pleasant, and Clarence Jasper. Dixon says he made more money playing nightclubs as a member of the Magnificents than he ever did touring with the Dukays. After his association with the Magnificents, Dixon tried to continue in the business as a single artist but couldn't make headway. Edwards never gave up his love for music, continuing his interest as a choir director in a church.

*   *   *

The success that the Bel Aires, the Sheppards, and the Dukays experienced with Bill Sheppard was varied. On one hand they all had rhythm and blues hits, but these songs pointed in opposite directions—forward to the era of soul and backward to the period of doowop. The groups looked to the future as they began to depart from the common rock 'n' roll language of the late 1950s and early 1960s to create a new separate black soul style. In casting a look backward, the groups were creating some of the last great rock 'n' roll hits of the doowop era.

The Bel Aires' "Rockin' an' Strollin'" was always considered a part of rock 'n' roll, and most listeners never even thought of it as an R&B song. The Sheppards, in "Island of Love," created one of the most memorable rock 'n' roll ballads and would appear on many later rock 'n' roll oldies collections. The Dukays' "Duke of Earl" was the culmination of doowop as a form of rock 'n' roll and ranks as one of the all-time biggest doowop hits. After that song would come soul, and rock 'n' roll would largely discard its doowop heritage.

Notes

1. Information on Sheppard's early career is sketchy, as Bill Sheppard has been uninterested in sharing his remembrances with researchers.

2. Simpkins interview, January 16, 1979.

3. Information about Mad Records comes from "R&B Ramblings," December 28, 1957; "'Mad Man' Jones Sets One Disc Outlet"; Tommy Jones interview.

4. This and subsequent remarks by Tommy Jones quoted in this chapter come from the interview with him.

5. Dick Shurman, unpublished liner notes, Memphis Slim album, Delmark, April, 1980.

6. Carl Davis interview, 1982.

7. Sheppard's operations with Carl Davis during the soul years were extensively covered in my book *Chicago Soul*. Other sources include Abbey, "Behind the Scenes"; Carl Davis interviews.

8. Information about the Bel Aires comes from Pruter, "Collectible Bel Aires"; Millard Edwards, Isaac, and Perkins interviews.

9. Millard Edwards interview.

10. Ibid.

11. Information about the Sheppards comes from Pruter, "Island of Soul"; Perkins and Isaac interviews.

12. This and subsequent remarks by O. C. Perkins come from the October 24, 1977, interview with him.

13. Cocks, "Sounds Like Old Times."

14. Information about the Equallos comes from the One-derful papers, *Living Blues* archives; O. C. Perkins interviews.

15. Information about the Dukays sources comes from Pruter, "The Dukays" and "Gene Chandler"; Chandler, Carl Davis, Charles Davis, Dixon, and Earl Edwards interviews.

16. This and subsequent remarks by Earl Edwards quoted in this chapter come from the interview with him.

17. This and subsequent remarks by Carl Davis quoted in this chapter come from the 1982 interview with him.

18. Charles Davis interview.

19. Chandler interview,

20. Dixon interview.

21. Charles Davis interview.

10

Deejays, Theaters, and the
Advent of Rock 'n' Roll

The year 1955 was a turning point in the history of black popular music in Chicago. A new music called rock 'n' roll had emerged, spawned largely by rhythm and blues and directed at teenagers. Chicago deejays were actively playing this new music on the airwaves and were promoting and emceeing dances and concerts in various theaters, skating rinks, and dance halls in the city. It was not uncommon to find vocal groups performing in such clubs as Martin's Corner and the Club Delisa as late as 1954, but by the end of 1955 it seemed an alien concept. Vocal groups were now considered a part of rock 'n' roll, and they sang a type of music for kids.

The golden age of Chicago's black and tans was coming to an end. In the 1940s one could find such clubs as Martin's Corner, Joe's Deluxe Club, the Beige Room, the Ritz Show Lounge, as well as the Club Delisa, all offering a fully produced floor show with a chorus line. But in 1955 that scene had virtually disappeared. The *Chicago Defender* ran a story that year about the demise of the chorus line, and the headline said it all: "Facts and Figures Tell Why Chorines Are Making Their Final Curtain Call: The Cuties Are Disappearing and But Fast."[1] Only the Club Delisa and Grand Terrace still had chorines. The Delisa had begun with a chorus line of fourteen dancers, later reduced it to twelve, and in 1955 was featuring only eight. The Grand Terrace in May 1955 went through one of its periodic reopenings, but with spectacularly bad timing. Resurrecting the concept of produced floor shows with a variety of acts and a chorus line, the Grand Terrace was an anachronism the day it reopened.[2]

Taking a little gloss off the older nightclubs and the Sixty-third Street stroll was the opening of two major nightclubs in 1955. Herman Roberts opened the Roberts Show Club at 6622 South Parkway, and Art Sheridan

and Ewart Abner Jr. started the Sutherland Lounge in the Sutherland Hotel at Forty-seventh and Drexel. These clubs did not feature floor shows,
relying instead on the drawing power of their major stars to bring in the
customers. But unlike the Crown Propeller Lounge of a few years earlier,
they never booked vocal groups.

In 1956 Chicago's black nightclubs reacted to the emergence of rock
'n' roll with alacrity, but also with an utter misunderstanding of what was
going on. Just as Kaye Starr exploited the trend with a puerile and inane
pop tune, "Rock and Roll Waltz," the nighteries responded in a similarly
ridiculous fashion. In May the Grand Terrace presented a "Rock & Roll
Revue" and in September the Roberts Show Club mounted a "Rock 'n' Roll
and Mambo Revue," while the Club Delisa offered "Rock & Roll Capers."
None of these shows had anything to do with rock 'n' roll music or with
any vocal groups or other rock 'n' roll acts. "Rock 'n' roll" was just a phrase
attached to the shows in order to appear trendy. The venerable Pioneer
Lounge at 57 East Fifty-first was renamed the House of Rock 'n' Roll but
pursued a blues policy, booking Memphis Slim and Howlin' Wolf. The
closing of the Club Delisa in 1958 put an end to Chicago's great era of the
black and tans, but by then the kind of entertainment the Delisa represented had become passé.

The area around Cottage Grove and Sixty-third Street was still viable
as a live music center during the late 1950s, for Basin Street (6312 South
Cottage Grove), Budland (6412 South Cottage Grove), and the Crown Propeller Lounge (868 East Sixty-third) were going strong. But the area was
beginning its decline. In December 1956, the deejay McKie Fitzhugh took
over the Strand Lounge (6325 South Cottage Grove) and opened in its stead
McKie's Disc Jockey Lounge, which presented a jazz policy but was really dedicated to celebrating the achievements of the city's disc jockeys.[3]
Every month or so Fitzhugh would spotlight one of the city's jocks and
would post his photo on the wall, among shots of his illustrious counterparts. Disc jockeys playing rock 'n' roll and rhythm and blues had become
the new stars of black nightlife.

The Deejays

The deejays who took center stage in Chicago during the mid-1950s were
broadcasting over several ethnic radio stations. The stations featured black
deejays playing rhythm and blues and jazz interspersed with Greek, German,
Lithuanian, Polish, Czech, and Spanish language programming. The city
could boast of having more hours of black radio programming than any other
metropolitan center, even if that programming was divided among several
radio stations and aired in a myriad of time slots.[4] The premier ethnic sta-

tion for rhythm and blues broadcasting was WGES (1390 on the dial), with studios on the West Side on Washington Boulevard and Sacramento Avenue. Its star deejay, Al Benson, broadcasted from his building at 4030 South State. The station's powerful five-thousand-watt signal from a tower in the western suburb of Evergreen Park could be heard throughout the Chicago area, and its deejays, which besides Benson, included Sam Evans, Richard Stamz, and Ric Ricardo, were the biggest in the black community.

Three other, less important ethnic stations were WSBC (1240), WHFC (1450), and WOPA (1470). Station WSBC was founded in 1925 and, like WGES, broadcasted a variety of ethnic programming. It was a black programming powerhouse in the 1940s when the city's first black deejay, Jack L. Cooper, held sway. Its studios and transmitter were at Madison and Western on the West Side. By the 1950s the station was a minor player, with the aging Cooper and his wife, Gertrude, winning an audience share that decreased every year.

Station WHFC was originally located in Cicero, but around 1947 it set up studios and a transmitter at Thirty-fifty and Kedzie in Chicago. Its schedule was predominately filled with foreign language programming, but such deejays as Cooper and Herb Kent broadcasted on that station. Station WOPA was formed by Egmont Sonderling in 1950 and had its studios in the Oak Park Arms hotel in the western suburb of Oak Park, which abuts the city's West Side. Its deejays, Big Bill Hill and later Purvis Spann, who played a heavy diet of blues, tended to appeal to an older working-class black audience rather than to teenagers. The station's signal was limited and reached mainly the West Side.

The Chicago-area black community was also served by two other small stations with a full schedule of black-appeal programming, WBEE (1570), and WAAF (950). Station WBEE (1570) was founded in suburban Harvey in 1955 by O. Wayne Robbins and was the first station in the Chicago area to devote its entire programming schedule to black listeners, airing a combination of jazz and rhythm and blues shows. The station ran a remote from the Trianon Ballroom, at Sixty-second and Cottage Grove, where Herb Kent provided a well-received afternoon show for teenagers. The station was handicapped, however, by its limited range, which could not reach the West Side, and by its daylight-only hours. Station WAAF, founded in 1922, was predominately a jazz station that featured Daddy O'Daylie, but in the 1940s some of its deejays played rhythm and blues.[5]

Most of the deejays in the Chicago area worked on a brokered system, buying the time from the station and then soliciting advertising to support the shows. The brokered system was typical of all ethnic programming. Deejays who were not good salesmen could not last, and Richard Stamz, a deejay himself, recalled seeing many pass through, noting that there must have been fifteen who may have stayed on the broadcasting scene just a month or two.[6] According to another deejay, Lucky Cordell, "Brokering also required a lot of dedication besides salesmanship. It can be feast or famine, if you hit a period when your sponsors drop off before you get other sponsors to replace them. But once you've gotten established and have gotten a name, and have proven yourself somewhat, the station occasionally will put an ad on your show, because someone will call in and will want to be on your show. But until that time you have to really work for those accounts."[7]

The deejays would work for the usual local advertising accounts, such as those of dry cleaners, food stores, and clothing stores, but they all aspired to garner national or major accounts, usually a beer or soft drink producer. Stamz had Seven Up, Ricardo had Pabst Blue Ribbon, and Benson's first big national account was Canadian Ace. The competition for those accounts was fierce. Stamz recalled that the first station to get national accounts was WGES, when Benson got Coca-Cola and Evans won Pepsi-Cola. The rivalry between Benson and Evans was intense. Evans was able to grab the Pepsi-Cola account from under the nose of Benson, who was pursuing the account when he purchased some stock in the soft drink company.[8]

A variation of the brokerage system was used at WGES. Herb Kent recalled, "You did not buy the time—you sold commercials and they gave you 30 per cent. Loosely, it was brokerage. To the full extent of the word, it wasn't. It was like you were paid on commission instead of salary."[9]

Radio surveying was not used much in the scattershot brokering system of the 1950s, so how did a national account determine whether or not a deejay was proving himself? Cordell explained that "the sponsors went by the movement of their product in your marketplace. If they were moving 50 cases a day when they took you on, and a few months later if they are moving 150 to 200 cases, they know that you're responsible." He also said that it was more difficult to "prove yourself" with local accounts, but, he noted, "if you could get yourself a major account—after you prove yourself to them—they would be willing to endorse you. Give you letters of recommendation, that kind of thing."

Black radio was pioneered in Chicago by Jack L. Cooper, who in the early 1940s was the only black presence that listeners could find on the dial. He was born in Memphis, Tennessee, and raised in Cincinnati, Ohio. He began as a song and dance man in vaudeville but entered journalism in 1924 when he joined the *Chicago Defender* staff as a theatrical editor. Transferred to the paper's Washington, D.C., office in 1925, he got into radio when he debuted a "dialect" show on WCAP. Back in Chicago the following year, he began broadcasting from WWAE in Gary, Indiana. In 1929 he joined

WSBC and started a show called "The All Negro Radio Hour." At first he presented live entertainment, but in 1931 he began playing some records, which made him the first black disc jockey in the nation. He also began broadcasting over WEDC (which shared the 1240 frequency with WSBC) in 1933, added time on WHFC in 1938, and started playing rhythm and blues records on WAAF in 1947.[10] By this time Cooper was on radio some forty hours a week with thirteen separate programs. In contrast, the fast-rising Al Benson was on twenty hours a week with five separate programs.[11]

Arnold Passman wrote in a 1992 essay about Cooper that the deejay adapted to the changing tastes of his listeners in the 1940s by playing blues and the rougher-edged rhythm and blues. Passman noted that "Cooper bound himself to another choice of no choice: to play the requested commercial recorded music of the Mississippi Delta that perhaps embarrassed him, but which, streetwise that he was, he was not ashamed of, and which he knew that black (and later white) folks of all classes couldn't resist."[12] Reading between the lines only a little, it is obvious that Cooper was dragged into playing more blues and earthier music, probably in reaction to the tremendous success that Al Benson was enjoying at the time because he played that music.

Passman quoted Cooper's wife, Gertrude "Trudi" Cooper, as saying, "Jack's decision on airplay was respectful," and noted that Cooper refused a run of requests to repeat a play of Jay McShann's "Confessin' the Blues." Mrs. Cooper explained, "They were mainly young girls, who were crying because it wouldn't be played again that day. The song was also considered risqué."[13] Given the conservatism of Jack Cooper, it is not surprising that he would be superseded by Benson and new young deejays who would establish themselves on radio in the late 1940s.

Cooper gradually lessened his broadcasting duties after the forties. During the 1950s, WSBC and WHFC presented shows by Jack Cooper but also shows by Trudi Cooper and Larry Wynn. Some of these shows were sub-brokered, that is, the deejay would buy time from Cooper. In 1953, for example, Lucky Cordell sub-brokered a show on WHFC from Cooper, and Wynn's show was undoubtedly sub-brokered as well. Cooper was the mentor for Wynn, who started working with Cooper and then graduated to his own show in 1957. Wynn moved to WBEE in the early 1960s. Cooper stayed on the air at WHFC and WSBC until 1961, and thereafter maintained a behind-the-scenes role. Trudi Cooper stayed on the air until 1968. Jack L. Cooper died in 1970, by which time WSBC had eliminated its black programs and devoted its day to foreign language programming.

The biggest radio personality of the 1950s was Al Benson, who dominated the market from the late 1940s to the late 1950s. He was the first to make an impact in the rapidly growing rhythm and blues market, but like

many of the early African American disc jockeys, he took a long and cir-
cuitous route to the job. Benson was born Albert Leaner on June 30, 1908,
in Jackson, Mississippi. He attended Jackson College, where he reportedly was a standout at football and baseball, and then became the chief of
recreation for all the black schools in Jackson. Moving to Chicago, he attended Loyola University, where he took courses in criminology. That led
to a job as a Cook County probation officer. Before he entered radio he also
was a cook on the Pennsylvania Railroad, an interviewer for the Works
Progress Administration (WPA), and a pastor of a nondenominational
church.[14]

Benson joined WGES in 1945 with a gospel music show, but it was not
successful. Then Elizabeth Hinzman, the operation's commercial station
manager, suggested he do a popular record show, and it took off. Benson's
tag was "The Old Swingmaster." By 1947 he was also broadcasting from
WJJD (at 1160) and was airing a total of three and a half hours a day.
Benson was at the height of his popularity in 1948 when he won the *Chicago Defender* "Mayor of Bronzeville" poll with a staggering 1,460,000
votes, an unheard-of figure for the annual contest. In a feature story that
December, the *Defender* reported that Benson had "33 employees, from
chauffeur, cook, secretary and bookkeeper to the people connected with his
radio shows."[15]

Lucky Cordell, who entered Chicago radio in 1952 through an association
with Benson, explained how the older disc jockey achieved such success:

> What happened, Al Benson saw a need, an opening, and filled it.
> There was no one at the time playing blues on radio. There was only
> one other deejay in Chicago and that was Jack L. Cooper. He played
> jazz and/or ballads; Ella Fitzgerald, Dinah Washington, acts like that.
> He would not play what he considered "gut bucket blues." Benson
> came on and started playing all those blues artists that so many of
> the people who migrated from the South wanted to hear. But the only
> place they could hear them was to buy a record and play it at home.
> So when he came on it was instant success.[16]

Benson was a controversial figure when he was first heard on the air-
ways. His thick dialect, use of crude black slang, and preference for playing the rougher styles of rhythm and blues were not universally accepted
in the late 1940s. Many black leaders thought of him as an embarrassment
to the race. Benson prided himself on what he called "native talk." He
would open his show by saying in his usual mushmouth manner, "If you've
got plenty of geets on you, go right into the store. Walk heavy and talk
heavy." The *Defender* reporter noted in the 1948 feature article that "during our interview, Benson was halted by several phone calls. One was from

a crank. She didn't like his music and didn't like the way he talks." Benson replied to the reporter, "I have had other people rake me about the way I talk and my records. Out among the people I found that most of them use slang and racy language, so why not Benson. They like bop and jazz, so bop and jazz it is. After all there are more ordinary people than so-called big shots."[17]

These points were echoed by Cordell: "Many of the people who listened to Benson talked just like him. They were from an area where they talked liked that. The number of people who were embarrassed—the professional blacks and the more educated blacks—didn't matter. Benson had enough 'just average' people to make him a huge success."

Much of Benson's success was built on teen appeal. The *Defender* had noted in July 1947 that Benson "had become a favorite of teenagers."[18] Throughout the 1950s, as the leading deejay, Benson promoted and emceed most of the biggest rhythm and blues packages featuring rock 'n' roll and R&B acts that came to Chicago and played the Regal. Herb Kent attested, "He was the epitome of black deejays that got on the air and played music, had charisma. He'd say little things like 'you jump here, you jump there, you jump everywhere,' and it was colorful, you know. It sounded good. It was something you get off from school and do your homework to, the familiar sound of Al Benson and his music."[19]

Benson stayed with WGES until 1962, when it was purchased and turned into a top-forty station and the new owners fired most of the old deejays, except for Lucky Cordell and Roy Wood. As Cordell explained, "Benson and Stamz and the others did not fit the format. They had an old-fashioned type of delivery and enunciation, things like that."[20] Benson moved to WHFC, and when Leonard Chess bought that station and changed it to Chicago's first twenty-four-hour black-appeal station, WVON, Benson joined the air staff. The famed deejay worked only a month at WVON and then announced his retirement. Benson later did little-noticed shows on WAIT, WWCA (Gary), and WIMS (Michigan City). He died in 1978.

Sam Evans, whose broadcasts over WGES in the late evening are still fondly recalled by many Chicagoans, was one of the giants of Chicago black radio and one of Benson's biggest rivals. He was born in 1912 in Chicago and graduated from Phillips High. He attended Fisk University for two years and then went to Northwestern University, majoring in business administration. For several years in the 1930s Evans worked as a dining-car waiter, in those days a job held by many blacks with underutilized talents. In 1939 he got a job as a salesman for Calvert Distilleries in Chicago. He served four years as a military officer during World War II, and after the war he headed to Los Angeles, where he operated a restaurant. He returned to Chicago in 1947 and started as an advertising salesman for the *Chicago Defender.*

Evans began his radio career in November 1948, when he went on station WAAF for a half-hour in the morning. By the end of the year he was on WGES in the evening and had established himself as an institution. From early 1951 to late 1953, Evans had his "Jam with Sam" on WGN (720) from 11:30 P.M. to midnight, but, following a brief stay at a Gary station, WWCA (1270), he returned to WGES for the remainder of his career. In 1955 his show, which by then ran from 10:00 P.M. to midnight every evening, was the highest-rated black program for that time period, according to the Pulse survey.[21]

Rick Sleep, writing in *Record Exchanger* magazine, fondly recalled the show:

> *Jam with Sam* show was greasing the airwaves with recordings by the Flamingos, Ravens, Danderliers, and all the great groups of the time, who were waxing solid jumps and smooth ballads. After he had played vocal group recordings from 10 to 11 PM, he stopped smoothly and mellowly oiling the megacycles with spiels for Gold Medal flour and velvet intonations of "I love you madly." Then, through the speaker came the first haunting bars of Little Walter's great chromatic Hohner wailing "Blue Light" as the theme for the next hour of music. Now Sam went down in his basement and told us how he had on nothing but a soft blue light, and how he was sitting on a beat-up old orange crate in that soft glow at the blue light. He'd always tell of how he hadn't much to eat, just some greasy greens and side meat, or grits and black-eyed peas, and he was going to eat them with the light turned down real low and hear some blue light music. Then we really got down there as he put on disc after disc by Sonny Boy Williamson, John Lee Hooker, the Howlin' Wolf, Billy Boy Arnold, Jimmy Reed, Smokey Hogg, Lightnin' Slim, and Muddy Waters.[22]

In his many promotions Evans would often have the same disparate styles, vocal groups, and blues singers.

Evans came from a middle-class professional background, so his routine on radio was something of a shtick. Cordell said, "Sam spoke very well, but Sam intentionally talked down. I don't know where he got the impression—I guess studying Benson—that people would like him better if he talked down. He actually spoke very well and was very cultivated."

By the turn of the decade Evans was through as a force in the business. As big and successful as he was, he could never step from behind the shadow of Al Benson. Richard Stamz has stated that Evans and Benson were bitter rivals and that the great success of Benson exacted a toll on Evans, causing him to drink excessively. Stamz alluded to some other personal problems that Evans was experiencing but wouldn't elaborate. Evans was eventually fired because of his drinking and other difficulties. He was given a second chance by WGES but his drinking got him fired again, unfortunately, permanently.[23] Evans died a forgotten man in 1981.

Richard Stamz, like most disc jockeys of his era, got into the field relatively late in life, at age forty-five, when he joined WGES in 1951.[24] He was born April 6, 1906, in Louisiana, to a Chickasaw father and a black mother. He could claim that he was literally born in the swamps. His father worked on a barge on the Mississippi repairing levees, and his mother used to take his father food and clothes. During the flood of 1906 she was isolated on a barge, and that was where Stamz was born. Stamz was raised in Memphis in fairly middle-class surroundings, but at age of sixteen he left home to join the Silas Greene Minstrels. He performed with the troupe as the end man, in which he said he "did a little dancin', a little banjo pickin', and a little joke crackin'." In the mid-1920s he attended LeMoyne-Owen College in Memphis and played football and tennis at the school. In the late 1920s Stamz ended up in Chicago, working in hotel lounges.

During the Depression Stamz traveled across the country and ended up stranded in Mexico, the circumstances of which Stamz has kept private because he considered this the lowpoint in his life. He ended up in Hollywood, where he found work on poverty row, at the Monogram and Republic studios, and he performed as an extra in B westerns. He would play an Indian one hour, get shot off a horse, and the next hour might portray a cavalryman chasing an Indian. For three years in the 1930s Stamz also traveled around with Ann Sothern, working with the band, working the stage, and serving as a majordomo.

Around 1941 Stamz returned to Chicago. Eventually he purchased a sound truck, and he would drive through the black neighborhoods, his truck loaded with advertising signs and his loudspeaker going to promote various products. His truck was also used by the deejay Jack L. Cooper to announce and broadcast black baseball games of Rube Foster's American Giants. Stamz was so successful with the truck that in 1951 WGES contacted him to be a deejay, since he showed a talent for generating advertising revenue.

During most of the 1950s Stamz was established on WGES, from noon to 1:00 P.M. daily, where he was known as the "Crown Prince of Disc Jockeys." He took the title "crown prince" because he knew that Benson was the king, and he knew Benson *knew* he was the king. So the title served both to honor Benson and to avoid a conflict with the deejay. Stamz always trod lightly around Benson. When the powerful deejay had a hit sheet (a printed survey of the biggest-selling records played by a disc jockey or a station), Stamz refrained from putting out a rival one. But as soon as Benson dropped his, Stamz began one. The hit sheet produced a big profit for Stamz and was highly successful for several years. He expanded the operation to produce hit sheets for various black disc jockeys in some thirty cities.

Stamz stayed with WGES until it was purchased by Gordon McClendon in 1962 and turned into a top-forty station, W-YNR. The deejay went briefly to WOPA and then to WBEE before he retired from on-air work.

McKie Fitzhugh was born in 1915. He came to Chicago at the age of twelve and later graduated from DuSable High School. In 1942 he began the first of his dance promotions, at the Parkway Ballroom, and quickly became one of the biggest dance promoters in Chicago. By the late 1940s he was managing the prestigious Savoy Ballroom, where he promoted such acts as Nat King Cole, Duke Ellington, Stan Kenton, Lionel Hampton, and Woody Herman. He met Al Benson, who gave him his start in radio in 1948, on WGES. After switching to WHFC in 1951 and then back to WGES, Fitzhugh began working at WOPA in 1954. In 1955 he was broadcasting from 2:00 to 4:00 P.M. daily, and the following year he added a midnight to 4:00 A.M show.[25]

In 1956 Fitzhugh was operating a record shop he'd established four years earlier at Forty-seventh and South Parkway, two restaurants, and, according to the *Defender,* a "solid business in dance promotions." Also in 1956 he opened McKie's Disc Jockey's Lounge and began running his show from the place. At that time the *Defender* noted that "for nearly 16 years, he has been a fixture in the community as a result of these dances, and his radio stints . . . The dances, which are part of his answer to how to keep teen agers in wholesome activity, have earned him the title 'Champion of the Teen Agers.'"[26] Stamz felt that McKie never became a top jock because he overextended himself with too many other interests, including concert promotions and taverns.[27]

Stamz may have been showing too much of his old competitive streak in his evaluation of Fitzhugh, but Herb Kent was an admirer. Kent said of Fitzhugh:

> He was something between Benson and myself in his enunciation and articulation. He was a bit more contemporary than Benson. He sounded like an emcee in his announcing style. He would broadcast from his record shop at Forty-seventh and South Parkway, and he would sit in his window, and when the cars would come he would describe the car, "Well, here comes a 1954 brand new yellow Cadillac with white walls, honk your horn." And the guy would honk his horn. And

people would get in their cars and just drive by. It was a hell-fire gimmick. A thing like that wouldn't mean shit today, but you know he became very big on that and he sold a lot of records.

When he was on WOPA he had *McKie's All Night Roundup.* The show would go to different taverns and they would play blues records, or sometimes they would have a live pickup of a blues band, or they would have a guy there spinning records for a half hour. They'd go on the West Side, they'd go on the South Side, and that was popular. I used to listen to *McKie's All Night Roundup,* it was interesting. You would in effect go to this nightclub and you wouldn't have to leave the house. He'd have Larry Steele's Revue come on the show. He'd have all kinds of fabulous jazz people. He was jazz oriented, jazz and blues. So he was very innovative.

In 1960 Fitzhugh was back at WGES but lost his job there when the station became top-forty W-YNR in 1962. During the 1960s he was employed by WVON, mainly in advertising but occasionally on the air. Fitzhugh died in 1970.

Stan "Ric" Ricardo was a deejay as early as 1952, sharing the mike duties with Eddie Plique on WENR live from the Pershing Lounge. He was the first deejay honored when McKie Fitzhugh opened his lounge in late 1956. Ricardo was on WGES through much of the 1950s and could be said to have arrived in 1958 when he got a national account with Pabst Blue Ribbon Beer for his nine o'clock morning show on WGES. Stamz saw Ricardo as a sharp and aggressive individual who wouldn't hesitate to grab rival deejays' sponsors with cut-rate deals.[28]

Kent drew a more complimentary take on Ricardo:

Ric was a fast-talking jock, just talked fast. He was a hell of a salesman. He'd beat the streets all the time and sold for a living. I used to hang with him at night. He was fast, he was very glib. I remember he saw this pretty checkout girl. She was gorgeous. He said, "I got to have that girl." He laid down ten bucks and said, "Leave with me." She said "I don't do stuff like that." He made it fifty, upped it, and finally put down two hundred dollars. She put her coat and hat on, and you should have seen that woman hopping over that coatroom barrier. He taught me something about life. He went down to Mexico and married a Mexican movie star, and brought her back up here.

When WHFC became WVON in 1963, Ricardo was made advertising sales manager, which ended his career behind the mike.

Herb Kent dominated black radio in Chicago in the 1960s as the kingpin of the evening time slot at the mighty WVON, but in the 1950s he had been one of many deejays who aspired to Al Benson's throne. By the end of that decade Kent had emerged as the powerhouse deejay. Kent was born October 5, 1928, in Chicago, and grew up in the middle-class community of Hyde Park, attending the prestigious Hyde Park High in the early forties. He actually broke into radio while still a high-schooler. The Chicago Board of Education in 1944 had inaugurated an educational radio station, WBEZ, and as part of its educational function the station used students from the system's high schools to put on a portion of the programming. Some fifty students were chosen in auditions, among them Herb Kent. Kent was very surprised to be selected, both because he was insecure about his own abilities and because he did not think a black person had much of a chance in those days. But it proved to be a valuable learning experience, since Kent and other students were trained to put on historical dramas.[29]

Kent then moved to NBC radio, where he first worked in the mail room. During this time he attended Northwestern University. At NBC he made valuable friendships within the industry, including one with Hugh Downs. Kent's first professional experience came in 1949, when he joined the Gary station, WGRY. But that association lasted only a year and he was back at NBC. Instead of returning to the mail room, he was working on the air, acting in dramas and other productions.

In 1954 Kent joined WGES. He said, "I worked for an hour for Sam Evans, from 11:00 to 12:00 in the morning. He sold and I sold. I did so well that the station took me away from him and put me on my own time, which was still 11:00 to 12:00. It was only one hour and I wanted to have more time. But the station was so crowded it was hard for me to get any additional time, so I left to join the newly opened station WBEE. I was on salary and started at only eighty-seven dollars a week; I was only making thirty-five dollars a week at WGES."

When WBEE came on the air in October 1955, Kent was given the most valuable time slot, 3:00 P.M. to 7:00 P.M., directly opposite Al Benson's show on WGES. Kent's show was called "Rock & Roll on the Bee Hive Show," and he worked from a remote booth in a storefront in the Trianon Ballroom building at Sixty-second and Cottage Grove. "The transmitter was at 159th and Campbell, in Harvey," Kent said, "but they wanted studios in Chicago because they felt they wanted to show the disc jockeys off, and they would get more business by being in Chicago. They had a big picture window, because it was a storefront, then they had a big room with seats and chairs, and then they had the studio. Kids would come from school and peer through the front window and watch the jocks work the booth." WBEE fired Kent in 1958. "I don't know why they did that," he said, "I was late for work or something. I went to WJOB in Hammond, Indiana, and pulled all the listeners. And so they brought me back by giving me more money." That was in February 1959.

Kent moved to WHFC the next year. He recalled, "We had a strike out at WBEE, and the way that strike was broken, I got an offer for another job at WHFC and I took it. I was on twice a day at WHFC. The prime time at that time was the afternoon, and so I was on from 3:00 to 6:00, something like that. Then I came on in the evening, from 8:00 to midnight. It was the best deal I ever had up to that time. I made union salary plus I got a percentage of the selling. I really started making money for the first time in my life."

These moves signified that Herb Kent had arrived as the top jock in the city, after building up a tremendous listenership at WBEE. Kent noted, "I was teen acclimated. This stuff that I did was very young, young gimmicks, and I just pulled a lot of kids. It was something about me, my charisma, there was that appeal to youngsters." Cordell said, "He was always a teen jock; he always appealed to the teens." This popularity with the young made him the most important rhythm and blues jock in the city during the rise of rock 'n' roll. Kent believed that near the end of the 1950s Benson "was fading a little bit" and thought that the top jock was "possibly" himself. Kent said, "I did a telephone call-in one time on WBEE, and blew out the whole exchange. People would listen through the static. I was more contemporary than Benson with what was happening in music and the kids, and closer to it than he. He was more into selling radio time and doing other things. I played everything the kids wanted. I was just dead on it."

Black radio jocks traditionally have chattered frantically, jive-talked in a rhyming cadence, or used some other artificial patter to relate to their audiences. Kent didn't adopt any of these common modes. A thin, somewhat dapper man, he relied instead on his warm, conversational, everyday manner. His popularity could be attributed to the fact that he always seemed to be communicating directly with his listeners rather than presenting himself as a show. Whereas some of the other deejays would play music (namely blues) directed to adults, Herb Kent was wholly devoted to the playing of vocal groups and music for teenagers.

When Leonard Chess purchased WHFC in 1963 and turned it into WVON, the station centered on the appeal of Kent. Kent boasted, "I was the catalyst for the sale of that station, which nobody realized." And in the 1960s, Kent became a giant of the airwaves, the "Al Benson" of the day, playing music for the teens.

In 1959 the *Chicago Defender* reported that the primary music played by Chicago's black deejays was "rock 'n' roll." An article in the paper advised, "If you are wondering what goes in radio broadcasting circles particularly on the South Side, take time out and listen to [the] majority of disc jockeys beaming music directed at the section sometimes known as 'Bronzeville.' You will discover the major kick is rock 'n' roll music. Running a close second . . . is the blues."[30]

The Chicago deejays established their association with rock 'n' roll by emphasizing their identification with vocal groups. Each sponsored a particular group. Kent recalled, "Just about every disc jockey had a group. I had the Kool Gents. The Orchids were Al Benson's, the Magnificents were the Magnificent Montague's, and the Clouds were McKie Fitzhugh's. Sam Evans didn't have one, but he was one of the few who didn't."

The Theaters and Rock 'n' Roll Venues

Before the advent of rock 'n' roll, Chicago's African American theaters, notably the Regal, provided occasional shows with a revue format directed primarily at adults. For example, in 1954, a benchmark year when rock 'n' roll was just emerging, the Regal presented five shows. February saw Dinah Washington headlining a package that included the Four Checkers, Pegleg Bates, Eddie "Cleanhead" Vinson, and Cootie Williams and His Orchestra. In April there was a package of Sugar Ray Robinson, Ruth Brown, Clyde McPhatter and the Drifters, and Butterbeans and Susie, and May had the Pearl Bailey show. October featured the Sammy Davis Jr. show, and in November there appeared Larry Steele's Smart Affairs, which included the Five Keys and Bullmoose Jackson. Most of these acts dated at least from the 1940s (Butterbeans and Susie were from the 1920s) and were directed at adult fans. A few vocal groups were on the bills to provide some teen appeal.[31]

There was something new in the air, apparently, but the bookers at the Regal seemed not to have picked up on the latest trends in the entertainment world, mainly the advent of rock 'n' roll. A story in the January 8, 1955, *Chicago Defender,* headlined "Small Crowds Cause Theaters to Change to Pix Only Program," painted a negative picture of the previous year's stage presentations. The paper noted that weeks would go by without a single "flesh act," to use the vernacular of the day, and that the few stage shows presented "did not fare any too well." The article noted that "Sammy Davis Jr. and Will Maston trio did a fair business but not what was expected of such an attraction and especially since no other house carried a stage show. The Larry Steele 'Smart Affairs' spent a low gross week at the Regal and so did another attraction or two." Steele's show was the old-fashioned variety show that was fading as a force in black entertainment. Had he presented an assortment of hot rhythm and blues vocal groups, who knows what kind of crowds he would have attracted.[32]

The *Defender* noted a few successful presentations, notably a show at the Trianon Ballroom, about which the paper reported, "no one knows how many were turned away from the rhythm and blues show starring Roy Hamilton. As it was, more than 7,000 jammed the newly [re]opened Trianon ballroom that normally accommodates 4,500."[33] The Roy Hamilton show in August featured, besides Hamilton, acts such as the Drifters, LaVern Baker, Faye Adams, the Spaniels, Big Maybelle, Memphis Slim, Muddy Waters, Little Walter, Rusty Bryant, and Erskine Hawkins. Although the show had a somewhat mixed appeal for both adults and teens, the presence of several chartmaking youthful groups on the bill made that presentation the first "rock 'n' roll" package concert in Chicago.

Hand in hand with the rise of vocal groups came a new sort of stage presentation in Chicago and nationwide: the packaging of a host of singing and musical acts with teen appeal, directed for the first time toward a youth audience. Vocal groups, because they were mostly associated with the rise of rock 'n' roll, tended to be marketed to teenagers, and therefore package rock 'n' roll shows invariably featured many of them. Herb Kent said, "Back in those days there were guys who were just big teen idols, and I was one. And being a big teen idol I thought when I did a show, I would put on vocal groups. A show like I did at Hyde Park High, I would pay five hundred dollars for a whole lot of groups—the Kool Gents, Spaniels, El Dorados, Moroccos, Magnificents. I would book artists like Jimmy Reed and Howlin' Wolf, but the ones I really loved were the groups."

During 1955, the Regal Theater was a bit slow in joining the rock 'n' roll revolution. It was the city's premier theater for African American entertainment and had been under the management of Ken Blewett since 1939. The theater was devoid of "flesh acts" for much of 1955, apparently while those in charge tried to figure out the market, but in September the Regal launched its first package rock 'n' roll show, presented and emceed by deejay Al Benson. The ad in the *Chicago Defender* declared "Stage Shows Are Back" and said, "Al Benson presents 'Rhythm and Blues' with a host of terrific recording stars." The package included the Buddy Johnson Orchestra, LaVern Baker, the Spaniels, the Four Fellows, Ella Johnson, the Orchids, Lou Mac, and J. B. Lenore. The last three were acts recording for Benson's Parrot/Blue Lake operation.[34]

The September show was followed in November by another Benson-sponsored show, which the *Defender* advertisement dubbed an "All-New Rock 'N Roll Jamboree" and added, "Al Benson presents the MOST in Rhythm & Blues." Again the teen appeal of the package was evident in the acts featured, notably Chuck Berry, Nappy Brown, Big Maybelle, the Nutmegs, the Cardinals, Dusty Brown, and Red Prysock and Orchestra. Dusty Brown was a blues act from Benson's Blue Lake label and probably was uninteresting to most of the kids in the audience.[35]

These developments at the Regal, in which Benson sponsored big teen-oriented package shows, reflected a national trend during 1955. On February 4, 1956, in a special section devoted to the rise of rhythm and blues,

Billboard included an article whose headline said it all: "DJ Emerges as Powerhouse Promoter on R&B Personals." The piece noted that "promoters have utilized more and more deejay promotion to push R&B shows during the last couple of years, but it wasn't until spinner Alan Freed of WINS, New York, chalked up big-time box-office grosses in three local stageshow appearances last year that the deejay really moved into a position to throw his sales weight around in the R&B personal appearance field."[36] The article used the terms "R&B" and "rock and roll" interchangeably, and in another piece in the special section a writer referred to "so-called rock and roll" and defined it as a "popularized form of R&B."[37]

Despite these trends, in 1956 the Regal featured only two shows, a teen package show with a weak lineup in April, and a Pearl Bailey show in December. In the last week of February 1957, Al Benson was back in the rock 'n' roll stage-show business, with a production advertised as a "Rock 'N Roll Rhythm and Blues Revue." Acts in the show included Big Joe Turner, Arthur Prysock, Screamin' Jay Hawkins, Gene and Eunice, the Tab Smith Orchestra, and three Vee Jay acts—the Spaniels, the El Dorados, and Priscilla Bowman.[38] The *Defender* announced the following week that "attendance records were shattered last week at the B&K Regal Theater where Al Benson staged a star-studded show." The show pulled in 31,750 tickets.[39] In April or May, Benson followed with another blockbuster show. Instead of showing the usual Hollywood western or such, Benson screened *Shake, Rattle, and Rock,* featuring Fats Domino. The theater opened at 10:30 on Saturday morning, May 18, to provide a two-hour show billed as a "Teenage Rock 'n' Roll round of rhythm entertainment."[40] Benson presented three more teen package shows in 1957, in August, November, and December. The Spaniels appeared on the August show and the Dells on the November show.

These shows were variously called "Rhythm Revue," "Rock 'N Roll Revue," or "Rhythm and Blues Revue." The term "rock 'n' roll" was used to engender teen appeal and to indicate modernism, as it was deemed a more up-to-date designation than "rhythm and blues." But to indicate the music's appeal to the African American audience, other terms, such as "rhythm and blues" or simply "rhythm," were plugged into the promotion. The term "rock 'n' roll" was used at least until 1963 to designate such stage shows, and the *Chicago Defender* writers often applied it to any rhythm and blues act with primarily teen appeal.[41] Until the emergence of the soul culture around 1963–64, black teens considered their music indistinguishable from "rock 'n' roll."

One fiction that has been disseminated in the past two decades in motion pictures, television shows, and other popular media is that the chitlin' circuit theaters and venues were inhospitable to white performers and white fans, and that such performers as Buddy Holly were breaking racial barriers by appearing at the Apollo. Hollywood, in particular, has presented some sort of fantasy of the African American community by trying to show that in the entertainment industry there was black racism that mirrored the prevailing white racism. Thus, in *The Buddy Holly Story,* a 1978 film starring Gary Busey, Buddy Holly and the Crickets are seen struggling to win the approval of an Apollo crowd who reacts negatively to their pale faces. But the truth of the situation is that the difficulties Buddy Holly and the Crickets encountered at the Apollo had to do with their poor performance, not the color of their skin. In another film, *Crossroads* (1986), in a silly scene, we see Ralph Macchio attempting to enter a southern juke joint and meeting an overtly hostile crowd, and in *Adventures in Babysitting* (1987), an utterly ludicrous scene has Elizabeth Shue and her small charges meeting with cold silent stares from the adult black nightclub audience when they find themselves accidentally on stage.

Such scenes are far from the truth. Marvin Junior of the Dells recalled, "Buddy Holly, when he worked the Apollo, he worked with us. You must understand, back in the fifties, black and white acts worked together in a lot of places—they worked the Apollo, they worked the Regal, you worked the black houses and the white houses together. The only place we didn't work together was when he started doing the dancehalls and in the South. But the big theaters in the north, you worked with white acts."[42]

The Regal featured white acts from the beginning of its existence. For example, an August 1951 show featured Stan Getz; a November 1951 show had Buddy DeFranco; and Benson's November 1957 rock 'n' roll extravaganza had the Mello-Kings. In 1960, both the Bill Black Combo and Dion and the Belmonts appeared at the Regal; and throughout 1961, the Capris, the Chimes, Jerry Lee Lewis, and the Mar-Keys each appeared in separate shows on the Regal stage. In short, a white act at the Regal was no big deal, and no big deal in any other northern chitlin' circuit theater.[43]

In the 1950s, the most serious rival to the Regal for the teen package shows was the Trianon Ballroom, which was opened in 1922 by two Greek immigrants, Andrew and William Karzas, at Sixty-second and Cottage Grove. The ballroom, built at a cost estimated at $1,200,000, was lavish in its design. Nancy Banks, writing in *Chicago History* magazine, described the building:

A formal staircase at the far end of the palatial reception lobby, which was furnished with imported tapestries and chairs upholstered in brocaded velvet, led to a "grand salon" adjoining the ballroom upstairs. The dance floor, surrounded by a line of Corinthian marble columns, measured 100 by 140 feet. The domed ceiling was bathed (a little garishly, some thought) in an ever changing display of colored lights, and overlooking the dance floor were boxes hung with crimson velvet, several parlors, and a tea room capable of serving 560 people.[44]

In 1926 the Karzas brothers built the lavish Aragon Ballroom at 1196 Lawrence Avenue on the North Side. The Trianon and Aragon provided memorable experiences for several generations of Chicagoans during the big band era. In 1947 the management of the two ballrooms boasted of catering to "more dancers each week than all other Chicago ballrooms combined."[45] By that time, however, both dance palaces were actually on their last legs, especially the Trianon, which served a neighborhood that was changing from white to black. The Karzas brothers had a policy of not booking black bands and of turning away blacks at the door.[46] In the early 1950s, civil rights organizations brought pressure to allow the entry of black patrons. In 1952, the Trianon closed its doors and the building was put up for sale.

In May 1954, the Trianon Ballroom reopened with a policy of catering to the black community. Banners in a *Defender* ad asserted: "Fabulous grand opening," "Under new management & new policy," "Everyone, but everyone is invited!"[47] The code for anyone to read was "blacks, this venue is now yours and you are invited." The grand opening act was Count Basie with the singer Bixie Crawford. The Horace Henderson Orchestra was the house band. This first engagement obviously appealed to adults, but within a few months, as "rock 'n' roll" groups emerged, the Trianon began developing a reputation for its teen-appeal packages. In August 1954, the Trianon could boast of its Roy Hamilton extravaganza as "The Biggest Rhythm and Blues Show."

Herb Kent said of the Trianon,

> They had two stages, they had one all the way in the back and they had a stage on your left-hand side as you entered. It was the most gorgeous place, beautiful hardwood floors. Like if they brought in Dinah Washington or Bill Doggett, adults could sit down. They would set it up with chairs and tables, cabaret style, with waiters, bartenders, and bars. And in front of the stage where the performers entertained there was maybe a small area for dancing. With teens, we wouldn't give them a lot of chairs and tables, because teens then liked to fight. We figured chairs and tables were just something to throw. The attitude was, they were young and they could stand up.

On August 8, 1954, during the same month as the Hamilton show, the Trianon played host to a "Teenage Jamboree" sponsored by three teenage clubs. Captain Walter Dyett and his orchestra was used to back the Five

Stars, described as a "sensational teen-age singing group."[48] The Five Stars later would go on to fame as the El Dorados. This initial "Teenage Jamboree" was followed regularly every Sunday with a "Teen-Age Ball." In October the Trianon launched a regular Saturday night show for teenagers. The *Defender* reported, "The Trianon ballroom has inaugurated a teen-age party for Saturday night when the youngsters will be admitted at a special price of 50 cents. Only adults admitted will be those accompanying the teenagers." However, the Trianon was still booking adult-appeal shows, with Dinah Washington playing on October 15.[49]

In January 1955 the Trianon hosted a traveling revue sponsored by Lou Krefetz. The "Top Ten Rhythm & Blues Revue," as it was billed, included Faye Adams, Joe Turner, Bill Doggett, Lowell Fulson, Paul Williams and his band, as well as two vocal groups, the Clovers and the Moonglows. Lou Krefetz returned once more to the Trianon with a package tour in October.[50] In July 1956 a national package tour called "Top Stars of 1956" came through, featuring Carl Perkins, Al Hibbler, Frankie Lymon and the Teenagers, Cathy Carr, Chuck Berry, Shirley and Lee, Della Reese, Illinois Jacquet, Bobby Charles, the Spaniels, and the Cleftones. The *Defender* said the show was "most appealing to rock and roll fans" and that critics were calling it the "greatest package of the year."[51]

Meanwhile, some local deejay promoters began booking the Trianon with shows. Sam Evans presented a show in May 1955 featuring Ruth Brown, Amos Milburn, Bo Diddley, and the Moonglows. Al Benson came back in July 1955 with a show featuring Floyd Dixon, Billy Boy Arnold, L. C. McKinley, Dr. Jo Jo Adams, Eddie "Cleanhead" Vinson, the Diablos, and the Orchids. Evans put on a show on May 19, 1956, with Richard Stamz as emcee. For the music, it featured Ray Charles, Muddy Waters, and Eddie Boyd, and for teen appeal, two local vocal groups, the Five Chances and the Kool Gents. Evans came back in August with a lineup of Ruth Brown, Muddy Waters, and the Cadets, and in September with Ray Charles, Chuck Willis, and two Chicago-based acts, the Calvaes and J. B. Lenore. In December Evans presented a show featuring Bill Doggett, Muddy Waters, plus three local groups, the Prophets, Danderliers, and the Moonglows.[52] Sandwiched in between the Evans shows was a McKie Fitzhugh package on Thanksgiving, consisting entirely of local acts, namely Otis Rush and five Chicago vocal groups—the El Dorados, Kool Gents, Clouds, Calvaes, and Magnificents.[53] It is clear from the foregoing survey of Trianon bills that the vocal groups had become essential for any rock 'n' roll promotion, large or small.

The Trianon peaked in 1956 with teen-appeal package shows, in part because the Regal was unusually quiescent that year. The Regal came back with solid shows in 1957, but the Trianon booked few shows during the later 1950s. Around 1964 the Trianon closed for good, and in 1967 the building was demolished as part of an "urban renewal" project.[54]

Far less competitive in the package show sweepstakes was the Park City Bowl, at Sixty-third and South Parkway (345 East Sixty-third), a roller rink that occasionally presented shows. The owner of the venue was Jimmy Davis, a longtime skating enthusiast and impresario. In the late 1930s Davis was an assistant manager at the Savoy Ballroom at Forty-seventh and South Parkway. That venue featured dancing to big bands and boxing matches and for many years drew a mixed patronage of blacks and whites. Davis prevailed upon the management to introduce roller skating, making the Savoy the first black roller rink in the city.[55]

There was another rink on the South Side, the White City Bowl, at Sixty-third and South Parkway. The rink was the remaining facility of the famed White City Amusement Park, a major South Side attraction from the time of the World's Columbian Exposition in 1893 (known as "the White City" because of its light-colored buildings and its night-time displays of electric lights) up until the late 1920s, when it was destroyed by a fire.[56] By the early 1940s, even though the surrounding neighborhood had become all black, the White City Bowl maintained a Jim Crow policy. But after a long campaign of picketing and protesting that began in 1942, White City lifted its color ban in June 1946.[57] In September 1947 a new management took over and brought in Jimmy Davis to oversee the venue, under the new name of Park City Bowl (the name "White City" obviously too redolent of its previous Jim Crow history).[58]

After an initial flurry of shows presented by McKie Fitzhugh, which started with white bandleader Tony Pastor, the rink settled down to being just a roller rink. But in the early 1950s, Davis, by then the rink owner, began getting involved in the surging rhythm and blues scene. Besides featuring shows at his Park City Bowl, he even started a record label, called Club 51. Davis's program began modestly in October 1953, when he booked the Orioles and advertised the show as being "for the younger set."[59] Most of the package shows that followed were booked and sponsored by Fitzhugh. The first of a series of shows, beginning in May 1955, featured Roy Eldridge, Amos Milburn, the Danderliers, the Clouds (a Fitzhugh-managed group), and Bobbie James and Her Buddies (a Davis-recorded act).[60] In January 1956 Fitzhugh teamed up with Ric Ricardo to present a "rock 'n' roll" show featuring Jimmy Witherspoon, Etta James, and the Clouds, among others. In March Fitzhugh and Ricardo promoted another "rock 'n' roll" show, featuring Bo Diddley, Ben Webster, the Clovers, the Drifters, and two local groups, the Clouds and the Pastels (the United label group). The *Defender* story noted that the show would feature "several 'battles' staged between singing groups."[61]

The last big show at the Park Bowl was a promotion of McKie Fitzhugh, Richard Stamz, and Big Bill Hill, on Easter Sunday, April 21, 1957. The *Defender* headlined its advance story as "Rock 'n' Rollers Hit Park City Bowl," and the lineup was large and designed to have the broadest appeal. According to the ad, the show featured three shake dancers, five bands (Paul Bascomb, Jack Cooley, Al Smith, Madman Jones, and Billy Cannon), three blues singers (Memphis Slim, Lil "Upstairs" Mason, and Harold Burrage), and ten vocal groups (including the Clouds, Serenades, Vicounts, Gay Tones, and Five Echoes).[62] In 1958 the neighborhood had deteriorated and Davis closed the Park City Bowl.

The Indiana Theater (219 East Forty-third) represented an older tradition in black entertainment with Saturday midnight stage shows that began after the last film feature. Few of its midnight acts had teen appeal, and it would seem that not many 1950s vocal groups ever played there. Aside from the Five Chances, who performed there fairly regularly, the Flamingos and only a handful of others appeared at the theater. In the 1950s the Indiana never put on a daytime or early evening stage show. The manager, Joe Clark, would recruit talent from the clubs. The *Defender* said that "never is there a big-time act that passes through or plays Chicago that he does not contact with a contract to try to get to appear then or at a later date. Sometimes he has to wait as long as six months for an act or an actor."[63] The midnight shows began in 1933 and by the 1950s had achieved truly exalted status.

Danny Overbea, a rhythm and blues star for Chess, remembered playing at the Indiana in May 1956 as his fondest memory of all. He recalled, "Oh, that was beautiful. That was an old vaudeville house and that was beautiful because in between shows you rushed down and do your thing and get back to your regular job. They used to book whatever name entertainers were in the city. It was run by Joe Clark, a good businessman and very warm. Playing there was an honor because as a kid I had been to the Indiana and watched great acts like Butterbeans and Susie. Oh, this was a thrill. I would have done it for free—they didn't know it at the time. It was such a legendary venue."[64]

Ken Blewett, manager of the Regal Theater, surprised Dempsey J. Travis, a black real estate mogul and historian, when he told him that "whenever he wanted to see show business at its best, he went to the Indiana Theater. It was known as a theater for entertainers who wanted to be entertained. Every Saturday, a 'Midnight Ramble' was held, where comedians, singers and dancers put on their 'bluest' jokes, their 'special material' songs, and their most revealing dance routines for the midnight audience. Occasionally the dancing would get so wild that the police would stop the show and warn the performers to turn down the burner."[65]

The bills at the Indiana were modest. For example, the Flamingos appeared in 1952 and 1953, when they were first starting. On the bill with them in July 1953 was the dance team of Leonard and Leonard and the notable Chicago blues singer Lil "Upstairs" Mason.[66] The Five Chances appeared in a November 1956 show with the jazz-blues combo Cool Breeze and His Four Breezes, singer Frank Butler, bluesman Heavy Duty, and shake dancer Dot Adams. Generally, an Indiana show represented the nightclub entertainment in the city at the time.[67]

The Rena Theater (4015 West Roosevelt) on the West Side took a few stabs at presenting shows, but generally that area of Chicago was poorly served. In October 1955 the Rena began a policy of presenting midnight shows on Saturdays. Their first show featured a chorus line of girls as well as little-known local acts, such as Lil Brooks, Jackie Turner (a mimic), Hattie Randolph, and George Williams, but little was heard from the Rena after that.[68] In June 1957 Sam Evans sponsored a midnight show at the Rena featuring Billy "The Kid" Emerson, Sonny Boy Williamson, Magic Sam, the Dells, and others.[69]

Evans had other promotions in West Side venues. In April 1956 he presented a show at the Madison Rink (2560 West Madison) that featured Ray Charles, the Diablos, and some local acts, the Moroccos, the Kool Gents, Lou Mac, and the Daps.[70] In September 1957, at a show at the Senate Theater, Evans presented what *Cash Box* called his fourth show on the West Side, which included a heavy blues lineup (largely from Louisiana) of Lonesome Sundown, Jimmy Reed, Slim Harpo, Lightnin' Slim, Carol Fran, Lazy Lester, Sonny Boy Williamson, Jody Williams, Flatfoot Sam, and the Five Chances.[71]

Sometimes local high schools served as venues for teen-appeal package shows. The largest such show was presented by McKie Fitzhugh at Corpus Christi High (4600 South Parkway) in September 1954, featuring mostly blues singers and vocal groups among the twenty or so acts. The bluesmen included Muddy Waters, Little Walter, Eddie Boyd, and Jimmy Rogers, and the vocal groups, advertised as taking part in a "battle of the singing groups," included the Five Echoes, El Dorados, Five Chances, Fasinoles, Five Buddies, and Kingslettes.[72]

Herb Kent became closely associated with vocal groups, mentoring such groups as the Kool Gents and presenting shows in the area. His biggest show, which took place in April 1957 at Hyde Park High (6220 South Stony Island), presented seven local groups—the Danderliers, Moroccos, Debonairs, Debs, Dells, Kings Men, and Magnificents—and Dee Clark, Roy Gaines Band, Charles Jones, and Ahmad Jamal.[73] Regarding Ahmad Jamal, a fine jazz musician but one who lacked teen appeal, Kent said, "He hardly got any applause. They couldn't wait until he got off."

In a show organized a month earlier, at the Grand Ballroom (6351 South Cottage Grove), Kent presented a dance featuring the Spaniels, the Dream Kings, the Kings Men, J. B. Lenore, and the Willie Dixon band.[74] This venue, however, rarely featured rock 'n' roll shows. Kent said, "It was a social club thing. Social clubs would rent it and like have a band. You could hire Red Saunders. He would have six bands that he fronted, so on the weekend he'd make a lot of money. You'd have these big bands, an emcee, maybe a fashion show. That's what they basically did at the Grand Ballroom."

The Opera House in downtown Chicago had, for a time in the late 1950s and early 1960s, the biggest package R&B and rock 'n' roll shows. In April 1957 Sam Evans promoted a big show with a lineup of Little Richard, Buddy Knox, the Del Vikings, and Jimmy Bowen, augmented by a solid local contingent of Sunnyland Slim, Otis Rush, Jimmy Reed, the Spaniels, and the Dells. The *Defender* noted that there were more "names" than in previous Evans-promoted shows and pointed to the presence of "rock 'n' roll attractions out of New York."[75] In June, Marty Faye, a white deejay, and McKie Fitzhugh presented "The Show of '57 Rock 'N Roll," featuring Mickey and Sylvia, LaVern Baker, Bobby Charles, Annie Laurie, and Dale Hawkins, plus locals Willie Dixon, the Dells, Harold Burrage, Paul Bascomb, and the Spaniels.[76] In April 1958, the deejay Alan Freed came into town and presented a "Big Beat" show at the Opera House that offered Jerry Lee Lewis, Buddy Holly, Chuck Berry, Frankie Lymon, the Diamonds, Danny and the Juniors, Billy and Lillie, the Chantels, Larry Williams, Screamin' Jay Hawkins, Dicky Doo and the Don'ts, the Pastels, and Jo Ann Campbell.[77] During the next month, Sam Evans also presented a show at the Opera House, this one with the banner headline "The Biggest Show of Stars for 58," carefully avoiding any "rhythm and blues" references. Bernie Allen, a deejay from WJJD, the top-forty station in the city, served as emcee. The acts included Sam Cooke, the Everly Brothers, Paul Anka, Clyde McPhatter, LaVern Baker, George Hamilton IV, Frankie Avalon, the Silhouettes, the Royal Teens, the Storey Sisters, the Crescendos, the Monotones, Jimmy Reed, and Jackie Wilson, among others. Both of these rock 'n' roll shows were advertised in the *Defender.*[78]

The Opera House was jumping in 1958, but the Regal that year was obviously not competing effectively for package shows. In February 1959, the honchos at B&K let go the theater's longtime manager, Ken Blewett.[79] The theater also was extensively remodeled and B&K announced it was ready to aggressively continue stage show presentations.[80] In May, Al Benson presented two big shows, the latter called "Rock 'N Roll Jamboree of '59."[81]

Blewett became manager of the huge B&K Tivoli Theater, at Sixty-third and Cottage Grove, described by the *Defender* as "the flagship of the South Side" and "long one of the country's most luxurious theaters."[82] Blewett proceeded to launch the Tivoli on a policy of presenting stage shows. After a Pearl Bailey show in March, the theater presented its first package rock 'n' roll show in April. Billed as a "rock 'n' roll stage extravaganza," the acts included Fats Domino, Priscilla Bowman, Big Maybelle, Joe Medlin, and the Cadillacs. A June show featured Dave "Baby" Cortez, Frank Virtue and the Virtues, Sam Hawkins, the Moonglows, Valerie Carr, and Sonny Thompson and his band.[83] Generally, many of the Tivoli shows featured older acts with less teen appeal than the Regal, perhaps because of Blewett's old show business background, and thus the Tivoli was always considered second-best by the biggest audience for popular black music, the teenagers.

All this activity did not go unnoticed by the *Defender,* which reported in June 1959, "The current parade of 'live' talent on stages of the Regal and Tivoli has meant plenty to Broadway talent agents as well as the stars they represent. Over [the] past several seasons there was only a limited outlet for such shows. The Apollo in New York was the only house playing shows regularly. . . . Now comes the Regal and Tivoli with almost weekly presentations of 'live' programs."[84] In August, the Regal and Tivoli officially formed a "live chain" with the Apollo in New York, the Howard in Washington, D.C, and other chitlin' circuit theaters. The *Defender* praised the Regal and Tivoli for their new activity and then noted that "other cities have been making the big switch to live shows. In Boston, Cincinnati, Detroit, and several other major cities there have been like decisions that meant [the] return of live shows." The purpose of the chain was to develop a single package that would make a "round robin" tour of the participating theaters.[85]

An item in a November 1959 issue of the *Defender,* headlined "Theater Owners Praise Southside Surge to Top," reported that "several delegates to the National Association of Theater Owners spoke glowingly of the jump in business on Chicago's Southside in recent months. Evidently the speakers had been observing the increase in business since the Regal and Tivoli went on the 'presentation kick' with stage shows being presented along with top pictures regularly."[86] In August 1960 a *Defender* reporter wrote still another story on the phenomenon, headlined "Live Shows Make Chicago Unique," saying, "Chicago's claim to the title of 'live show center of the nation' can hardly be questioned. Week after week Southside theaters are bringing in live attractions that cannot be matched any place."[87] There was a little hyperbole to the story, but it conveys the sentiment of the day.

By the 1960s, large package stage shows were largely concentrated in the Regal, and throughout the decade the Regal shows became synonymous with the best in soul music. Packaged shows largely died in the white community as self-contained bands became the preferred way of making music. At the Tivoli, shows continued through the early 1960s, but by 1962 the theater was concentrating on more adult fare with such acts as the Jimmy Smith Trio, Della Reese, and Damita Jo.

The conferring of star status on radio deejays, the growth of package teen-appeal shows, and the emergence of vocal groups all came together in the last half of the 1950s to produce the rock 'n' roll revolution in popular music. Clearly, rhythm and blues vocal groups in Chicago were at the forefront of that revolution.

Notes

1. Hill, "Facts And Figures."
2. "Grand Terrace Opens."
3. "Disc Jockey Citations."
4. Newman, *Entrepreneurs of Profit and Pride,* p. 82.
5. Information about Chicago radio stations can be found in Bellavia, *Capsule History.*
6. Unless otherwise noted, all remarks from Stamz quoted in this chapter come from the March 16, 1993, interview with him.
7. This and subsequent remarks by Cordell that are quoted in this chapter come from the interview with him.
8. Stamz interview, May 13, 1978.
9. Unless otherwise noted, all remarks from Kent quoted in this chapter come from the March 31, 1993, interview with him.
10. Information about Jack Cooper comes from Hunter, "74 And Blind"; Passman, "Jack Cooper."
11. "Disc Jockeys: 16 Sepia Spielers," p. 44.
12. Passman, "Jack Cooper," p. 49.
13. Ibid., p. 48.
14. Information about Al Benson comes from "Benson Quits"; Davis, "Al Benson"; Hunter, "Has Al Benson's Star Set?"; "Rites Set For Al Benson"; Kent and Cordell interviews.
15. Davis, "Al Benson."
16. Cordell interview.
17. Davis, "Al Benson."
18. [photo item], *Chicago Defender,* July 26, 1947.
19. Kent interview, March 31, 1993.
20. Cordell interview.
21. Information about Sam Evans comes from "A New Star"; Reed, "The Most"; "Sam Evans Went from Press to Radio"; Sleep, "Sam Evans"; "Truth About Sam Evans' Hit Show"; Cordell and Stamz interviews.
22. Sleep, "Sam Evans," p. 14.
23. Stamz interview, March 16, 1993.

24. Information about Richard Stamz comes from "Richard Stamz Rates"; Stamz interviews.

25. Information about McKie Fitzhugh comes from Hunter, "Night Clubs Fail"; "If You Wanta Get on Radio"; Pegue, "*Soul* Mourns"; Stone, "Personality Spotlight"; Kent and Stamz interviews.

26. "If You Wanta Get on Radio."

27. Stamz interview, March 16, 1993.

28. Ibid.

29. Information about Herb Kent comes from "Herb Kent, Radio's Bee"; Kenning, "One 'Kool Gent'"; Pruter, "How Herb Kent Got Burned"; unpublished bio sheet about Kent; Kent interviews.

30. "Local Radio 'Jockeys.'"

31. Regal ads, *Chicago Defender,* February 20, April 17, October 23, and November 20, 1954.

32. "Small Crowds Cause Theaters to Change."

33. Ibid.

34. Regal ad, *Chicago Defender,* September 3, 1955.

35. Regal ad, *Chicago Defender,* November 26, 1955.

36. Bundy, "DJ Emerges."

37. Simon, "Term R&B."

38. Regal ad, *Chicago Defender,* February 23, 1957.

39. "Benson Sets Gate."

40. "D.J. Al Benson."

41. Regal ad, *Chicago Defender,* February 23, 1963.

42. Junior interview, 1993.

43. Regal ads, *Chicago Defender,* August 4, 1951; November 17, 1951; November 9, 1957; June 25, 1960; November 26, 1960; February 25, 1961; April 20, 1961; May 20, 1961; and October 21, 1961.

44. Banks, "The World's Most Beautiful Ballrooms," p. 207.

45. Ibid., p. 212.

46. Ibid.

47. Trianon ad, *Chicago Defender,* May 15, 1954.

48. "'Teenage Jamboree'"

49. "New Teen Age Parties."

50. Trianon ads, *Chicago Defender,* January 29 and October 8, 1955.

51. "Top Record Stars of '56."

52. Trianon ads, *Chicago Defender,* May 19, August 11, September 1, and December 1, 1956.

53. "Trianon Dance Classic."

54. Jackson, "Old Memories."

55. O'Hara, "Skating through the Color Barrier."

56. Lowe, *Lost Chicago,* p. 211.

57. "White City Rink."

58. "The Park City Skate Arena Opens."

59. Park City Bowl ad, *Chicago Defender,* October 22, 1953.

60. "Amos Heads Allstars."

61. "'Rock 'n' Roll' to Park City."

62. Park City Bowl ad and article, "Rock 'n' rollers Hit Park City Bowl," *Chicago Defender,* April 20, 1957.

63. "Midnight Shows at Indiana."

64. Overbea interview.

65. Travis, *Autobiography,* pp. 163, 165.

66. Indiana Theater ad, *Chicago Defender,* July 16, 1953.

67. Indiana Theater ad, *Chicago Defender,* November 17, 1956.

68. "Rena Theatre Launches Midnight Show Program."

69. *Cash Box,* June 29, 1957.

70. Madison Rink ad, *Chicago Defender,* April 7, 1956.

71. *Cash Box,* September 7, 1957.

72. "McKie's Variety Show" ad, *Chicago Defender,* September 15, 1954.

73. "Herb Kent and WBEE Blues and Jazzville Concert" ad, *Chicago Defender,* April 13, 1957.

74. "R&B Ramblings." p. 42.

75. "Little Richard's Package."

76. Opera House ad, *Chicago Defender,* June 22, 1957.

77. Opera House ad, *Chicago Defender,* April 26, 1957.

78. Ibid.

79. "Herb Hopkins"; Dempsey J. Travis in his *Autobiography of Black Jazz* provides an illuminating portrait on Ken Blewett, devoting a full chapter to his career, pp. 157–78.

80. "Regal Theatre Changes Management."

81. Regal ads, *Chicago Defender,* May 9 and 30, 1959.

82. "Tivoli Theatre Plans the Big Switch."

83. Tivoli ads, *Chicago Defender,* April 25, May 30, and June 13, 1959.

84. "Regal and Tivoli Live Show Parade."

85. Roy, "Regal, Tivoli Join with New York."

86. "Theater Owners Praise Southern Surge."

87. "Live Shows Make Chicago Unique."

Afterword

"Vocal groups were the transition from rhythm and blues to rock 'n' roll," Art Sheridan said, without any prompting from me. This one-time record man, whose Chance operation was the subject of the first company profile in this book, was present at the dawn of the doowop era and has seen firsthand the entire history of the rhythm and blues and rock 'n' roll scene. He has a perspective on the subject that is shared by few observers. A couple of years ago he and his wife attended a concert by the Four Tops and the Temptations. "What excited me about that," Sheridan reflected, "was to watch people of that generation who are a little younger than I but fairly old people, late fifties, really out there dancing in the aisles, white and black. I turned to my wife and said, 'My God, what we created in those early years.' When you're doing it you don't realize the impact it leaves. I mean that very humbly."[1]

It has become clear, after more than thirty years of research and writing by fans of doowop, that this despised vernacular form was on the cutting edge of the rock 'n' roll revolution. The articles and books that have focused on vocal groups have shown systematically that this is a valid conclusion. The authors of these works have understood better than writers for the mainstream press the true nature of the rock 'n' roll revolution.

Research into doowop's history began in the 1960s, carried out by lovers of vocal harmony who were largely of the working class. These researchers investigated not only doowop but the various harmony styles that preceded it, going back to the nineteenth century. The early research was unsophisticated, but over the years it has matured as the doowop followers have become more knowledgeable researchers and writers. These people were energized because they were eager to tell the true story of rock 'n' roll and doowop.

Fan magazines of the 1950s directed at the rhythm and blues and rock 'n' roll audiences were concerned more with the personalities in the vocal groups and the superficialities of the doowop phenomenon than with their history, influences, and styles. When the rock press of the 1960s and 1970s looked back at the earlier era, writers did not analyze the various vocal approaches of the groups. They concentrated instead on finding the "true auteurs" of the groups, usually the composers or the producers. Because the vocal groups tended not to play instruments and had repertoires that were heavy on ballads and old pop standards, most later rock fans, led by the rock critics, tended to place the vocal groups outside the critical mainstream.

The one exception to this critical indifference was the attention paid to vocal harmony groups by fans on both coasts in the 1960s, people who had been raised on rock 'n' roll in the previous decade. Alienated from the middle-class appeal of the British invasion groups, such as the Beatles, doowop fans sought to recapture the early days of rock 'n' roll, when it was considered music for working-class youth and when vocal harmony groups were in the forefront. Lamenting the passing of that era, they sought first to revive and later to preserve interest in classic doowop in self-published amateur magazines that many now call "fanzines" (fan magazines). Such publications as *Bim Bam Boom* (1971–74), *Big Town Review* (1972), *Record Exchanger* (1969–83), and *R&B Magazine* (1970–71) were among the first to carry detailed histories of the old vocal groups and to analyze what it was in each group's sound that made its vocal harmony so appealing. Major early contributors to this pioneering work were Marcia Vance, Bob Galgano, Steve Flam, Jack Sbarbori, Lenny Goldberg, and the team of Mike Redmond and Marv Goldberg.

There have also been several important early books on the subject. *They All Sang on the Corner,* by Phil Groia, a schoolteacher, ranks among the best works on the subject. Centered largely on the vocal groups that arose in the various boroughs of New York City, the book provides the deepest analysis and most detailed history of a regional vocal group scene currently in print. Originally published in 1973, the book appeared in a much-improved, revised edition in 1983 and is worth consulting. Another discussion of doowop with a regional focus can be found in Paul Lepri's *The New Haven Sound: 1946–76* (1977), which covers various self-contained rock bands and both white and black vocal groups. Lepri's presentation is undermined, however, by his unfortunate decision to cover the scene rigidly year-by-year.

An outstanding general work is *Rhythm and Blues* (1971), by Lynn McCutcheon. McCutcheon concentrates on the principal vocal groups and provides an interesting sociological study of the phenomenon as well as a history of the genre. His book was somewhat marred by his tendency to mention the releases of innumerable vocal group rarities without examining the records' import, or lack thereof. Another fine work was Ed Engel's look at Italian-American vocal groups from New York, *White and Still All Right* (1977). The publisher's choice to run only half of Engel's group profiles in a far-too-thin book deprived the reader of what could have been a near-definitive resource.

Rap Attack, a brilliant history of the origins of rap, a definitive urban-based African American music, appeared in 1984. The English writer David Toop carefully showed that doowop was one of the important strands of African American culture that contributed to the development of rap. He discussed the affinities of doowop and rap, their aesthetics and common street origins. By discussing doowop in the same breath with such a cutting-edge music form as rap, Toop unwittingly helped raise doowop's cachet within the mainstream press.

Contributions to vocal music research came from the magazines *Story Untold,* published by Roy Adams from 1977 to 1986; *Yesterday's Memories,* published by Marv Goldberg, Mike Redmond, and Marcia Vance from 1975 to 1977; *Echoes of the Past,* published by Bob Belniak since 1987; *Record Collector's Monthly,* published by Don Mennie since 1982; and *Cat Tales,* published by Greg Milewski from 1989 to 1994. In addition, such general record-collector magazines as *Goldmine* and *Discoveries* have devoted coverage to doowop group histories. Contributors to vocal group research in the 1980s included Peter Grendysa (whose work centered mainly on 1940s and early 1950s groups), Bob Diskin (who wrote on Italian-American groups in the New York area), and Jim Dawson (who mined the California scene). My own work has long concentrated on developments in Chicago.

A peculiar facet of black popular music, whether it be jazz, blues, soul, or doowop, is that little historical or analytical writing on the subject has been done by blacks. It has largely fallen to white observers, many of them overseas, to develop magazines, draft liner notes, and write books attempting to explain the importance and artistry of various black vernacular musics. The output among blacks has largely consisted of autobiographies by the performers and musicians, so when a book by an African American appears that provides analysis and historical perspective, it is a real treat. *Du-Wop* (1991), by the former doowop singer Johnny Keyes, is such a book. Although Keyes's career in music has been fairly extensive, doowop fanatics know Keyes primarily as the lead singer of the Chicago vocal group the Magnificents, who were best known for "Up on the Mountain."

At first glance, Keyes's hundred-page book appears to be a memoir of the singer's career in the music business; it is not. Keyes, using his personal experiences as the model, wants to provide insights on what it was like to be in a doowop group during the 1950s, and he systematically explains how a doowop group practiced, how it prepared for a recording session, how a recording session went, what a tour was like, what a group's breakup was like, and many other facets of the experience. This is an invaluable ethomusicological contribution to doowop research.

In 1992 there appeared the most complete history of doowop groups to date, Jay Warner's massive *The Billboard Book of American Singing Groups: A History 1940–1990,* in which the bulk of the coverage is devoted to 1950s rhythm and blues vocal groups. The book does not take a straight narrative form. Rather each decade is introduced by several pages of general history, followed by dozens of individual group histories in alphabetical order.

The year 1992 also saw the appearance of an analytical examination of doowop music from Anthony J. Gribin and Matthew M. Schiff in their important work *Doo-Wop: The Forgotten Third of Rock 'n' Roll.* The authors present an original thesis that doowop should not be considered a part of rhythm and blues but one of three subcategories within rock 'n' roll. Doowop thus constitutes the "forgotten third of rock 'n' roll," the other two-thirds being rhythm and blues and rockabilly. Gribin and Schiff provide a useful and enlightening breakdown of stylistic shifts in the music, from its emergence in the early 1950s to its revival in the early 1960s, as well as a sociological examination of doowop groups (the latter largely from second-hand sources).

Most vocal groups have not garnered the widespread fame necessary for a publisher, even a specialty house, to chance putting out a book about them. But there have been a few such publications: two books by the British writer Bill Millar, *The Drifters* (1971) and *The Coasters* (1975), and another book on the Drifters called *Save the Last Dance for Me: The Musical Legacy of the Drifters, 1953–1993* (1993) by Tony Allan and Faye Treadwell. It seemed unlikely that a book would ever come out about any of the Chicago groups, but in 1995 a small New Jersey press published a book on the Spaniels, *Goodnight Sweetheart, Goodnight: The Story of the Spaniels,* written by Richard D. Carter, an East Coast journalist.[2] Carter does an excellent job in telling the story through the words of all the participants, but the book is slightly flawed by some errors and by the absence of any vintage photos.

In 1993 Rhino Records put out a boxed set of doowop recordings, called *The Doowop Box,* which presented four CDs containing 101 titles dating from the late 1940s to the late 1980s. This well-received set included five informative essays by experts in the field—namely Bob Hyde (who compiled the collection), Billy Vera, Wayne Stierle, Donn Fileti, and David Hinckley. The writers set out the history of doowop and made the case why doowop ought to be respected and appreciated. The thick essay booklet plus the intelligently programmed set provided one of the most thorough examinations of doowop ever published.

In addition, several membership organizations devoted to the perpetuation of doowop harmony have sprung up, mostly on the East Coast, the home of the United in Group Harmony Association (UGHA), based in New Jersey, and the Rhythm and Blues Rock 'n Roll Society, Inc., in Connecticut. Florida can also boast of such an organization, the South Florida Group Harmony Association (SFGH), formed by ex–New Yorkers and ex–New Jerseyites. In the Los Angeles area there is the Doo-Wop Society of Southern California (DSSC), headquartered in Seal Beach. These organizations usually publish newsletters or magazines, present radio shows, and put on live concerts of revived vocal groups. Gribin and Schiff, two inveterate attendees of such shows, reported that "even though it is rare to find more than one original member in each group, the vocals remain true to form," and they ironically noted that "most of the groups are working more and some are doing better financially than they did when their records rode the charts."[3]

Overseas, there has been far less research into vocal groups. For some years, many writers abroad viewed rock 'n' roll as being southern-influenced with a heavy emphasis on the sound of the electric guitar and the sax. They tended to overlook the vocal groups, whose balladic approach was a barrier to aesthetic appreciation. Gradually, foreign writers, notably in Great Britain, warmed up to the form. They began by learning to appreciate the many jump sides put out by 1950s vocal groups and then extended that appreciation to the ballads as well. Various stories on vocal groups were published in the late eighties and early nineties, mostly by Seamus McGarvey in *Juke Blues, Blues and Rhythm,* and the premier British vintage rock 'n' roll magazine *Now Dig This,* attesting to a belated interest in the groups.

Around the same time that Gribin and Schiff's *Doo-Wop* was published, the *New York Times* published a feature article by Martin Gottlieb called "The Durability of Doo-Wop." The author, who did an excellent job in surveying the early 1990s subculture of doowop appreciation, began his essay by remarking that the music has not received respect. "Doowop is so submerged in caricature and deprecation," he said, "that shadings of Rodney Dangerfield color its very name." Gottlieb noted that "it was easy for teen-agers to emulate, but it also led to broad parody, mediocrity and to many critics, a creative cul de sac that caused pop music to move on without it." He added that "nostalgia played a huge part in bringing most people back to doo-wop." Gottlieb also noted that "the doowop world exists in a string of specialty record shops, private record collections, small club dates and gatherings of devotees sprinkled through the blue-collar byways of the New York region . . . an audience made up heavily of classic Reagan Democrats—white, middle-aged, working-class men—and the black performers most fans venerate."[4]

In Gottlieb's observations we have some clues as to why doowop has been mostly ignored or dismissed by the mainstream rock critics: the fact that it represented a cultural byway; its vintage quality; and the class bias, validation, and nostalgia associated with the music. Doowop indeed reached a cul de sac, as did rockabilly and, many would say, blues. That, of course, is the fate of many forms of popular music. The essential quality of popular music is its evolutionary nature, but rock criticism treats this evolution as a consciously progressive one. In the late 1960s and early 1970s, when rock criticism took shape, there was almost a cult of "progressivism." Today, ironically, many of those same critics are still pining over that same music, much as the doowop fans yearn for old vocal group records.

Rock 'n' roll was born a blue-collar music, but in the mid-1960s it was appropriated by the middle class as its own. The "embarrassing" music of the 1950s would not do. As the middle-class kids of that decade reached college age and then adulthood, they shrugged off the declassé blue-collar styles of their adolescence to adopt a new form of rock music that was heavily influenced by folkie and fine-art pretensions. During their college years they might have become fans of folk music or jazz, but by the mid-1960s rock 'n' roll had become hip, and so the young people appropriated the new music as their own. There came a wave of middle-class folkie performers, such as members of the Byrds, the Lovin' Spoonful, and the Grateful Dead, who entered the rock field by electrically amplifying their music.

Joni Mitchell was at one time considered the "first lady of rock," and her understanding of rock 'n' roll history reflected the attitudes of the new middle-class followers of rock. She expressed this outlook in 1991 when she told *Musician* magazine that doowop represented a "wave of superficiality [that] was followed by the more earnest sound of the folk boom, like the Weavers, Kingston Trio, Dylan."[5] Mitchell's assertion that her folkie favorites were "earnest" and that doowop was "superficial" is remarkable. She did not understand that doowop was likewise a folk form and not a mere record company contrivance. But her views were shared by a large proportion of the educated middle-class and the people in her milieu.

Members of the middle class rejected old rock 'n' roll forms like doowop in the belief that they had better taste than their blue-collar counterparts, and that the "vapid" lyrics and "simplistic" music of the form could not possibly appeal to those with more educated and sophisticated musical tastes. Critics believed that the "caricature and deprecation" associated with doowop was eminently deserved, if one paid attention merely to the lyrics and did not consider nuances of the falsetto tenor, the deep bass, and the textures of harmony. But doowop writers and fans listen with different ears. They evaluate doowops on how they are sung and harmonized, not on what they say. The demand for sophisticated lyrics in such songs basically misses the point. If songs were simply lyrics, could many of the crude blues or old-time country tunes hold up without the context of presentation?

There seems to be a bias at work here that is tied up with the notion of validation. Validation is an important element in the creation of taste in popular music. Most people develop their self-image and measure their self-esteem by their own tastes, and they often look to their peers in developing their tastes. If a music is deemed incorrect among their circle, it cannot be acceptable to them. In the realm of rock criticism, the element of validation looms as large as the element of critical judgment.

Mainstream critics frequently condescend to doowop by connecting it with nostalgia for the innocent 1950s, as though there could no musical reasons why the genre could be valued. Gottlieb was careful in his essay to moderate his associating doowop with nostalgia by quoting Donn Fileti, a co-owner of one of the leading doowop reissue companies, Relic Records. Fileti asserted that the doowop fandom went beyond wistful longings for the past to a "genuine appreciation for the music."[6] But when Rhino released the four-CD *Doo Wop Box* in 1993, and both *Rolling Stone* and the *New York Times* felt compelled to take note of it, the nostalgia connection was, sadly, made once more. Stephen Holden's essay in the *Times* concentrated on the form as a source of nostalgia, referring to "nostalgically potent" songs and asserting that "doo-wop has long been synonymous with '50s nostalgia." He ended his essay on a diffident note, by raising a question about the song "Earth Angel": "Is it one of the most magical records ever made—or is it just nostalgia?"[7] Holden tried to be respectful of the music, but as a middle-class critic he had to show a distance from it as well, once more connecting doowop with nostalgia. Although New York City was the principal center of doowop music, the *New York Times* has not reviewed books on doowop, thereby failing to contribute to the public record for future historians of popular music.

The general bias against doowop is reflected in the difficulties the Rock and Roll Hall of Fame has had in admitting famous doowop groups. By 1995, only one true doowop group, Frankie Lymon and the Teenagers, had made it into the Hall of Fame. The group was admitted only because the nominating committee—after years of sending the name to the voting members, only to have it rejected—voted in the group directly. Other vocal harmony groups in the Hall of Fame are the Orioles, the Drifters, the Coasters, and the Platters. The Flamingos and the Moonglows clearly belong, and possibly in the next few years the nominating committee will see fit to induct them, but their admittance likely will not come from the voting members.

It is encouraging, however, that appreciation and knowledge of doowop are occasionally expressed by mainstream cultural commentators. For example, the popular-music critic of the *New York Daily News,* Dave Hinckley, regularly reviews doowop releases and writes appreciative obituaries when group members die. The national political/cultural columnist Jeff Greenfield sometimes mentions his appreciation of doowop harmony groups.

Much education needs to be undertaken to illuminate and define the role of doowop in the history of rock 'n' roll. We must listen to the voices of those who appreciate and defend doowop, as well as to the voices of those who first recorded the form. I hope that they will prevail in this cultural dialogue.

Notes

1. Sheridan interview, July 3, 1992.
2. The book carries a publication date of 1994, but it was not actually released until May 1995.
3. Gribin and Schiff, *Doo-Wop,* p. 15.
4. Gottlieb, "The Durability of Doo-Wop."
5. Resnicoff, "Front Woman."
6. Gottlieb, "The Durability of Doo-Wop."
7. Holden, "'The Deep Forbidden Music.'"

Appendix 1:
Discography of Chicago Vocal Group Reissues

This discography concentrates on vocal releases that are available on CD. Where certain vocal group sides are not on CD, I have noted the vinyl formats in which they can be found: original singles and albums, counterfeit singles and albums, and legal reissue albums. "Counterfeits," also called "boots," are illegal releases put out by record collectors to supply copies of records to other collectors who can not afford to pay the high prices for the originals (which can run into thousands of dollars for many Chicago-group releases) or who can not find copies of the originals. Generally, these records are issued with counterfeit labels to look like the original issues.

Many common hits by some of the biggest vocal groups remain unavailable on CD, yet a number of obscure and previously unreleased songs can be obtained. This is due to several factors. Certain masters are unavailable because they cannot be found or because their ownership has not yet been determined. Some owners of the masters feel the market does not merit reissue. Sometimes compilers of reissues do not have sufficient knowledge of the field and thus omit certain sides or groups from anthologies. Despite such deficiencies, the owner of these CDs in the mid-1990s has more reissues available on Chicago doowop groups than were ever available on reissue vinyl.

Chance Groups

The vocal group offerings from the Chance catalog have been mostly unavailable, except for material by the Flamingos and the Moonglows, which has been released by Vee-Jay Limited Partnership and other firms. The complete catalog of the Flamingos and Moonglows on Chance is available on a Vee Jay reissue, *The Flamingos Meet the Moonglows "On the Dusty Road of Hits": The Complete Twenty-five Chance Recordings.* The sound is superb, making the records far more accessible to contemporary ears than might have been supposed. The essay by Billy Vera is only adequate, however. Chance material on the Flamingos can also be found on a Rhino reissue from 1990 called *The Best of the Flamingos* (four selections) and an Instant 1993 reissue from the United Kingdom, *I'll Be Home* (seven selections). Chance material on the Moonglows can also be found on a Chess/MCA reissue from 1993, *Blue Velvet: The Ultimate Collection* (three selections). One side of the Moonglows' first single on the Champagne label can be heard on a Flyright anthology reissue from the UK called *I Always Remember* (1992); the side is "I've Been Your Dog."

The Five Blue Notes, the Five Echoes, and the Five Chances so far have been neglected in reissue programs and may be unavailable. Collectors over the years have been making these artists available on counterfeit singles, and Constellation in 1964 came out with an album of the three groups called *Groups Three,* part of its collectors showcase series of reissued Chance recordings. The *Taste of Doo-wop* series, put out by Vee-Jay Limited Partnership in the early 1990s, provided all of the Five Echoes material that appeared on Vee Jay in either alternate takes or issued versions.

Chess Acts and Groups

The Chess catalog was taken over by MCA in 1986, and MCA has done a terrific job of reissuing the company's famed blues catalog. It has been less systematic and complete with regard to the doowop catalog, undoubtedly because the market for doowop is deemed smaller than that for blues. However, the company has done the Moonglows proud, putting out the magnificent collection *Blue Velvet: The Ultimate Collection* in 1993. It contains forty sides that the group recorded in its various incarnations from 1954 to 1959, plus three sides the group earlier recorded for Chance. The liner notes essay by Peter Grendysa is the best ever written on the group, although it does skirt the songwriting credit controversies. MCA has also reissued the first Moonglows album put out for Chess back in 1959, called *Look!—Its the Moonglows* (1988), but unless one is seeking to complete a collection or looking for a bit of memorabilia, the *Blue Velvet* collection makes this one superfluous. Bobby Lester put together a group for one of the Moonglows' later incarnations for the East Coast revival circuit. Relic put out a live recording of one of their sets, *The Moonglows: On Stage* (1992), but it is more of a memorial for Bobby Lester than an engaging listening experience. In 1994 Chess/MCA released an anthology boxed set, *Chess Rhythm and Roll* that includes both big hits and selected alternate and rare sides, among them the Moonglows hits "Sincerely" and "See Saw" and the previously unissued "No One."

MCA has neither reissued the original Checker album on the Flamingos, *The Flamingos* (1959), nor put out a collection on the group. In 1976, when Chess was owned by All Platinum in New Jersey, the label put out a wonderful reissue LP, *The Flamingos,* but one must look in resale shops for that one. Rhino put out a *The Best of the Flamingos* collection (1990) that contains three of the group's best known Checker songs—"I'll Be Home," "A Kiss from Your Lips," and "The Vow." Instant, a Charly subsidiary, put out a complete Checker collection, *I'll Be Home,* in the UK in 1993. It contained eleven sides along with Parrot and Chance material but inexplicably omits "The Vow." Also it mistakenly put a photo of the Dominoes on the package instead of the Flamingos and used the later cut version of "I'll Be Home" instead of the original. The *Chess Rhythm and Roll* boxed set includes "I'll Be Home," as well as a previously unissued alternate take of "Need Your Love."

The Flamingos' End material, recorded in New York, is outside the scope of this book, but it is available on various Collectables reissues. The Sequel 1991 reissue, *I Only Have Eyes for You,* not only contains the best anthology of the group's End sides but contains the best liner notes essay, by Donn Fileti, who writes of their Chicago years with particular acuity.

The Bo Diddley catalog is almost fully available for most of the doowop songs discussed in this book. A good start for collectors would be Chess/MCA's boxed set, *Bo Diddley* (1990), which contains a spectacular previously unissued doowop, "You Know I Love You." Another reissue compilation is the collection of rarities called *Rare and Well Done* (1991), which contains the alternate version of one of Diddley's best doowops, "No More Lovin'." The following original albums (all available on CD reissue by Chess/MCA) also augment the Diddley doowop oeuvre: *Bo Diddley* (1958) and *Go Bo Diddley* (1959), which are paired in a two-fer; *In the Spotlight* (1960), and *Bo Diddley Is a Gunslinger* (1960). The reissue of *Bo Diddley Is a Lover* (1961) appeared on a UK label, See for Miles, in 1994, but is hardly considered essential. Not available so far on CD are the original LPs *Bo Diddley's a Twister* (1962), *Bo Diddley* (1962), and *500% More Man* (1965), all containing doowops, although hardly the most inspiring.

Only a few songs by the lesser groups in the Chess catalog are available. There is no Vibrations CD; only their biggest hit, "The Watusi," has been put out on several collections, the most readily available being the *Best of Chess Rhythm and Blues Volume 1* (1988). If one can find the group's one Checker LP, *Watusi!,* one must weigh the prospect of acquiring a thin selection against paying an exorbitant price because of its rarity. Both the *Best of Chess Vocal Groups Volume 2* (1988) and the *Chess Rhythm and Roll* boxed set contains "Peanut Butter," the hit the group made as the Marathons. The box also contains a previously unreleased gem, "You're Mine," but since "Oh Cindy" remains unavailable, that is small consolation. The Coronets' "Nadine," sadly, is currently unavailable on CD. Curiously, though, a previously unreleased side by the group, "Should I," is readily available on the *Rhythm and Roll* boxed set. "Nadine" can be found also on an excellent two-fer LP, *The Golden Age of Rhythm and Blues.* A straight reissue of this great 1972 collection of Chess vocal groups on CD would be most welcome, as it also contains the Five Notes' "Show Me the Way." The song was also briefly available on a mini-CD reissue in 1987, *Chess Doo-Wop II,* but the mini-CD failed to catch on, making the reissue almost as rare as the original. The flip, "Park Your Love," which is even better, is not available in any format.

On the boxed set one can find previously unavailable sides by the Daps, the Four Tops, the Kents, the Brothers, and many group sides that Chess picked up in leased deals. But it doesn't contain the Checker sides by Donald Jenkins and his Fortunes group, which are not available anywhere.

Parrot Groups

Practically the entire Parrot/Blue Lake catalog of doowop music is available on three CDs put out by Relic Records in the early 1990s. On *The Golden Era of Doo-wops: The Groups of Parrot Records, Part One* (1993) can be found all the recordings of the Five Thrills and the Earls, and most of the Orchids and Flamingos output. The Flamingos songs not on the collection are "I'm Yours," "Ko Ko Mo," "I Found a New Baby," and "If I Could Love You." *Parrot Records Part Two* (1994) includes these remaining Flamingos songs as well as all the company's recordings of the Five Chances, Swans, Parrots, Pelicans, Fortunes, Clouds, Maples, and Fascinators. Also included on the collection are some alternate takes of songs by the Orchids. *Rockin' at Midnight* (1992) contains some marginal vocal group work that is duplicated in the two *Parrot Records* collections.

United/States Groups

Most of the United/States catalog of vocal group material has been unavailable. Currently it is in the hands of Delmark Records, which, since purchasing the masters from the original owner, Leonard Allen, in 1975, has reissued much of the blues and jazz that came out on the label but not the doowops. The company has not chosen to lease the masters to other companies, either. Delmark owner Bob Koester and I put together an album of

Five Cs and Hornets material in 1977, and this material was released in Japan on LP in 1983, as *Chicago Doo-Wops: Five C's vs. Hornets.* But this LP remains virtually unavailable, even in Japan. As of the mid-1990s, however, the album has not received a domestic release.

A bootleg LP of Danderliers and Moroccos material was made available in the early 1970s, but it is almost as rare as the original releases. Calvin Baron of the Moroccos later formed the Cosmic Rays, and one of the group's sides, "Bye," is available on *A Million Dollars Worth of Doo-Wop, Volume Three* (1994). Many of the United/States groups have been put out on counterfeit single releases that surface now and then at record shows. There is much interesting unreleased material as well as wonderful released sides by the Five Chances, the Palms, the Sheppards, and the Pastels that deserves to see the light of day.

Vee Jay Groups

The Vee Jay catalog has been the beneficiary of an extensive reissue program during 1992–93, when the company under the name Vee-Jay Limited Partnership operated as a reissue label. Before suspending operations in late 1993, the company reissued two CDs on the Spaniels, one on the Dells, and one on the El Dorados, along with a continuing anthology series, called *A Taste of Doowop,* that has been making available the remainder of the doowop catalog.

The Spaniels were well supported on CD in the early 1990s. Vee Jay put out two CDs in 1993, *Goodnight Sweetheart, Goodnight* and *Heart and Soul,* and both should be purchased for a complete hearing of the Spaniels on Vee Jay. As with many doowop groups, the Spaniels history has been one of disbandings and reunions as the group appeared in shows on the East Coast doowop circuit. One such show in Boston was put out on CD, called *The Spaniels Recorded Live* (1992). It came out in France on Fan Club Records and is recommended only for those seeking to complete their collections. *The Spaniels Fortieth Anniversary 1953–1993* is highly recommended. It was recorded by Pookie Hudson with the original group of Spaniels in 1993, with mostly remakes of old Spaniels tunes. This material, called *The Ultimate Acapella Collection!* (1993), was reissued and remixed in a cappella form by Wayne Stierle for his Juke Box Treasures label. Undeniably, the set offers something to a capella fans, but doowop sung to accompaniment is preferable, and so is the *Fortieth Anniversary* set. Consumers may still find in stores *Play It Cool* (1990), the set put out by Charly Records in the United Kingdom. It contains twenty-six original Vee Jay recordings, although one, "Why Don't You Dance," does not appear on the Vee-Jay Limited Partnership reissues.

Most of the Dells' Vee Jay catalog has been made available on a CD called *Dreams of Contentment* (1992). Some of the remainder, eight selections in all, have been made available on *A Taste of Doowop Volume Three* (1993). "Time Makes You Change" is notable. One side of the Dells' first record, which the group made as the El Rays on Checker, can be found on the boxed set *Chess Rhythm and Roll* (1994), namely "Darling I Know." A faster version of the song can be found on a 1972 Chess double-LP, *The Golden Age of Rhythm and Blues.*

The El Dorados are readily available on a Vee Jay reissue, *Bim Bam Boom* (1992), but its version of "At My Front Door" has audio problems. Vee Jay has made a pristine version of the song available on *A Taste of Doowop Volume Two* (1993), where it included a previously unissued side. In 1993 George Paulus released an exciting album of new recordings by the El Dorados (the lead, Pirkle Lee Moses, is the only original member) called *Street Corner Blues and Rhythm.* The group does remakes with traditional instrumentation of some of the bluesier material put out by Chicago groups in the early to mid-1950s. If some of the rare releases cannot be obtained, one can get a sense of the sound by listening to the El Dorados do their take on such songs as the Five Cs' "Whoo-wee Baby," the Sheppards' "Mozelle," the Debonairs' "Mother's Son," and a batch of Moonglows' Chance sides.

The Kool Gents music has been spread around a bit on reissue, so the ideal situation would be to have a single CD of their entire output. It does not look like that will happen, however. The songs on which Dee Clark led are available on some Clark reissues, most notably the *Charly R&B* CD from 1987 called *Raindrops,* which contains "I Just Can't Help Myself," "When I Call on You," "Just Like a Fool." The Vee Jay reissue from 1992, also called *Raindrops,* contains only "I Just Can't Help Myself." Vee-Jay Limited Partnership has made other Kool Gents songs available on their *Taste of Doo Wop* series, comprised of some six sides, but most are previously unissued alternate takes (the original masters apparently are unavailable). Two of the sides the group did as the Delegates are available on *Volume Three* in the series.

All of the Magnificents work on Vee Jay has come out on CD, albeit on three *Taste of Doo Wop* anthologies, where "Up on the Mountain" and "Caddy Bo" appear on volume one, six sides are on volume two, and three more sides are on volume three. Some are alternate takes from the issued versions, apparently because the masters are missing. Eight sides of the Magnificents on one release can be found on a 1984 Solid Smoke LP, *Magnificents and Rhythm Aces: Fifteen Cool Jewels.*

The Rhythm Aces are available on CD in *A Taste of Doo Wop, Volume Three* with alternate takes of "Whisper to Me" and "That's My Sugar." The

1984 LP on Solid Smoke, *Magnificents and Rhythm Aces,* contains their whole body of work on the label. Both *A Taste of Doo Wop* and the Solid Smoke LP contain "Joni" and "Be Mine" by the later Rhythm Aces group.

All of the Prodigals' and Falcons/Lyrics' Vee Jay output is available on *A Taste of Doo Wop,* volumes one and two, as are two sides by the Orioles, on volume three. The only things that Vee Jay neglected to reissue are the wonderful sides by the girl group the Capers. Two of their sides can be found on a three-volume Japanese reissue of Vee Jay material on the P-Vine label, called *Vee-Jay Records: Ten Years of Chicago Street Corner.* Volume three of this series contains two Goldenrods sides, their local hit, "Color Cartoon," and a previously unissued song, "The Football Game." Other odd groups on the *Ten Years* records include the Dontells, the Twintettes, Miss Mello and Heavy Drama, and recordings by the above-mentioned groups.

Vee-Jay Limited also put out a boxed set in 1993, *Celebrating Forty Years of Classic Hits: 1953–1993,* that included the most notable sides by the Spaniels, El Dorados, Five Echoes, Kool Gents, Magnificents, Dells, and Orioles, besides many sides by the label's blues, jazz, and soul artists.

Small Entrepreneurs Groups—Citywide

By virtue of the Hambone Kids' association with a major label, Columbia, their "Hambone" is readily available on the 1989 CD reissue of a 1982 vinyl two-fer, *OKeh Rhythm and Blues.* The other Hambone Kids numbers are not available. Willie Dixon's work with the Big Three Trio has been extensively documented on disc and can be found on two LPs of recent vintage, *I Feel Like Steppin' Out* (1985) and *The Big Three Trio* (1990). A Five Breezes number, "Minute and Hour Blues," can be found on *The Human Orchestra* (1985).

The Club 51 output can be obtained on a vinyl reissue by Relic called *The Golden Groups—Part Thirty-five: The Best of Club 51 Records.* Besides the Five Buddies and Kings Men sides, the LP also contains various acetates and tapes of as yet unidentified groups who came into Jimmy Davis's shop to make a record. Donn Fileti of Relic says that he has no plan to reissue the LP on CD although he will eventually place the masters, but not the acetates, in a Chicago compilation.

The Hepsters on Ronel and the Marvellos and the Sheppards on Theron have appeared on counterfeit releases. As for the Marvellos on the Marvello and Stepheny labels, only counterfeit singles are available, except that "I Need a Girl" appears on CD on the compilation designed for the hardcore collector, *A Million Dollars Worth of Doo-Wop, Volume One* (1993). The Vals side, "The Song of a Lover," is on *A Million Dollars Worth of Doo-Wop, Volume Four* (1994). Other Chicago groups not discussed in my text but which appear in these various *Million Dollar* collections include Little June and the Januaries ("Hello!," originally on Salem, and "Oh What a Feeling," originally on Profile), the Debs ("A Star in the Sky"), the Epics ("Summer's Coming In," originally on Bandera), and the neo-doo-wop Stimulators ("Warm Summer Nights," originally on Sound-O-Riffic). The Daffodils on C. J. are unavailable because the masters had been lost by the owner, Carl Jones.

The Cobra catalog of blues has been extensively reissued, but virtually none of the vocal group material has been made available. The most notable single reissue of the catalog is *The Cobra Records Story,* the boxed set issued by Capricorn Records in 1993, which includes one previously unissued alternate take of the Clouds' "Born with Rhythm." No songs by the Rip-Chords or Calvaes, however, appear in the box. The Rip-Chords' "I Love You the Most" can be found on a release by the Austrian-based Wolf label, *Abco Chicago Blues Recordings,* released in 1994. Counterfeit copies of the Clouds, Calvaes, and Rip-Chords occasionally appear in record shows, however.

The Faith Taylor and the Sweet Teens sides on both Federal and Bea and Baby are not available. The Federal recording has been counterfeited but the Bea and Baby release has not. In either case, the records are hard to find. Those are supposedly the only two releases on Faith Taylor and the Sweet Teens, but all the published sources indicate one more Bea and Baby release. I have not found one collector, however, who has two Bea and Baby releases. It would seem that Bea and Baby originally intended to put out two releases, numbered 104 and 105, but instead decided on one release, combining the two strongest sides from the two intended releases.

Regarding the releases of Formal Records, two Masquerades songs are available on *A Million Dollars Worth of Doo-Wop, Volume Three* (1994), which contains "Fanessa," cut for Don Talty in Chicago, and "Nature's Beauty," cut for Ike Turner in St. Louis, both dubbed from vinyl. Don Talty, owner of the masters, died in 1979, and the masters are in the possession of his daughters in a small community in northern Illinois. The release of unissued recordings by the Masquerades would really be an event for doo-wop collectors. The Trinidads' "Don't Say Good Goodbye" is available on *A Million Dollars Worth of Doo-Wop, Volume Eleven* (1995).

Most of the group sides released on Lenny LaCour's Lucky Four and Six-Twenty labels are unavailable on reissue in any form. Only two sides by the Uniques, "Cry, Cry, Cry" and "Silvery Moon," are available, on *A Million Dollars Worth of Doo-Wop, Volume Five.* There have been no known counterfeits of the records either. A consumer not plugged into the collector community, where a kind and helpful individual could make a tape of his rare sides, would find it a hopeless task to locate LaCour's music.

Small Entrepreneurs Groups—Neighborhoods

The very nature of most of the small neighborhood labels leaves little prospect that any substantial proportion of this music will become available to the consumer. Most of the records are extremely rare, and in order to study them I was forced to find the music on counterfeit copies or on tapes made by collector friends. None of the records ever became large enough hits for a record company to search out the original masters and put them on reissue compilations. They are appealing only to the hardcore doowop collectors.

For the groups in the Altgeld Gardens area, only counterfeit copies of the Park label groups (Four Gents and Quintones) are available. This is true likewise of the Nobles release on Sapphire. Of the Near North groups, namely the Von Gayles, Medallionaires, Serenades, and Players, only the Players can be found on CD. Their two hits, "He'll Be Back" and "I'm Glad You Waited," appear on *The Minit Records Story* (1994). A 1993 Collectables reissue of their *He'll Be Back* LP is also available. The Serenades have been released on counterfeit recordings, but the other groups have not. Theoretically, Paula/Jewel in Shreveport, Louisiana, would have the Serenades songs, but the company has not included them in any of its many compilations of Chief, Profile, and USA material.

The Gems on Drexel are the only Evanston group available on counterfeits. One side of the Gay Notes on Drexel, "Pu Pa Doo," is available on *A Million Dollars Worth of Doo-Wop, Volume Four* (1994). On the same disc is "Blue Island" by the Rannels, which originally appeared on Evanston's Boss label, but the group was not discussed in the text.

Nike and Erman Groups

The Nike catalog is unavailable on CD, nor has it ever been available on LP. The sales were so localized on the Daylighters that there is no incentive for any company to risk trying to market the group. The owner of the catalog, Charles Colbert Sr., is now dead, and the masters are believed to be in the possession of his son, Chuck Colbert.

The Erman catalog for the Cortland and Witch labels, unfortunately, is likewise unavailable. The owner of the masters, Bill Erman, has kept all of them in storage in Chicago since the closing of his label in 1965. The Blenders, the Versalettes, the Ideals, Donald Jenkins, and other doowop groups' material can be picked up only at record collector shows on rare occasions and at high prices, except for one Jenkins side. Jenkins and the Delighters' "Elephant Walk," is available on the CD *Itzy Records Presents Pittsburgh's Greatest Hits,* the title of which indicates that the record had particular popularity in the Steel City. The CD from the early 1990s is a reissue of a double-LP that came out in the mid-1960s.

Bill Sheppard Groups

The Sheppards are available only on a poor package put out by Collectables, *Island of Love: Golden Classics* (1994), which contains eighteen sides including their excellent OKeh single, "Pretend You're Still Mine." A fine package is a Solid Smoke vinyl release from 1980, *The Sheppards,* with good liner notes and superb mastering from vinyl originals. Of the Bel Aires and Equallos, only two sides on the Equallos are available, "Underneath the Sun," which appears on *A Million Dollars Worth of Doo-Wop, Volume One* (1993), and "Patty-Patty," which appears on *A Million Dollars Worth of Doo-Wop: Volume Eleven* (1995).

The songs by the Dukays with the Gene Chandler as lead, specifically "Duke of Earl," "Festival of Love," "Nite Owl," and "The Big Lie," can be found on Chandler albums and are easily obtained. The most comprehensive collection of Chandler's Vee Jay output is *The Duke of Earl* CD from 1993, put out by the later reissue company, Vee-Jay Limited Partnership. Charly R&B has a CD collection, *Stand By Me* (1987). The Vee Jay release, however, contains a later Chandler solo version of "Nite Owl." The original version of "Nite Owl," as well as "Duke of Earl," can be found on *Nothing Can Stop Me* (1994) on Varese Sarabande. All of these collections are deficient because of the absence of "Girl Is a Devil." Later Dukays songs on Vee Jay and Jerry O have not been made available in album form and one must search oldies record shows and shops for the singles.

*   *   *

As mentioned in the afterword, in 1993 an extraordinary boxed set called *The Doo Wop Box* was released by Rhino Records. It contained four CDs programming 101 mostly hit doowop songs from the late 1940s to the late 1980s. More than half dated from the golden age of rock 'n' roll, 1955 to 1959. Chicago vocal groups were represented by the Flamingos (with "Golden Teardrops," "I'll Be Home," and two End sides), the Moonglows ("Sincerely" and "Ten Commandments of Love"), the Spaniels ("Goodnite Sweetheart, Goodnite"), the El Dorados ("At My Front Door"), and the Dells ("Oh What a Nite"). Also in the set is Jerry Butler and the Impressions' "For Your Precious Love," which is more a proto-soul record than a doowop. *The Doo Wop Box* provides tremendous entertainment value, but with its extensive liner notes booklet and intelligent programming it also offers enough material to provide doowop fans and collectors with a real education.

Appendix 2:
List of Interviews

Except where noted, the following were telephone interviews conducted by the author. The locations given indicate the places from which interviewees spoke. All transcripts and notes are in the author's files.

Abner, Ewart; Los Angeles Calif.; March 15, 1995.
Allen, Leonard; personal interview with Jim O'Neal; Chicago; 1976.
Allen, Leonard; personal interview; Chicago; November 2, 1980.
Barksdale, Charles; Chicago; February 21, 1981.
Barnes, Prentiss; Jackson, Miss.; September 26 and 27, 1992; January 12, 1993; July 27, 1994.
Bell, Albert; Chicago; July 16, 1978.
Black, Carlton; Evanston, Ill.; July 16, 1977.
Blake, Cicero; Chicago; June 23, 1981.
Brackenridge, Joe; August 28, 1991; September 19, 1991; October 25, 1992.
Bradley, Jan; Country Club Hills, Ill.; November 11, 1994.
Brown, Devora; Detroit; July 13, 1986.
Burnett, Hiawatha; Gary, Ind.; March 22, 1995.
Butler, Herbert; Chicago, October 5 and 25, 1992.
Butler, Jerry; personal interview; Chicago; April 21, 1982.
Butler, William; personal interview; Chicago; June 5, 1974.
Carter, Clifton; Chicago; March 2, 1980.
Carter, Johnny; Chicago; August 9, 1978.
Cary, Zeke and Jake; personal interview with Carl Tancredi; Philadelphia; 1971.
Catron, Bob; Memphis, Tenn.; January 23, 1988.
Chandler, Gene; personal interview; Chicago; February 6, 1979.
Clark, Dee; personal interview; Chicago; December 19, 1979.
Clay, Don; personal interview with Jim O'Neal; Chicago; February 25, 1982.
Colbert, Charles; personal interview; Chicago; August 20, 1974.

Colbert, Charles; Chicago; January 22, 1988.
Coleman, Gloria; Chicago; June 14, 1992.
Cordell, Lucky; Chicago; March 21, 1993.
Davis, Carl; personal interview with Dave Hoekstra; Flossmoor, Ill.; 1982.
Davis, Carl; personal interview; Flossmoor, Ill.; April 27, 1986.
Davis, Charles; LaGrange, Ill.; January 27, 1978.
Dixon, Bernard; Chicago; April 27, 1980.
Dixon, Richard; personal interview; Chicago; June 11, 1977.
Edwards, Earl; Chicago; July 18, 1977.
Edwards, Millard; Chicago; September 8, 1981.
Erman, Bill; Atlanta, Ga.; July 23, 1988.
Frank, Theresa Legg; Lithonia, Ga.; December 10, 1992.
Giardini, Angelo; Wheeling, Ill.; July 23, 1988.
Gideon, Tony; Birmingham, Ala.; August 8 and 9, 1976; January 20, 1988.
Gordon, Reggie; Chicago; August 1, 1993.
Hawkins, Jimmy; Berkeley, Ill.; August 1, 1993.
Hudson, James; Gary, Ind., February 8, 1984, and Washington, D.C., March 28, 1991.
Hunter, Rufus; Chicago; August 7, 1993.
Isaac, James Dennis; Chicago; February 18 and 20, 1978.
Jackson, Reggie; personal interview; Bellwood, Ill.; July 29, 1978.
Jenkins, Donald; Chicago; February 23, 1977.
Jenkins, Levi; Chicago; February 9, 1980.
Johnson, Lawrence; Chicago; July 3, 1979.
Johnson, Ralph; Chicago; February 21 and 28, 1993.
Johnson, Tommie; Chicago; October 23, 1992.
Jones, Hilliard; Chicago; December 23, 1988; November 1, 1989.
Jones, Tommy; Chicago; May 25, 1993.
Junior, Marvin; Harvey, Ill.; March 20, 1984.
Junior, Marvin; personal interview with Seamus McGarvey; Harvey, Ill.; 1993.
Kent, Herb; Chicago; April 8, 1977.
Kent, Herb; personal interview; Chicago; March 31, 1993.
Keyes, Johnny; Chicago; August 7, 1993.
LaCour, Lenny; personal interview with Wayne Jancik; Chicago; June 6, 1984.
LaCour, Lenny; Oakbrook, Ill.; June 22, 1984, by Wayne Jancik.
LaCour, Lenny; personal interview with Wayne Jancik; Oakbrook, Ill.; June 22, 1984.
LaCour, Lenny; Westmont, Ill.; November 15, 1993.
Lewis, Earl; personal interview; Maywood, Ill.; March 24, 1978.
Malone, Peggy; Boulder Creek, Calif.; January 11, 1993.
Manor, Ularsee; Chicago; August 5, 1993.
McElroy, Sollie; personal interview; Chicago; June 1, 1976.
McGill, Lucius; Harvey, Ill.; February 22, 1991.
McGill, Michael; Harvey, Ill.; January 15, 1981.
McGrier, Sammy; Chicago; May 6, 1980.
McKnight, Charles; Chicago; April 2, 1980.

McVickers, Janice; personal interview; Sandwich, Ill.; January 8, 1989.

Mitchell, Leonard; Maywood, Ill.; September 12, 1978.

Moore, Johnny; interview with Marvin Goldberg; June 6, 1979.

Morrow, Melvin; Chicago; August 17, 1978.

Moses, Pirkle Lee; Chicago; October 18, 1982.

Nelson, William; Chicago; February 21, 1993.

Nesbary, Sherman; Chicago; September 22, 1991.

Overbea, Danny; Chicago; June 26, 1992.

Palm, Norman; Chicago; May 16, 1976.

Perkins, O.C.; personal interview; Chicago; October 24, 1977.

Perkins, O.C.; Chicago; November 13, 1977.

Perry, Charles; Evanston, Ill.; November 17, 1994.

Pitman, Howard; Chicago; May 21, 1995.

Potter, Jerry L.; Detroit, Mich.; March 4, 1990.

Prayer, George; personal interview; Chicago; September 5, 1978.

Pritchett, Louis; Chicago; February 21, 1991.

Pruitt, John; Chicago; April 27, 1978.

Robinson, Kathleen Spates; Duluth, Ga.; December 10, 1992.

Robinson, R. C.; Evanston, Ill.; April 10, 1989.

Scott, Howard; Chicago; January 15, 1989.

Scott, Robert; Chicago; January 15, 1989.

Sheridan, Arthur; personal interview; Oakbrook Terrace, Ill.; July 3, 1992.

Simpkins, Maurice; Chicago; August 7, 1977; January 16 and December 3, 1979.

Smith, Marvin; personal interview; Bellwood, Ill.; December 9, 1979.

Smith, Reggie; Chicago; September 28, 1989; October 11 and 15, 1989.

Spraggins, Wesley; personal interview; Chicago; June 10, 1976.

Stamz, Richard; personal interview; Chicago; May 13, 1978.

Stamz, Richard; Chicago; March 16, 1993.

Steele, Stacy, Jr.; Chicago; August 28, 1991.

Sullivan, Eddie; Chicago; August 16 and September 13, 1980, August 23, 1990, July 2, 1993.

Talbert, Homer; Los Angeles; November 20, 1992.

Tharp, Robert; personal interview; Bellwood, Ill.; July 29, 1978.

Toole, Cornelius; Chicago; January 9, 1993.

Tucker, Nathaniel; Chicago; April 27, 1978.

Vanorsby, Stanley; Chicago; February 28, 1993.

Wallace, Vera Regulus; Chicago; July 11, 1991.

Walton, Charles; Chicago; March 24, 1993.

Williams, Freddie; Chicago; March 10, 1993.

Works Cited

Abbey, John. "Behind the Scenes with Carl Davis." *Blues and Soul,* August 3–16, 1973, pp. 22–24.

———. "The Vibrations." *Home of the Blues* 1 (May 1966): 8–9.

Abbott, Lynn. "'Play That Barber Shop Chord': A Case for the African-American Origin of Barbershop Harmony." *American Music* 10, no. 3 (Fall 1992): 290–325.

"Amos Heads Allstars into Park City Bowl." *Chicago Defender,* May 21, 1955.

Anderson, Will. "The Carnations." *Bim Bam Boom* 8 (December 1972): 33.

Baker, Cary. "The C.J. Records Story." *Goldmine,* March–April 1977, p. 7.

———. "The C.J. Records Story." *Goldmine,* March 1982, pp. 26–27.

Banks, Nancy. "The World's Most Beautiful Ballrooms." *Chicago History,* Fall–Winter 1973, pp. 206–15.

Beauchamp, L. 'Chicago Beau.' "Interview with Billy Boy Arnold." *The Original Chicago Blues Annual* 5 (1993): 14.

Beckman, Jeff. "Teenage Tenor Leads." *Bim Bam Boom* 12 (1974): 38–43.

Bellavia, Roy J. *A Capsule History of Past and Present Radio Stations in the Chicagoland Area.* Chicago: WSBC Broadcasting Company, 1978.

"Benson Quits Radio after Sixteen Years." *Chicago Defender,* April 27, 1963.

"Benson Sets Gate Record for Regal." *Chicago Defender,* March 5, 1957.

Bernholm, Jonas. Liner notes, Big Three Trio, *I Feel Like Steppin' Out.* Dr. Horse H-804, 1985.

Braunstein, Bill. "Bo Diddley Bo Diddley, Where Have You Been?" *Chicago Tribune Magazine,* June 6, 1980, pp. 18–21.

Bundy, June. "DJ Emerges as Powerhouse Promoter on R&B Personals." *Billboard,* February 4, 1956, p. 54.

Bushnell, George D. "Chicago's Magnificent Movie Palaces." *Chicago History,* Summer 1977.

Caldarulo, Mike. "The Moonglows: A Definitive Biography." *Harmony Tymes* 3 (Winter 1987): 4–11.

Callahan, Mike. "Both Sides Now, the Story of Stereo Rock and Roll, Vee Jay Records." *Goldmine,* May 1981, pp. 170–72.

———. "Vee Jay Is Alive and Living in Burbank." *Goldmine,* May 1981, pp. 161–63.

———. "The Vee Jay Story, Part 1: Scenes from a Family Owned Company." *Goldmine,* May 1981, pp. 6–18.

Calloway, Earl. "Entertainment World Mourns 'Red' Saunders." *Chicago Defender,* March 7, 1981.

———. "Red Saunders, a Pivotal Figure in Music." *Chicago Defender,* April 1, 1978.

Carter, Richard G. *Goodnight Sweetheart, Goodnight: The Story of the Spaniels.* Sicklerville, N.J.: August Press, 1994.

Cocks, Jay. "Sounds Like Old Times." *Time,* January 5, 1981, p. 75.

Coleman, Gloria. "The Black Gold Coast: The Rise and Fall of the DuSable Hotel, an Oral History." Chicago *Reader,* November 9, 1984, pp. 1, 30–42.

"D.J. Al Benson Presents Socko 'Package' Show." *Chicago Defender,* April 13, 1957.

Dance, Stanley. *The World of Earl Hines.* New York: Scribner, 1977.

Davis, Charles A. "Al Benson, Mayor of Bronzeville, Old Swingmaster, the Real Story." *Chicago Defender,* December 11, 1948.

Davis, Chuck. "Platters" [column]. *Chicago Defender,* March 18, 1961.

Diddley, Bo. Liner notes, "Bo Diddley on Bo Diddley." *Bo Diddley* (boxed set), Chess/MCA CH2–19502, 1990.

"Disc Jockey Citations on Tavern Parade Dec. 7." *Chicago Defender,* December 8, 1956.

"Disc Jockeys: Sixteen Sepia Spielers Ride Kilocycle Range on Twenty-one Stations." *Ebony,* December 1947, pp. 44–49.

Engel, Edward R. *White and Still All Right.* Scarsdale, N.Y.: Crackerjack Press, 1977.

"Faith Taylor Cited by Radio's Roy Wood." *Chicago Defender,* November 12, 1958.

"Faith Taylor, Nine Stars on Video." *Chicago Defender,* October 4, 1958.

Fileti, Donn. Liner notes, *Golden Groups—Part 35: The Best of Club Records.* Relic Records 5059 [1985].

———. Liner notes, The Flamingos, *I Only Have Eyes for You: The Best of the End Years.* Sequel Records NEMCD 609, 1991.

"Five Hepsters, Cleveland R&B Quintet, Prove Practice Makes Perfect." In *The History of Rhythm and Blues, Volume 6: 1956,* edited by Galen Gart, p. 22. Milford, N.H.: Big Nickel, 1991.

"Foster Brothers" [caption]. *Chicago Defender,* November 23, 1957.

Fuchs, Aaron, and Dan Nooger. "Harvey Fuqua: The Motown Days." *Goldmine,* March 15, 1985, pp. 18, 20–22, 24.

Galgano, Bob. "El Dorados and Kool Gents." *Bim Bam Boom* 2 (October–November 1971): 8–9.

Galkin, Peter. "Black White and Blues: The Story of Chess Records, Part One." *Living Blues* 88 (September–October 1989): 22–32.

———. "Black White and Blues: The Story of Chess Records, Part Two." *Living Blues* 89 (December 1989): 25–29.

Gart, Galen. *ARLD: The American Record Label Directory and Dating Guide.* Milford, N.H.: Big Nickel, 1989.

————. *First Pressings: The History of Rhythm and Blues,* Vol. 1, 1951; vol. 2, 1952; vol. 3, 1953; vol. 4, 1954; vol. 5, 1955; vol. 6, 1956; vol. 7, 1957. Milford, N.H.: Big Nickel, 1991, 1992, 1989, 1990, 1990, 1991, and 1993.

————, ed. and comp. *First Pressings: Rock History as Chronicled in Billboard Magazine, Volume 1, 1948–1950.* Milford, N.H.: Big Nickel, 1986.

————. *First Pressings: Rock History as Chronicled in Billboard Magazine, Volume 2, 1951–1952.* Milford, N.H.: Big Nickel, 1986.

Given, David. "Moonglows." In *The David Given Rock 'n' Roll Stars Handbook,* pp. 211–20. Smithtown, N.Y.: Exposition Press, 1980.

Goldberg, Marv. "'Coronets' Smooth Style 'Copied' by Orioles; No Magic from Alan Freed 'Management.'" *Record Collector's Monthly* 45 (December 1989): 12–13.

————. "The Jay Hawks/Vibrations." *Bim Bam Boom* 5 (April–May 1972): 12.

————. "The Orioles." *Whiskey, Women, and . . .* 12/13 (December 1983): n.p.

————. "The Rhythm Aces." *Goldmine,* February 8, 1991, pp. 24, 42.

————. "The Rip-Chords." *Goldmine,* April 1979, p. 36.

Goldberg, Marv, and Mike Redmond. "The Five Blue Notes." *Yesterday's Memories* 4 [1975]: n.p.

Goldberg, Marv, and Rick Whitesell. "Fred Buckley and the Pastels." *Goldmine,* April 1979, p. 39.

Gottlieb, Marvin. "The Durability of Doo-Wop." *New York Times,* January 17, 1993.

"Grand Terrace Opens amid Socko Applause." *Chicago Defender,* May 21, 1955.

Greensmith, Bill. "Red Holloway," part 1. *Blues Unlimited* 117 (January–February 1976): 4–10;

————. "Red Holloway," part 2. *Blues Unlimited* 118 (April–March 1976): 9–14.

Greggs, LaTicia D. "Lead Singer of the Magnificents Recalls Du-Wop." *Chicago Defender,* June 15, 1991.

Grendysa, Peter. "Blues and Jazz Collide in Chicago: Cats 'n' Jammers; Four Shades of Rhythm." *Record Collector's Monthly* 8 (April 1983): 1, 10.

————. "The Four Jumps of Jive and the Big Three Trio." *Classic Wax* 4 (August 1981): 4–5.

————. Liner notes, *The Moonglows: Blue Velvet/The Ultimate Collection.* Chess/MCA CHD2 9345, 1993.

————. "The United and States Labels: A Collector's Guide." *Goldmine,* February 13, 1987, pp. 79, 82, 89.

Grendysa, Peter [company history essay], and James Marshall [artists' biographies essay]. Liner notes, *The OKeh Rhythm and Blues Story 1949–1957.* Epic/OKeh/Legacy E3K 48912, 1993.

Grendysa, Peter, George Moonoogian, and Rick Whitesell. "The Cats and the Fiddle." *Yesterday's Memories* 6 [1976]: 12–17.

Gribin, Anthony J., and Matthew M. Schiff *Doo-Wop: The Forgotten Third of Rock 'n' Roll.* Iola, Wis.: Krause, 1992, p. 15.

Groia, Phil. *They All Sang on the Corner.* West Hempstead, N.Y.: Phillie Dee Enterprises, 1983.

Haig, Diane Reid, and Don Snowdon. Liner notes, *The Cobra Records Story.* Capricorn Records 9 42012-2, 1993.

"Hambone Kids." *Ebony,* June 1952, pp. 71–76.

Hep [pseud.]. "Night Beat" [column]. *Chicago Defender,* October 30, 1954.

"Herb Hopkins New Manager Regal Theatre." *Chicago Defender,* February 18, 1961.

"Herb Kent and WBEE Blues and Jazzville Concert." Advertisement, *Chicago Defender,* April 13, 1957.

"Herb Kent, Radio's Bee Back on Local Station." *Chicago Defender,* February 3, 1959.

Hill, Luther. "Facts and Figures Tell Why Chorines Are Making Their Final Curtain Call: The Cuties Are Disappearing and But Fast." *Chicago Defender,* August 27, 1955.

Hinckley, David. Liner notes, "R-E-S-P-E-C-T," *The Doo Wop Box.* Rhino Records 71463, 1993.

Hinckley, David [with Marv Goldberg]. "The El Dorados." *Goldmine,* April 1979, pp. 35–36.

———. "The Kool Gents." *Goldmine,* April 1979, pp. 42–43.

———. "The Other Four Buddies." *Goldmine,* April 1979, pp. 38–39.

Hoekstra, Dave. "Flamingos Return to the Home Nest." *Chicago Sun-Times,* April 3, 1987.

Holden, Stephen. "'The Deep Forbidden Music': How Doo-Wop Casts Its Spell." *New York Times,* May 29, 1994.

Hopkins, Charles. "Wax and Needle" [column]. *Chicago Defender,* June 25, 1953.

Horlick, Richard. "The Spaniels." *R&B Magazine* 4/5 (July–October 1970): 47–51.

———. "The Spaniels—Revisited." *R&B Magazine* 6/7 (November–February 1971): n.p.

Hunt, James. "The Moonglows." *Record Exchanger* 2 (March 1970): 6–11.

Hunter, Bob. "Has Al Benson's Star Set as Top Deejay?" *Chicago Defender,* October 2, 1962.

———. "Night Clubs Fail, But McKie Still Makes It." *Chicago Defender,* November 12, 1962.

———. "Seventy-four and Blind, Jack L. Cooper, First Negro Deejay, Still Airs Radio Show." *Chicago Defender,* May 14, 1963

Hyde, Bob. Liner notes, "Compiler's Notes," *The Doo Wop Box.* Rhino Records 71463, 1993.

"If You Wanta Get on Radio, Then See McKie Fitzhugh." *Chicago Defender,* February 16, 1956.

Italiano, Ronnie. "The Splendid Spaniels." *U.G.H.A. Selection No. 2* [pamphlet], December 1978, pp. 1–10.

Jackson, Arthur. "Old Memories to Fall with the Trianon." *Chicago Tribune,* January 2, 1967.

Jackson, John A. *Big Beat Heat: Alan Freed and the Early Days of Rock and Roll.* New York: Schirmer, 1991.

Janusek, Carl and Nancy. "Prodigals." *Echoes of the Past* 13 (Fall 1990): 5–10.

Jones, Wayne. "Nate Nelson of the Flamingos." *Goldmine,* March 1978, pp. 12–13.

Kenney, William Howland. *Chicago Jazz: A Cultural History, 1904–1930.* New York: Oxford University Press, 1993.

Kenning, Dan. "One 'Kool Gent.'" *Chicago Tribune,* August 7, 1990.

Keyes, Johnny. *Du-Wop.* Chicago: Vesti Press, 1987.

Lee, Alan, and Donna Hennings. "The Spaniels." *Yesterday's Memories* 6 [1976]: 4–7.

Lenehan, Mike. "Conversations with the Dells: Twenty-eight Years of Rhythm and Blues, from Doowop to Disco." Chicago *Reader,* November 14, 1980, pp. 1, 20–40.

Lepri, Paul. *The New Haven Sound: 1946–1976.* New Haven, Conn.: By the author, 1977.

"Little Richard's Package at Civic Twice on April 12." *Chicago Defender,* April 13, 1957.

"Live Shows Make Chicago Unique." *Chicago Defender,* August 20, 1960.

"Local Radio 'Jockeys' Keep Rock 'n' Roll Tops." *Chicago Defender,* January 27, 1959.

Loder, Kurt. "Bo Diddley: The Rolling Stone Interview." *Rolling Stone,* February 12, 1987, pp. 76–80, 98, 100.

Lowe, David. *Lost Chicago.* Boston: Houghton Mifflin, 1975.

"'Mad Man' Jones Sets One Disc Outlet; Hits." *Chicago Defender,* May 31, 1958.

Marchesani, Jim. "Time Capsule." *Bim Bam Boom* 3 (December–January 1972): 21.

Marion, Jean-Charles. "Listening In: The Moonglows." *Record Exchanger* 30 [1982]: 24, 27.

"The Masquerades" [caption]. *Chicago Defender,* February 15, 1958.

McCutcheon, Lynn Ellis. *Rhythm and Blues.* Arlington, Va.: Beatty, 1971.

McGarvey, Seamus. "The Flamingos Story." *Now Dig This* 97 (April 1991): 28–30.

———. "Jump Children." *Now Dig This* 42 (September 1986): 5–7.

———. "Knocking at the El Dorados' Front Door . . ." *Now Dig This* 132 (March 1994): 15–17.

"McKie's Variety Show." Advertisement, *Chicago Defender,* September 4, 1954.

"Medallionaires" [caption]. *Chicago Defender,* February 1, 1958.

"Midnight Shows at Indiana in Broadway Step." *Chicago Defender,* March 8, 1952.

Millar, Bill. *The Coasters.* London: W. H. Allen, 1975.

———. *The Drifters.* New York: Collier, 1972.

"Music Personalities A–Z: The Musician." *Chicago Tribune,* February 3, 1980.

Newman, Mark. *Entrepreneurs of Profit and Pride: From Black-Appeal to Radio Soul.* New York: Praeger, 1988.

"A New Star Is Born! It's Sam Evans, Your Lucky Man." Advertisement, *Chicago Defender,* February 12, 1949.

"New Teen Age Parties at Trianon Saturdays." *Chicago Defender,* October 2, 1954.

"Nite Beat." *Chicago Defender,* December 12, 1953.

Oates, Max. Liner notes, The Four Jewels, *Loaded With Goodies.* BJM Records, 1985.

O'Brien, T. C., ed. "Church of God and Saints of Christ." In *Corpus Dictionary of Western Churches,* p. 192. Washington, D.C.: Corpus Publications, 1970.

O'Hara, Delia. "Skating through the Color Barrier." *Chicago Sun-Times,* April 29, 1987.

"OKeh Handled by Twenty Indies." *Billboard,* November 1, 1952, p. 17.

O'Neal, Jim. "Narvel Eatmon (Cadillac Baby)." Obituary, *Living Blues* 101 (January–February 1992): 32–33.

———. "You Must Be the Man from God. You Are Cadillac Baby!" *Living Blues* 6 (Autumn 1971): 23–29.

Palmer, Robert. Liner notes, "Bo Diddley: The Overview," *Bo Diddley* (boxed set), Chess/MCA CH2–19502.

"The Park City Skate Arena Opens Friday." *Chicago Defender,* September 6, 1947.

Passman, Arnold. "Jack Cooper: The First Black Disc Jockey." *Popular Music and Society* 16, no. 2 (Summer 1992): 43–49.

Pegue, Richard. "*Soul* Mourns the Loss of Chicago Correspondent McKie Fitzhugh." *Soul,* January 11, 1971, p. 16.

Penny, Dave. "Rudy Greene—The Blues Imitator." *Blues and Rhythm: The Gospel Truth* 43 (March 1989): 18–20.

"Petrillo Nixes Art Sheridan's Disking License." *Billboard,* May 19, 1951, p. 13.

Piper, Don. "Remembering Dee Clark." *Goldmine,* February 8, 1991, pp. 48, 50, 52.

Propes, Steve. "The Moonglows: The Commandments of Doo-Wop." *Goldmine,* February 8, 1991, pp. 11–13, 32.

Pruter, Robert. "Bo Diddley: The Doo-Wopper." *Goldmine,* April 16, 1993, pp. 24–28, 48.

———. "Chicago's 'First' Sheppards Patterned after Flamingos by Producer Andre Williams." *Record Collector's Monthly* 46 (April 1990): 1, 4.

———. *Chicago Soul.* Urbana: University of Illinois Press, 1991.

———. "Collectible Bel Aires Disc Precursor of R&B/Soul Hits by Chicago's Sheppards." *Record Collector's Monthly* 37 (February–March 1986): 4.

———. "The Danderliers Define Chicago Soul on Tiny R&B Label Run from Tailor Shop." *Record Collector's Monthly* 47 (August–September 1990): 1, 6–7.

———. "The Daylighters." *Goldmine,* February 1981, pp. 12–14.

———. "The Dee Clark Story." *Goldmine,* May 1981, 19–20.

———. "Donald Jenkins' Story." *Record Exchanger* 28 [1979]: 14–15.

———. "Don Talty and Formal Records." *Juke Blues* 19 (Spring 1990): 6–11.

———. "The Dukays." *Record Exchanger* 27 [1978]: 4–7.

———. "Early Chicago Groups." *Record Exchanger* 29 [1981]: 12–15.

———. "The Early Dells: Party Staged by Female Fans Inspires 'Oh What a Nite,' Group's Biggest '50s Hit." *Record Collector's Monthly* 50 (November–December 1991): 1, 4–5, 9.

———. "The Eddie Sullivan Story." *Goldmine,* April 1981, p. 19.

———. "El Dorados Make Rock-and-Roll History in the '50s, and Survive Today Still Fronted by Their Original Lead." *Record Collector's Monthly* 41 (June–July 1988): 1, 4–6.

————. "The Emergence of the Black Music Recording Industry, 1920–1923." *Classic Wax* 3 (May 1981): 4–6.

————. "Evanston Soul: Patti Drew and the Drew-vels." *Record Exchanger* 26 [1978]: 22–24.

————. "The Fascinators." *Goldmine,* November 16, 1990, pp. 28, 112.

————. "The Five Chances and Their World of Chicago R&B." *Goldmine,* April 6, 1990, pp. 19–20, 33.

————. "The Five Echoes." *Goldmine,* April 1979, pp. 37–38.

————. "The Five Thrills." *Goldmine,* February 8, 1991, pp. 22, 42.

————. "The Flamingos: The Chicago Years." *Goldmine,* April 6, 1990, pp. 28, 30, 108, 116.

————. "Formal and Other Label Releases Associated with Don Talty." *Juke Blues* 20 (Summer 1990): 16–19.

————. "Gene Chandler." *Goldmine,* January 1980, pp. 13–17.

————. "The Hambone Kids." *Goldmine,* September 1980, pp. 180–81.

————. "How Herb Kent, the Kool Gent, Got Burned." Chicago *Reader,* April 16, 1977, pp. 11, 17.

————. "Island of Soul: The Sheppards." *Time Barrier Express* 27 (April–May 1980): 69–73.

————. "The Jewels: The Most Angelic Voices Ever Waxed." *Goldmine,* January 2, 1987, pp. 14, 20.

————. "Moonglows' Sound, Solidly Based on Rhythm-and-Blues, Adapts to Teen Audience as Rock-and-Roll Era Begins." *Record Collector's Monthly* 51 (July–August 1992): 1, 4–7.

————. "Moroccos Career Starts with R&B Wax, But First Success Comes with a Road Show in Australia." *Record Collector's Monthly* 38 (September–October 1987): 12–13.

————. "Nolan Chance." *Goldmine,* July–August 1978, p. 23.

————. "Palms Undercut by Dying Label; Best Material Never Released." *Record Collector's Monthly* 40 (March–April 1988): 10.

————. "Pastels' Promise Eclipsed by Managers' Marital Problems." *Record Collector's Monthly* 45 (December 1989): 7.

————. "Prentiss Barnes Recalls Early Moonglows; Compensation, Credit Eluded Most Members." *Record Collector's Monthly* 52 (February–March 1993): 7–8.

————. "The Spaniels: Great Googley Moo!" *Goldmine,* February 21, 1992, pp. 42, 44, 102.

————. "Windy City Soul." *Goldmine,* February 1979, pp. 11–13.

Pruter, Robert, and Marv Goldberg. "The Hornets: The Group behind the $18,000 Record." *Goldmine,* April 6, 1990, p. 33.

Pruter, Robert, and Jim O'Neal. "Leonard Allen and the United/States Story, Part One." *Living Blues* 92 (July/August 1990): 37–40.

————. "Leonard Allen and the United/States Story, Part Two." *Living Blues* 93 (September/October 1990): 34–36.

————. "Leonard Allen and the United/States Story, Part Three." *Living Blues* 95 (January/February 1991): 41–46.

Rainsford, Mike. "Doin' the Boogie Twist: The Cal Valentine Story." *Blues and Rhythm: The Gospel Truth* 94 (November 1994): 4–7.

"R&B Ramblings." *Cash Box,* March 23, 1957, p. 42.

"R&B Ramblings." *Cash Box,* December 28, 1957, p. 54.

Red Book. Chicago: Donnelley, 1954, 1955.

Reed, Granville, III. "The Most" [column]. *Chicago Defender,* June 21, 1958.

"Regal and Tivoli 'Live' Show Parade Astounds the Nation." *Chicago Defender,* June 11, 1959.

"Regal Theatre Changes Management on Mar. 1; Plan [*sic*] Many Improvements." *Chicago Defender,* February 7, 1959.

"Rena Theatre Launches Midnight Show Program." *Chicago Defender,* October 22, 1955.

Resnicoff, Matt. "Front Woman: Joni Mitchell." *Musician,* March 1991, p. 7.

Richardson, Clive. "The Dells." *Shout* 61 [December 1970]: n.p.

"Richard Stamz Rates Top as Radio Jockey." *Chicago Defender,* September, 22, 1956.

"Rites Set for Al Benson, Black Broadcasting Pioneer." *Chicago Tribune,* September 8, 1978.

Ritz, David. *Divided Soul: The Life of Marvin Gaye.* New York: McGraw-Hill, 1985.

"Rock 'n' Rollers Hit Park City Bowl." *Chicago Defender,* April 20, 1957.

"'Rock 'n' Roll' to Park City March 11." *Chicago Defender,* March 8, 1956.

Rowe, Mike. *Chicago Breakdown.* London: Eddison, 1973.

Roy, Rob. "Call Debonairs Youthful Quintet with Promise of Brilliant Future." *Chicago Defender,* August 10, 1959.

———. "Joe Hughes' Club Changes Policy." *Chicago Defender,* June 24, 1950.

———. "Meet Faith Taylor Who Rates Cherished Crown as Singer of Tomorrow." *Chicago Defender,* January 21, 1960.

———. "Regal, Tivoli Join with New York, Washington to Form Major 'Live' Chain." *Chicago Defender,* August 29, 1959.

"Sam Evans Went from Press to Radio—Still a Salesman." *Chicago Defender,* February 15, 1956.

Sbarbori, Jack. "The Dells . . . Twenty-three Years Later." *Record Exchanger* 22 [1976]: 4–11.

———. "Sollie McElroy: Flamingos—Moroccos." *Record Exchanger* 19 [1975]: 18–20.

Schuller, Tim. "The Al Braggs Story." *Juke Blues* 9 (Summer 1987): 22–25.

Seroff, Doug. "Polk Miller and the Old South Quartette." *78 Quarterly* 1, no. 3 [1988]: 27–41.

———. "Pre-History of Black Vocal Harmony Groups," part 1. *Goldmine,* March–April 1977, p. 17

———. "Pre-History of Black Vocal Harmony Groups," part 2. *Goldmine,* October 1977, p. 10.

S[h]urley, Ralph. "The Danderliers." *Bim Bam Boom* 8 (December 1972): 39.

Simon, Bill. "Term R&B Hardly Covers Multi-Material So Grouped." *Billboard,* February 4, 1956, p. 55.

"Six of a Kind" [caption]. *Chicago Defender,* September 1, 1960.

"Sixty-third Street Goes Broadway: Propeller Is Star Studded Swing Center." *Chicago Defender,* August 18, 1951.

Sleep, Rick. "Sam Evans . . . I Love You Madly." *Record Exchanger* 22 [1976]: 14–15.

"Small Crowds Cause Theaters to Change to Pix Only Program." *Chicago Defender,* January 8, 1955.

Southern, Eileen. "James ('Jim') Bracken." *Biographical Dictionary of Afro-American Musicians.* Westport, Conn.: Greenwood Press, 1982, pp. 43–44.

Stallworth, Robert. "Five Thrills on Parrot; Classic Chicago R&B." *Record Collector's Monthly* 20 (May 1984): 5.

———. "The Gems and the Drexel Label." *Yesterday's Memories* 6 [1976]: 9–10.

———. "R&B Rarities on 'Red Wax' Are Really Deejay Promos." *Record Collector's Monthly* 16 (January 1984): 7.

———. "Vals, Supremes Rarities Documented; Chance Also Home to Rare City Blues." *Record Collector's Monthly* 38 (September–October 1987): 15, 20.

———. "Yes, It Does Exist!" *Record Collector's Monthly* 31 (June–July 1985): 1, 5.

Stone, Theodore C. "Personality Spotlight" [column]. *Chicago Defender,* January 6, 1960.

Tancredi, Carl. "The Flamingos: The Early Years." *Bim Bam Boom* 4 (February–March 1972): 4–7.

Taylor, Mark. "Smithsonian Tunes into the Spaniels." *Post- Tribune,* February 20, 1991.

"'Teenage Jamboree' at Trianon Saturdays." *Chicago Defender,* October 2, 1954.

"Theater Owners Praise Southside Surge to Top." *Chicago Defender,* November 11, 1959.

"Tivoli Theatre Plans the Big Switch; Live Stage Shows Included." *Chicago Defender,* February 23, 1959.

Toop, David. *Rap Attack 2: African Rap to Global Hip Hop.* London: Serpent's Tail, 1991. 2d, rev. edition of *Rap Attack,* Pluto Press, 1984.

"Top Record Stars of '56 Appear at Trianon July 27." *Chicago Defender,* July 14, 1956.

[Topping], Roy, and [Richardson], Clive. "The Tommy Hunt Story." *Shout* 74 (February 1972): n.p.

Travis, Dempsey J. *An Autobiography of Black Jazz.* Chicago: Urban Research Institute, 1983, pp. 25–37, 111–21, 157–78, 192.

"Trianon Dance Classic Set for Tomorrow Night." *Chicago Defender,* November 21, 1956.

"Truth About Sam Evans' Hit Show 'Jam with Sam.'" *Chicago Defender,* August 23, 1952.

Twain, Mark. *Life on the Mississippi.* New York: Harper, 1917.

"Vee-Jay Boss Joins Urban League Board." *Chicago Defender,* July 9, 1962.

Vera, Billy. Liner notes, "What Is Doowop?" *The Doo Wop Box.* Rhino Records 71463, 1993.

"Vivian Bracken, 69; Brought Records of the Beatles to U.S." *Chicago Sun-Times,* June 15, 1989.

"Vivian Carter, Disc Jockey, Moves to WWCA." *Chicago Defender,* February 13, 1954.

Wang, Richard. "Jazz in Chicago: A Historical Overview." *Black Music Research Bulletin* 12, no. 2 (Fall 1990): 8–11.

Warner, Jay. *The Billboard Book of American Singing Groups.* New York: Billboard Books, 1992.

"The Well-Known Fascinoles" [caption]. *Chicago Defender,* September 29, 1956.

White, Cliff. "Harvey Fuqua: The Man behind Sylvester." *Black Music and Jazz Review,* November 1978, pp. 24, 31–32.

"White City Rink Race Ban Dropped." *Chicago Defender,* June 1, 1946.

Whitesell, Rick. "The Lewis Bronzeville Five." *Goldmine,* November 1980, pp. 158–59.

———. "The Three Bits of Rhythm." *Classic Wax* 2 (January 1981): 8–9.

———. "The Three Sharps and a Flat." *Goldmine,* March 1980, pp. 10–11.

Whitesell, Rick [with Marv Goldberg]. "The Magnificents." *Goldmine,* April 1979, pp. 33–34.

Whitesell, Rick, Peter Grendysa, and George Moonoogian. "The Four Vagabonds." *Yesterday's Memories* 7 [1976]: 7–10.

"Willie Wright Makes Long Trip from Slums to Plush Night Club." *Chicago Defender,* February 21, 1963.

Index

ROBERT PRUTER is a senior editor in the Social Science Department of New Standard Encyclopedia in Chicago. He earned a master's degree in history from Roosevelt University. He has written numerous articles that have appeared in journals such as *Goldmine, Living Blues, Juke Blues, Record Collector's Monthly,* and *Record Exchanger.* Pruter is the author of *Chicago Soul.*

Books in the Series
Music in American Life

Only a Miner: Studies in Recorded Coal-Mining Songs   Archie Green

Great Day Coming: Folk Music and the American Left   R. Serge Denisoff

John Philip Sousa: A Descriptive Catalog of His Works   Paul E. Bierley

The Hell-Bound Train: A Cowboy Songbook   Glenn Ohrlin

Oh, Didn't He Ramble: The Life Story of Lee Collins, as Told to Mary Collins
Edited by Frank J. Gillis and John W. Miner

American Labor Songs of the Nineteenth Century   Philip S. Foner

Stars of Country Music: Uncle Dave Macon to Johnny Rodriguez   Edited by
Bill C. Malone and Judith McCulloh

Git Along, Little Dogies: Songs and Songmakers of the American West
John I. White

A Texas-Mexican Cancionero: *Folksongs of the Lower Border*   Américo Paredes

San Antonio Rose: The Life and Music of Bob Wills   Charles R. Townsend

Early Downhome Blues: A Musical and Cultural Analysis   Jeff Todd Titon

*An Ives Celebration: Papers and Panels of the Charles Ives Centennial
Festival-Conference*   Edited by H. Wiley Hitchcock and Vivian Perlis

Sinful Tunes and Spirituals: Black Folk Music to the Civil War   Dena J. Epstein

Joe Scott, the Woodsman-Songmaker   Edward D. Ives

Jimmie Rodgers: The Life and Times of America's Blue Yodeler   Nolan Porterfield

*Early American Music Engraving and Printing: A History of Music Publishing
in America from 1787 to 1825, with Commentary on Earlier and Later Practices*
Richard J. Wolfe

Sing a Sad Song: The Life of Hank Williams   Roger M. Williams

Long Steel Rail: The Railroad in American Folksong   Norm Cohen

*Resources of American Music History: A Directory of Source Materials from Colonial
Times to World War II*   D. W. Krummel, Jean Geil, Doris J. Dyen, and Deane L. Root

Tenement Songs: The Popular Music of the Jewish Immigrants   Mark Slobin

Ozark Folksongs   Vance Randolph; edited and abridged by Norm Cohen

Oscar Sonneck and American Music   Edited by William Lichtenwanger

The Sound of the Dove: Singing in Appalachian Primitive Baptist Churches
Beverly Bush Patterson

Heartland Excursions: Ethnomusicological Reflections on Schools of Music
Bruno Nettl

Doowop: The Chicago Scene   *Robert Pruter*